"As American politics becomes more polarized and as more areas of life become politicized, it starts to feel like there's no escape. But if there's a way out of this situation—where politics is increasingly extremist, defamatory, and conspiratorial—surely it's not going to come by just picking a side in the culture wars and trying to impose our own political and moral vision. Surely we need to better understand where we've all gone wrong. For anyone hoping for a way out of the current political mess, Jim Belcher's *Cold Civil War* is a must-read, and it's clearly the product of the author's many years of curiosity about and careful consideration of diverse moral and political views. Belcher offers a new way of classifying political orientations. He argues that the four main political orientations act as countervailing forces that strengthen the country when in their more centrist forms but tear the country apart in their more extreme forms. The way forward isn't to abandon our ideologies entirely or for us all to agree with one another, but the country does need to move toward the 'vital center.' And Belcher offers a vision of how to do so."

Bradley Campbell, professor of sociology at California State University Los Angeles and coauthor of *The Rise of Victimhood Culture*

"As the current pastor of Godspeak Church in Thousand Oaks, California, and the former mayor of the City of Thousand Oaks, I have always viewed my political opponents not as my enemy but as an opportunity. I groped in the darkness to understand how to apply civility in the political arena. Having read Jim Belcher's book *Cold Civil War*, I now possess a clear understanding of what I longed for but could never fully articulate. American Christianity has abandoned their presence in the public square because politics for most is simply a blood sport. Jim Belcher's book gives a clear road map back to our needed participation in the public square. Civility is the key and wisdom is our strength. I am so grateful personally for this timely work and rejoice wholeheartedly in endorsing it."

Rob McCoy, senior pastor of Godspeak Church and former mayor of Thousand Oaks, California

"Our country is divided. Jim Belcher in this thoughtful book helps us understand what and who is making the polarization worse. Our country is divided, and Jim helps us consider a new vital center, one that will heal and not fracture. *Cold Civil War* is an important book to help Christians recover a vibrant public philosophy, one that will empower Christ-followers to lead our society from the tumultuous to the virtuous. *Cold Civil War* is a hopeful book. Read it."

Barry H. Corey, president of Biola University and author of *Make the Most of It: A Guide to Loving Your College Years*

"Jim Belcher offers an innovative and empathetic framework for understanding our polarized moment in this thoughtful synthesis of public philosophy and political debate. This introduction to the ferocious argument between left and right is essential reading for anyone concerned about our nation's future."

Matthew Continetti, senior fellow at the American Enterprise Institute

"Reflecting both his preparation as a political philosopher and his skills as a theologian, Jim Belcher has given us a timely and thoughtful proposal to address public square issues by rebuilding a new vital center for America. Examining the ideas, trends, and developments that have brought about the current philosophical, political, and cultural divide, Belcher offers a bold, challenging, and hope-filled framework to move beyond the fragmentation and polarization on the right and the left. Grounded in an appeal to reclaim the place of both special revelation and natural law, and drawing on insights from Tocqueville, this important volume, while not naive to the difficult road ahead, provides much-needed guidance for shaping a public theology, enabling the church to reclaim its mission, overcome cynicism, and take responsibility for helping to bring healing to the nations. *Cold Civil War* is worthy of serious reflection and engagement by those on all sides of the issues. Highly recommended!"

David S. Dockery, president of the International Alliance for Christian Education and distinguished professor of theology at Southwestern Baptist Theological Seminary

FOREWORD BY
JOHN D. WILSEY

JIM BELCHER

COLD CIVIL WAR

OVERCOMING POLARIZATION, DISCOVERING UNITY, AND
HEALING
THE
NATION

An imprint of InterVarsity Press
Downers Grove, Illinois

InterVarsity Press
P.O. Box 1400, Downers Grove, IL 60515-1426
ivpress.com
email@ivpress.com

InterVarsity Press® is the book-publishing division of InterVarsity Christian Fellowship/USA®, a movement of students and faculty active on campus at hundreds of universities, colleges, and schools of nursing in the United States of America, and a member movement of the International Fellowship of Evangelical Students. For information about local and regional activities, visit intervarsity.org.

Scripture quotations, unless otherwise noted, are from The Holy Bible, English Standard Version, copyright © 2001 by Crossway Bibles, a division of Good News Publishers. Used by permission. All rights reserved.

While any stories in this book are true, some names and identifying information may have been changed to protect the privacy of individuals.

New Vital Center quadrant graph © Jim Belcher 2019, used with permission.

The publisher cannot verify the accuracy or functionality of website URLs used in this book beyond the date of publication.

Cover design and image composite: David Fassett
Interior design: Daniel van Loon
Images: black ink roll out: © IntergalacticDesignStudio / E+ / Getty Images
  tan texture: © Katsumi Murouchi / Moment / Getty Images
  red texture: © LoudRed Creative / E+ / Getty Images
  flag: © Vectorios2016 / DigitalVision Vectors / Getty Images

ISBN 978-0-8308-4764-8 (print)
ISBN 978-0-8308-4765-5 (digital)

Printed in the United States of America ♾

InterVarsity Press is committed to ecological stewardship and to the conservation of natural resources in all our operations. This book was printed using sustainably sourced paper.

Library of Congress Cataloging-in-Publication Data
A catalog record for this book is available from the Library of Congress.

P	25	24	23	22	21	20	19	18	17	16	15	14	13	12	11	10	9	8	7	6	5	4	3	2	1
Y	43	42	41	40	39	38	37	36	35	34	33	32	31	30	29	28	27	26	25	24	23	22			

To Jordan, Jonathan, Lindsay, and Meghan

and their American futures

CONTENTS

Foreword by John D. Wilsey   *1*

Introduction   *3*

PART ONE

HOW WE GOT INTO THE COLD CIVIL WAR · 19

1 The Evangelical Dilemma and the Search for Public Philosophy   *21*

2 The End of the Vital Center   *41*

PART TWO

MAPPING OUR DIFFERENCES · 57

THE QUADRANT FRAMEWORK SYSTEM

3 Freedom Left 2   *63*
The Theory of the Godless Constitution

4 Freedom Left 3   *80*
From Open Society to Closed Society

5 Order Left 2   *95*
The Rise of the Welfare State and the Great Society

6 Order Left 3   *110*
The Reified Postmodernism of Antiracism

7 Freedom Right 2   *124*
Libertarians and the Quest for Open Borders

8 Freedom Right 3   *142*
*Radical Libertarians, the End of the State, and
the Rise of Utopian Technocracy*

9 Order Right 2   *161*
Poison Pill Conservatives

10 Order Right 3   *180*
The Illiberal New Right

PART THREE

FORMING THE NEW VITAL CENTER · 199

11 The New Vital Center   *203*

   The American Synthesis and the Four Souls

12 Patriotic Citizenship   *227*

   The Sweet Offer for Resident Aliens and Alienated Residents

13 Christianity   *246*

   The Second Constitution

Conclusion   *265*

   The Heroic Role for the Church

Acknowledgments   *275*

Notes   *277*

FOREWORD

JOHN D. WILSEY

For the past few decades, Americans have been fighting each other in a culture war. Pat Buchanan, giving the keynote address at the 1992 Republican National Convention that nominated George H. W. Bush for the presidency, declared, "There is a religious war going on in this country. It is a cultural war, as critical to the kind of nation we shall be as the Cold War itself, for this war is for the soul of America."[1] More recently, the federal elections of 2016, 2018, and 2020 were the backdrop for many expressions of this cultural war between Americans identifying with the political right and left. But increasingly, we witness local and state jurisdictions serving as the platform for the conflict. Our communities are dividing over critical race theory, Drag Queen Story Hour, and the presence of monuments in public places. Local jurisdictions have also become ground zeros all around the country as the Covid-19 pandemic raged. Debates about the pandemic are but one iteration of the culture war that has been ongoing since the early 1990s.

Jim Belcher is right to classify this conflict as a cold civil war, one that has been promulgated by issues swirling around race, sexuality, gender, public health, immigration, climate, religious expression, and political correctness. News outlets proliferate, but they are widely untrusted. Social media platforms like Facebook and Twitter police their patrons for what they say in the interest of purging the internet of "fake news" and "misinformation." Big corporations such as Coca-Cola, Nike, and Delta Air Lines are "woke." People live in fear of being canceled, a contemporary colloquialism that simply means having your life ruined over your political and social views. Billionaires such as Richard Branson and Jeff Bezos race one another into low-earth orbit, while others of their ilk retreat to private islands to escape the Delta variant.

Where does all that leave the rest of us? It leaves us mired in a cold civil war that nobody can see the way out of and nobody can foresee how it may end. But few of us think it will end well. Conservatives and progressives alike fear for the future and fear for the world their children and grandchildren will be inheriting from us partisans in this cold civil war that very few of us asked for or wanted. Yet here we are, and Christians are more often than not considered by the culture at large as part of the problem, not the solution.

Christians and non-Christians alike often use the term *post-Christian* to describe our contemporary state of affairs in America. I've never thought of the term as particularly helpful, nor historically accurate. A term like *post-Christian* implies that Christians have never faced anything like what we are facing now. Such a term has always seemed to me terribly ignorant of church history, especially the history of the church in its first three centuries. It was during this time that the churches in the Roman Empire faced a hostile culture, and they looked to their own resources derived from the Scriptures and general revelation to serve as salt and light in a world that hated them.

What Jim Belcher is offering us in this book is a word of hope for American churches as they seek to recover their mission to be salt and light in a culture that is on the brink of an open civil war rather than a subtle one. Belcher's quadrant system, in which he skillfully diagnoses American social divisions and identifies a new vital center that serves as a beacon through the storm of strife we are confounded by, outlines the contours of American divisions in the early twenty-first century and offers a productive way forward.

Our times are not unprecedented. Christ's bride has, by his grace, faced myriads of grave existential challenges, many of them like the ones she is faced with today. She has not only survived, she has thrived. This is in fulfillment of the Lord's promise that "the gates of Hades will not overpower it" (Matthew 16:18 NASB). Belcher's work on our current state of affairs in cultural discourse, marked by hyper-partisanship, incivility, and political, social, and moral instability, contributes a needed perspective borne of clear, careful, and charitable thinking. It is reflective of deep thought and research that has obviously been ongoing for many years, and I'm certain it will spur further dialogue among scholars in the academy and citizens in the public square for years to come.

INTRODUCTION

AMERICA IS IN THE MIDST of a cold civil war.[1] Unlike a hot war that uses tanks and bullets, this cold civil war is about cultural conflict, the clash of worldviews, protests, and riots. It's about two rival views of America, two different views of the Constitution, two opposing cultures, and two ways of life. Because of this cold civil war, America is coming apart at the seams. As Jonathan Haidt says in his bestselling book *The Righteous Mind*, "The country now seems polarized and embattled to the point of dysfunction."[2] We see this polarization on cable news, social media, talk radio, and in our national politics. It's like the two sides in the conflict are talking about two different countries and two different political realities. As Haidt contends, over the past decade and a half there has been "a decline in the number of people calling themselves centrists or moderates . . . a rise in the number of conservatives . . . and a rise in the number of liberals."[3] He says we are in the middle of a culture war that is tearing at the national fabric, the unity needed to sustain a workable democratic republic.

A 2018 report, "Hidden Tribes: A Study of America's Polarized Landscape," found that "America is deeply factionalized . . . and Washington is gripped by a sense of permanent crisis regularly compared to that of the Watergate era." The authors believe "this reflects America's profound polarization, in which any and every issue can be channeled into an us-versus-them conflict between warring factions and where partisan ends justify any means."[4]

By the middle of 2020, the last year of the Donald Trump presidency, after months of urban protests and riots, the pandemic crisis engendering widespread conflict over masks and medicine, and hourly online battles on social media, America was deeply divided, obvious to everyone. Random strangers got into shouting matches in grocery stores over masks. Some people wore masks while driving alone in their cars and some never wore masks at all, each showing solidarity to their political tribe. Some put signs in their yard, letting the world know of their political righteousness, like talismans warding off evil spirits.

In July of 2020, Bari Weiss, a well-known left-of-center journalist, resigned from the *New York Times*, citing years of bullying and harassment by her colleagues and bosses because she dared to challenge the reigning progressive narrative of the *Times*. In her resignation letter, she decried the straight jacket of progressive orthodoxy destroying freedom of the press and thought, warning of its danger.[5]

Six months later, following the January 6, 2021, riots at the Capitol in Washington, DC, she wrote that we are living through "The Great Unraveling," described as "the unraveling of the old truths, the old political consensus, the old order, the old conventions, the old guardrails, the old principles, the old shared stories, the old common identity."[6] She now realizes she has more in common with those on the right, thinkers she "once regarded as my ideological nemesis," than many erstwhile former allies who no longer share a commitment to historic liberal norms like freedom of speech, a free press, and religious freedom. Unlike her radically progressive former colleagues, her new allies "see clearly that the fight of the moment, the fight that allows for us to have those disagreements in the first place, is the fight for liberalism."[7]

But Weiss contends that the term *great unraveling* doesn't even quite capture what has happened over the past few years, for "it fails to capture the takeover and the unimaginable strength of the new powers that have superseded the old ones." Ultimately, she claims, what we are witnessing is the complete takeover, by any means possible, of our liberal democratic system, a hijacking by a monopolistic oligarchy of big-tech corporations and a professional class after one thing: power.

I was pondering this "great unraveling" the day of President Biden's inauguration, wondering what he would do to seek the unity he mentioned, curious if he would find common ground. But I was disappointed. Before the day was over, President Biden signed seventeen executive orders that overturned some of President Trump's policies or advanced progressive policies.[8] Many wondered if he would govern as a moderate. These first executive orders said otherwise.[9] The impact and scope were breathtaking, even for progressives who welcomed them with surprise. But my surprises weren't over for the day.

That night, as I watched the speech again, I noticed something; when he talked about the "uncivil war," the word order jumped out at me. Biden said "red against blue . . . rural versus urban, conservative versus liberal," making it seem to me, due to the word order, that he was insinuating who is causing the uncivil war.[10] Clearly the vast majority of Americans are against extremism and political violence and believe that those who committed acts of violence at the Capitol on January 6, 2021, should be prosecuted (every major conservative and liberal voice immediately denounced what happened).[11] But while condemning "white supremacy" and "domestic terrorism," why didn't President Biden also condemn Antifa and Black Lives Matter, who had openly planned riots in Portland and Seattle on the night of his inauguration? Was this an oversight of his speechwriter? Or is extremism only found on the right?

This made me nervous, for political violence is never the answer, whether on the left or the right. But if President Trump should have been more careful with his language on January 6 before the riot at the Capitol, shouldn't President Biden have been more careful in his inauguration speech?[12]

But I didn't have to wait long to get an answer. As I sat watching the news, former CIA director John Brennan, a paid commentator on MSNBC, spoke about what he thought Biden meant. Brennan said that the enemies of unity, the aggressors in this uncivil war, are the "unholy alliance" of "religious extremists, authoritarians, fascists, bigots, racists, nativists, even libertarians" and that they need to be rooted out.[13] According to Brennan, a man who still holds the nation's highest security clearance, newly appointed members of the administration had already begun "in laser-like fashion" to "uncover as much as they can about what looks very similar to insurgency movements that we have seen overseas."[14] And he didn't mean extremists on the left, proving my nervousness was warranted.

Brennan cast a wide net (even including libertarians, he said), catching in it not just the Capitol rioters but potentially all seventy-four million people who voted for Trump or hold to conservative or populist positions.[15] Glenn Greenwald, a civil libertarian and a man of the left, believes Brennan's comments are extremely dangerous. Greenwald believes that we are witnessing an unholy alliance of big tech, big government, and big military under the guise of fighting a war on domestic terrorism, going after anyone who doesn't toe the new party line, accusing them of sedition and insurrection.[16] And if you don't agree with the ruling coalition, you are guilty of sedition.

What exactly is this bipartisan ruling coalition that Greenwald mentions? Well, for Greenwald the ruling coalition is *not* just made up of Democrats but also includes Republicans. As he said on the night of the inauguration, we need to get away from seeing Washington as two parties warring against each other. Rather,

> there is a Ruling Class elite that is extremely comfortable with the established ways of both parties; they love Nancy Pelosi and Chuck Schumer every bit as much as they love Mitch McConnell and Mitt Romney and Marco Rubio and Paul Ryan. Those are the people they (the Ruling Elite) fund equally because those are the people who serve their agenda.[17]

If this ruling coalition wants to control the way we think, speak, and associate, this is bad news. By lumping all Republicans into one camp, argues Greenwald, now anyone who opposes the ruling elite fall into either one of two categories—either crazy conspiracy people or insurrectionists—there is no third option and dissent of any kind is no longer allowed. Even challenging the ruling class policy is out of bounds. Yet for Greenwald, there remains an entire group of people with legitimate concerns who are not conspiracy-theory people or insurrectionists but the working class and middle class, who hold many of the views that are now deemed domestic terrorism. There is an entire group of people, he argues, who are hurt by the bipartisan ruling elite, "whose cares and concerns are ignored."[18]

In short, he argues that this new war on domestic terrorism isn't a battle between Democrats and Republicans or ultimately over getting rid of domestic terrorism (which everyone agrees is bad); rather, in their attempt to shut down all views that threaten their power, the ruling class is conducting a new class war. And as Warren Buffet, a member of the plutocratic class once famously said, "There's class warfare, all right, but it's my class, the rich class, that's making war, and we're winning."[19]

Ten years ago, in his book *The Ruling Class: How They Corrupted America and What We Can Do About It*, US intelligence expert Angelo Codevilla warned readers about the bipartisan ruling class—politicians from both parties, the permanent bureaucracy in Washington, DC; lobbyists, multinational corporations; and the ruling intelligentsia in the university and journalism—that runs America and are waging class war against the majority of Americans.[20] In 2020, former Democrat Joel Kotkin picked up this contention in *The Coming of Neo-Feudalism: A Warning to the Global Middle Class* and describes how the new oligarchy, made up of the plutocrats, the superwealthy, and their allies composed of Washington politicians, government bureaucrats, journalists, activists, and university professors—what he calls the "clerisy class"—wage economic, political, and cultural war against the working and middle class.[21] The new oligarchs monopolize all the wealth and power and reduce everyone else to serfs, dependent on the government for a living wage.[22] On the right, conservative Michael Lind makes a similar case in his 2020 book, *The New Class War: Saving Democracy from the Managerial Elite*, where he also claims that a technocratic elite has taken over America's politics, economics, and culture, rigging the system to keep them in power.[23]

Looking at a few of Biden's executive orders, we see they cover these three categories—politics, economics, and culture. Biden signed orders on immigration and the border wall (politics), the termination of the Keystone XL pipeline and rejoining the Paris Climate Accord (economics), and solidifying the right of transgender biological males to participate in women's sports and strengthening the right to abortion (culture). These all fit with progressive politics of the left. But from the right, the Republican Senate leader Mitch McConnell, neoconservative Bill Kristol, and Republicans on Wall Street remained almost completely silent, demonstrating their consent and the bipartisanship of the ruling elite. On all three levels—politics, economics, and culture—the ruling class, the new oligarchy, appears to reassert its control over America, further fueling polarization, division, and our cold civil war. No wonder many working- and middle-class Americans feel like their life is under siege from the ruling class, their way of life threatened.

What is going on? Why do the working and middle classes feel like they are being squeezed politically, economically, and culturally? Over the last decade a group of mostly left-of-center scholars who write for the *Small Wars Journal*, led by USC professor Robert J. Bunker,[24] devised an interesting concept about the threats to democracy and the rise of resentment and anger among so many Americans, causing so much polarization among groups. Their original idea is that the threats to social stability and democratic societies come from two main places, above and below, causing those in the middle to be attacked from both sides.

From below, governments allow and sometimes utilize gangs, crime, violence, and riots, causing the corruption of the judicial and political system and the hollowing out of the state, destroying trust among the population. From above, the high-tech "Plutocrat Insurgency" (on the left and right) wages war on our political and economic systems, rigging the system in favor of the plutocrats, while the clerisy helps them dismantle the middle-class culture and values that undergird a democratic constitutional republic. So for Bunker and his colleagues, American democracy, which depends on a stable working and middle class, is under attack from below and above, causing widespread unhappiness, societal division, and political polarization. And as we are going to see, our ruling class, while they would prefer stability, often use all the chaos in the streets, in the media, and in politics to increase their own control and power and wealth. After all, "never let a crisis go to waste."[25]

WHY WALL STREET CHOSE JOE BIDEN

In June 2019, while campaigning for his party's nomination, then-candidate Biden addressed a group of wealthy donors at the Carlyle Hotel in Manhattan,[26] of whom many were looking for an alternative to Bernie Sanders and his populism. Biden put them at ease, assuring them not to worry about his commitment to a green energy policy. "No one's standard of living would change," Biden told them.[27] "Nothing would fundamentally change." Writing for NYMag.com, Eric Levitz contended that what Biden really meant was that since "inequality had reached such exceptional levels, he [Biden] could redistribute significant income from the rich to the poor without putting a dent in the former's living standards."[28] Once assured of where Biden's loyalty stood, the plutocrat class in Washington and Wall Street switched their support to Biden, opposing Bernie Sanders, who promised to increase taxes on the rich. And by the time of the presidential election in November, the vast majority of firms on Wall Street, including many of those run by Republicans, backed Biden, turning their back on the working and middle classes.[29]

And why are the working and middle classes so threatening to the oligarchic class? Well, according to all the authors I have mentioned, if the plutocrats are going to maintain their position atop the hierarchy, they can't have a vibrant middle and working class that wants to share political, economic, and cultural power. They can't have a class that appeals to the Constitution for rights or a church that wants religious freedom and the right of free association, or people who want to defend girls sports, or workers questioning the offshoring of jobs to China. All of these positions of the middle and ruling class get in the way of the bipartisan ruling class and their quest for more power and wealth. They are the new robber barons.

In fact, according to Lind, Kotkin, Codevilla, and Bunker (two thinkers on the left and two on the right), the plutocratic oligarchs want the destruction of the middle class, ripping away the ladder of upward mobility so the poor can never reach the middle class and the middle class can never rival the plutocrats for control. To achieve this, the plutocrats wage "twin insurgency" mentioned above—a war from below and a war from above, squeezing the middle class from both sides, the goal being submission.[30] With the middle class out of the way, the poor will have no ladder to climb out of poverty and will need a living wage, "generously" provided by the plutocrat class, thus staving off a revolution and keeping them in power.

Yet even President Trump, for all his populist positions that angered the plutocrat oligarchs (e.g., tariffs on China, reducing immigration, opposing wars in the Middle East, restoring manufacturing and energy jobs to the middle of the country), doesn't get off the hook when it comes to the ruling class, especially their control over Wall Street. When he could have broken the hold of the economic ruling class, his 2017 tax-cut bill did the opposite, giving a massive tax cut for the huge Wall Street hedge funds. And he signed yearly bloated budgets, each one further expanding government and its control over the population.[31]

Just a few weeks after the national lockdown due to the pandemic began in March 2020, Joel Kotkin predicted that the pandemic would hurt the middle and working classes, putting many out of work and closing their businesses. And at the same time he predicted that the lockdown would benefit the technological oligarchy, who stood to make millions through online shopping, grocery buying, and entertainment, providing them "with opportunities to gain control of a whole set of coveted industries."[32] In hindsight, the facts bear that out. The tech oligarchs got even richer during the pandemic.[33] "Like the barbarians who seized control of land during the demise of Rome," Kotkin remarked, "they seem well-positioned to benefit from the emerging social distance-driven recession."[34] Time will prove if Kotkin's predictions about the middle and working classes are spot on, because already thousands of small businesses have shuttered forever.[35]

It wasn't just in the area of economics that the pandemic provided potential to solidify wealth and power. There was also potential to increase political power. In his "7 Ways Governments Used the Coronavirus Pandemic to Crush Human Rights," journalist John Hayward highlights the potential dangers from the ruling class during crises such as a pandemic, as seen in government examples around the world, suggesting similar actions within the United States. And what is so scary, contends Hayward, is that "coronavirus lockdowns created power structures that can be used to enforce the will of the State in countless other areas. Skepticism that any of those 'emergency' dictatorial powers will be relinquished after the Wuhan coronavirus recedes is warranted."[36] The oligarchs may simply repurpose these new powers, curtailing our civil liberties for their benefit. To understand how much this view may be shared by those on the *left* as much as the *right*, one only has to see the bipartisan support to recall California governor Newsom, who has overseen one of the most comprehensive shutdowns of any of the fifty states.

And this brings us back to where I began this introduction—we are in a cold civil war. The partnership of big government, big tech, and big military, the new ruling class, have formed an oligarchy to wage war against the middle and lower classes of both parties. Writing just ten days after the tragic Capitol riots, Joy Pullman accused them of "using the excuse of an unrepresentative group of fools criminally ransacking US Capitol offices" to push a communist-style social credit system on Americans.[37] It appears, she says, "that global oligarchs have decided to not only collude with China's totalitarian control over society, but to export that social control to formerly free nations such as the United States." Yet as scary as this sounds, there are voices on the left that welcome it. According to Pullman, "one of the leading lights of leftism, the *New York Times* and columnist Tom Friedman, welcome with open arms" because "it silences all those pesky dissidents who just get in the way of enlightened policymaking." A decade ago the civil libertarians on the far left would have been raising alarms. Not anymore, it seems.[38]

Yet if unity for the oligarchs means everyone must agree with them or be banished, then our "uncivil war," as Biden called it, will never end. If unity only means that everyone has to agree with the ruling class, we will never have true unity but an untenable peace that will remain a powder keg waiting to explode, on both the left and the right. What is the solution? How do we end this class war, put an end to extremist violence on the right and the left, and find common ground for all Americans? Can we end the cold civil war? Is it too late? Has the oligarchic ruling class won?

How Do We Move Forward?

At the end of Codevilla's strongly pessimistic book *The Ruling Class*, he is not totally devoid of hope. But the solution for getting back our country will include more than politics. While he believes we need to take practical politics seriously, that is, our responsibility for self-government, he argues there remains something even more important.

As a first step, if we want to take on the ruling class and not be cowed, co-opted, and corrupted by them, we must know exactly what we are fighting against and what we are fighting for. Politics is not just a battle for power and control; if it becomes all about raw political power or even violence, then we are fighting on their terrain and we will lose. No, it is first and foremost a moral and spiritual battle, a conflict of visions for ideas, the kinds of ideas that undergird our constitutional republic, the principles that are the foundation of our natural rights, the grounding for being a Christian, an American, and a nation. What guides us? What justifies our system? What is our standard of life together? Where do we get right and wrong, true and untrue, good and bad, beautiful and ugly? These are concepts of truth, justice, and goodness. We have to fight here first, says Codevilla. Our argument—our fight—must be moral, philosophical, and theological.

"Only by mobilizing . . . against it on a principled, moral basis," contends Codevilla, can we successfully take on the ruling class.[39]

> Because aggressive, intolerant secularism is the moral and intellectual basis of the Ruling Class' claim to rule, resistance to that rule, whether to the immorality of economic subsidies and privileges, or to the violation of the principles of equal treatment under equal law, or to its seizure of children's education, must deal with secularism's intellectual and moral core.[40]

I agree with him. For all the bipartisan ruling class's pragmatic quest for power and wealth, at the heart of their project is a worldview—a view of the world (globalism), a way of knowing (pragmatic instrumentalism) and vision of the future (the great reset), all of which will be explained in the pages ahead. If we don't understand this, and if we don't take them on over the nature of their "morality," we will not have the insights or the inspiration to stick it out, to stay in the game for the long haul. Slave abolitionist William Wilberforce fought the slave trade for decades in the face of yearly defeats, and never gave up because he knew he was waging a spiritual and moral battle; he knew exactly who and what he was fighting, and he understood on what grounds he stood. That must be our inspiration too. But it is not going to be easy.

As Codevilla points out, the reality is that as soon as we object to the ruling class on the basis of morality, law, or religion, the ruling class will accuse us of being irrational, unscientific, stupid, and of trying to set up a theocracy. As Codevilla concludes his book, he says this battle "lies beyond the boundaries of politics." He is right. The battle ultimately begins in the realm of public philosophy.

In fact, almost three decades ago, University of Virginia sociologist James Davison Hunter wrote in his book *Culture Wars* that at the heart of this cultural conflict is the question of *ultimate authority*.[41] What guide or standard or foundation determines what is good and bad, true and untrue? Is it the Bible? Natural law? Our founding documents? Science? Individual choice? Social justice? Elite experts? Moreover, by what authority do we define what it means to be a citizen in the United States? Writing a quarter of a century ago, Hunter held that "the meaning of America—who we have been in the past, who we are now, and perhaps most important, who we, as a nation, will aspire to become—is at the center of the cultural war."[42] Yet the question of authority and the "meaning of America" are even more contested today. If anything, our cultural divide has become greater and our incivility even more marked. As the two sides become more calcified, the worst of tribal politics is on display.

As the "Hidden Tribes" study contends, "millions of Americans are going about their lives with absurdly inaccurate perceptions of each other." Stoked by the media and our national political culture, the authors conclude, "We are long past the point where these differences are contributing to a healthy and robust democracy. The intolerance for the other is a grave threat to our democratic system . . . both sides have absorbed a caricature of the other."[43] How do we move beyond this? The "Hidden Tribes" authors believe that combating this "us-versus-them tribalism and polarization may be one of the greatest social and political challenges of the digital age." While they don't provide a blueprint for ending this dangerous polarization, they are able to show "how much such a blueprint is needed."[44]

At the end of their study the "Hidden Tribes" authors assert that "America has one great asset unrivaled in the world: a powerful story of national identity that, at its core, is idealistic, hopeful and inclusive. It's a story that calls the nation and its people to act with virtue and against division; that speaks to the better angels of our nature." If "America today needs a renewed sense of national identity," a national identity "that fosters a common vision for the future in which every American can feel that they belong and are respected," then I am convinced the church has much to offer in reaching this renewed sense of identity.[45] We have the resources, through a new vital center, to help end the polarization.

Is there a way forward? Can we overcome this cold civil war and avoid a hot civil war and regain a new vital center? I believe we can, but it is a long-term project. I agree with Codevilla. For us to be successful, our project "must deal with secularism's intellectual and moral core." It must begin with public philosophy. We must understand how we got into our mess, who and what are making it worse, and what renewal looks like.

For this our nation's political, business, cultural, and religious leaders need to step back and do some thinking. Religious leaders should have the most to contribute but, more often than not, are either silent or have defaulted to mindless tribalism. But this right-left spectrum is not only not helpful in understand the ruling class, but it often is used as political theater, to distract from the fact that the ruling class is apolitical, will co-opt both parties to achieve what they want, and that this political theater is used during every election to get people to vote.

But it is a sham. Both political parties have more in common, particularly in the area of economics, than we know. There are many reasons why the church has provided so little leadership in our cold civil war and has gotten caught up in tribal politics, but the main reason is a lack of deep thinking about public philosophy and what it means to be salt and light in the area of politics, economics, and culture. And the church will never regain its ability to lead until it does some hard thinking and begins to champion a public philosophy capable of challenging this bipartisan ruling class.

THE STRUCTURE OF THE BOOK

The plan of the book is to do three things. First, I will explain in part one why understanding public philosophy is vital to understanding our times. I will define *public philosophy* as those first principles that are beyond the day-to-day world of politics—principles that define, guide, and justify. In short, these principles undergird our entire life together as a nation. Along with being the grounding and glue for our political, ethical, and economic life together, public philosophy provides the narrative that defines who we are as a people and what our true ends are. Public philosophy is the philosophic and religious key to understanding our Constitution, how and why we share power, and America's role in the world. For centuries America shared a common vital center, regardless of how many enemies wanted to destroy it or turn it into an oligarchy. But this vital center has been slowly eroded and has been replaced, first with pragmatic instrumentalism and now increasingly with postmodern power. Once this erosion had taken place, we opened the door for the agents of polarization, on the right and the left, to divide us, pulling us further and further away from unity and the ability to balance rights and responsibilities toward one another.

In part two I will explain that once we lost our vital center, that shared public philosophy, the extremes on the left and right pulled apart the American project. I will demonstrate why the key to understanding this polarization is my breakthrough quadrant and my discovery that the left-right spectrum is inadequate for explaining our current polarization. In this section I will also show how the left-right spectrum is better understood when it is a quadrant and that both the right and the left have two sides, a freedom side, and an order side. Thus, like a person who has been drawn and quartered, our society has been drawn and quartered by four extremes on the left and the right.

I will also prove that the bipartisan ruling class has been using and exploiting these four extremes to destroy the vital center—not just its grounding, its public philosophy, but also the institutions, associations, and civic virtue built on this grounding, all things vital to providing a buffer between the middle and working class and the ruling elites. The more the grounding and the institutions and associations it rests on are weakened, the easier it is for the ruling elite to solidify and maintain their power, control, and wealth. It is vital that whether we vote Republican or Democrat we move beyond seeing this as a battle solely between Democrats and Republicans, but rather that polarized positions exist on both sides, that the enemies to our constitutional republic—the oligarchic class—are bipartisan and will side with whichever party or candidate lines up best with their views. Corrupted officials exist on both sides of the aisle.

My goal is to help you see that the real threat to our system is oligarchy, those that hate our constitutional republic, and that the enemies of our republic exist in both parties, sometimes in equal measure and sometimes more in one party than the other. But until we recognize the threat, we will never appreciate, defend, and restore our constitutional republic, and we will never regain a new vital center, one capable of holding together a diverse, multiethnic, and commercial republic.

In part three I will lay out the new vital center, one that transcends our partisan divide. I will demonstrate how this new vital center is capable of providing us a renewed public philosophy, one capable of grounding, guiding, and shaping our life together, our identity as individuals, and our common story as a nation. Made up of the "Four Souls," this new vital center is our last best hope for unity, a unity that is capable of protecting the rights of all people, inspiring responsibility toward one another, and providing a vision of America where the ends we pursue bring true freedom, liberty, and justice for all. In this section I will also sketch out how the church and its leaders have a unique opportunity to lead the nation in this discussion and in the discovery of a new vital center, and at the same time reestablish the church as an important voice in our culture.

Who Is This Book For?

And this leads me to the question of my audience. I am writing for two primary audiences. First, I am writing for pastors and Christian leaders in all walks of life, including in politics, business/economics, and culture/education, who see this polarization tearing apart their congregations and organizations. They desperately want unity but don't know how to find a new vital center. And they long for an organization that is truly missional, one guided by a public philosophy of civic and public life, providing a road map for lasting impact.

Moreover, it is written for those who realize that if evangelicals, one of the largest voting blocks in America, fail to lead, they will continue to be tossed to-and-fro on the waves of partisan political polarization, incapable of helping the country rediscover a viable public philosophy and bring the country together. In fact, I contend that we are in trouble as a nation and a church if evangelicals don't regain a public philosophy, one capable of diagnosing our cold civil war, one that can call out our political polarization on both sides (and how the ruling elite exploits it) and clearly articulate a new vital center based on natural and divine sources.

But along with pastors and Christian leaders, this book is for all those who care deeply, whether on the left or the right, about the best of America: our constitutional republicanism and civil liberties, our civic republican tradition, the sharing of power between all classes in society, a robust working and middle class, and ultimately the fight against oligarchy in all its manifestations throughout American history.[46] It is for those who are saddened by the cold civil war, by the takeover of our country by the ruling class, afraid of what it means for civil liberties of all people. It is for those who believe deeply that grounding our politics and social and economic life in more than pure power is important and that a renewed public philosophy is desperately needed, and they want to be part of this new movement. To this end I believe my new quadrant system, clearly showing how polarization on the right and left is tearing us apart and what a bipartisan new vital center must look like, will be an aha moment for many, helping open up all kinds of dialogue with erstwhile enemies that are now allies.

My Hope

My hope in writing this book is that it is not too late to call America back from the brink of total oligarchy, an impending hot civil war, and the total destruction of our constitutional democracy. It is my hope that it is possible to step back from the abyss, the threat of the total destruction of our republic in the name of revolution, whether from the far left or the far right.

I am well aware that many thinkers are not optimistic that we can end our cold civil war.[47] Many on the left say that only violence can transform America into a nation of racial equity. Some of the right believe that the American regime has already been captured and only a revolution will win it back. Claremont McKenna professor Charles Kesler is one of those thinkers on the right who contends the culture war may be too great to overcome, that in fact our republic has already been lost. If this is indeed true, he believes there are only two real options—one side secedes from the nation or, worse, our cold civil war turns into a hot civil war and we begin to kill one another in a second civil war.[48] Kesler realizes we need a different path and writes, almost wistfully, "Let us pray that we and our countrymen will find a way to reason together and to compromise, allowing us to avoid the worst of these dire scenarios—that we will find, that is, the better angels in our nature."[49] Yes let's hope our better angels can and will prevail. But here's the thing: even if the republic has been lost (or never existed, as the Far Left says) or we need to split apart to avoid a real civil war, those who love constitutional republicanism will still need to regain the new vital center, at least to strengthen and safeguard the newly created nation, whenever and wherever it is formed.

Two hundred years ago Alexis de Tocqueville, the greatest observer of American democracy, observed that "the most powerful, most intelligent, and most moral class of the nation have not sought to take hold of it so as to direct it. Democracy has therefore been abandoned to its *savage instincts*."[50] In fact, while some of our best leaders have failed to protect our public philosophy, others have purposely corrupted it for their own plutocratic ambitions. Like Tocqueville, I believe what we need today is a "new political science," one "to instruct democracy, if possible to reanimate its beliefs, to purify its mores."[51] One that will provide the grounding to justify our system, the glue to hold us together, and the God-ordained norms found in nature, discovered by right reason and strengthened and made clear in revelation, protecting our rights and inspiring our responsibilities. This is the new vital center.

Like Tocqueville I hope to make clear that "this book is not precisely in anyone's camp . . . to serve or contest any party" but "to see . . . further than the parties," and in the process "ponder the future."[52] In the end, this book is about principle, not party, and my argument is open to anyone who mourns the loss of a vital center and wants to understand why we are being polarized and how we can regain a new vital center.

I invite you to come along with me and see that despite how polarized we are, how strong the ruling class has become, and why we may be in the eleventh hour of our country, we must remain hopeful. Ultimately, we are not guided by uncontrollable forces; we are actors that have real agency and real voices, and we need to use them. And that when we see that this struggle is a moral and ethical and spiritual battle, we will have the courage not to give in but to work for a better day. I hope it is not too late.

PART ONE

HOW WE GOT INTO THE COLD CIVIL WAR

1

THE EVANGELICAL DILEMMA
AND THE SEARCH FOR
PUBLIC PHILOSOPHY

Evangelicals are divided over politics. They are experiencing their own cold civil war in the pews, afraid to talk to one another, angry, wounded.[1] A year ago, I had lunch with a fellow church member, an extremely successful veteran Hollywood producer. He self-describes as a left-of-center, pro-life, registered independent, politically engaged, non-Trump voter. As he sat down he seemed preoccupied, so I asked him how he was doing. Not well, he said. He told me that he just had a long conversation with an old friend, a long argument, really, where his friend condemned him for *not* supporting the president, practically calling him a traitor to America. He couldn't believe it. He felt attacked, misunderstood, and hurt.

After sympathizing with his hurt over this political rift with his friend, I told him that my Facebook feed is filled with the same kind of derision in the other direction. Not a day goes by that my Trump-hating Christian friends, many of them pastors and Christian leaders, some I've known for years, attack Trump supporters, calling them hypocrites, accusing them of lying, being conspiracy theorists, and being brainwashed in a cult.

No wonder people in the pews avoid discussing politics and avoid one another. And even if we are willing to take the attacks from friends, defending ourselves is futile—social media makes rational dialogue impossible. As soon as someone tries to point out the other candidate did the same thing, they are accused of dodging the issue, of being guilty of the dreaded *whataboutism*, the new term for excusing the behavior of one's favorite candidate by pointing out the behavior of the opposing candidate.

But the real goal of slinging around whataboutism is to avoid the charge of hypocrisy. No one wants to be seen as inconsistent, but even more important no one wants to jeopardize their side's hold on power or give the other side ammunition, so they remain silent about the infractions of their side. After years of condemning Bill Clinton for his character, conservative evangelicals were suddenly willing to give Donald Trump a pass on his three marriages. For the past four years we heard nonstop about how Trump was a danger to the institutions of democracy, and now progressive evangelicals say nothing about Biden, who in his first one hundred days has signed more executive orders, bypassing Congress, than any president in history.

At some level, when it comes to electoral politics and our favorite candidate, we are all tribalists. And this tribalism prevents us from having calm, rational discussions with those across the political aisle. The partisan divisions have grown worse over the years, fraying friendships and even marriages.[2] Moreover, it seems that every month there is a new issue to divide evangelicals. Conflicts over Trump's character, the Russia conspiracy, the Brett Kavanaugh hearings, immigrant children at the border, the first impeachment, the pandemic lockdowns, church shutdowns, and mask wearing—these divided evangelicals over the course of the Trump presidency. Now disputes over election fraud conspiracies, vaccine mandates and vaccine passports, and mass immigration at the US–Mexican border continue to divide evangelicals. Christians online and in the media take sides. People dig in, their views already confirmed by bias, and more division results. Divided, Christians stop talking to one another, and the unity of the church is splintered. And who wins when this happens? Certainly not the church, nor our witness, nor our ability to impact the world around us.

And in the midst of all this division, many pastors have no idea what to do. Some decide, having been deeply affected by the Black Lives Matter protests after the George Floyd death, that it's time to educate their congregation about racism and white supremacy, pleasing some in the congregation, angering others. Other pastors decide it is time to teach on Christian patriotism and love of country, again pleasing some and pushing away others. Churches now are taking part in their own version of the "big sort," not sorting over doctrine or worship styles but political affiliation, blue versus red, Trump versus never-Trump.[3] And still other pastors, desperately wanting to hold on to unity, avoid politics at all costs and stick to preaching the gospel text—keeping the application limited to the individual, afraid that any reference to our current political situation will alienate a large portion of the congregation. Doing this, however, avoids one problem only to engender another. By ignoring the challenges and suffering, the anxiety and the fear, the economic hardships and political disagreements, these pastors neglect to shepherd their members. They miss out on an opportune time to teach a biblical worldview—a worldview that would give tools to understand our current polarization, how to be salt and light in the midst of it, and how to bring renewal. And, even worse, their silence affirms the status quo.

A few months before the 2020 election, I drove to San Diego to spend four hours on a Saturday morning with one of my former associate pastors, Steven Cooper, and a handful of his leaders from the center-city church he was pastoring at the time. As a pastor he understood his responsibility to address the struggles of his members and teach them to think Christianly about every area of life, including their civic and political responsibilities. Yet, not wanting to alienate anyone in his congregation over politics, he didn't know what to do. He was honest about the struggle. The current political climate had become so contentious, so complicated, and so confusing on both sides of the political spectrum that it was hard to even know where to begin. And he felt like no matter how much he followed national politics, how much he read, or how hard he tried to understand the polarized views in his congregation, he just did not know enough to bring the two sides together. So it was safer not to say anything about politics, hoping things would get better and heal over time. But he knew it probably wouldn't. So I ventured down to San Diego to see if I could help.

Even before I got there, I knew how hard it would be. There are a myriad of forces that encourage polarization, many that monetarily benefit from it and even more who see polarization as part of a plan to change society. Big media has discovered that polarization and fearmongering pays big bucks.[4]

Social media outlets like Twitter seem to thrive on nastiness. Politicians stoke the us-versus-them divide to build party loyalty and destroy opponents. Big business has become woke. Education is now politicized. Polarization is everywhere—in professional sports, fashion, architecture, pop culture, Hollywood, and even the military. There doesn't seem to be any safe space anymore, any free-speech zone, any place in our society where we can get away from the culture war. All of life is political. And in early 2021, it only got worse. Now, if we step out of line on social media, we can be deplatformed, demonetized, destroyed. Now, if a pastor or a church holds a position that just a year ago would be considered mainstream, or if we challenge the ruling class in anyway, we are in trouble and could earn the appellation of "domestic terrorist."

How dangerous is it getting for pastors and churches? Recently, the *New York Times* proposed the Biden administration adopt a "Reality Czar" to help our nation determine what reality is and what is not, what thoughts and actions are acceptable, and what ones are out of bounds, dangerous to the norms and institutions of our democracy.[5] Facebook has appointed a vice president of civil rights to keep all content and users in line with the founder's vision of the world.[6] Google polices speech through their secret algorithm.[7] The result: some Hollywood and music stars are being canceled in social media and fired from their jobs. We now have a confluence of big government, big media, and big tech joining the post-9/11 surveillance state to root out views not acceptable to the ruling class. In fact, someone criticized a politician on Twitter to later have the police show up at his door.[8] In early February 2021, the new US defense secretary ordered a stand-down to begin rooting out anyone who holds views similar to those of the people who stormed the Capitol whether they were there or not.[9] The FBI and CIA are already rooting out domestic terrorists in our country. How soon before church websites, sermons, and mission statements are next, particularly for those who believe in constitutional republicanism?

But as I arrived at Steven's backyard patio for discussion, on a cool September day, a nice ocean breeze blowing, I resolved one thing: in spite of all the dangers of the cancel culture or that even this conversation could increase polarization, Christian leaders must have these conversations, learning to understand the context of their ministry and what must be done to train their members. Fear of persecution, the dread of cancel culture, or the reluctance of offending the ruling class or further dividing members can't be an excuse for avoiding politics. They must take the risk. But if pastors are going to take the risk, it begins by equipping themselves. If they are going to have productive conversations, understand the who-what-why of polarization, and lead their churches and organizations to have real impact in their towns and cities, then they must be trained. They can't give away what they don't have. But this is the problem. They aren't trained—most are theologians, not political philosophers.

When George Floyd died in spring 2020, and protests and riots erupted, I kept waiting for the church to speak into the situation, to say something, to lead, to save our cities. I wanted to see churches give the people in the pews some guidance on what was happening. But I only saw more partisan divide. As the media politicized it, so did Christian leaders. I was shocked how ill-equipped the evangelical church was, unable to provide any national leadership, reacting more than leading.

And as the summer progressed, with riots spreading to dozens of cities, the country teetering on breakdown, the coronavirus creating more economic hardship, battles increasing over how to end the pandemic, and disputes about science and medicine growing, it was obvious to anyone paying attention that the church was unprepared to provide national leadership on any of these issues. Instead what it provided was tribal, politicized, and polarized. It seemed like every conversation came back to Trump, either blaming or excusing him. And then when the Capitol riots happened, it exposed the church again, for its lack of training, its inability to understand what was going on and speak with one voice; instead the event became one more polarizing issue, political theater for advancing partisan agendas. Why is the evangelical church so ill-equipped to provide leadership in times of national crisis? Why are so many pastors unable to help their congregations think through so many tough civil and cultural issues?

Over the past few years I have surveyed what books have shaped pastors' politics and which of those, if any, they recommend to curious congregation members who want to understand politics. Sometimes they can think of one or two, but typically they draw a blank. Part of the problem is the dearth of books written by evangelicals on politics. So few evangelicals are trained to write them; without the resources, pastors aren't trained, and when pastors aren't trained, they can't disciple their members on civic issues—how to think about them, what to do about them, being salt and light within them. Here is a partial list of recent issues that Christians are facing on a daily basis:

- not wearing masks versus wearing them
- obeying emergency measures versus civil disobedience
- colorblindness versus antiracism
- nationalism versus globalism
- climate change skepticism versus climate change acceptance
- biological binary sex versus gender fluidity
- free speech versus cancel culture
- equality versus equity
- capitalism versus socialism
- border walls versus open borders
- woke schools versus patriotic schools

I could add more items to this list: these are everyday issues that Christians encounter on social media, cable news, and podcasts, and in discussions with their neighbors, on their jobs, and while educating their children. In fact, in my Pasadena neighborhood, every other house seems to have a sign in their yard supporting BLM and open immigration, broadcasting to everyone what side of the culture war they are on. On our Nextdoor app, people rage against those not wearing masks while walking their dogs alone. And yet in the midst of all this social conflict, most churches remain silent on these issues, giving little help to their members to think and act Christianly. Why? Some of it is because of fear, terrified of dividing their church. Some of it is fear of being canceled by the culture or fined.[10] But I think it is deeper than a lack of courage. At its heart, the problem is that evangelical leaders lack a public philosophy, a well-thought-out philosophy of civic thought and action, a worldview that includes the issues of citizenship and civics and civility; without this, most (but not all) pastors don't have the confidence to lean into these issues.

THE GREAT EVANGELICAL WEAKNESS

In his helpful book *Evangelicals in the Public Square*, J. Budziszewski puts his finger on the problem: "Although evangelicals," he says, "have long played a part in the public square, *they have never developed a clear, cohesive, and Christian view of what politics is about*."[11] Some of this is because evangelicals have historically put the stress on individual conversion and not paid as much attention to the broader culture: "If only everyone were converted, the public square would take care of itself."[12] But more importantly, he contends, among evangelicals "orderly political reflection has not yet risen to the task."[13] What keeps evangelicals from having lasting influence in politics and culture, "from offering a serious challenge to the dominant political theories of the secular establishment," argues Budziszewski, "is that it has failed to ask many of the most essential questions, failed to answer many of the questions it *has* asked, and thrown away half of its resources for answering them."[14] Evangelicals lack a thought-out and detailed political philosophy. To begin, writes Budziszewski,

> adequate political theory . . . would include three elements: (1) an *orienting doctrine*, or a guide to thought, explaining the place of government in the world as a whole; (2) a *practical doctrine*, or a guide to action, explaining in broad but practical terms how Christians should conduct themselves in the civic realm; and (3) a *cultural apologetic*, or a guide to persuasion, explaining how to go about making the specific proposals of those who share the other two element plausible to those who do not.[15]

Included in this apologetic, he continues, is the understanding that the evangelicals' commitment to truth will clash with secularism, and ultimately there will be a conflict of visions. Budziszewski is calling evangelicals to do the hard work of formulating a public philosophy. He contends that a coherent political theory or public philosophy must include a theoretical component—the roles of government and civil society and the ends to which the society is committed; a practical component—a theory of governance, that is, how people should conduct themselves in the public square; and a grounding or a cultural apologetic—the underlying justification for our life together, that is, what provides the ultimate authority for our life together and why this agreement is necessary to provide unity and consensus.

So often, however, when I bring up the need for pastors to develop a public philosophy, they push back, arguing that they don't need one, the Bible is their textbook. "We don't need political philosophy. We just need to faithfully preach the text," they say. "And if someone has the wrong political views, it is because they are not faithful to the Bible." And there are a number of books out there that reinforce this view.[16]

But here's the problem. Both partisan sides have the Bible, and both sides appeal to it, sometimes using the exact same verses, on government (e.g., Romans 13), on immigration, or on what makes a godly leader, to defend their side. Yet how is it possible, then, that the same Bible can be used to defend such divergent, polar opposite political views? How is it possible that Christians like David French and Eric Metaxas come to such divergent political views on former president Trump? How can theologian Wayne Grudem and journalist Michael Gerson, or conservative activist Franklin Graham and progressive theologian Ron Sider, see the political world so differently? Or how is it that author Jemar Tisby believes that critical race theory can help us understand biblical justice and yet pastor Voddie Baucham contends it is a Trojan horse inside the evangelical church?[17] How can historian John Fea argue that America was never a Christian nation, but historian David Mark Hall believe it was?[18] If the Bible is all we need for politics, why does it mean so many different things to so many different people?[19]

TWIN PROBLEMS OF ACCOMMODATION AND INFLATION

According to Budziszewski, the reason is simple: most evangelicals fall into the error of "projective accommodation." That is, evangelicals accommodate Scripture to their own political views "by reading those views into the biblical text."[20] Over the centuries, he contends, evangelicals have found warrant for monarchies, republics, democracies, and many other forms of government. But here's the truth, at once shocking and liberating. When it comes to the proper form of government, "Scripture provides no criterion." This is the evangelical dilemma:

> The problem for evangelical thinkers is not that the Bible contains no political teaching (for it does) but that the Bible does not provide *enough by itself* for an adequate political theory. Although important general

principles about government can indeed be drawn from Scripture, the list of such principles is short.[21]

After listing ten general biblical principles, he notes that while "these ten principles are sufficient to give a jolt to secularist political thinking . . . they fall far short of an adequate doctrine of politics, . . . in fact, not a single requirement of political theory is satisfied."[22] Here's the rub for Budziszewski: the Bible does not give us an adequate orienting doctrine, an adequate practical doctrine, or an adequate cultural apologetic.

> The ten principles tell us precious little about the place of government in the world as a whole, still less about how Christians conduct themselves in the civic realm, and almost nothing about how to make Christian cultural aims and aspirations plausible to those who do not share the biblical worldview.[23]

And because the Bible does not include everything needed for a robust political theory and evangelicals are unwilling to admit this (for fear that they may somehow undermine the sufficiency of Scripture), evangelicals are confident that they can fill in what is missing. But what happens, contends Budziszewski, is that "they try to draw more money than the bank contains" and thus are guilty of "inflationary" tactics: taking aspects of the Bible like "God's code for ancient Israel," or the biblical theme of covenant, or particular "policies adopted by biblical rulers" and inflating them into a full-blown political theory.[24]

> What all such methods have in common is that they make the normative political teaching of the Bible seem more ample than it is. They read into it principles that are not really there that really come from the intuitions of the interpreter . . . in the political thought of evangelicals, much of what passes for biblicism is really intuitionism in disguise.[25]

Thus, evangelicals hold certain political or social views or belong to a particular political persuasion and then *find* in Scripture what *we want* in order to baptize it with the Bible. Examples of inflationary tactics from both sides, in history and present times, can easily be found.[26] When evangelicals connect the Bible to current cultural views, they think that this demonstrates a high view of Scripture, when in fact it often shows that culture is the more powerful factor, enticing evangelicals into accommodation and inflation.

THE EVANGELICAL DILEMMA

Why is it so easy to fall into these twin errors of accommodation and inflation? According to Budziszewski, "Although evangelicals are rightly committed to grounding their political reflection in revelation, the Bible provides insufficient material for the task."[27] It's that simple. Yet evangelicals do not want to admit this fact, and thus the twin errors of inflation and accommodation remain at the heart of the "evangelical dilemma." According to Budziszewski, the answer to the dilemma, if they are willing to admit it, "lies in the recognition that the Bible is only part of the revelation." Along with *special revelation* in the Bible that God has provided to the people of faith, he has also provided *general revelation*, which is found in nature and our use of reason, making his revelation evident "not only to believers but to all humankind."[28] Budziszewski mentions Psalm 19:1 as a good example: "the heavens are telling the glory of God; and the firmament proclaims his handiwork" (NRSV). We see this same knowledge of general revelation in Romans 1:19-20 where Paul writes, "What can be known about God is plain to them, because God has shown it to them. For his invisible attributes, namely, his eternal power and divine nature, have been clearly perceived, ever since the creation of the world."

Because this knowledge of God and his creation is known, Paul goes on to say that when people outside of the family of faith "who do not have the law, by nature do what the law requires. . . . They show that the work of the law is written on their hearts" (Romans 2:14-15).[29] Budziszewski calls this knowledge "natural law," which he defines "as an ordinance of reason, for the common good, made by him who has care of the community."[30] In Reformed circles this has always meant that God has embedded his creational norms into the world, that these norms, the way things ought to be, can be discerned and carried out, though often imperfectly and with great difficulty.[31] General revelation or natural law, then, is the conviction that design permeates the natural realm in general, and human beings in particular; that our conscience bears witness to its existence; and that when we violate natural law we not only know it intellectually, often suppressing it, but we experience it with deep feelings of guilt and brokenness.[32] Through cultivating a heart of wisdom, humans can read God's general revelation and know God's design for the world. Yet many evangelicals are unfamiliar with the concept of general revelation, thus they struggle to work out a full-orbed public philosophy.

In holding up natural law, Budziszewski is not saying that the Bible is defective. He takes pains to say that "the Bible is indispensable."[33] Without the Bible we don't know where to go for forgiveness when we break the law and our conscience condemns us. Special revelation tells us not only where to go for absolution but who absolves us, laying out the plan of salvation. But just as natural law needs the Bible, the Bible depends on natural law, taking for granted that its readers bring a certain natural knowledge with them when they encounter the Bible. The Bible can't contain all truth about all subject matters, so the Bible takes "for granted that we know certain large truths." Natural law exists; and we can't but know it.[34] Thus both forms of knowledge, general revelation and special revelation, work together. For Budziszewski, God communicates through *both* general and special revelation. We can't have a full view of knowledge, ourselves, and our responsibilities without both, each complementing and enhancing the other.[35]

And here we get to the crux of Budziszewski's argument—why evangelicals fall into the twin errors of accommodation and inflation and why they lack a full-orbed political theory. Without a natural-law doctrine, without these first principles, rooted in both special revelation *and general revelation*, evangelicals will never be able to work out a coherent public philosophy. And without it they will continue to force the Bible to say more than it is capable of, inflating biblical passages that confirm a political bias. But even more importantly, without a public philosophy, which takes hard work and deep thinking, Christians will not have the resources to transcend polarization, staying stuck in tribalism almost by default. And when this happens, Christians add to the cold civil war we are experiencing, increasing the echo chamber. If we evangelicals are going to avoid this polarization, we must rediscover a robust vision of general revelation, that is, natural law, and do the hard work of formulating a public philosophy, one that is faithful to both divine and natural revelation.

MY SEARCH FOR PUBLIC PHILOSOPHY

I didn't know it at the time, but my search for a public philosophy started as an undergrad at Gordon College, a small, Christian liberal arts school in

New England where I majored in politics. As a fairly new believer fascinated with politics, I wanted to develop a well thought-out worldview, one that would help me understand politics. I admired political thinkers, who, regardless of the political issue, could fit most issues into a consistent political philosophy. I wanted that skill. In my classes, my professors introduced the thought of Dutch theologian and prime minister Abraham Kuyper (1837–1920), who taught extensively on common grace.[36] In Kuyper I found someone who had worked out a public philosophy based on both general and special revelation.

Following college I enrolled at Fuller Theological Seminary to suss out the connection between these creational norms and public philosophy. At Fuller I learned more about common grace and natural law tradition under the tutelage of Richard Mouw, who a few years later would became Fuller's president and remain in that post for twenty years. He introduced me to the twentieth-century neo-Kuyperian tradition, comprising those who took their cues from Kuyper and tried to apply his principles to the issues of the day.[37]

After Fuller, I attended the PhD program at Georgetown University, set among grand nineteenth-century buildings, manicured lawns, tree-canopied walkways, and founded in the Catholic tradition.[38] With a strong tradition of natural law, which overlapped a great deal with my Kuyperian views on common grace, I decided to major in political theory. My mentor was Professor George Carey, a nationally renowned expert on *The Federalist Papers*. Under his tutelage and that of Father James Schall, a Jesuit priest, I was able to dig deeper into natural law. Both professors impressed on me what the rejection of this tradition meant for our nation.

One essay by Carey had a huge impact on me. In his "On the Degeneration of Public Philosophy in America," Carey argues that public philosophy, rooted in natural law "provides transcendent standards for society: standards to set goals, serve as restraints, and as measures of society's health."[39] Therefore, "the loss of the public philosophy . . . has created a disorder within the 'soul' of modern society that weakens its cohesion and moral sensibilities."[40] I began to realize that this "disorder within the soul," brought on by the rejection of natural law was at the heart of our nation's disintegration and polarization.

A short time later, I came across another helpful essay, "What Is the Public Philosophy?," by University of Virginia's James Ceaser, a nationally recognized scholar of the presidency.[41] Ceaser contends that for a public philosophy to be effective, it must address the following questions:

> What is the bond or social glue that constitutes Americans as a people; what are the ends—and their rank order . . . equality, freedom, order, justice and virtue? What are the respective roles assigned to government and civil society, or the public and the private spheres, in promoting these ends; how is political authority conceived and allocated, which is sometimes referred to as a "theory of governance"?[42]

Another way to express this is that "the public philosophy may therefore be conceived as a system in which the parts bear certain connections to each other."[43]

For Ceaser these represent the "political elements" of a public philosophy. And different public philosophies will differ on the question of ends, roles, and theory of governance. Yet for Ceaser, it would be easy for us to stop at "this list of recognizable practical political elements."[44] But understanding public philosophy raises deeper questions. For example, what justifies any decision on political arrangements about power sharing, liberty, and law? Here we get to the question of justification or what he calls "grounding," that is, what is the ultimate authority to answer questions of means and ends. How public philosophies are grounded "are integral parts of the public philosophy."[45] To further define the term he continues,

> a grounding refers to a philosophical or theological foundation that derives from a first principle about the character of the world as a whole or of social existence. . . . A grounding is deemed to be so fundamental that it supplies a starting point in need of no further justification; it answers the "why" question that anyone might pose.[46]

Grounding, thus, was key.

Because of this overlap of "grounding" with natural law and general revelation, I wanted to attend Georgetown and no other university. If I just wanted to understand the parts of a government and how politics worked, apart from a grounding, I could have gone to any graduate program that offered programs in political science. There I could have learned about the parts and studied politics from a scientific point of view. But I wanted to understand more than just the parts. I wanted to understand how these parts were grounded, and how they fit together, almost by design. And for that I had to find one of the few graduate programs that still valued normative questions and hadn't eliminated their political philosophy programs, reducing politics to the mechanics of a science, devoid of first principles, relying on opinion surveys and sociology. I knew that questions of grounding are ultimately religious.[47] Because whether one believes in God or not (or something else, whether it be nature, natural rights, history, culture, expressive individualism), the grounding of any system is ultimately a religious one. Faith is put in something to justify the political system. The crisis of this grounding—fundamental disputes about first principles—is at the heart of our public philosophy. Because if we no longer have the correct grounding, we no longer have a vital center; instead we are in the midst of a culture war.

Public philosophy, then, is about how humans get along, how they form and maintain a common life together, how they handle conflict and disagreements, and ultimately what law and conception of justice they appeal to in order to not only ground life together but settle ongoing conflict.[48] As James Hunter points out, our cultural war today is ultimately a crisis of authority, a crisis over what Ceaser calls grounding. What is the authority (grounding) that ultimately governs our life together? What was the grounding of our founding, and what grounds our democratic project today? Ultimately, this question, even more than the particular parts of our life together (constitutional government, separation of powers, checks and balances, federalism, associational life) is at the heart of our debates over public philosophy and our political polarization.

MY BIG BREAKTHROUGH

Returning to our discussion of the evangelical dilemma, how does my discovery so many years ago—the need for a well-thought-out public philosophy, one grounded in natural law—help the church and its leaders, both pastors and marketplace leaders? How does it help us move beyond the evangelical dilemma we experience? To start, it means we must realize that we need both general revelation, natural law, *and* divine revelation, the Bible. And this means that if we are going to understand what has been revealed to humans in the area of general revelation, we have to study the history of political thought.

That is why I went to Georgetown and why I have spent a lifetime reading political philosophy. I glean insights from general revelation, integrate these insights with what the Bible says, and formulate a public philosophy, one that grounds our political system and gives us a framework for living as citizens, all the while trying to avoid the twin errors of inflation and accommodation. But it hasn't been easy. From the start I knew that if I were to work out a public philosophy to guide me and help the evangelical church, I needed a framework for making sense of the history of political thought. So I set about devising one.

Mapping the Right-Left Spectrum

One of the more interesting classes I took at Georgetown was A Symposium on Conservatism, taught by George Carey, a class that attempted to help us map the different conservative views on public philosophy. I learned that modern conservatism was basically a reaction to the way modern liberals had, according to conservatives, hijacked the classical liberal position. It was a history of their attempt to get it back. That conservatives were the original classical liberals and that modern liberals are actually progressives, desiring to break with the liberalism of the founders, was at the heart of conservatism. Yet even within conservatism, I quickly discovered, thinkers differed widely about their understanding of classical liberalism; for example, what had gone wrong in American, when it went wrong, who was to blame, and how to fix it.

During the class I recall my attempt to map what I was learning, placing each of the conservative thinkers on the liberal-conservative spectrum. But I struggled to do so. If, as Carey taught, the original founding and the Constitution balanced order and liberty, calling it "ordered liberty," was it possible to put the Left on the side of liberty and the Right on the side of order? I tried this, but it posed problems.

For example, where would I place libertarians, committed to individual and economic freedom? Would I place them on the liberty side (the left) or the order side (the right)? And what about liberals who champion extreme expressive individualism, and yet at the same time want more government control of the economy, some going so far as calling for socialism? Would I place them on the left (liberty) or on the right (order) side of the spectrum? And where would I put social and cultural conservatives, who stress the need for morality and virtue? Would I place them on the order (right) side?

And where would I place myself, as a neo-Kuyperian? After all, I was highly critical of both the expressive individualism of the left (liberty side) and at the same time in favor of the need for morality and virtue in society (order side). Yet I was also against the administrative state ordering the economy and in favor of economic freedom. Was I on the order side, the liberty side, or both? Was I a classical liberal or a cultural conservative or both? At the time, I began to realize that the left-right spectrum was inadequate, but I didn't have an alternative. So when I left Georgetown my attempt at discovering a framework was sadly incomplete. But I kept working on it for decades.

During the two-plus decades that followed my graduate work at Georgetown, I continued to rely on my understanding of the left-right spectrum, doing my best to overcome its limitations in my own public philosophy. For the most part, modern political liberals continued their drumbeat for more and more personal autonomy, breaking away from all traditional authority structures like the family and church, especially in the area of sexuality and morality, described so well in Robert Bellah's *Habits of the Heart* and Allan Bloom's *The Closing of the American Mind*. From Hollywood movies to Madison Avenue to postmodern relativism in the universities to expressive individualism being enshrined in our judicial law, liberalism trumpeted personal gratification and desire. Liberals constantly decried the conservative attempt to legislate morality, infringing on the individuals' right to determine their own morality, truth, and good life.

In the 1990s the liberal commitment to personal autonomy and liberation was at the heart of the Left's hatred of the Christian Right. Since there was no standard for the good, individuals must be free from all traditional authority, particularly traditional religion to pursue their own ideas of the good life. "If it feels good, do it" was the liberal mantra. This continued through the 2000s during the George W. Bush years. Then, around 2008, I noticed something curious: the Left's message began to change. Suddenly, the Left seemed to discover a vision of the good, not just for the individual but for society as a whole. It turns out there is a morality after all, there is a way all people *should* live, there is a cosmic vision of justice and the good. But there was a twist.

This new progressive vision didn't include the founding documents of America. In fact, instead of seeing the Declaration of Independence and the Constitution as allies for personal autonomy and expressive individualism, as the Left had done for decades, the Far Left decreed these documents and the entire founding of American as evil, compromised from the start. Now the founding fathers were seen as racist, the Constitution as endorsing slavery, and the entire system corrupt.[49] All of a sudden, I noticed the Left wasn't appealing to our founding in order to call Americans back to its guiding principles (as Martin Luther King Jr. did in his famous "Letter from Birmingham Jail"), that is, to live up to its ideals, but that these very ideals were evil. If America was ever to be a place we could be proud of, it had to decry its past, erase its history, tear down its monuments, root out all racism, homophobia, misogyny, destroy capitalism, and begin anew, creating a new socialist utopia. The Left went from being against those who wanted to legislate morality to legislating their own type of morality.

Then, around 2009, the Left's vision of justice began to influence the church.[50] As the Christian Right was waning, the Christian Left was waxing. Books about justice started to appear, many of them wanting to revive Walter Rauschenbusch's social gospel teaching, a helpful charge to serve the poor but a deeply flawed theologically account of the Christian's life and the state's responsibility.

Then I noticed another change. Around 2015, books from the Christian Left were not just calling for the government to spend more money on the poor, to increase the size of the welfare state, but were calling the entire American system, root and branch, into question. They too were condemning the Constitution, claiming that any document that protected slavery must be rejected.

But as the Left was moving further left, the Right seemed to become more radical as well, demonstrating a loss of faith not only in our current system but calling into question the founding.[51] This was new. In condemning the illiberal takeover of the Constitution, Christian thinkers on the right were calling for illiberal solutions, sometimes radically libertarian solutions. To burn it all down. So even as evangelicals on the left were moving further left, Christians on the right were moving further right.

MY BREAKTHROUGH

In 2018, halfway through the Trump presidency, in the midst of so much polarization in our nation and the church, I began sketching out this book, wanting to explain polarization and why the evangelical church needed a public philosophy. But I ran into a problem. If I were to explain polarization, I needed a better framework than the left-right spectrum. But nothing better existed. I was still using the outdated left-right spectrum.

That is when I had a breakthrough. What if the left (freedom) and the right (order) don't sit on opposite sides of the freedom-order continuum; what if each have an order and a freedom side? If this were true, it would explain why it was so hard to map them on an axis. So at that moment, I took out my crude drawing of the left-right spectrum and drew a line right down the middle, bisecting the left and right, thus creating a quadrant with two axes, not one. On one side of the new axis was order and the other side freedom, showing that the left and the right both have two sides—order and freedom. Thus the left and the right both had an order side and a freedom side. Immediately, my mapping started making sense. I no longer struggled with deciding where to put thinkers and authors; plotting them on the quadrant became fairly simple.

But then I discovered something else. Within each quadrant some representatives were more radical than others in the quadrant. So I took out my pencil again and drew a line, dissecting each quadrant, radiating out from the center axis. On this line I drew three positions. I could have had more, but these categories seemed enough to show the progression from the middle out to the extremes.

Looking at the extremes in each quadrant (the #3 position), I realized that these four extremes are pulling further and further away from the center. They are the ones speaking with the loudest voice, abetted by our national media. Furthermore, I noticed that all four extremes have a strong proclivity to illiberal solutions, favoring a type of elitist oligarchy over democracy, the rule of the elite over the many, and opening them up to the charge of fascism or totalitarianism.

But I didn't just notice the existence of the four extremes on the left and the right. As I began to place certain thinkers in the first positions (closest to the center), I began to see something curious. Thinkers in these spots, unlike the four extremes, didn't reject the natural-law tradition; they recognized the need for some kind of grounding and were much more open to returning to the founding documents, rooted as they were in an antecedent authority, one that transcended oligarchy (rule of the elite) and democracy (rule by the voice of the people). In different ways, from different angles to be sure, the four positions were defending a kind of constitutional republicanism, a tradition, certainly, that needed to be reformed or recovered but one worth fighting for nonetheless.

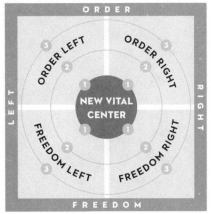

So just like that, I had a system to help understand the groups, thinkers, and ideas that are causing our polarization, and for organizing those quickly. I now had a tool to understand how we lost the vital center and what it looks like to regain it. And, finally, I had discovered a framework to develop a public philosophy capable of unifying Americans, including evangelicals, giving the church a road map for mission, a guide to impact, and the vision to overcome cynicism.

The New Vital Center Quadrant

After spending four hours with Pastor Steven and his leaders in San Diego, laying out the quadrant framework, explaining how we lost the vital center leading to so much polarization, and how we could regain a new vital center rooted in natural law, they seemed to experience a breakthrough. Finally, here was a tool, a framework that could revolutionize how they discipled their members and trained them to impact the city.

In fact, on my way home, Steven called me on my cell phone, explaining that his leaders were so empowered by the quadrant framework that they wanted to share it with the rest of the congregation and begin formulating how their church, using the new insights, could live out the new vital center, influencing the city and the citizens who lived there. The quadrant framework gave them a plan, empowered them, inspired them.

I will explain in more detail this framework, my quadrant system. But first, we need to understand how we lost the vital center in our country and how this started us on the road to polarization. It is to that story that we now turn.

2

THE END OF THE
VITAL CENTER

WHOSE COUNTRY IS IT? And who gets to define what it means to be an American? Just weeks before the 2016 presidential election between Hillary Clinton and Donald Trump, Jeet Heer, writing in the left-of-center *New Republic*, accused the Right of giving up on democracy, voting for a candidate who was a fascist authoritarian. Heer wrote,

> One of the few positives about Donald Trump's run for president is that he forced us to see aspects of American culture that many instinctively turn away from. . . . Anti-democratic sentiment [is] a growing threat. . . . Beyond this election, beyond even the fate of the Republican party, there is a significant minority of Americans who are giving up on democracy because it doesn't serve their purposes of upholding a white Christian patriarchy.[1]

While Heer saw Trump only as a symptom of this growing anti-democratic sentiment, what really worried him was that "even if [Trump] fades as a political force after the election, the underlying disease will remain, and indeed will likely spread."

Now after four years of the Trump presidency and his defeat in the 2020 presidential election, critics were still seeing Trump as a symptom, and even more worried about the growth of the antidemocratic sentiments, not in a small minority fringe of the electorate, but possibly seventy-four million people. And while critics were relieved that Trump was defeated, many pointed to the riots of January 6, 2021, as proof of the fascism that had been growing for years. In many ways, the impeachment of Trump may have been less about him and more about his supporters. Trump was a symptom; what they really feared was Trumpism, now embraced by half the electorate and that threatens to take over the entire Republican party.[2]

Consider the opinion piece by Republican never-Trumper Michael Gerson, writing at the time of the impeachment hearings, and making it clear the real threat is no longer Trump but his legion of supporters: "Trumpism Is American Fascism." After apologizing for going there, Gerson makes clear that anyone who supports and believes in Trump's populism is really a fascist, clinging to "the betrayal of American identity." According to Gerson, "the 45th president and a significant portion [how big he doesn't say] of his supporters have embraced American fascism." While Gerson doesn't think Trump came "close to success," he contends that "the influence of his treacherous ideology is still being spread" and "American fascism needs to be aggressively marginalized."[3]

Writing in the left-leaning *Atlantic*, MSNBC commentator Chris Hayes contends that "the Biden era of American politics is shaping up as a contest between the growing ideological hegemony of liberalism, and the intensifying opposition of a political minority that has proved willing to engage in violence in order to hold power." According to Hayes, "This fight isn't ultimately about policy . . . it's about whether the United States will live up to the promise of democracy—and on that crucial question, we've rarely been so divided." Yet we can't lose hope; there is no way around this division, and "there is no way to avoid that fight if we're to defeat the growing faction that seeks to destroy majority rule." We must, he tells his readers, continue to fight, for "no substantive victories can endure unless democracy is fortified against its foes." So that is the task, according to Hayes—defeating those who oppose democracy, those who resist the "ideological hegemony of liberalism," and thus rooting out that small minority who get in the way of America reaching its democratic promise.[4]

Conservative John Daniel Davidson pushes back on Hayes.[5] Davidson, contra Hayes, contends that the division in America *really is* about policy, and our divide is actually "widening, not narrowing," and this demonstrates there is a "growing faction" that opposes "Democrat efforts to dismantle our constitutional system." At the heart of this opposition are differences over the very meaning of democracy itself, which Hayes equates with far-left progressivism, propagated by a one-party ruling class. And opposition to this majoritarian progressivism is really opposition to the will of the people, and this makes a person antidemocratic. Davidson rejects this equation. "You can smear [certain] Republicans as 'radicalizing against democracy,'" Davidson writes, "but it's really that Republicans are radicalizing against *direct* democracy," and "they know it is the only way to save the republic."[6]

Another conservative, Seth Barron, makes a similar case but notices something else. "A curious turn of phrase," writes Barron, "has slipped into discourse over the last few years."[7] It is the phrase "our democracy." After chronicling the use of this phrase in current discourse, Barron contends:

> Democrats seem not to be so worried about American democracy in general so much as their version of it, which is centered round an agenda of "equity"—meaning careful allocation of all society's plums to favored demographic categories—open borders, the erasure of sex difference, and a globalized economy.

In this sense, "our democracy" has a very definite meaning and it does not mean constitutional republicanism or what I will describe later as the new vital center.

How did we get so polarized? When did we lose any sense of a shared definition of "our democracy," that is, what it means to be an American? How did we lose our vital center? That is the story of this chapter.

How We Lost the Vital Center

I grew up in the 1970s, living in a small coastal town in New England. After school most days I would play for hours with the neighborhood kids, free from parental oversight; some afternoons we roamed freely around the neighboring woods, built forts, or rode our bikes through trails; we played stick ball, street hockey, or played in neighbors' backyards. An hour before dinner my mom would ring a bell, and we knew it was time to go home and wash up before family dinner. It was a great time to grow up. But it wasn't perfect, and it was changing fast.

The ideas unleashed in the 1960s, including the sexual revolution, were already being felt at that time, changing the culture. Our nation's political life was in turmoil. By the time I was ten (1975), America was divided over the wars in Southeast Asia, shocked by the deaths of Martin Luther King Jr. and Bobby Kennedy, stunned by Watergate, and offended by Hollywood's campaign to disrupt traditional values. Our economy was racked by double-digit inflation and lines at the gas pump.

But in spite of the changes happening in American culture, politics, and economics, in spite of the fact that America had a long way to go in providing equality for African Americans, growing up in an American suburb in the 1970s was still fairly idyllic. I look back on my childhood with nostalgia. Is it wrong to look back to those mid-century decades for guidance today?

Yuval Levin thinks so. In *Fractured Republic*, he says that "our political life is now exceedingly nostalgic. . . . This nostalgia is at the core of the frustration that so overwhelms our politics now."[8] Traditional liberals, he says, look to the fifties as a golden era when government and the economy worked well together, unions were strong, and we seemed on the verge of achieving the "Great Society." Conservatives look back and see a time of traditional values, strong families, God in school, and the freedom to pursue economic dreams. Both sides are now disappointed with the present crisis in politics and culture, and thus, he says, we look back to the fifties with nostalgia. Yet Levin says this is a mistake. It keeps us from dealing with the present challenges of modern life, devising solutions to our real life in America now, which he points out will never again look like the 1950s after so much technical advancement, "diffusion," and "deconsolidation" in American life. "If we could see our way past it, we might gain a much better grasp of the nature of the problems we face and the shape of potential solutions."[9]

Time and again Levin hammers away at nostalgia, calling his readers not to a golden age of the fifties but to a realistic assessment of our present discontents. Let's roll up our sleeves and get to work solving the problems that beset our society. Until we give up this longing for a bygone era, we can't move forward. But what if in moving forward we solve more problems and gain more technical sophistication but in the process we lose something even more important, something that unified all Americans, a common political culture? By losing this political unity, aren't we just creating more problems?

So could it be that it's *not* a misguided nostalgia that has led to a fractured nation but the fact that we have nothing in common, no consensus, to facilitate working and living together? He raises this possibility: "If the problem we have is not that we are increasingly failing to live up to our own moral standards, but that we increasingly do not have such standards in common, then wholesale solutions become ever more difficult to imagine."[10] While he doesn't spend much time pursuing this line of argument, he is right. Without a common consensus on moral standards, it is difficult to get anything done in politics. If we can't even agree on the basics, it is hard to work together, and the last time we had some agreement was the mid-twentieth century. So is it possible that our nostalgia for the fifties isn't for the economy or even the culture but for something else: a longing for a lost vital center, a common creed, a mutual covenant, a shared history, a glue that bound us together? This common consensus is now gone.

THE END OF *UNUM* AND THE RISE OF *E PLURIBUS*

In his book *The Twilight of the American Enlightenment: The 1950s and the Crisis of Liberal Belief*, historian George Marsden says that

> the 1950s would look like a sort of golden age for American intellectuals. An ideal was still intact—the notion that the culture of the nation might be guided by a broad inclusive national consensus—and academics and other intellectuals were more on the inside of that project than not.[11]

This national consensus was what Walter Lippmann called "the public philosophy." Lippmann and other proponents of this public philosophy "were passionately committed to principles such as individual freedom, free speech, human decency, justice, civil rights, community responsibilities, equality before the law, due process, balance of powers, economic opportunity, and so forth."[12]

No book captured this consensus better than Democrat historian Arthur Schlesinger's *The Vital Center*, published in 1949.[13] As Marsden writes, "Schlesinger represented the antidogmatic liberal consensus of the era as well as anyone."[14] Trying to find a middle ground beyond the totalitarianism of the Soviet Union and the unlimited freedom of market capitalism, Schlesinger said democracy supported a healthy balance between individual fulfillment and community responsibility and was "a process, not a conclusion [that] . . . dedicates itself to problems as they come, attacking them in terms which best advance the human and libertarian values, which best secure the freedom and fulfillment of the individual."[15]

Marsden points out that Schlesinger's audience in the book is clearly the radical progressive of his own liberal Democratic Party, whom he worried about. Signs that the progressive left threatened his vital center were everywhere, and Schlesinger wanted to shore up a commitment to the American creed before it was too late.[16] Like others who stood in this mid-century vital center Schlesinger stood in continuity with the American founders, and the "new radicalism" of the 1950s threatened this continuity.

Schlesinger wrote *The Vital Center* to warn the mainstream Left about the Far Left that threatened this consensus. The progressive left was pushing a view of human nature that denied original sin and the depravity of man, that promoted socialism, that believed a "new man" was possible if the social structure was changed, that was ultimately utopian. Schlesinger rejected this view of human nature as naive and dangerous, and it threatened to overturn everything our founders fought for: "the conception of the free society—a society committed to the protection of liberties of conscience, expression and political opposition—is the crowning glory of western civilization." He continues, "Centuries of struggle have drawn a ring of freedom around the individual, a ring secured by law, by custom and by institutions."[17] Yet Schlesinger feared this view was under attack by certain segments of the political left, the radical progressive side of his party who were embracing totalitarian thought, and he wanted to shore up the glories of the democratic liberalism of the founders. Yet while he is constantly warning his readers about the danger democracy faces, his book is infused with a certain optimism, a confidence that his view of liberalism will prevail. He had no doubt that the vital center would hold.[18]

But the center did not hold. The 1960s unleashed a tidal wave against the vital center. Andrew Hartman, a man of the left and sympathetic to the changes the sixties brought, writes in *A War for the Soul of America* that "the sixties gave birth to a new America, a nation more open to new peoples, new ideas, new norms, and new, if conflicting, articulations of America itself."[19] Others were not as sanguine about the changes. Roger Kimball, literary critic, writes in *The Long March: How the Cultural Revolution of the 1960s Changed America* that these "new ideas" and "new norms" have been a disaster for our country. "We owe to the 1960s," he contends, "the ultimate institutionalization of immoralist radicalism: the institutionalization of drugs, pseudo-spirituality, promiscuous sex, virulent anti-Americanism, naïve anti-capitalism, and the precipitous decline of artistic and intellectual standards."[20]

Of course this could be dismissed as right-wing hyperbole. But listen to Andrew Hartman: "The New Left blew a deep crater into the surface of traditional American culture. Normative America, though still large, still powerful, was nonetheless disfigured beyond repair."[21] How did they do this? he asks. Not primarily by changing the political system but by changing American culture. When the New Left realized that they couldn't do away with our system of checks and balances, the Constitution, and separation of powers, they focused their attention on changing culture, succeeding, says Hartman, in "reorienting American culture."[22] New Left intellectuals helped the movement see that the American founding was corrupt at its roots and that it needed to be washed away. As new leftist Theodore Roszak claimed,

> The counterculture is the embryonic cultural base of New Left Politics, the effort to discover new types of community, new family patterns, new sexual mores, new kinds of livelihood, new aesthetic forms, new personal identities on the far side of power politics, the bourgeois home, and the Protestant work ethic.[23]

In fact, the New Left was attacking the vital center, a consensus that believed what the founders had bequeathed us was good, noble, worth preserving, even though flawed. The New Left wanted a clean break, rejecting the history of America as one of genocide, racism, sexism, patriarchalism, materialism, greed, and power.

In the 1980s the Christian Right rose up against this rejection of the vital center and the ideas of the founders. They decried the cultural revolution of the sixties, pointing out its effects on the individual, the family, and the nation, and called for a return to Hartman's "normative America" or Jerry Falwell's "Moral Majority," or what other believers have called Christian America. But not all evangelicals agreed. A tiny but growing minority of progressive evangelicals objected to the Christian Right, throwing in their hat with the forces that rejected "normative America," and accused the Christian Right of protecting racism, patriarchalism, and imperialism under the guise of "family values" and traditional religion.[24]

By the late 1970s conservative evangelicals saw the cultural decay all around them and wondered what had happened to their country. They, says Hartman,

> were confronted with a perfect storm of secular power that they deemed a threat to their way of life and to the Christian nation that they believed the United States once was and ought to be again. This realization, more than anything else, led religious conservatives to take up arms in the culture wars.[25]

This desire to "take back America" led Protestant religious conservatives into political alliances with Catholics, Jews, and Mormons, groups that differed in their religious outlook from evangelicals and each other but nonetheless became cobelligerents in the fight to reclaim America.

The highpoint came in 1980 with the election of Ronald Reagan. But by the end of his two terms, evangelicals still bemoaned the rapidly decaying culture—the loss of God in the public square, the breakdown of the family, the secularization of education, rampant abortion, the degrading of biblical views on sexuality, and the increase in those who claimed no faith. They felt that not enough had been done to turn the tide and they blamed people in the GOP for not doing more. But even as they blamed certain politicians, the religious Right was unable to see how much they had contributed to the erosion of the culture.

In their opposition to creeping socialism and the growth of big government, they didn't see how their alliance with big business engendered market forces that dissolved civic virtue and harmed the working and middle classes. In their marriage with utilitarian libertarians, crony capitalism, unrestrained greed, and putting profits over the common good destroyed much of what conservatives valued. In placing their bets with free trade, unrestrained immigration, and deregulation of hedge funds, the Christian Right, quick to praise the benefit of cheap consumer goods and a growing economy, didn't realize that these would be achieved by offshoring jobs and the destruction of small towns, hollowing out the working and middle classes in the process. What has followed is decades of high unemployment, widespread drug addiction, broken families, and the dis-integration of entire towns.[26]

So, while the progressive left was attacking our common culture and re-defining politics, big business, championed by forces on the right, was un-doing the very culture that religious conservatives wanted to preserve. And bipartisan members of Congress and the clerisy class worked hand in glove with the titans of Wall Street to transform the economics of our country. Eventually these transnational corporations and their CEOs grew tired of the religious Right, and its foot-dragging over globalization and the attempt to tie trade with China to improvements in human rights, and abandoned the Republican Party altogether, aligning with the Democrats and further angering the Right. But that story will be told later.[27]

THE HEART OF THE CULTURE WAR

In the 1990s, no one described the frustration and anger over cultural change better than James Davison Hunter, an evangelical who teaches at the University of Virginia. Writing twenty-five years before Hartman's *A War for the Soul of America*, Hunter recognized the cleavage at the heart of the conflict.

> The nub of political disagreement today on the range of issues debated—whether abortion, child care, funding for the arts, affirmative action and quotas, gay rights, values in public education, or multiculturalism—can be traced ultimately and finally to the matter of moral authority.[28]

What Hunter means by moral authority is "the basis by which people determine whether something is good or bad, right or wrong, acceptable or unacceptable, and so on." Hunter says these conflicting views of moral authority and the worldview it engenders create "the deep cleavages between antagonists in the contemporary culture war."[29]

For Hunter, while there are many worldviews competing in the public square, they basically can be boiled down to two main impulses—"*the impulse toward orthodoxy and the impulse toward progressivism.*"[30] By orthodoxy he means a commitment to an "*external, definable, and transcendent authority,*" whether that is the Bible or natural law. "Within cultural progressivism, by contrast," he says, "moral authority tends to be defined by the spirit of the modern age, a spirit of rationalism and subjectivism."[31]

Generally, those who embrace the orthodox view are conservatives and those who adopt the progressive view are liberals. And while these two camps differ on a host of social and political issues, "the source of the conflict is found in different moral visions." And this conflict of visions spills over into what it means to be an American, how we order our lives together in this country, our national identity, and the meaning of America itself.[32]

While the 1980s and 1990s saw the Christian Right push back on progressive liberalism, they had little success, other than defining the battle. The Left marched on, winning one cultural political battle after another. As Hartman says, with approval, the 1960s counterculture has won. What Hayes called the "ideological hegemony of liberalism"[33] is a reality. Commentators on the right, with deep sadness, would agree.[34]

Why the Center Couldn't Hold

So, clearly, the vital center of the 1950s didn't hold. Why not?

According to Marsden, while Schlesinger and other classical liberals warned their camp about the radicalism of the New Left and ultimately put their faith in liberalism to triumph, they were naive about the power of the New Left and the threat that it would metastasize into something more radical, eventually calling not for reform but wholesale revolution, the upending of everything Schlesinger found dear.

While Schlesinger and other vital-center thinkers on the center-left diagnosed the dilemma well—a choice between the radical New Left on the one hand and totalitarian Right on the other—their prescriptions were inadequate. "These moderate-liberal thinkers," writes Marsden, "who stood near the center of the cultural establishment, were living in the last days before a cultural revolution."[35] They saw the "deep crisis regarding the quality of their civilization" (agreeing with some of the protests of the student new left movement), but "in retrospect, we can see that they had no solutions beyond more of the same."[36] While many of these vital-center thinkers stood in continuity with much of what the founders established (something not shared by many of those on the left today)—that is checks and balances, federalism, property rights, and so on—they did not share the underlying grounding (to use Ceaser's term) of the American project. They wanted the fruit without the tree.

Most of the founding fathers "took for granted that there was a Creator who established natural laws, including moral laws, that could be known to humans as self-evident principles to be understood and elaborated through reason."[37] Yet Schlesinger and other mid-century moderate liberals had left this view behind, instead, adopting *pragmatism*, the view that human societies develop their own laws "rather than discovering them in a fixed order of things."[38] To these thinkers the vital center was ultimately grounded on "shared ideals" that could shape the national character and hold the vital center together. They wanted a public philosophy, one that championed American democratic values, but without the grounding of revelation or natural law.

But as we have seen, by the end of the 1960s this vision had proved fanciful, according to Marsden.[39] How did they not see this outcome? Marsden asks a similar question:

> How was it possible for so many liberal thinkers of the mid-century to retain their faith in what amounted to the enlightenment conclusions of the founders ("liberty and justice for all," and the like) while dismissing the enlightenment foundation on which those conclusions rested? Why did they not, like Lippmann or conservative thinkers of the day, see that the edifice on which they were building their pluralistic consensus was about to collapse? How could they be both skeptics regarding fixed first principles *and* believers in the principles of the American way?[40]

Marsden is right. So was Lippmann. They knew that you could not have the fruit of the founders' project without the roots. You can't have the edifice without the foundation. And the edifice couldn't endure much longer "without the foundations on which the founders had built."[41] The 1960s would not only continue to attack these foundations, the grounding, but eventually the edifice, the very democratic republic of the founders.

THE TRIUMPH OF PRAGMATISM

Sadly, Schlesinger tried to warn his own party about the threat of the progressive wing, but he, along with his party, didn't seem to have the stomach to root them out. And by not doing so, they allowed the radical progressives to eventually control the party and attack the very thing Schlesinger was so committed to—the classical liberal ideal. "It is not hard to see why the center could not hold," concludes Marsden. It was based on pragmatism. "But the

problem with pragmatism is that . . . it does not provide much basis for es-
tablishing first principles or deciding among contending moral claims."[42]

This became evident in the late sixties when different groups started
claiming their own first principles, even when they were at odds with the
founder's vision of what it meant to be an American.[43] Pragmatism has no
way of adjudicating the conflicting claims, says Marsden.[44] Lippmann understood this and tried to point it out. So did many conservative thinkers.
But Schlesinger and other centrist liberals didn't want to listen. By the time
they realized what had happened, it was too late.

Prophetic Voices on the Left Went Unheeded

Interestingly, Schlesinger seems to admit this fifty years after writing *Vital
Center*. By the 1990s, he had lost his confidence that reason and rationality
and deliberation alone would be enough to maintain the vital center. In the
forward to his 1998 *The Disuniting of America: Reflections on a Multicultural
Society*, he asks, in the face of pluralism, "What holds a nation together?"
Without a common purpose to bind a fractured nation together, "tribal an-
tagonisms will drive them apart."[45] And they have.

Schlesinger saw this happening. In sharp prose he contends that the "cult
of ethnicity" or identity politics, while bringing some welcome change to
America and an appreciation of other cultures, had gone too far—rejecting
"the unifying vision of individuals from all nations melted into a new race."[46]
Schlesinger seems shocked that his call for a common vision, a vital center,
could be tossed aside for an agenda of separatism, tribalism, and group
antagonism, and that the history profession, public schools, and universities
were being used to promote this destructive agenda that was tearing the
nation apart. Multiculturalism had become a "cult, and today it threatens to
become a counter-revolution against the original theory of America as 'one
people,' a common culture, a single nation."[47] But the threat of a counter-
revolution is now a reality. It has happened. Mark Lila's *The Once and Future
Liberal: After Identity Politics* shows the total triumph of multiculturalism
and identity politics today.[48]

Schlesinger wants to avoid this fate, so he stresses the ideals that for centuries have helped us transcend ethnic, religious, and political division,
ideals rooted in our democratic republic. And he remains optimistic "that

the historic forces driving toward 'one people' have not lost their power. . . . The belief in a unique American identity is far from dead."[49] But he seems incapable of realizing that these ideals, for most of the founders, were based on a "grounding," and once these first principles were jettisoned, so would be the democratic edifice on which they stand. Pointing the nation back to the "goal of one people," while noble, isn't enough to overcome the ideology of multiculturalism that is hell-bent on dividing people into different groups. If the goal isn't "one people," he asks, then "what is the future?—disintegration of the national community, apartheid, Balkanization, tribalization?"[50] The answer seems to be yes.

But the larger question is why do proponents of Balkanization want this? If indeed "the cult of ethnicity has reversed the movement in American history, producing a nation of minorities . . . less interested in joining with the majority in common endeavor than in declaring their alienation from an oppressive, white, patriarchal, racist, sexist, classist society," then what is their goal in sowing all their division, asks Schlesinger?[51] What is their real goal? If Schlesinger knows, he doesn't say. But, as we have contended, the goal is ultimately a "twin insurgency" by the ruling class.

While Schlesinger never answers his own question, he is willing to say what is needed. Our only hope, our only solution, he counsels, is to return to "ultimate bond of union," to the "democratic social ideal."[52] He describes this ideal: "democratic principles provide both the philosophical bond of union and practical experience in civic participation."[53] He is right. But unfortunately, other than referencing the Constitution and our democratic principles, he doesn't go any further than liberal pragmatic principles. He does say that the nation needs to recover and rally around the "American Creed." But he seems to think that just affirming these propositions will be enough, that reasonable people can be persuaded to adopt the creed, that is, a belief in democracy and the ideal of one people. But even here he seems to be reluctant to ground the creed in anything more than pragmatism, shorn of any groundings or first principles. Yet without first principles he doesn't have the resources to understand what is happening and what is needed to reverse the problem.

Here's the problem. Pragmatism, shorn of a stronger grounding like natural law, natural right, or biblical revelation, isn't strong enough. And even then one has to wonder if the creed, reduced to a set of propositions (i.e., we were founded on an idea) is enough to unify America.[54] Others argue that the creed, while helpful and important, is not enough. Our nation has always been grounded on more than propositions. It has included our common history, character, and religion, which were handed down to us from British and European sources, forged by centuries of English common law, custom, natural-law thinking, and constitution making. You can't have the American creed without a particular culture.

The problem is that this is exactly what the proponents of multiculturalism don't want. They reject this grounding, desiring to do away with it so they can create something entirely new, a new kind of democracy. So to appeal, as Schlesinger does, to values that "work for us" but are not true for all people everywhere is to cling to pragmatism that will wilt in the face of multiculturalism, political correctness, and the cancel culture. The ruling class believes it is right, and they will fight for their vision of reality.

In the end, as helpful as his critique of multiculturalism is, Schlesinger's commitment to secularism wouldn't allow him to admit that the Western ideals of individual freedom, political democracy, and human rights must be grounded in something other than pragmatism. He doesn't have the tools to turn back the arguments of multiculturalism or those who are redefining democracy. In sum, Schlesinger knows that America has lost its reigning public philosophy, and he wants it back. But he wants it back without the first principles that historically have underpinned it, first principles rooted in culture, history, and religion. But it doesn't work that way.

What Schlesinger and other mid-century, left-of-center liberals would not admit is that the vital center held together not because of the American creed, as important as that was, but because moral capital born of Christianity still existed in America—a moral capital that both sides could appeal to in their deliberations, a moral capital that animated this American creed, moral capital that rooted individual liberty, democratic institutions, and human rights in a theological tradition of virtue. But now this moral capital is gone, and the pragmatism that worked well at mid-century now seems naive, replaced by cynical power politics of one group fighting another.

Is the American Covenant Broken?

According to sociologist Robert Bellah, we are now living with a broken covenant.[55] In *The Broken Covenant*, Bellah, a man of the left, clearly spells out what others like Schlesinger won't admit.[56] The covenant is dead. The America creed has been rejected. The public philosophy of the founders has been rejected. And this is why Americans are so polarized, so divided over the definition of democracy and what it means to be an American.

Like Schlesinger, Bellah agrees that a common consensus is needed to make us "one people." "Any coherent and viable society rests on a common set of moral understandings about good and bad, right and wrong, in the realm of individual and social action."[57] But, unlike Schlesinger and the other pragmatists of mid-century, Bellah holds that "these common moral understandings must also in turn rest upon a common set of religious understandings that provide a picture of the universe in terms of which moral understandings make sense."[58] Here he speaks of the grounding of public philosophy. In fact, for Bellah "moral understanding" constitutes in America the "external covenant" of democratic republicanism. Yet, if this external covenant is not continuously renewed by the "invisible covenant," that is, a common set of religious understandings or grounding, the external covenant will collapse. "But in a republic an external covenant alone is never enough," he argues, contra Schlesinger.[59] "The external covenant must become," he posits, "an internal covenant and many times in our history that has happened."[60]

But with the internal covenant dead, the external covenant is also moribund, and no matter how much thinkers like Schlesinger are hopeful it can be revived, Bellah argues that "the external covenant has been betrayed by its most responsible servants and, what is worse, some of them, including the highest of us all, do not even seem to understand what they have betrayed."[61] Nonetheless, the covenant is broken, both internal and external, and all hell has broken loose. Thinkers on both the left and the right have predicted our present predicament and tried to warn us. But their warnings went unheeded. We are now reaping the whirlwind.

So here we find ourselves right back to Hunter and his belief that our current polarization is a clash of two worldviews. Two groundings. Two sets of first principles. Two different views of democracy. Two different external covenants. Two differing edifices. This clash of worldviews is on display daily in our politics.

Ultimate Authority

We are in a cold civil war; we live in a fractured republic; our covenant is broken.

What we are living through is a crisis of civilization. We not only disagree about what America stands *for*, but we disagree about what exactly our nation stands *on*. Hunter warned us that the culture war was fundamentally a clash over ultimate authority.

But those writing in the twenty-first century, those who want to return to a common external covenant, thinkers like Levin, make the same mistakes—they want this external covenant without seeing the need for the invisible covenant to breathe life into it. But Lippmann, Hunter, Bellah, and Marsden have shown this won't work; it hasn't worked.

Levin wants to move beyond the invisible covenant. We are just too pluralistic, "diffused," to use his term, to agree on theological first principles.[62] He believes strongly that we can have deconsolidation and diffusion on the one hand and great community on the other. He proposes a vision of "deconsolidated subsidiary." But he can't explain how these communities won't be another version of Bellah's lifestyle enclaves, further fracturing our nation, bringing more Balkanization, more tribes, more identity groups. The external covenant is not strong enough to hold us together. We need the "invisible covenant." Levin wants none of that.

Next Steps

So we are locked in polarization, a cold civil war. We no longer agree on a shared definition of democracy or what America stands for. The Left believes it can reeducate half the population. Many of the right have given up hope. As Matt Walsh says, "It is Time to Face the Facts: We Cannot be United."[63] Others say it is time to burn it all down.[64] But if we aren't going to give up hope, one thing is certain: to restore a public philosophy that unifies the nation, our next step is to understand our current polarization—why it has gotten so bad and how it is used to tear us further apart, making any return to the vital center seem impossible. Moreover, we have to understand how the current debates in Washington, exemplified so well in the 2021 impeachment trial, are actually conducted not for unity, surprisingly, but to further divide us. And we have to ask the question, while Americans tear one another apart, who ultimately benefits?[65] Once we understand this, we might find our way back to a new vital center.

PART TWO

MAPPING OUR DIFFERENCES

THE QUADRANT

FRAMEWORK SYSTEM

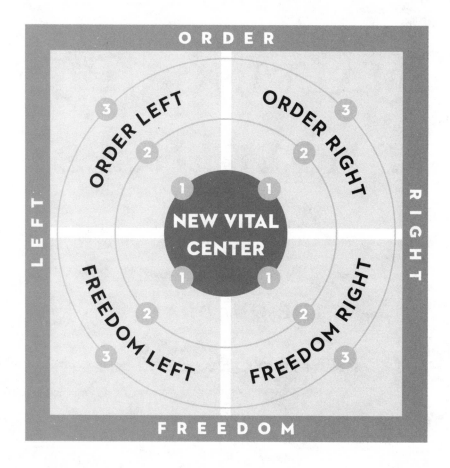

HAVING MADE THE CASE that we have lost a vital center, a shared understanding of the public philosophy, we now move to the largest section of the book and explain how the loss of the vital center engendered polarization, as all four quadrants distance themselves from the center and at the same time are pulled away by the ruling elite. Only when we understand this polarization and the ideas, forces, and people behind it, will we be ready to discover a new vital center. As we look at the polarized positions—the 2 and 3 positions of each quadrant—three things must be kept in mind.

First, in order to understand each polarized position, we need to understand its narrative. In his groundbreaking book *Moral Believing Animals*, Christian Smith persuasively argues that all worldviews have a narrative; they tell a story.[1] And all narratives have in common the components of a good story, that is, a beginning ("Once upon a time"), a middle ("how we fell from the golden age"), and an end ("a plan for recovery").

Along with this basic narrative structure, Smith argues that narratives stress the existence of enemies, that is, the person or group that causes the loss of the golden era and the person or group that impedes recovery, which more often than not is the same person or group. The narrative of loss and recovery not only helps identify enemies, but it also helps identify natural allies, people who share the declension narrative and the desire for a new golden era, who have enemies in common and can work together. Behind every position, every political point of view, is a narrative, a story, that has shaped each group.

Furthermore, I realize that if we are going to understand how we lost our public philosophy, how our public life has become mired in polarization, tribalism, and rage, we have to first understand the narratives behind each of the four quadrants. Could it be that part of our incivility, part of our difficulty in having conversations that don't descend into acrimony, is that we don't understand the deep stories animating those we disagree with? Simply trying to win arguments, using facts and policy positions, doesn't get to the root of the matter. Until we understand the narratives that shape each tribe, how these narratives shape our views on politics and the emotional connection we have to them, we won't be able to have civil conversations that don't engender name-calling, distrust, and hurt feelings.

Second, as we look at each polarized position, I will attempt to be as fair as I can. Since it is so hard to talk about politics without our brains immediately reacting in tribal defensiveness, if I want each side to take self-examination seriously, then the best chance I have is if voices on each side provide the necessary critique. So only the Right will self-critique the Right; and only the Left will self-critique the Left. As the reader will notice later, the voices that are providing the critique, by and large, are coming from the new vital center (the 1 positions on the graph). Some of these thinkers we will return to in part three.

I realize by laying out four extreme quadrants I may be accused of creating a "moral equivalency." Those on the right will contend that the Far Left is the biggest challenge to democracy and that extremism on the right is small in comparison. Those on the left will contend that the Far Right poses the greatest challenge, and that comparing extremism on the left to the Far Right is a "false moral equivalency." Since at present we don't have an accurate number of people in either the Far Left or Far Right we can't answer the "moral equivalency" argument.

The bottom line is that there exist people and thinkers on both extremes, and thus it is worth discussing them and seeing that the extremes are always a threat to our constitutional republic. And extremism can wax and wane; sometimes it exists more on the right and sometimes on the left. What matters is having the framework to spot it, reject it, and champion a new vital center, one built on constitutional republicanism.

Having said all this, these critiques may hit too close to home for some of my readers. And I realize by starting with the left side of the quadrant graph, I may lose progressives, particularly progressive evangelicals. Thus, my suggestion is that if you identify as a progressive evangelical, you might begin with the chapters on freedom right and order right (chapters seven through ten), and then return to chapters three through six.

Finally, as the forces of polarization attack the vital center, we will see that there is a symbiotic relationship between the polarized positions on the left and the right. Writing in *National Affairs* in 2018, Jason Willick argues that both sides in our politically polarized environment tend to gravitate toward illiberal solutions and are willing to side-step long held democratic and constitutional practices to achieve their goals.[2] This is true of the Right and the

Left; both sides flirt with and in some cases embrace illiberal solutions. Relying on a thinker named Peter Viereck, Willick points out that by themselves none of the polarized positions are strong enough to threaten our democratic republic, to threaten our democracy. But, and here he is quoting Viereck, "Freedom is destroyed when both [the Left and the Right] attack at the same time." According to Viereck, the system is threatened when both sides produce a "mutually reinforcing radicalism that amplify one another. . . . The backing of one such extreme only nourishes the growth of the other extreme," he wrote.

What happens, as both sides attack the other side, is that it "gradually corrodes the legitimacy of the existing regime and opens the door to a genuine authoritarianism somewhere down the line." Here is how it happens: "Between a far right that denigrates Western values of pluralism and equality before the law," argues Viereck, "and a far left that denounces Western civilization as a white-supremacist construction, between multicultural identitarians and white identitarians, between thought controllers of various stripes, the space for rooted liberalism is shrinking." And it is shrinking because voices on the right and the left, some that contain helpful critiques of our system, when combined, "tag team" to bring down our system and close off what Viereck called "rooted liberalism" or what we have been calling a new vital center. To understand how this tag team works and how it is exploited, we need to understand the polarized positions on the quadrant system.

One last comment. As I lay out each quadrant and the different positions in each, it is important to note that I am not a neutral observer. My task in this book is to explain how we lost the vital center, how the cold civil war has been stoked, and, persuasively I hope, to show how we can move beyond it to a new vital center. So there is a negative project that needs to happen before we get to the positive project of renewal. But clearing away much of the polarized ground will make it easier to plant the seeds of the new vital center, which will produce a harvest of constitutional republicanism. But before we lay out the new vital center, which our country so desperately needs, we must first clear away the polarization. And it is to that clearing that we now turn.

3

FREEDOM LEFT 2

THE THEORY OF THE GODLESS CONSTITUTION

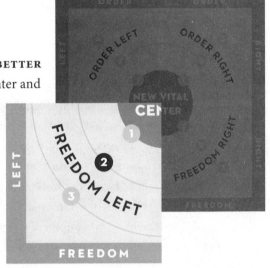

NOTHING DEMONSTRATES BETTER the breakdown of the vital center and centrifugal polarization than the fight over our constitution, particularly its justification and interpretation. What grounds it and who decides its meaning are both contested questions. And nothing gets to the heart of this contest better than the confirmation hearings for Amy Coney Barrett.

During the Seventh Circuit confirmation hearing in September 2017, Senator Dianne Feinstein made headlines when she challenged Barrett's strong Catholic faith, saying "the dogma lives loudly within you, and that's a concern." Feinstein feared that Barrett would mingle law and faith, allowing her piety to compromise her legal decisions. Critics jumped on Feinstein, accusing her of imposing a "religious test."[1] Others said it was fair game. Three years later, when Barrett was nominated to the Supreme Court, Feinstein and the other senators steered clear of questions of faith.

However the media wasn't so reticent, painting her faith as scary, raising questions about her family's involvement in People of Praise, a community within the Catholic Church, and erroneously claiming it was the inspiration for

Margaret Atwood's dystopian novel *The Handmaid's Tale*.[2] If Barrett is confirmed, one critic implied, we should be worried about her imposing this dystopian vision on America, a vision where abortion is illegal, women are subservient to men, and a new theocracy is imposed.[3] On the other side of the political aisle, Republican senators defended her qualifications, pointed to her stellar professional résumé, and celebrated her accomplishments as a mother of six, but strenuously avoided questions of her faith, not wanting to stir the pot.

But the questions remained. What was it about her faith that worried the Left so much? It wasn't just her Catholicism. After all, many Democrats in Congress are Catholic, and for them it doesn't pose any conflict with progressive policies. And it couldn't really be the People of Praise, which after a decade of involvement, hadn't turned Barrett into a mindless slave. By all accounts she had a lovely marriage and a healthy family. And it couldn't have been her commitment to originalism because, even as Justice Elena Kagan said, "We are all originalists now," endlessly discussing "dubious claims about events centuries in the past," thus giving the impression that it is a wax nose, a technique of neutrality, which could be pushed in either direction.[4] No, what worried Feinstein and the media critics was something else. Something, in their minds, far more sinister. But what was it?

In a lengthy essay in the center-left *New Republic*, Peter Hammond Schwartz sheds light on what bothers Democrats so much about Barrett.[5] It's not her originalism, which he says is nothing more than a tool, "a vehicle for other legal principles," for embedding a "deeper structure." But it is this deeper structure which is the real concern. And at the heart of this deeper structure is something called *natural law*, a system of moral and ethical thinking tied to religion.

In his "Originalism Is Dead. Long Live Catholic Natural Law," Schwartz argues that "Barrett represents more than a simple link" to other originalists, like her mentor Justice Scalia, but in fact "represents the alarming future of the conservative legal project," one that sees the Constitution and the entire American system grounded upon natural law.[6] It is this grounding so closely tied to a religious view of the world that they fear. While natural law has been with us for centuries, in the past, says Schwartz, it was mostly agnostic, often acting as a nonreligious guide on issues like civil rights, social justice, and universal human rights.[7] But not anymore.

As Schwartz argues, "Catholic theorizing about natural law swung hard right in the 1960s, assuming a new and more sinister synthesis in the new natural law, or NNL, that emerged from the religious and political turmoil of the 1960s."[8] It was then that conservative Catholics transformed natural law "into a rigid, reactionary, punitive, and self-righteous propaganda platform for the most conservative elements of the Catholic Church and its intellectual apologists."[9] Built on this new natural-law foundation, conservatives (including many evangelicals who followed their lead and leaned on their scholarship), have "constructed an intellectual scaffolding that has inspired powerful critiques of liberalism and modernity."[10]

It is this "intellectual scaffolding," this grounding, this destruction of a "neutral space" in the civic realm, that seems to terrify those on the left, including Schwartz. And it terrifies him because it can only lead to one thing: theocracy. For Schwartz, this NNL "would obliterate church-state barriers and superimpose a terrestrial layer of morality and control, under the auspices of natural law, to root out deviance and knit together the republic."[11] What we are witnessing, he argues, is "a new post-liberal vision of what American society would look like stripped of its current impediments and illuminated by . . . natural law."[12] In sum, then, in his fear that the naked public square will be clothed and that all civil and religious liberty will be wiped out, Schwartz drives home the point that to cling to NNL—a view that sees all law, but particularly our constitution, grounded in a transcendent source—can only lead to one place: a second inquisition; it couldn't but lead to this.

According to Schwartz, NNL is authoritarian, illiberal. And in order to make this point more dramatic, either on purpose or to cause confusion, he downplays, buries in long lists, or simply ignores the natural law thinkers who defend the Constitution and Bill of Rights. Instead, he lumps them all together in the most extreme, most illiberal of positions, downplaying the nuance of thinking that exists in natural-law circles.[13] Doing so helps build his case that NNL threatens or may even have destroyed the golden age of liberalism, and in the process it is wiping out decades of progress in civil liberties and the welfare state.

Put simply, in uncovering the real reason for the opposition to Amy Coney Barrett, Schwartz not only provides a helpful summary of why liberals fear her view on natural law but also constructs a window into the freedom left 2 position in general, providing a number of the telltale signs that we will explore in this chapter. In rejecting all proponents of the NNL (even those who champion constitutionalism), he rejects, whether knowingly or not, the original grounding of the founders and thus contributes to the loss of the vital center. This opens the door to the more radical elements of postmodernism. But before we get there we need to step back and understand why the Left reacts so strongly to the new natural law, and to do this we need to go deeper into the genealogy of the progressive Left.

ONCE UPON A TIME: THE GOLDEN AGE OF FREEDOM LEFT 2

The story begins, according to Harvard's Michael Sandel, around 1900, when the Left felt that America, for all its economic achievements, had fallen short in reaching its promises.[14] Throughout the Industrial Revolution, while America was experiencing tremendous economic prosperity, a significant portion of the population was being left behind. Certain historians, professors, and politicians were startled by so much economic and racial injustice all around. And they wondered why after 150 years America still hadn't fulfilled her promise that "all men are created equal." As these progressive elites looked for something to blame for the injustice, they came to the conclusion that what had gone wrong was not the *promise* of the Declaration but the *mechanism* of the Constitution, setting their sights on the separation of powers and checks and balances, which put too many roadblocks in the way of achieving progressive ends.

Initially, they tried to get rid of the Constitution and start anew, but when they realized that wasn't possible (Americans love and revere their Constitution), they decided the best they could do was to change what it means, to redefine it, so that it lined up better with progressive ends, that is, the economic equality of all people.

So they set to out to redefine it, knowing that once they redefined the Constitution, they could then transform economics and politics. In the early twentieth century, progressives like John Dewey began teaching that if our society was going to become radically equal, human nature had to be changed. But this posed a problem, for human nature was grounded on an outside authority, whether that authority went by the name nature, reason, or God. So, the first step for Dewey was to reject this grounding and make the case that rights are purely secular, formed through "social conditions." "They [the founders] put forward their ideas," wrote Dewey, "as immutable truths good at all times and places; they had no idea of historic relativity."[15]

Ultimately Dewey, inspired by Hegel and German philosophy, saw the repudiation of natural right and natural law (and God) as necessary to achieve his vision of the progressive utopia. Once he got rid of the founders' grounding, the Constitution became flexible, and it could easily be manipulated. And over the first half of the twentieth century that is what progressives did. Judges and legislatures began reinterpreting the Constitution in a completely different way, one guided by a radical vision of justice. Equality was no longer about equal treatment before the law. This had produced too much inequality. And it meant that people started at completely different places in life, so some had more opportunity than others. So now equality would mean equal outcomes and would be achieved through the government leveling the playing field.

As President Lyndon Johnson said in 1965, "We seek . . . not just equality as a right and a theory but equality as a fact and equality as a result."[16] And this meant massive redistribution from the "haves" to the "have-nots." In order to achieve equality of results, rights had to be redefined as economic rights, the rights to the basic necessities of life: a livable wage, housing, education, medical care, food, and so on.

Following Dewey, Franklin Roosevelt took the next big step, arguing in his economic bill of rights that "certain conditions were prerequisites for the freedom of each person to choose his ends for himself."[17] And for these economic rights to become a reality, a huge state apparatus would need to be built because unless people have these rights met, they are not truly free and certainly not equal. Of course, in order to achieve this massive redistribution, what became known as the welfare state, the government's administrative function would balloon over time into a massive administrative state, staffed by experts, our version of Soviet apparatchiks.

But, according to Sandel, bypassing the plain words of the Constitution and thus transforming legal rights into economic rights would not have been possible without another significant change: a cultural transformation that went from trusting religion to define the good to allowing the state to protect rights based on neutral conception of the good. Progressives realized that if they wanted to change the historic definition of rights from equality of opportunity to equality of outcomes, the very definition of *good* had to be changed. And since it was religion, in large measure, that gave shape to the idea of the good, it had to be kept out of the public realm.

Starting in the 1940s, according to Sandel, progressives stopped talking about the good, because it had been tied historically to Christianity, and instead started stressing the ideas of rights and choice. Americans, they believed, must be free to choose their own ends. "Government [through the support of religion] could not impose on its citizens any particular conception of the good life."[18] In a dispute over the meaning of patriotism in a 1940 case, the court concluded, "no official, high or petty, can prescribe what shall be orthodox in politics, nationalism, religion, or other matters of opinion."[19]

For Sandel this was a sea change. It meant there was no longer a grounding, a standard, to judge politics or the good; only individual choice mattered. The individual self was supreme. "Patriotism would now be a matter of choice," concludes Sandel, "not of inculcation, a voluntary act by free and independent selves."[20] But for this to happen, religion had to be downgraded.

Seven years later, in 1947, came an even more important watershed moment; the court ruled for the first time that the government had to remain neutral toward religion, never endorsing one brand over another. The individual's choice was now the sole authority. "Religious beliefs worthy of respect are the product of free and voluntary choice by the faithful."[21] For Sandel, if individual choice is paramount, the state can have no tutelary role in cultivating virtue. The priority of individual rights took precedence over the good of society. And this meant that the law had to remain neutral, not taking sides. During this time Thomas Jefferson's "wall" came to mean an extremely high wall, and the complete "bracketing out" (Sandel's phrase) of religion from public life, keeping religion away from politics altogether.

By the end of the twentieth century, then, the progressive transformation of economics, politics, and culture was complete. They had achieved their golden era. To pull it off, the new progressive Left (freedom left 2) had reinterpreted the founding away from a grounding in natural rights (and natural law) to that of secular individual rights, a grounding based solely on a voluntary conception of the self. No longer was there a conception of the good based on natural law or a religious conception of life or an outside lawgiver to provide guidance on how to live our lives. Now, everything was reduced to individual choice. And for the government not to infringe on individual choice, the government was seen to be secular or neutral. This alone would help the nation reach its true goal, to live up to its original promise. During the progressive era, America was finally living up to its promise, the promise of a democracy for everyone.[22] Even if the nation had not completely reached its golden era, for there was still much to accomplish, the "arc of justice" was bending in the right direction.

GODLESS CONSTITUTION

When trying to spot someone in the freedom left 2 position, one of the telltale signs is how they view the Constitution and its grounding. If it is a purely secular grounding, devoid of natural law and natural rights, un-tethered from religious notions of the good, they are most likely in the freedom left 2 position. They believe in a "godless constitution," a phrase coined by professors Isaac Kramnick and R. Laurence Moore in their book *The Godless Constitution: A Moral Defense of the Secular State*.[23]

In the main, the authors describe a similar progressive genealogy as Sandel but with one twist. Instead of saying that the progressives changed the plain meaning of the Constitution, Kramnick and Moore contend that the early progressives believed strongly that they were simply defending the original meaning of the Constitution, one that had been clouded over, lost in the first 150 years of the nation. For Kramnick and Moore, progressives contended that the founders based the Constitution not on a natural-rights grounding, as erroneously thought, but on "the autonomous independent individual as the center of the social universe, for whom social and political institutions are self-willed constructs whose purpose and function are to secure the rights and interest of self-seeking individuals." Kramnick and Moore contend that the founders viewed the government's role as solely negative—"It keeps the peace and order in a voluntaristic, individualistic society" and never seeks "to promote the good of the moral life."

In this view the founders rejected that government should "nurture and educate its subjects in the way of virtue, or preside over the betterment or im-provement of men and society," or "defend and propagate moral and religious

truths." The founders, argue Kramnick and Moore, pushed "morality and religion outside the public realm to a private realm of individual preference."[24]

Religious freedom, then, could only mean one thing: keeping religious
influence from the state and its laws. For Kramnick and Moore, Thomas
Jefferson wanted a high and impenetrable wall, a godless constitution
wherein the individual decides what is good and has the freedom to choose
it. Only then will individuals achieve happiness, and only then will our
nation maintain the American Dream, a golden era of liberalism rooted in
individual reason and a rational state. It has always been thus, and it needs
to remain thus.

THE GODLESS CONSTITUTION UNDER SIEGE

But just when the godless-constitution view had reached its zenith, around
1980, the religious Right began to spoil it. Thinkers like Richard John
Neuhaus challenged this view of neutrality, pointing out its harmful effects
on American culture. In his bestselling book, *The Naked Public Square*,
Neuhaus sounded the alarm, warning the nation that a *naked square*, a
public square devoid of religion, was dangerous because once the benefits
of religion were pushed to the side, the square wouldn't remain naked but
would be flooded with secularism; it would end up at the cultural bottom.[25]
And that is what was happening, said Neuhaus. Ethically and morally,
America was rotting from within.

But if this weren't bad enough, the naked public square was only transi-
tional, for no public square can remain neutral. Eventually it would be highjacked by forces more totalitarian than even the most extreme religious
expression. Throughout his book Neuhaus counters the pernicious doctrines of the progressive Left, contending that a secular America (and
godless constitution) was revisionist history, a myth concocted by the Far
Left to push Christianity into the private realm. In fact, to Neuhaus and
those of the Christian Right, both Catholic and Protestant, America was
founded on Christian principles.

But it was this contention, that America was a Christian nation, that
particularly enraged those of freedom left 2. For them the idea that
America is a Christian nation is a lie and destroys what progressives have
achieved. Because the Christian Right "refuses to recognize secularism as

a fundamental principle of American government," they have become the sworn enemy of those in the godless-constitution camp.[26]

PROGRESSIVE EVANGELICALS JOIN THE CAUSE

After thirty years of the religious Right turning back the clock, progressive secularists weren't the only ones who were angry. Surprisingly, they had unlikely allies—progressive evangelicals. Many of these progressive evangelicals, having grown up in fundamentalist and conservative evangelical churches, brought firsthand grievances to the debate.

A good example is Dartmouth professor Randall Balmer and his book, *Thy Kingdom Come: How the Religious Right Distorts the Faith and Threatens America.*[27] "I write as a jilted lover," shares Balmer, and "the evangelical faith that nurtured me as a child and sustains me as an adult has been highjacked by right-wing zealots . . . who have failed to appreciate the genius of the First Amendment."[28] Moreover, "the effect of this right-wing takeover has been the poisoning of public discourse and a distortion of the faith."[29] Not only is his book a personal lament that the Christian Right now defines what it means to be an evangelical, but he is also angry that fellow Baptists, heirs of Roger Williams, who were once the strongest proponents of the First Amendment and the separation of church and state, have traded this once proud heritage for the lure of political power.

In his chapter "Where Have All the Baptists Gone?" he traces the history of Roger Williams and other well-known Baptist preachers who he says influenced Thomas Jefferson and James Madison in the formation of the First Amendment and the separation of church and state.[30] Treading on ground similar to Kramnick and Moore, Balmer interprets the First Amendment as a secular document that keeps the state and the church separate for the good of both, protecting religious liberty and prohibiting the establishment of any religion.

Holding this position for almost two hundred years, in the late 1970s Baptists did an about-face. "Lured by the prospect of political power during Reagan years, the leaders of the Southern Baptist Convention steadily whittled away at their Baptist heritage and moved the denomination into the orbit of the Religious Right."[31] No longer was the goal to stay away from politics; these new Baptist leaders now sought "to impose their religious views on all Americans, thereby violating not only the First Amendment but the very principles that define their own religious heritage."[32] This pernicious vision threatens America.

But if Balmer seems angry at fellow Baptists, he is furious at another group of right-wing zealots—theonomists. Describing *theonomy* as "a social ethic . . . that advocates restructuring civil society according to the laws contained in the Hebrew Bible,"[33] he says this group of religious-right leaders (infatuated by the founder of theonomy, Rousas John Rushdoony) don't just "want to reconfigure the line of separation between church and state. They want to obliterate it altogether."[34] They want a theocracy. But to accomplish this the religious Right must "dismantle the First Amendment" and impose "its own theocratic vision" on America.[35] Not only does this scare Balmer, but it angers him. He calls for "true Baptists" to stand up and protect the First Amendment, staying out of politics for its own good and the good of democratic pluralism.[36]

Thus, in the end it isn't progressives who are altering America, it is the religious Right, the Christian nationalists. Progressives vehemently disagree with the Christian Right that the United States needs to return to its Christian origins.

> If the United States was set up as a Christian nation, then critics of Christianity can be painted as radicals who want to change the basic nature of our society. But if it was set up under the umbrella of religious freedom, then it is the critics of Christianity who are fighting to preserve the basic nature of American Society.[37]

If this view is true, then "it would be cultural conservative activists who would be the radicals attempting to alter the basic nature of American Society."[38] And as social scientists, Yancey and Williamson discovered progressives claiming that "the Christian right is altering the basic nature of our society with their assertions about the primacy of Christianity."[39]

So, if the Left is going to return to the golden era, it will need to root out religious conservatives, meaning any conservative who believes that our founding was grounded on natural law or Christian principles or that Christianity has a role in shaping our public life. Those who hold these views are extremists, Christian nationalists, and dangerous to democracy.

So there the freedom left 2 narrative is clearly laid out.[40] All the telltale signs are present, making it an easy mark. A progressive golden age, a downfall caused by the religious Right, a recovery through the reinstatement of the high wall of separation between church and state—all part of the freedom left 2 narrative. But are they right?

WARNINGS GO UNHEEDED

Reading Balmer and other progressives leaves no question as to who their enemy is and what they fear. And to defeat this enemy they can't brook even the slightest intrusion of religion in the public square because just giving it the slightest foothold might open the door to theocracy.

This fear is at the heart of their opposition to Justice Barrett—that isn't hard to see. But what is hard to fathom is the marriage between secular rationalists and progressive evangelicals. In their desire to keep religion out of the public square, progressive evangelicals have formed an alliance with the most secular of thinkers, progressives who have redefined the very nature of our constitution, the self, and the good and possess a strong antipathy to Christianity. (These progressive secular rationalists in the freedom left 2 position would include atheists like Sam Harris and Christopher Hitchens.) And yet they seem unaware of the downside, the dangers posed to formal religion and the nation.

Moreover, what I find even more interesting in the freedom left 2 position, especially among progressive evangelicals, is their unwillingness to admit any weakness in their position, even after it has been clearly spelled out by critics, many on their own side. They are so sure of their enemies, religious conservatives of any kind, and so confident in their position, a godless view of the Constitution, that they seem blind to the problems that this position entails. Let me explain.

I first came across liberal self-criticism at Georgetown in the early 1990s when I read an essay, "The Search for a Defensible Good: The Emerging Dilemma of Liberalism," penned by Professor Bruce Douglas, a Democrat.[41] Douglass acknowledges that the liberal commitment to prioritizing individual moral autonomy over the good, promoting a view of neutrality that allows individuals to decide what is ultimately good, is problematic—it is the Achilles' heel of the progressive narrative. Douglas argues that there is no such thing as a neutral state, for even a "secular" state has a conception of what the good is. By giving priority to liberal individual choice, progressives are ruling other views of the good as out of bounds. "The liberal good turns out, above all, to be a certain kind of freedom" that itself rests on a certain teleology or the best end of a human life. And once this view of freedom is adopted, it turns out, ironically, that liberalism "is in actuality not nearly so tolerant or neutral as it first appears . . . certain goods—and ways of life—are promoted at the expense of others."[42]

At the time I was Douglas's student I didn't realize that he, standing in the liberal tradition, had great reservations about the "one-sided priority attached to the good of freedom." This priority rules out different and deeper conceptions of the good, other claims from teleology (what the best human being and society should look like), and claims that the liberal project can't sustain itself without a deeper public philosophy in which to ground itself. Without this public philosophy, liberalism is "incompletely grounded," and lacks "*any* sort of deeper support."[43]

And this incomplete grounding has led to dire results, which progressive evangelicals seem to ignore. In fact, says Sandel in *Democracy's Discontent*, our present unhappiness is not because the religious Right has infringed on freedom of speech. Rather it is due to a huge shift in classical liberalism carried out by the progressive movement, a shift from an old version of liberalism based on a civic republican view of self-democratic rule, to a new vision of America, one that fundamentally reshaped how we looked at the individual, the good, and the purpose or end of government.[44] Sandel believes that historic liberalism's "core thesis" has now become the view that "a just society seeks not to promote any particular ends, but enables its citizens to pursue their own ends, consistent with a similar liberty for all."[45] Government must then remain neutral, holding no conception of the good. No longer is government guided by a conception of the general welfare, the greatest happiness or cultivating virtue, but rather its standard is the "concept of right, a moral category prior to the good, and independent of it."[46] While the godless-constitution view sees this as a good thing, Sandel sees it as the degradation of a noble tradition.

For Sandel, this prioritizing the *right* over the *good* for the individual has meant one thing: the "unencumbered self." Rejecting an older conception of the self that finds its identity in God's law, the family, and the church, city, and town, the unencumbered self is a self "prior to and independent of purposes and ends."[47] "For the unencumbered self, what matters above all, what is most essential to our personhood, are not the ends we choose but our capacity to choose them."[48]

THE LONELY SELF

The self then is prior to the good. The self must determine its own identity apart from any restraint placed on it from the outside, whether God, the family, or the community. No longer is the individual tied down to obligations to others; it can now experience total liberation. We are now free to choose our ends, our purposes, totally unencumbered by any outside authority. And for Sandel, to guarantee the right over the good, the self over the telos, a certain kind of government must be set up, and certain changes in our Constitution and laws need to be enacted to support the unencumbered self—and this new government is the "Procedural Republic" (another memorable phrase),[49] a state that remains neutral, brackets out religion, doesn't propose or legislate any particular conception of the good or purpose of life, allowing the liberated individual to choose for themselves, free from the constraints that traditionally shaped the individual. How has this worked out? Not well.

As Sandel tells the story, the unencumbered self, now flush with its new freedom and rights, initially likes the new liberation but soon realizes it is all alone, having broken away from the family, the town, and the church.[50] Isolated, it turns to the government for support, both to protect its rights and also to find financial support when difficult times arrive. Attaching itself to the state, the isolated individual is willing to give up some of its freedom for security. And the administrative state is all too happy to come to the rescue, the heroic protector of individual rights, engendering a massive bureaucracy to protect and support the unencumbered individual.

But where does this leave the individual? The unencumbered self, says Sandel, is left "lurching . . . between detachment on the one hand, entanglement on the other."[51] So-called liberation has turned into slavery. The individual is now less free than ever before—on the one hand it is a slave to loneliness, detachment, and isolation, and on the other it is encumbered by an expansive government that now controls its life. "In our public life, we are more entangled, but less attached, than ever before."[52]

THE LOSS OF FREEDOM AND THE GROWTH OF GOVERNMENT

This is the modern dilemma. The "freer" the individual becomes, the bigger the government becomes. The more elite experts become empowered, the less free becomes the individual. And here we see how we have moved from the unencumbered self to the "rights talk" at the heart of our society.[53] The more individuals fight for their rights, the more government has to get involved. In fact, the more the government grows, the more it must keep growing, creating more and more dependence. It creates an ever-increasing dependence by destroying the mediating structures that once cared for the individual. Once these structures are gone, the individual has no choice but to turn to the state. Sandel observes that as individual rights have morphed from free-speech rights and the right to choose one's best life to economic rights—the right to some of the spoils of capitalism, the right to a certain level of economic security—the larger the government grows to protect these new rights.

Ironically, the more economic and political rights the unencumbered self gains, the more detached, isolated, and lonely that self becomes. So, says Sandel, for solidarity and protection the isolated self joins with other isolated individuals to form a group, and together they appeal for more rights for their group. Thus the concept of group rights is born.[54] Now, instead of having individuals fighting each other, we have groups fighting each other for the spoils of capitalism. And these group rights, often called identity politics, whether on the left or the right, have fueled our present polarization.

PROGRESSIVE EVANGELICALS IGNORE THE WARNING SIGNS

But Douglas and Sandel's critique has gone unheeded. In fact, progressive evangelicals like Balmer, unwilling to admit that it has led to the unencumbered self, the procedural republic, the growth of the administrative state ruled by elites, and the rise of the cancel culture, has confidently doubled down on this view of the godless constitution. In his 2021 book, *Solemn Reverence: The Separation of Church and State in American life*, Balmer makes the case that Christian nationalism, fueled by the erroneous view of a Christian founding, continues to be the greatest threat to democracy in America.[55] Christian nationalists have wrecked religious freedom, attacking the First Amendment, that wonderful marriage between rationalists and

evangelicals, which has "bequeathed to the United States a vibrant and salubrious culture unmatched anywhere in the world."[56] And we got this
culture because of the godless constitution.

But in placing all the blame on religious conservatives, Balmer is not only
oblivious to the warnings of people like Sandel, and what this marriage really
has given us, but he is also unaware that the naked square, far from remaining free, has been filled with a new established "religion," that of woke
progressivism. Far from admitting this has taken place, an obvious fact for
anyone with eyes to see, Balmer instead continues to focus on the problem
of the theocratic Right.[57] In doubling down on his solution, the godless constitution, he spends most of his book showing how key founders like Jefferson, Madison, and Roger Williams set up a "high wall" of separation, con-
veniently showing how they line up with his view. The problem is, however,
he is perpetuating a dangerous myth—our nation's secular founding.[58]

Canadian philosopher Charles Taylor, a thinker well respected by evangelicals on the left and the right, a man who converted to Christianity late
in life, contends that at its most fundamental level the godless-constitution
thinkers misinterpret the First Amendment, reading back into it—in an
anachronistic way—a view that the founding fathers would *not* have recognized, even Thomas Jefferson and James Madison.[59] Jefferson, Madison, and
Baptist preacher Isaac Backus wanted to prevent the federal government
from aligning with one denomination or one confession, and thus they
posited a view of the First Amendment that opposed confessionalism. "The
Separation of church and state did not have to mean bracketing out God or
religion," claims Taylor.[60] Originally the goal was just as much about protecting Christianity from the state.

In fact, from its inception America has always seen a close connection
between the "spirit of liberty and the spirit of religion," to quote Tocqueville.
But today this view has changed—"many people see it as a bracketing
today."[61] But this is an incorrect reading of the First Amendment, says Taylor,
that has lodged in the minds of many people today and had overtaken the
Supreme Court in the 1950s. The court had taken deconfessionalization and
turned it into privatization, "a rejection of religion as such from the public
sphere." What was adopted for the purpose of disestablishment has been
"subsumed as a stage in privatization" and this is "seriously to distort it."[62]

Agreeing with Sandel that this secular view of the First Amendment comports well with the unencumbered self and the neutral procedural-republic state, Taylor concludes that "civic freedom cannot accommodate this bleeding of the public domain of all significance" because the public realm "requires strongly held common values," a strong notion of what the good is.[63] So not only is the loss of these common values problematic, Taylor argues that this absence of values leaves a vacuum for "a minority of determined atheists who try to construct an entire alternative outlook."[64] And it is the construction of this "entire alternative outlook" that Balmer and other progressive evangelicals either don't see or are unwilling to recognize, fearing it would play into the hands of Christian nationalism. So they take a see-no-evil view of the Far Left.

But the consequences of this secular myth have been catastrophic. The procedural republic has led to the hollowing out of individuals, growing the power of the state, and enshrining a new ruling class. For some reason, progressive evangelicals have gone along with this and joined in the attack with progressive secularists on religious conservatives. In fact, during Barrett's confirmation hearing, Randall Balmer not only didn't defend a fellow believer, he reminded Justice Barrett in slightly condescending terms that "one of the crowing achievements of the founders, as embedded in the Constitution, was the rejection of majoritarianism, the notion that the majority dictates the rights and the behavior of everyone else."[65] Clearly, he was worried that her judicial commitment to natural law might "compromise the rights of others."

But he didn't have to remind her of the dangers of majoritarianism or compromising the rights of others, especially since it was the Far Left that had been slandering her and her family for weeks on end. If she weren't so gracious, a trait recognized even by those who disagree with her, she might have said to critics like Balmer, "You might want to look in a mirror yourself" or even "physician, heal thyself." But I'm not sure it would have helped.

In the end, while progressive evangelicals continue to bang the drum against a mythic theocracy, setting up a straw man, lumping all conservatives into the most radical positions, they are unwilling to admit that their own majoritarianism has already devolved into a far more dangerous handmaid's tale, one of woke political correctness.[66] How this happened is the story of the next chapter.

In Sum

- For those in the freedom left 2 position, America was founded on a secular, godless constitution, one that is under siege by conservative religious forces, who want to turn it into a theocracy.

- Freedom left 2 believes that the only way America can reach its true promise is to continue to bracket off religion, maintaining a government that is neutral on the question of the "good," which allows the individual the final choice in determining the good life, questions of right and wrong, and ultimate purpose.

- While progressive evangelicals share many of the same transcendent norms as conservative believers, they too believe in the godless-constitution view, contending it is the best way to protect religious freedom. So these progressive evangelicals side with the freedom left 2 godless-constitution thinkers to fight against religious conservatives, seeing them as the greatest danger to our constitution.

- Yet we have seen many voices on the left who contend that the godless-constitution view is not the original view of our founders, that it has been smuggled in by progressives and in the process it has led to an "unencumbered" self, the growth in government, and the enslavement of individuals, who are less free, more entangled, and more lonely than ever.

- Moreover, what we have learned is that the radical push for an "open society" has not led to freedom, but to a "closed society," and it was the godless-constitution view that was the Trojan horse, promising freedom built on a neutral procedural government, but in fact it has brought us something entirely different, the rise of the oligarchic elites and the loss of freedom.

4

FREEDOM LEFT 3

FROM OPEN SOCIETY TO CLOSED SOCIETY

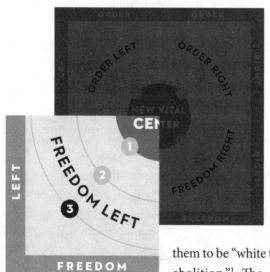

As the second year of the pandemic and lockdowns began in New York City, and the patience of parents of school-aged children wore thin, a group of parents received a message from their kids' school principal, Mark Federman, asking them to be "white traitors" and to push for "white abolition."[1] The email contained a colorful graphic showing eight stages of white identity development—moving from the low end of "white supremacist" to moderate forms of "white confessional" and "white traitor" to the highest form of "white abolitionist." According to the creator of the graphic, Northwestern University professor Barnor Hesse, the purpose of the exercise is to root out the "regime of whiteness" and "subvert white authority," making sure that they don't allow "whiteness to reassert itself." In his letter, principal Federman made clear he wants to abolish whiteness as a social construct but acknowledges this might be impossible because their racism is implicit.

After the email and graphic leaked to the media, one parent expressed outrage over the blatant indoctrination of their child, saying "we need to stop indoctrinating our youth and radicalizing them."[2] But this kind of instruction has now migrated out of the city and spread to upstate New York, where the Buffalo Public Schools has adopted a Black Lives Matter curriculum for its K-12 schools. Their stated goal is to educate their children in the tenets of BLM, including the dangers of Western civilization, the white supremacy of the nuclear family, and the justification of violence as an acceptable method of protest against injustice. The goal is teaching students from a young age how to become "anti-racist."[3]

What is happening in the New York public schools is spreading all across the country, claims Max Eden, as more and more school districts adopt these types of curriculums.[4] Yet "for many parents, this might sound like an unobjectionable appeal to moral progress in the wake of a tragic injustice [the death of George Floyd]."[5] But they are beginning to see that teaching antiracism is more than teaching a form of the Golden Rule, treating everyone with respect. Rather it contains a specific method on how to be antiracist and teaches that silence is not an option, for to remain silent is to promote racism. "It's an all-encompassing ideology" that demands total commitment. It means burning down the old curriculum and adopting a more just one. As part of its "toolkit to help foster productive conversations about race and civil disobedience," the Chicago Public School included a quote by Angela Davis: "In a racist society, it is not enough to not be non-racist, we must be anti-racist."[6] You have to pick your side, there is no in-between. Education now means the "constant questioning of one's own actions and motives and the actions and motives of others, with total vigilance about one's own purportedly implicit racial biases."[7]

For those who believe that our country was born in racism and that its curriculum continues to perpetuate "white supremacy," then "flood[ing] our children with counter messages" is the right thing to do.[8] As the National Council of Teachers of English contends, "there is no apolitical classroom," and thus public school teachers must make their classrooms laboratories of reeducation, and not stop until all racial and economic and educational inequalities have been addressed.[9] If we are going to change this country, we must imprint, they believe, this teaching onto the next generation of students before it is too late. And that means completely transforming the curriculum, rejecting the old one based on Western civilization that promoted white supremacy, and adopting a new one, based on the ideas of antiracism, which include specific ways of looking at politics, economics, and culture.

Journalist Max Eden interviewed parents who wondered "how our public schools became propaganda mills" for one political persuasion. "The answer," he says, "to paraphrase Hemingway, is two ways: gradually, then suddenly."[10] As Eden says, "Critical race theory was largely pioneered in US schools of education; a generation of teachers has been trained" in its doctrines. Then, after George Floyd's death, school districts across the nation "publicly vowed to imprint" these teachings on the next generation.[11] And they don't want to waste any time doing it. Yet, as more parents, even Democrats, find out what is being taught in schools and what they are being asked to accept, more and more families are fleeing the public school system, adding to the polarization in our country.[12]

This polarization over antiracism is not confined to public schools. It is happening in corporate America, the US military, professional sports, and once institutional bastions of liberalism like Smith College and the newsroom at the *New York Times*.[13] And the church is not immune to the conflict. On the progressive side of evangelicalism, *Relevant* magazine founder, Cameron Strang, was forced to take a sabbatical when staffers accused him of being "insufficiently woke" and later apologized for his own "toxicity and insensitivity," promising to engage in "learning."[14] Progressive Jim Wallis of *Sojourners* magazine got into trouble with his own staff for holding opinions deemed unsatisfactory in this new radical culture.[15]

Along with progressives, some of the most conservative enclaves of evangelicalism are now entangled in the conflict, sorting along ideological lines as if they are being chosen for separate houses in a Harry Potter movie: those that are woke and adopt the antiracism teaching and those who reject it, claiming it is alien to the historic teachings of Christianity.[16] This conflict has led a well-known African American pastor to drop out of his Southern Baptist seminary because the seminary president rejected critical race theory.[17] In the Presbyterian Church in America, one of the largest conservative denominations in the country, there are those who embrace antiracism and those who are worried it will destroy the denomination.[18]

Evangelical leaders are not alone in dividing over being woke. People in the pews are feeling the tension. Recently, blogger Rod Dreher posted a long letter from one of his readers who explains why he and his wife had no choice but to leave their church: "The driving factor," he says, "is something

I can only describe as 'our church got woke.'" They could no longer stand that "evangelicalism and identity politics are at war" and that identity politics is winning, gutting the once sound theology of his church.[19] But this divide cuts both ways. Progressive evangelicals are just as frustrated that their church leaders remained silent in the weeks after George Floyd's death and that they haven't embraced the new antiracism teaching.

Put simply, among church leadership and congregants, "This is the No 1 divide in evangelicalism in 100 years," says J. D. Hall, a pastor who runs *Pulpit & Pen*, a widely read blog. "The largest denominations in the country are splitting down the middle on this. . . . It's huge."[20] How did we get here?

Even those outside the church see the polarization and are worried about its effects on the body politic. In fact, professor and author James Lindsay, someone who might easily fit into the freedom left 2 position, contends this moment of reckoning, this explosion of conflict, is easy to explain. As the Left moved from believing in the norms of liberalism, rationalism, science, and free speech (freedom left 2) to a view that all truth is socially constructed, all politics is power, and that language must be carefully policed, they have adopted an entirely new politic (freedom left 3), setting themselves in opposition to mainstream liberalism. If someone adopts a political stance that "rejects all potential alternatives" for correcting inequality in society and then calls these alternatives racist, they create a situation where "all our relationships and social systems [are] extremely fragile and tense, ready to explode over a highly divisive issue."[21] With only one solution, says Lindsay, a solution that can never be fully achieved, the Far Left has set up a zero sum conflict of perpetual war, "like a black hole. No matter how much you give it, it cannot be filled and only gets stronger—and it will tear apart anything that gets too close to it." Again, how did we arrive at this spot? How did the Left, which just ten years ago was still fighting for equal rights, freedom of speech, and defending liberal democracy, end up here? And why are so many progressive evangelicals going along, contending these new views are acceptable, a welcome ally in the fight for social justice?[22]

ONCE UPON A TIME THERE WAS ONLY INJUSTICE

In my opening story we can see the main tenets of the freedom left 3 narrative. Once upon a time, there was no golden age, as America was born into sin, a racist nation. White supremacy was baked into the founding documents. As heirs of White Western civilization, America was ruled by White supremacists and from the start political, economic, and religious institutions helped perpetuate their oppressive rule, keeping Blacks and other minorities down, never allowing them to experience their fair share of material growth or civil rights.

With no golden age to look back to, there is no reason to "Make America Great Again," only a plan for the present and future: revolution (a total dismantling of our society) and reconstruction (a complete reordering of society along antiracist lines). Finally, the enemy is clearly seen—anyone who resists this call for revolution and reconstruction, clinging to their "White fragility," defending patriarchal Western civilization, or fighting for Christian nationalism.[23] That, in a nutshell, is the narrative of freedom left 3.

How did this narrative come about? To answer that, we need to dig a little deeper.

THE LEFT ADOPTS POSTMODERNISM

In chapter three we saw how liberalism had cut itself off from the grounding of natural rights, so closely tied to natural law, which provided the country with an idea of the "good." I chronicled how mid-century liberalism attempted to hold on to "America values," but, shorn of any transcendent grounding, it adopted a "godless-constitution view." Mid-century liberals wanted the fruit—liberal democratic values—but no longer wanted the tree that produced the fruit. Eventually, however, the unencumbered self and the naked public square were challenged by the Right, particularly the Christian Right.

What is often missed, though, is that this pragmatism of the left was also attacked by forces on the far left, those in freedom left 3, who contended that Enlightenment rationalism and science are just as oppressive as any of the worst tyranny on the right. America can't experience true liberation through the Enlightenment or liberalism or science or Christianity (all as offspring of Western civilization), which perpetuate oppressive systems. These metanarratives of power and injustice all have to be eliminated. Thus postmodernism was born. And postmodernism's first step is deconstruction, the tearing down of all metanarratives.

FROM MODERNISM TO POSTMODERNISM

Postmodernism, while difficult to pin down, is a philosophical movement that began in the 1960s and spread through literature departments in the 1970s and 1980s. Primarily it was an attack on the West's overreliance on Enlightenment rationalism (modernity) and empiricism (science and historical fact). At its heart, postmodernism taught that all epistemologies (groundings) were metanarratives of control and power. And they all need to be identified, unmasked, and destroyed; this included metanarratives on the left *and* the right.

In *Postmodernism: A Very Short Introduction*, Oxford University's Christopher Butler writes that postmodernism is an "incredulity toward metanarratives" of all kinds. For Butler these metanarratives are "some form of legitimization or authority," what we have been calling groundings.[24] Postmodernists reject all groundings. "The result," says Butler, "was that the basic attitude of postmodernism was a skepticism about the claims of any kind of overall, totalizing explanation."[25] Swept away in this negative project are all the ways America has traditionally grounded itself—reason, history, science, and religion. They have attacked liberalism as much as religion, the Left as much as the Right. They attacked those on the secular Left (the godless-constitution camp), rejecting their contention that liberalism could still establish a grounding apart from religion or natural law. To postmodernists, all metanarratives (even freedom left 2) are about power, using a particular grounding or overall story to control reality, to oppress people, and give the power to those who control the narrative.

As this more radical, postmodern thought was attacking secular liberalism, there were a few lonely voices on the left sounding the alarm, pushing back. Charles Taylor wrote the small book *The Malaise of Modernity* in which he tried to explain the shift from pragmatic rationality to more extreme views of liberation that would lead to the loss of the self, the complete loss of truth, and eventually the loss of freedom itself.[26] Others like Christopher Lash and Phillip Rieff joined the chorus of criticism.[27]

Even those on the left who were generally supportive of postmodernism, like Butler, couldn't ignore the contradictions within postmodernism. Since, "the central argument for deconstruction depends on relativism," meaning that "truth is always relative to the differing standpoints and predisposing intellectual frameworks of the judging subject," it can't help but become its own form of "irrationalism at the heart of postmodernism" and a "kind of despair."[28] This means that after they have deconstructed all the metanarratives, all the known groundings, there is nothing less than solipsistic despair for some postmodernists. And many never moved beyond this despair, becoming cynical about life. There were others, however, who, even though they were committed to postmodernism and its radical skepticism, needed something to give them hope, something to live for other than deconstruction. This was problematic, though.

POSTMODERNISM CAN DESTROY BUT IT CAN'T BUILD

Adopting a grounding of individual subjectivism and relativism doesn't provide a foundation to rebuild upon. Once the individual is freed from all outside authority—whether reason, history, or religion—individual life becomes a free-for-all, individuals scrambling to get their needs (rights) met. But standing alone, says Butler, is too isolating, so the lonely individual is forced to join with other likeminded lonely and isolated individuals, and thus the concept of group rights is born. If there was no higher meaning in life, at least the lonely individuals could suffer together, share their grievances, and hopefully get some of their material needs met. Yet, as Butler says, all these new identity groups, fighting to have their grievances heard, in the end, led to "isolated communities," groups divided from one another.[29] Balkanized. Polarized.

Without a grand narrative, a common consensus, and a public philosophy to attach themselves to, these disparate groupings have nowhere to look for meaning and purpose. "Once all these differences and different identities were established, they were cut off from any central harmonizing ideology."[30] What then would hold these groups together? For Butler this is problematic, "given the sustained and near anarchist hostility of many postmodernists to any overall theory or picture of society."[31]

In the end, what began as an exhilarating doctrine of liberation, freeing groups from the oppressive metanarratives, allowing more viewpoint diversity, and giving more people a seat at the table, eventually led to the complete absence of a common language or a common ethic or a common public philosophy to guide citizens. Public and civic life, particularly at universities, became a cacophony of voices, making it impossible to have conversations. So they stopped talking to one another. And this inability to communicate, to trust one another, eventually spilled out into our public life, leading to tremendous polarization. Would there be a way out of this dead end? The answer would come in the postmodern turn.

THE POSTMODERN TURN

According to Pluckrose and Lindsay's *Cynical Theories*—maybe the most helpful book on postmodernism and its evolution into critical theory and social-justice scholarship—postmodernism had three phases.[32] The high deconstructive phase ran from the late 1960s to 1980 and was based on radical skepticism that led to extreme cynicism, pessimism, and despair. The second phase, from roughly 1980 to 2000, was characterized by a "postmodern turn" to a more positive postmodernism, an attempt to construct a better world through "applied postmodernism," mainly through group identity politics. The third stage, what he calls "reified postmodernism" where a new metanarrative rises from the ashes of skepticism to provide a new vision of the world, one spelled out in social-justice scholarship, included a new moral imperative and map to give shape to the antiracism activism.

While I have been describing phase one and will cover phase three (see chapter six), here we will focus briefly on the second phase, the "postmodern turn," where pessimistic postmodernism took on a more positive turn and mutated into critical race theory.

POSTMODERNISM MUTATES INTO CRITICAL RACE THEORY

In a chapter on critical race theory, Pluckrose and Lindsay say that it is "at root, an American phenomenon," mostly set in American history and context. In brief, they posit that critical race theory "holds that race is a social construct that was created to maintain white privilege and white supremacy."[33] Similarly, in their primer on critical race theory, Richard Delgado and Jean Stefancic explain that "critical race theory questions the very foundations of the liberal order, including equality theory, legal reasoning, Enlightenment rationalism, and neutral principals of constitutional law."[34]

But critical race theory went further than postmodernism, which mainly attacked metanarratives worldwide, and turned its focus on the United

States, arguing that America among all nations is uniquely racist. Racism, America's original sin, was enshrined in its founding documents; White supremacy, at the heart of all its cultural, political, and economic institutions, was established by Whites to have power over Blacks and other ethnic minorities; and finally, "White fragility," the denial of complicity and ongoing bias, has characterized the White population since the start of the country. Only by coming to grips with this unjust system, rallying the oppressed minority groups to fight for racial justice, and pushing for change through equity, affirmative action, and redistribution of power and resources can the old system be toppled and a new one established.

PROGRESSIVE EVANGELICALS PLUNGE RIGHT IN

Surprisingly, in spite of its rejection of metanarratives and its commitment to radical skepticism and relativism, progressive evangelicals have been open to the postmodern turn into critical race theory. In my 2009 book on the emerging church movement, I included a chapter on postmodernism, trying to show how evangelicals were slowly adopting it and the ways they were open to it, seeing it as an ally against the arrogance of enlightenment secularism.[35] But while I argued it that was correct to point out the problems with Enlightenment secularism (freedom left 2), I also tried to warn the evangelical church that postmodernism was not the solution, as it swept away the Christian metanarrative along with the rest. At the time I was writing, others also warned of postmodernism in the church, thus putting the emergent church on the defensive.[36] With so much pushback, many progressive evangelicals dropped the term *postmodernism* and began stressing the term *missional*, calling for evangelicals to pursue justice. Soon books on justice began to appear.[37]

Almost as soon as the academic Left and the larger culture began gravitating from the high deconstructive phase of postmodernism to the more positive critical race theory, progressive evangelicals followed suit. As if they were wont to jump on the publishing trend, evangelical publishing houses began turning out book titles like *White Awake, Dear White America, The Myth of Equality,* and *Be the Bridge.* Yet many of these books worked to remain theologically orthodox, not fully adopting the new ideology, which created an awkward alliance. But as critical race theory entered the mainstream, making its devotees bestselling authors and spilling out onto the streets with Black Lives Matter, progressive evangelicals began to embrace critical race theory's totalizing narrative even more, closing the gap between it and the biblical view of justice.

I believe Jemar Tisby's book *How to Fight Racism* illustrates this accommodation.[38] After reading the book, I could only conclude that Tisby relies on critical race theory to understand America's racial past.[39] Tisby, a gifted communicator and passionate advocate for the church, parallels the main tenets of the critical race theory narrative in his book: America's racist founding, the nation built on White racism, White complicity in the oppression of racial minorities (the continuation of the original sin), the presence of "racial justice deniers," and the need for Whites to grow in racial awareness.

Tisby believes that social justice can only be achieved through the instruments of diversity, equity, and inclusion and that affirmative action social policies are needed to balance the scales of justice.[40] For Tisby, CRT is a helpful philosophy, one of many to aid in our cultural analysis. While some of his passion for critical race theory could be attributed to rhetorical passion, and his passionate desire to achieve racial equality, I see it at the heart of his entire narrative, animating and giving life to everything he says, guiding his analysis and determining his conclusions.

Yet, by making this bold move, I believe Tisby has slid into biblical inflation and cultural accommodation. And what if in adopting CRT, Tisby is contributing less to racial justice and harmony and more to an environment which leads to division, bitterness, and the fraying of the body politic, including in the church, and in the end contributing to the breakdown of the vital center and the rise of the oligarchic elites?[41]

How Critical Race Theory Divides and Destroys

A number of voices on the left have been making just this case, contending that critical race theory is divisive in six ways.[42]

First, by making everything about race—not class or grounding or citizenship or any number of important concepts—it has set up an environment where everyone is looking for racism everywhere and in every personal interaction, leading to a kind of race hysteria, a "racecraft" like the witchcraft of the Salem trials.[43] Once we find it, critics say, we must make the accusation, regardless of whether we have definitive proof or whether it ruins someone's life or divides the community.[44] This can be so destructive.

As Greg Lukianoff and Jonathan Haidt point out in their bestselling book, *The Coddling of the American Mind*, using race as the number one dividing line in our nation, expressed through the Marxist oppressor-oppressed axis, telling people that life is a battle between good people and evil people (those who are racist and those who are not), has *not* brought warring groups any closer together. Rather, it has engendered "an environment highly conducive to the development of a 'call-out-culture,'" in which we gain prestige for identifying small offenses committed by members of our community and then publicly calling-out the offenders.[45] It is a recipe for disunity.

Second, critical race theory claims that all politics is about power—who has it, who doesn't, and how the dominant class maintains it. Once they reject all metanarratives, whether found in the Enlightenment, Christianity, or natural law, they fearlessly claim that liberal values have always been a sham, a ruse, and are now more than happy to admit that power is all that matters.[46] As if they are no longer afraid to speak the quiet parts out loud, they have no trouble boldly announcing that the ends justify the means.[47]

Third, since the end of racial justice is noble and those who stand in the way are evil, critical race theory believes that to be tolerant of injustice or racism is actually a form of intolerance. To allow speech that is hateful is to allow intolerance to continue; to allow racist views to proliferate is to condone racism. In pure critical race theory, all voices of disinformation must be silenced or deplatformed. This also divides and destroys, eroding freedom of speech, religious liberty, and democratic participation.

Now that the gloves are off and the sham of liberal tolerance has been abandoned (freedom left 2), Marxist thinker Herbert Marcuse, "a German philosopher and sociologist who fled the Nazis and became a professor at several American universities," is experiencing a renaissance.[48] From a 1965 essay "Repressive Tolerance," by Marcuse, Lukianoff and Haidt note, "In a chilling passage that foreshadows events on some campuses today," the authors argue, "Marcuse argued that true democracy might require denying basic rights to people who advocate for conservative causes, or for policies as aggressive or discriminatory, and that freedom of thought might require professors to indoctrinate their students."[49] What Marcuse raised as a possibility has now become a reality on some campuses.

Fourth, critical race theory has moved from the liberal vision of the open society (freedom left 2) to a closed society (freedom left 3).[50] As James Lindsay, a man of the left, says, critical race theory is against free societies; instead, they want a society of control.[51] Politicians call big tech to clamp down on disinformation;[52] those who challenge the strategy of the pandemic lockdowns are silenced;[53] citizens who resist a policy on masks have their freedom of speech and assembly taken away;[54] small business owners who want to stay open and earn a living are fined and some put in jail.[55] Big tech spies on its customers.[56] And as investigative reporter Andy Ngo has chronicled in his new book, the Far Left uses Antifa as a new Stasi (East German secret police under communist occupation), turning a blind eye to its violence and destruction of property.[57] In twenty-first-century America, control is king, conformity is the rule, silence is mandated.

Finally, maybe the most ironic and harmful effect is that freedom left 3 and its commitment to applied postmodernism and critical race theory has become its own form of racism. As Lindsay argues, when Whites alone are racist and oversee a system of White supremacy and are unable to reach racial awareness because it is so intrinsic to them, and when Blacks can never be racist because they have no power, or when their violent actions can be excused in the name of racial justice, we now are living under a new system of racial hierarchy that favors minorities at the expense of the old majority power.[58] Yet, as history has shown us over and over again, minorities who grab power without the guardrails of natural law and the rule of law always turn right around and oppress the former oppressors. This is almost axiomatic. The former Soviet Union, China, Cuba, and Venezuela all attest to this reality.

Who Ultimately Benefits?

Those who embrace critical race theory like to ask the question: *Who benefits from a system of power?* The same question could be asked about critical race theory. By undermining the grounding of society, by reducing the self to group identity, by equating all politics to power, by separating us into oppressor and oppressed classes, who benefits? By saying that racism is everywhere, telling Black and minority students that all Whites play a part in perpetuating systemic racism, thus creating tremendous distrust between racial and ethnic groups, who benefits the most? When society is more controlled, locked down, or censored, who is benefitting? When freedom left 3 leads to distrust, division, and destruction in society, what group comes out ahead?

It's not the American people, the working class, the middle class, or the poor. It's neither minorities in the inner cities nor religious believers. Rather, it's the oligarchy, the new ruling class, and their clerisy who are using freedom left 3 as part of their larger campaign to wage war from below and above, their strategy of twin insurgency. Far from a harmless philosophy in the academy, I see the ruling class using critical race theory to extinguish our grounding, delegitimizing the American project in the eyes of the public. They are utilizing critical race theory to wear away our view of the biological self, to transform our views on gender, to erode the structure of the nuclear family, and to pit the races against one another, all with the goal of chipping away at middle-class values. In the end, their goal is to centralize and consolidate their own power. Undoubtedly, it's a dark vision. But it's brilliant. And it seems to be working.

A year before Andrew Sullivan left the *New York Times*, he wrote that "every now and again, it's worth asking about what the intersectional left's ultimate endgame really is." He concludes, "the ultimate aim seems to be running the entire country by fiat . . . [and] there is a word for this kind of politics and this kind of theory when it is completely realized, and it's totalitarian."[59] And people on the left are beginning to see what is happening. When a liberal feminist Democrat like Naomi Wolf goes on *Tucker Carlson Tonight*, not to disagree with the conservative host but to mutually decry what she calls the totalitarian takeover of our country under the guise of a national health emergency, we see strange bedfellows coming together, recognizing the breakneck speed with which the totalitarian oligarchy has seized the reins of power, possibly destroying our constitutional democracy forever.[60]

Many on the evangelical left (but not all, I admit) are slow to see what liberal critics like Lindsay, Butler, and Wolf have discovered: the danger of accepting critical race theory in toto. Instead, there are some pastors and scholars who continue to embrace the whole of critical race theory as an ally. Moreover, they don't see that the bipartisan oligarchs, made up of both

Republicans and Democrats, really have little interest in racial justice or helping minorities; their goal is something completely different—total power, allowing them to enforce a new vision on humanity. While it is not true of most who adopt CRT (many are sincere), there are some who cynically push it as a way to support the agenda of the ruling elites, benefiting financially from the ruling class through large government subsidies and the growth of the administrative state and other transfers of wealth.

Yet, the real goal of the ruling class, so often led by the new high-tech priests of progress, is not racial justice but something much greater and more sinister: to transcend the biological binary into a new transhumanism (with the help of artificial intelligence); to replace the nuclear two-parent family, substituting in its place the state; to build a neo-feudal society, one comprising dependent serfs and high-tech overlords; and to usher in a brave new world in which humans have become like gods, capable of living forever.[61]

In the end, progressive evangelicals are focused on the wrong enemy. They are worried about theocracy on the right or Christian nationalism, but the true enemy is the bipartisan ruling class, who are using critical race theory to divide and conquer, advancing their own cynical grab for power and control. And by the time progressive evangelicals realize it, it may be too late—for the church, the nation, and for parents, whether Democrat or Republican, tying to educate their children not to be angry activists but to be students, lifelong learners, successful adults, and citizens who love this great country, in spite of its flaws, and who know deep down that America is worth protecting and preserving for the next generation.

In Sum

- For freedom left 3, there never was a golden age, as America was born into sin, a racist nation from the start—White supremacy was baked into the founding documents. As heirs of White Western civilization, America was ruled by White supremacists and, from the start, political, economic, and religious institutions helped perpetuate their oppressive rule, keeping Blacks and other minorities down, never allowing them to experience their fair share of material growth or civil rights.

- Since there is no golden age to look back to, there is no reason to "Make America Great Again," only a plan for the present and future: revolution (a total dismantling of our society) and reconstruction (a complete reordering of society along antiracist lines).

- For freedom left 3 the enemy is clearly seen—anyone who resists this call for revolution and reconstruction, clinging to their "White fragility," whether they are proponents of Western civilization, Enlightenment rationalism, or Christian nationalism.

- In spite of its rejection of metanarratives and its commitment to radical skepticism and relativism, and a move from secularism to reified postmodernism most present in critical race theory, many progressive evangelicals have adopted the postmodern turn into critical race theory, believing it can be helpful for the church as it pursues racial justice.

- There are a number of voices on the left who have pushed back, showing how this postmodern turn into CRT has brought not more racial justice, but less; not more harmony, but less; not more freedom, but less.

- The more CRT pushes the nation away from the vital center, the more divided we become and the less justice all races experience.

- The ones who benefit from the division left in the wake of CRT are not racial minorities but the bipartisan ruling elites, who exploit racial unrest and division to consolidate their power in American society.

5

ORDER LEFT 2

THE RISE OF THE WELFARE STATE
AND THE GREAT SOCIETY

WHEN GEORGE FLOYD DIED at the hands of the Minneapolis police in May 2020, it was the spark that lit an inferno. Within days, protestors in a half dozen major cities—Minneapolis, Los Angeles, Philadelphia, Atlanta, New York City, and Washington, DC—took to the streets, carrying signs, shouting, calling for justice for George Floyd, and some demanding to abolish the police. But right from the start, when nightfall descended on these cities, peaceful protests turned violent, as people clashed with the police, burned police vehicles, threw rocks through storefronts, and looted hundreds of stores.[1] It went on like this for days, and then days turned into weeks, and weeks into months. Three months later, by the time the riots had subsided and thousands had marched in protest, twenty-four police officers were dead, hundreds more injured, and over $1 billion in damages had been inflicted on our cities.[2]

During the summer of 2020 the media downplayed the riots, claiming they were mostly a peaceful movement, even as the video playing behind their talking heads showed fires burning and people looting stores. They took pains to say these were peaceful protests, and many were. Yet, when the evidence of the violence became overwhelming, when they could no longer deny the rampant violence—video doesn't lie—they shifted their message and began condoning it. CNN's Chris Cuomo said on his show, "Please, show me where it says protestors are supposed to be polite and peaceful."[3] The Fairfax Democratic Party tweeted, "Riots are an integral part of this country's march toward progress."[4] *Slate* magazine blared "The Fight for Civil Rights Is Never 'Nonviolent,'" attempting to rewrite Martin Luther King Jr.'s nonviolent marches in the civil rights era. Even Democrat lawmakers such as then-Senator Kamala Harris said that "they're not going to stop."[5] And she was right; they continued. And when the year was over, "the per-capita murder rate climbed 30 percent in 2020 among thirty-four major cities surveyed by Richard Rosenfeld, a criminologist at the University of Missouri in St. Louis," reports Reuters.[6]

If endorsing violence wasn't shocking enough, reports were coming in that the mayors of these cities, all Democrats, were telling their police to stand-down, to let the rioting go on.[7] And in many cities the police became the enemy.[8] What was going on? Why would Democratic mayors not support the police and let their cities burn? Why would they allow people, many of them residents of their cities, destroy, maim, and kill, burning and looting and destroying the very city they live in?[9]

It didn't take long for people to notice that many of these cities, where the police and criminal-justice system were accused of oppression, have been run by Black mayors, Black city council members, and Black police chiefs, some for over five decades.[10] As an example, in Baltimore, a city experiencing two waves of riots, 40 percent of the police force was Black and it hasn't had a White mayor since the 1960s, meaning it has been under Black Democratic control for over sixty years.[11] And on top of this, no city has received more government aid over the decades. In 2014, through President Obama's stimulus package, Baltimore received 1.8 billion dollars in aid for education, police, welfare, and food stamps.[12] And what has all this money produced? Not much. The same could be said about all the cities experiencing riots. Billions have been poured into these cities since the mid-sixties and the reality for the residents has gotten worse.[13]

Yet it was in cities like Baltimore that the Democratic mayors had told their police to stand down, to give the rioters space to destroy, and therefore allowing their *own* cities to burn and their *own* people to be harmed. As one looter's sign read, "Eat the rich." But the "rich" includes small businesses, many minority-owned, the mom-and-pop shops that inner city residents frequent every day, thus in effect destroying their own neighborhoods, forcing themselves to travel miles for groceries. Why would mayors allow this? Aren't they sworn to protect their own?

SOME CLUES TO WHAT WAS HAPPENING

Back in summer 2020, as the uprisings continued, I got a clue to why mayors didn't step in to end the violence and looting. One evening I came across an interview with longtime civil rights leader and community activist Bob Woodson, now eighty-three.[14] His nonprofit, the Woodson Center, has been laboring for decades in inner cities, mentoring Black teenagers, and attempting to end intergenerational poverty. He tried to explain what was really behind the looting and violence.

In the early days of the civil rights movement, he said, civil rights leaders told themselves that if Blacks could only get elected to office, then they would do a better job running these cities and all Blacks would be better off. But, he argued,

> In the past fifty years $22 trillion has been spent on poverty programs. Seventy percent goes not to the poor but those who serve the poor. . . . So many of those people taking office use this money to create a class of people who are running these cities, and now after fifty years of liberal Democrats running the inner cities, where we have all of these inequities that we have, race is being used as a ruse, as a means of deflecting attention away from critical questions such as why are poor blacks failing in systems run by their own people?[15]

Sadly, the ruse has been working for fifty years.

So, for Woodson race is used as an excuse to cover their mistakes. But he also insinuates that it is more. It is not just covering over the fact of fifty years of bad policies that have made things worse, but it is also covering up something else—that they have used their positions of power to get rich and stay in power, and that they actually need the poverty to continue in order for the gravy train to continue. That is what he meant by 70 percent of the $22 trillion never going to the poor. It is going to the politicians and inner-city leaders who "help" them, the ones who show up at city hall or other governmental agencies driving luxury cars and living lavash lifestyles while all they help are poor.

These mayors, according to Woodson's interview, actually know what they are doing: inciting racial animosity, allowing the looting and violence, encouraging disrespect of the police, condoning the destruction of their cities. He says this leads to the flight of the working class, increasing the dependence on public housing, government subsidies, and daycare subsidies for those who are left behind, mainly unmarried women with children. And they do all this because in the long run it actually benefits politicians, covers over their bad policies and their money-making schemes, increasing their control and wealth and political power. All the while the lives of the poor never improve, no matter how much money is poured into these cities. It is without a doubt, says Woodson, that "poor people are being bamboozled by these race grievance politicians." This is what he meant that "racism is a ruse."

The Narrative of Order Left 2

To understand how we have arrived at the spot where city politicians stoke racial animosity to cover their unsuccessful record and increase their power, we need to step back in time and understand the genesis of the welfare state, why and how it was set up. Once we grasp the genealogy of this quadrant position, it will make sense why these mayors, who are supposed to protect all their citizens, allow a certain segment to terrorize not only the authorities but also the middle-class business owners who contribute so much to the fabric of these cities, increasing the economic woes of the inhabitants and stoking racial division.

As we saw in chapter three, Freedom left 2 supports a particular kind of freedom in which individuals attempted to get away from traditional authority—the church, the town, and the family. Freedom left 2 enlists a particular view of the self, the unencumbered self, and a particular view of individual rights and choice. You will recall that for Sandel, the procedural state prioritizes the right over the good, where government no longer cares about civic virtue. In this narrative, government "should be neutral among competing conceptions of the good life in order to respect persons as free and independent selves, capable of choosing their own ends," contends

Sandel."[16] Further, by bracketing out religion, government allows individuals the freedom to choose their own values and ends as long as they don't harm others.[17] This new emphasis on rights fueled much of the fight for civil and political rights after WWII. Installing this procedural republic that is neutral to the good and the proper ends has been at the heart of the godless constitution, the fight in the courts to keep religion out of the public square, and to keep conservatives from "legislating morality."

But this fight for the unencumbered self wasn't consigned just to the courts and matters of civil and political speech. According to Sandel, "It also figured prominently in the justification of the American welfare state as it emerged from the New Deal to the present," and the need for the government to intervene in the economic realm.[18] But how could intervention in the economy be consistent with a neutral state? It seems to be a contradiction. Not so, says Sandel,

> The advocates of the welfare state . . . appealed . . . to the voluntarist conception of freedom. Their case for expanding social and economic rights did not depend on cultivating a deeper sense of shared citizenship but rather on respecting each person's capacity to choose his or her own values and ends.[19]

And if each person is going to have this capacity and actually be able to choose, which is the first step needed to make one's own life, they must have a minimum level of material well-being. Thus the welfare state was born.

It Began with FDR

For Sandel, President Franklin Roosevelt most clearly articulated this momentous change in liberalism.[20] In his "Economic Bill of Rights," Roosevelt stated that the civic and political rights protected by the procedural republic were not enough to ensure freedom. How could people be free if they didn't have the basic necessities of life? "Among the social and economic rights necessary to 'true individual freedom' were 'the right to a useful and remunerative job, . . . the right to earn enough to provide adequate food and clothing and recreation, . . . the right of every family to a decent home, the right to adequate medical care, . . . the right to a good education.'" For FDR a certain level of economic security was necessary for a free individual to "choose their own values and ends."[21]

Thus welfare-state liberalism was born, moving the state from a position of neutrality to one of active involvement in the economy and the proliferation of new social programs to assist people from cradle to grave. In order to oversee this massive growth in government, the administrative state ballooned and the number of elites necessary to run the new welfare state did as well. According to Sandel, President Johnson in the 1960s continued to expand the welfare state with his Great Society and tied the procedural republic to welfare-state liberalism. For Johnson, "government liberates [the individual] from the enslaving forces of his environment." Thanks to the Great Society "every American is freer to shape his own activities, set his own goals, do what he wants with his own life, than at any time in the history of man."[22]

For Johnson, as for Roosevelt, says Sandel, "economic security is a prerequisite for individual liberty."[23] Sandel continues that Johnson contends, "The man who is hungry who cannot find work or educate his children, who is bowed by want—that man is not fully free."[24] Johnson defended the further growth of government handouts "in the name of enabling people to choose and pursue their ends for themselves," concludes Sandel.[25]

Johnson summarizes the move from the neutral state to the involved state perfectly: "For more than 30 years, from social security to the war on poverty, we have diligently worked to enlarge the freedom of man. And as a result, Americans tonight are freer to live as they want to live, to pursue their ambitions, to meet their desires . . . than at any time in all of our glorious history."[26] And to achieve this new activist government, the progressives, Sandel documents, had to reinterpret the Constitution not in the old civic republican way that stressed the cultivation of virtue and self-government, but in the new view of the procedural republic.[27] And once they were able to win in the courts, this new view became the framework for the welfare state and the growth of the administrative state to oversee all these economic programs. The more the government tried to make individuals free, the more it tied them to the state.

What has been the result for the individual? According to Sandel, the unencumbered self is now "lurching . . . between detachment on the one hand [and] entanglement on the other. . . . For it is a striking feature of the welfare state that it offers a powerful promise of individual rights," but instead entangles all citizens with the state. The individual loses freedom.[28] In other words, the more we rely on government handouts, the more addicted (entangled) we become and the less free we are. We have traded our freedom for economic security. But sadly, we have neither. On the one hand the individual is less free from government regulations and intrusions and dependency; and on the other, poverty and inequality still exist.

ONCE UPON A TIME

There is a direct link between freedom left 2 and order left 2. At their core they share a common narrative. Early twentieth-century progressives realized that the American dream wasn't working for minorities, many of them stuck in poverty, and until we ended poverty and our system shared the wealth better, our nation hadn't reached its promise. There had been no golden era, it was still a dream to be reached. So in order to reach this dream, progressives needed to transform the meaning of the Constitution, reshaping it to usher in a new era of economic equality and justice. At the heart of their new way of interpreting the plain words of the Constitution is a new way of looking at the self and the role of the state: as the freely choosing unencumbered self and the procedural republic.

For freedom left 2 the watchword was *freedom*, stressing personal liberation —from the family, the church, and the state. And in order to achieve this freedom the state had to be reduced to a position of neutrality, a procedural republic, never dictating what the good is for the individual, and this included bracketing out religion from public life, keeping the public square "naked." But this naked square never really stayed empty—it was filled with a new majority opinion, this time that of the secular Left. And this new progressive opinion not only included a secular view on culture but also views on economics and politics.

Far from staying neutral from making decisions on what is good for people, the progressive Left smuggled back into the debate a definitive view on what constitutes the economic and political good. In fact, the more it stressed freedom from any metaphysical grounding like natural law or Christianity, the more it seemed to get involved in the lives of its citizens, entangling them economically, politically, and socially.

While in chapter three I stressed the *freedom* side of this narrative, how it freed the self from all outside restraint or authority, here we see the *order* side, how it began to take on a new version of the good and impose it on the lives of its citizens. As Sandel pointed out, progressives did this in the New Deal and the Great Society. In the process they believed they had reached a new golden era. But for these progressives, this golden era didn't last long, as it was dismantled by deep cuts in the welfare state, starting in 1980, when President Reagan, the darling of the religious Right, took office. And here is where the narrative takes its next step.

If the golden age, which was lost in the rise of the religious Right (the biggest enemy), is to be regained, progressives need a plan for recovery. And they have one. The government, controlled and guided by elites, must regain its moral authority and continue to expand, redistributing more and more wealth to those most in need, including free health care, subsidies for public housing, and a living wage. And, along with meeting the economic needs of its citizens, the new elites must continue to shape in a progressive direction the cultural landscape, that is, the thoughts and actions of citizens, in order to provide the necessary runway to a new golden age.

Progressive Evangelicals Adopt Order Left 2

This progressive once-upon-a-time story is not just the narrative of secular thinkers, those of the godless constitution and new deal progressivism. Over the years there have been many progressive evangelicals who share it, championing the godless constitution, the unencumbered self, and the procedural republic. Over the years, some progressive evangelicals have defended and supported the welfare state and great society. Minority voices within evangelicalism—progressive evangelicals like Tony Campolo, Ron Sider, and Jim Wallis—believed that free-market capitalism, far from being a friend of the poor, had caused their poverty, unjustly trapping them into a life of misery.[29] Therefore, the best way to fix capitalism is by economic redistribution, transferring as much wealth as possible from the rich to the poor. Generally, these evangelical progressives endorsed the policies of the welfare state and the great society.

Young Progressive Evangelicals Carry It Forward

Another representative of the order left 2 position is Jonathan Wilson-Hartgrove, a second-generation progressive evangelical and someone who has built on earlier progressives like Sider and Wallis. In his two most recent books, *Reconstructing the Gospel: Finding Freedom from Slaveholder Religion* and *Revolution of Values: Reclaiming Public Faith for the Common Good*, Wilson-Hartgrove shares his strong love and desire to help the poor, the marginalized, and those left out of the material prosperity of the nation.[30] Throughout his books he cites, rightly, passages in the Bible about God's concern for the poor, the outsider, and racial justice. God, he reminds us, is on the side of the poor and against those who exploit the poor (i.e., the rich and powerful). God clearly takes sides, or at least puts a huge burden on the most fortunate to watch out for, care for, empower, and help the least fortunate. With these Bible verses he is on solid ground.

But instead of exhorting all Christians to do a better job in this area, he dumps all the blame for injustice on one group, which go by different names but are the same people—Republicans, conservative evangelicals, and the religious Right—all people who exploit the poor and reject God's mandate to care for them. And this accusation and condemnation is not subtle; like an Old Testament prophet speaking to corrupt and exploitive leaders, he thunders at evangelicals on the right, accusing them of pushing a "false narrative," "twisting Scripture," saying the Republican Party is evil, calling their pro-capitalism "Jim Crow, Esq.," being on the side of genocide and patriarchy, and guilty of "policy violence."[31] He is not subtle.

Following a narrative similar to freedom left 2 and 3, Wilson-Hartgrove tells us that America has been corrupt from the start, born into "genocide and slavery," that slavery is America's original sin, that from the start it was grounded in a "slaveholder religion," and that "Jim Crow and internment camps, mass incarceration and deportation, global climate change and inequality" have continued because America is still gripped by its original White racial sin.[32]

So, having made the case that there never was and has never been a golden era, what is Wilson-Hartgrove's plan for reaching one? As bad as it has been, Wilson-Hartgrove surprisingly doesn't seem to give up on America entirely. Numerous times he mentions Martin Luther King Jr. and how King "reclaimed the moral narrative" and pointed to the day when we would have a "more perfect union."[33] Wilson-Hartgrove contends there are still "things we should all work to conserve in the American republic."[34] Yet, while King frequently looked back to the Declaration of Independence and Lincoln's "rebirth of freedom," Wilson-Hartgrove doesn't make clear what is worth preserving and doesn't seem to share King's views of the nation's past.[35] Instead he seems frustrated with America's progress.

And here we move to the third act of the narrative, the plan for renewal. Wilson-Hartgrove doesn't agree that mid-century was a golden age, but he does agree, like other progressives in the order left 2 position, that the best plan for helping the poor is strengthening the programs of the New Deal and the Great Society.[36] In fact, he says America was making some progress toward alleviating poverty until the Christian Right, led by Ronald Reagan, scuttled the progress through cutting welfare programs and linking pro capitalist republicanism with Jim Crow racism.[37]

While he doesn't tell us exactly what system of economics he prefers, he does seem to favor a kind of social democracy, a plan of economic redistribution that far exceeds the current welfare state. Using Acts 2 as an example of sharing all things in common, he seems to call on Christians to support a much greater amount of redistribution. He says we should have all things in common, with the goal being "equality" in the economic realm.[38] An example he gives is the fight for a $15 minimum wage, recently proposed by the Biden administration. But beyond that, he is fairly vague, mentioning the right to "maternity leave and childcare, quality public education, access to birth control, affordable health care," and prison reform—all pretty standard planks in the Democratic Party.[39] Basically, for Wilson-Hartgrove the "revolution of values" means supporting a progressive vision for politics, economics, and culture.

In the end, Wilson-Hartgrove is trying to convince conservative evangelicals to turn away from their slaveholder religion, their false narrative of Christian nationalism, rooted as they are in political views born in the racist South, and return to God's side and his love for the poor.[40] Once we have our eyes opened, once we are born anew, we will see the need to end racism, stop hurting the poor, and join God's side in the battle for justice, and "stand with Jesus" against "the genocidal White supremacy and patriarchy that have compromised Christian witness throughout history."[41] This is question for us: Is this kind of White enlightenment, so needed among conservative evangelicals, really the best way to help the poor? While I don't doubt the sincerity of progressive evangelicals' commitment to helping the poor, I do question their wisdom. After sixty years of welfare society programs, the jury is *no* longer out. And the verdict is bad, truly terrible. Not only has it not eliminated poverty, it has created intergenerational poverty that seems almost impossible to wipe out.[42]

THE DISSENT OF A BLACK LIBERAL

While it is not very newsworthy when a conservative criticizes the welfare state—after all, they have been doing this for decades, and their rebukes are generally ignored by the Left—it is shocking when a dissident Democrat takes on the system, especially when he is a Black, tenured professor from an Ivy League college.[43] In 2005, Columbia professor of linguistics John McWhorter did just that, taking on the welfare system and its defenders in *Winning the Race: Beyond the Crisis in Black America.*[44] In a four hundred-page manifesto, McWhorter took on every progressive excuse for the persistence of the poor Black underclass in spite of decades of throwing money at the problem. Through exhaustive research, he takes on the common excuses for persistent poverty—the loss of inner-city jobs, the creation of tall public-housing buildings, the underfunding of schools, the introduction of crack cocaine, the bifurcation of neighborhoods by new freeways, and the high concentration of Blacks in certain neighborhoods caused by redlining—and demolishes them all.[45] And the biggest one of them all, White racism, while a continual irritation, he disabuses easily, showing how racial discrimination was magnitudes worse from 1920 to 1960, during which the Black community started to thrive, making substantial gains in every economic and cultural category.

So if none of these factors is responsible for the creation and continuation of the underclass, what is? Two things, and they both began during the 1960s: (1) a new Black self-identity vis-à-vis White America, and (2) the adoption of welfare as an economic solution to poverty. As he summarizes, "the nut of the issue is that black America turned upside down in a particular ten-year period, from 1960–1970, and that this era has left us a legacy much more damaging than anything racism [while it still exists, he says] has left us."[46] In a way that sounds like our description of the anti-authority revolution in mid-century, McWhorter says this anti-authoritarianism of the countercultural revolution took hold in the Black community like no other, combining a toxic mix of "therapeutic alienation" against the "White Man," with a type of "racial enlightenment" among Whites.[47]

Once the Black community grounded their identity on hatred for America, they began to opt out of the daily fight for survival, rejecting entry-level jobs, turning their back on education, rejecting the responsibilities of marriage, and distrusting the entire system as oppressive. With all these structures and institutions broken down and nowhere else to turn for economic survival, when welfare was offered, they jumped on it, which meant they could stay on the margins of American society. The percentage of Blacks on welfare skyrocketed.[48] And with it followed crime, murder, the breakdown of the once strong Black family, economic dependency, and the destruction of inner cities, turning them into "hells on earth."[49] In the end, he says, this "new way of thinking that infected blacks and whites alike . . . affected a massive transformation in cultural attitudes that discouraged millions of blacks from doing their best, while at the same exact time teaching concerned whites that supporting blacks in this way was a sign of moral sophistication."[50]

The problem, however, is that far from sophisticated, it was benighted, resulting in nothing short of a tragedy for Black America.[51] In fact, McWhorter says that prior to 1960 Blacks had made steady gains and were on a trajectory to middle-class prosperity when the goodwill of Whites got in the way, sliding Blacks "into the sinkhole of the permanent dole."[52] As he says, the twin changes of the 1960s—open-ended welfare and white America's expression of therapeutic alienation—did much more to bring down poor black America than any other factor, including the boogeyman of racism. Yet, as he says, resistance to this truth, a truth so plain and visible, is resisted at every turn, covered over with accusations of race and bigotry. As Bob Woodson posited, race had become a ruse.

Returning to our opening story on the riots, we now see that the inner-city mayors that condoned the violence were acting out a perverse incentive put in place decades before. Excusing the riots and blaming them on systemic racism made sense. Not only was it a way to cover up sixty years of destructive policies that have caused large-scale dependency among the Black underclass, dragging even the once-working poor onto the dole, it was an extremely effective tactic to grow this dependence and at the same time strengthen their power. And White progressive leaders, driven by guilt, had the perfect way to assuage their guilt and demonstrate how much they care, pushing more people into the underclass. When the riots struck in 2020, we shouldn't have been surprised.

McWhorter makes clear who benefits: the local politicians and bureaucrats. But as these riots caught on nationally, leading to looting and destruction in hundreds of cities, someone else had an incentive in the riots continuing. As we know, politicians are supposed to "never let a serious crisis go to waste." And they didn't. As mostly blue cities burned, politicians called on the national government for bailout money and the increase of welfare for the residents of these blighted areas.[53] We were told that if we are going to avoid riots like this in the future, we needed to provide free health care, more public housing, and a living wage for the poor, once again strengthening the welfare state and in the process solidifying the dependence of future generations of the underclass. It was the same old song and dance.

Who Benefits?

I want to return to something Wilson-Hartgrove is fond of doing in his books: linking the Republican Party and Christian Right with slaveholder religion. In doing this he makes the case that the modern-day Republican Party is the party of the Old South. Believing in "the lost cause" narrative, it resisted Reconstruction.[54] But historically he actually has it backward and is performing a sleight of hand like a magician who distracts the audience while executing a trick. In historical fact, it was the Democratic Party that supported slavery before the Civil War, resisted Reconstruction, and continued its racial segregation in the Jim Crow era, including its opposition to civil rights in the 1960s.[55]

However, the Republican Party was created in 1854 as the antislavery party and was the party that led the Union fight against slavery, supported Reconstruction in the South, and provided the largest voting block to help pass the civil rights legislation in the 1960s.[56] In fact, it was Democrat Lyndon B. Johnson, an avowed segregationist and racist, who switched his position on civil rights only after the winds of change were shifting, promoting it as a way to control Blacks, keeping them dependent on the Democratic Party.[57]

McWhorter contends that it was commonly known that welfare bureaucrats in the Democratic Party spent the sixties handing out welfare, convincing the working poor that they really didn't want to work, that those manufacturing jobs were beneath them, and that "whitey" was against them.[58] The goal of the bureaucrats wasn't a one-time hand up but rather to addict them to the dole forever, thus controlling them. And, of course, as the Black underclass became dependent on welfare, they became dependent on the Democratic Party and have voted overwhelmingly for Democrats for sixty years, seeing them as the protectors of, and the continuation of, the welfare state.[59] So Johnson was right, sadly.

Moreover, far from the modern Republican Party as the keepers of the slaveholder religion, it is the modern Democratic Party that supports transnational corporations, favors illegal immigration for cheap labor, the offshoring of entry-level manufacturing jobs (many now done by slave labor and women and children in China), and the destruction of middle-class businesses in the inner cities, all of which hurt working-class and poor Blacks the most.[60] By favoring top-down politics and economics of redistribution (the war from the top) and condoning and encouraging riots and crime (the war from below), the modern Democratic Party and its twin insurgencies are the modern equivalent of the southern oligarchy, keeping the poor in bondage. I believe if any narrative needs to be shattered it is the narrative of progressive welfarism, shared by elites in both parties.[61]

In making this point, I am linking the progressive Left (order left 2), which Sandel and McWhorter have criticized, with the oligarchy of the ruling class, which Lind, Kotkin, and Codevilla described in the introduction. In fact, along with Kotkin's article, "What Do the Oligarchs Have in Mind for Us?" (where he describes the ruling class as a marriage of big tech, big government, and the clerisy class), we could easily ask what the modern Democratic Party has in mind for us? And Kotkin's conclusion is telling: "Their social vision amounts to what could be called oligarchical socialism," a system based on the "hegemony of a left-wing identity-centered individualism," reducing everyone to "a scientific caste system" and "neo-feudal reality."[62] For Kotkin, a lifelong Democrat turned independent, this narrative is harrowing. But he says it is already here, and we are living it—a two-tier caste system in which the rich and the progressive Left have all the power and everyone else is a feudal serf, a slave. The poor of all races and ethnicities are addicted to government handouts. The rich elite live behind their secure gates. It's bread and circuses, cell phones and video games. And now we could add looted designer bags and Target merchandise.

While Kotkin is mortified by this reality, filmmaker Astra Taylor, writing in the progressive *New Republic,* is excited about this future. After describing what this new socialist system will look like, a system that will eliminate much of what we experience in free-market democratic institutions and individual rights and liberties, she can hardly contain her giddiness for this socialist moment. But, lest her readers think she has tumbled into sentimentality, she adds that she is embarrassed that "it all sounds terribly utopian."[63] Of course, she is right. It does, and it is utopian. And I wouldn't use the word *giddy*—it's more like *frightening*. Yet, sadly, too many progressive evangelicals are endorsing this radical narrative, this utopian vision, some not even aware of its larger long-term radical agenda. It's to that story, the true end game of the radical, polarized Left, that we now turn.

6

ORDER LEFT 3

THE REIFIED POSTMODERNISM OF ANTIRACISM

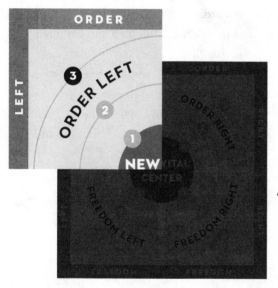

AFTER THE JANUARY 6, 2021, Capitol riots in Washington, DC, reporters Rebecca Sagar and Brie Loskota are convinced the greatest threat to democracy is the "mix of white, right-wing identity politics and nationalist Christianity" which have "been stirring for many years."[1] Turn on MSNBC or CNN and it is wall-to-wall coverage about White supremacy, militia groups, QAnon conspiracies, and security threats to the Capitol, all reasons that the military lockdown in Washington, DC, should continue. Director of the FBI, Christopher Wray, testified to Congress about the rise of domestic extremism on the right.[2] Four months into his presidency, Joe Biden, building on Wray's claims, contended that "according to the intelligence community, terrorism from white supremacy is the most lethal threat to the homeland today. Not ISIS, not al Qaeda—white supremacists." And since it is the number one threat to our democracy, his administration "will soon lay out our broader strategy to counter domestic terrorism."[3]

And so with White Christian nationalism on the rise in the Republican Party—an existential threat to American democracy—the time for polite discussion is over, contend many on the left. For those who care about "our democracy," the moment to choose is here; it is no longer acceptable to be nonracist, one must be *anti*racist, one must actively oppose White nationalism. White supremacy must be contained, and it must be done now, according to those in order left 3.

Governmental agencies in the Seattle area have heard this call to action. According to whistleblower documents, government officials in King County brought in a private consulting group called Racial Equity Consultants to hold "'listening sessions' to root out 'institutional privileges and systemic inequalities,'" apparently widespread in one of the most liberal sections of the country.[4] After people were sorted into segregated groups and discussion took place, "the senior staff have recently required employees to sign an 'equity and social justice' pledge and assigned 'continued training for white employees,' who must 'do the work' to 'learn the true history of racism in our country.'"[5] But that raises the question: What if they reject the view that they are racist or that Seattle is suffering under a regime of White supremacy? What if they refuse to sign the pledge?

One employee who attended the Whites-only workshop felt like he was sitting through a "firing squad" and that any resistance might lead to further retaliation. Others reported that the segregated training sessions "have created suspicion and distrust among employees." People undoubtedly were worried, scared of the taint of the racist label. Yet one gets the impression that for the senior administrators in King County, if things are going to finally change, they must oppose all policies and systems that promote racism or further unequal racial treatment, and they must work for policies that promote equity. Only when they do this will they be antiracist. Seen in this newfound activism, those in order left 3 have entered a new phase.

POSTMODERNISM'S THIRD PHASE

In chapter four, I mentioned James Lindsay's three phases of postmodernism. After looking at the first, the *high deconstructive phase*, and the second, the *applied postmodern phase*, we have now come to his third phase, what he calls the "reified" phase, where "abstract concepts are treated at though they are real."[6] Around 2010, in this third phase, under the banner of *social justice scholarship*, activists and scholars, in Lindsay's words "have come to take for granted a reification of the once abstract and self-doubtful postmodern knowledge principle and postmodern political principle." In other words, while postmodernism started out deconstructing all truth and metaphysical narratives, contending that objective knowledge was impossible and that "society is made up of systems of power and privilege," in this third phase the doubt and skepticism are gone, replaced with a new confidence in its grasp of truth, its guiding narrative, and its political ends. Its "principles are treated as fundamental truths," says Lindsay, becoming "*known-knowns*— ideas taken for granted as true statements about the world that people 'just know' are true."[7] What used to be a theory, a tool used to deconstruct all metanarratives, has now become a "belief" and an "objectively true statement about the organizing principle of society."[8]

Does this sound like a metanarrative? Does it sound like they are absolutely convinced their "once upon a time story" is correct and they grasp objective reality with certainty? That's because it *has* become an objective narrative. According to Lindsay, "social justice scholarship and its educators and activists see these principles and conclusions as *The Truth*" and are thrilled that "they have discovered the analogue of the germ theory of disease, but for bigotry and oppression."[9] They have discovered the key to understanding society, how all society is socially constructed around systems of power and privilege, and that in America this means systems of White supremacy, patriarchy, and heteronormativity, which are "literally structuring society and infecting everything," "present always and everywhere," often hidden below the surface.[10]

Now that they have made this startling breakthrough (a new "germ theory"), the key to overcoming systemic racism and bigoted policies is for those to be "constantly identified, condemned, and dismantled so that things might be rectified." This is the gospel of social justice,

> that express[es], with *absolute certainty*, that all white people are racist, all men are sexist, racism and sexism are systems that can exist and oppress absent even a single person with racist or sexist intentions or beliefs (in the usual sense of the terms). . . . That is the reification of the postmodern political principle.[11]

This means that the Left has gone from saying there is no objective morality (freedom left 3) and that all metanarratives are oppressive and must be deconstructed, to adopting their own *metanarrative*, one held in utmost confidence that must be adopted and actively applied by individuals and the state (order left 3).

Clearly, Lindsay's third phase is upon us. As he says, this "social justice scholarship has become a kind of Theory of Everything, a set of unquestionable Truths with a capital T," which becomes their new epistemology, their new theory of knowing and grounding reality, and becomes the basis for their new activism.[12] They think they have discovered the secret to exactly how the world works, a new knowledge which comes mainly from oppressed groups and their lived experience. And on this new epistemology of grievance, the pedagogy of the oppressed, they are able to condemn the past, to deconstruct the present, and to reconstruct the future. And since White, heterosexual men and women have none of the special knowledge of oppression that unlocks the key to reality, they are thus on the wrong side of the oppressed-oppressive divide and, in fact, are complicit in the systemic injustice of society, infected with a false consciousness, and therefore must be condemned.

While this third phase shares much of the once-upon-a-time narrative of the first two phases, what makes it so different is that any self-doubt or skepticism about objective reality has disappeared and has now *reified* into a definitive belief, a new metanarrative, and this now has been combined with the postmodern political principle, providing an evangelist's fervor in antiracism activism, one that no longer stresses freedom as much as order. And this *reified postmodernism* best describes the order left 3 position on our quadrant.

THE ANTIRACISM OF IBRAM X. KENDI

One of the best examples of this profound confidence in diagnosis and prescription is Ibram X. Kendi's bestselling book *How to Be an Antiracist*.[13] Along with Ta-Nehisi Coates and Robin DiAngelo, Kendi has shot to fame as one of the main evangelists for the antiracism theory of everything. Through dozens of compelling personal stories and anecdotes detailing America's racist past and present, Kendi takes for granted this third phase of postmodernism, known under the critical race theory banner.[14] With an evangelist's fervor, he passionately shares the breakthrough insight that racism, both individual and systemic, is objectively true and that nothing else could explain the continued racial disparities in America. For Kendi, to be racist means supporting racist policies built on capitalism and economic freedom, policies that engender economic disparities, and to be antiracist means actively opposing these very same policies and calling for antiracist policies that further equity.[15]

Yet, at much as Kendi pushes for new antiracism policy, he isn't under any illusion that changing some policies will end racism because, ultimately, if the racist system remains intact, it will continue to inculcate racist people. So, if we are going to get rid of racism altogether, the racist system will have to be replaced with a new one that assures diversity, equity, and inclusion of all racial groups. Until then, we must remain active to use the levers of political power to oppose racist policies. As Kendi says, "The only remedy to racist discrimination is antiracist discrimination; the only remedy to past discrimination is present discrimination; the only remedy to present discrimination is future discrimination."[16]

The bottom line for Kendi is that this new antiracism narrative is gospel truth, taken for granted, obvious to anyone who has the eyes to see. He believes that freedom from "false consciousness" begins with knowing the correct definitions of our nation's history, the true reality of racism in our country and its philosophical foundation.[17] Kendi, like the *New York Times* 1619 Project, believes that racism defines America; it was present at birth, it shaped our Constitution, and it grounds our systems today, having never been dismantled.

As we saw with Lindsay, this reality is the "germ theory" of racism and bigotry; it is the key to breaking through to a new dawn. According to order left 3, everything relies on this new definition, this new diagnosis. America's racist past, one that defines the nation *in toto*, must be rejected, but so must its present, as the racist system of the past has never gone away and continues to be propped up by a certain segment of the population: White men. So, to be antiracist means not only to reject America but the racists themselves, mainly White men, who want it to continue. And this means calling out them, their policies and systems, and actively condemning racism wherever and whenever it appears.

SARAH JEONG'S HATRED OF WHITE PEOPLE

Tech journalist Sarah Jeong heard this call to activism and was rewarded for it. In early 2018 the *New York Times* hired Jeong to be on their editorial board, hoping it would boost circulation. But then her tweets from the previous few years began to resurface.[18]

- "It's kind of sick how much joy I get out of being cruel to old white men."

- "Are white people genetically predisposed to burn faster in the sun, thus logically only being fit to live underground like groveling bilious goblins."

- "The world would get by just fine with zero white people."

- "Have you ever tried to figure out all the things that white people are allowed to do that aren't cultural appropriation, there's literally nothing . . ."

Many on the right accused her of racism against White people. Yet many on the left jumped to her defense, claiming that as a woman and a racial minority she can't be racist. Racism is "not a thing" for people like Jeong. Libby Watson wrote on the website *Splinter* that Jeong's tweets "were not racist" but merely "jokes about white people."[19] She went on to say that only those groups who have systematically oppressed people can be racist. Thus people of color and beleaguered minorities are not capable of being racist, only Whites are.[20]

Zach Beauchamp was Jeong's strongest defender. He claimed that what her critics don't understand is that the term *White people* does not mean a particular group per se but is code for the structure of society that White people control. "To anyone who's even passingly familiar with the way the social justice left trolls, this is clearly untrue," Beauchamp argues.[21] Because White people are complicit in a violent system of abuse, control, and oppression, it is okay to attack them, regardless of their guilt or innocence, and to do so is not racist. Since Sarah Jeong, an Asian woman and part of the resistance, is attacking the structure, she cannot be racist, no matter how many cruel things she says about Whites. This is a similar argument to justify violence against Whites in the riots.

And this is happening throughout society. Almost weekly there are new examples of this antiracism activism in action, destroying people's lives and careers, even those who are progressives.[22] For a certain group of Americans, including many on the left, we are witnessing in this new definition of racism the end of tolerance and free speech. Upon us now are the days of Orwell's *1984* "Two Minutes Hate," justified in the name of tolerance and antiracism.[23]

EVANGELICALS ON THE LEFT JOIN THE FIGHT

Early on, when this third phase was gaining steam in our universities and entering the culture through antiracism evangelists like Kendi, Coates, and DiAngelo, some evangelicals, many recent graduates from programs influenced by critical race theory, began utilizing critical race theory methods in their writings and books. When they were criticized for adopting "cultural Marxism," many of them vehemently denied it or said they were just "eating the meat and spitting out the bones."[24] But over the past few years, especially after the George Floyd protests and riots and the rise of Black Lives Matter as a major force in our society, a number of more progressive evangelicals seem to have gone from tentative embrace to strong adherence of critical race theory. In fact, one conservative critic of critical race theory, Neil Shenvi, recently tweeted: "I'm actually glad that many evangelicals are explicitly defending #CriticalRaceTheory. Just a few years ago, people were denying that these ideas had any influence among evangelicals. Almost no one is saying that today."[25]

Three months after the protests and riots began, the *New Yorker* magazine published the article "How Black Lives Matter Is Changing the Church," reporting that "a growing number of leaders in both evangelical and mainstream churches for whom Black Lives Matter has prompted a crisis in moral conscience."[26] Jemar Tisby is quoted in the article as saying, ""What Black Lives Matter did was highlight the racism and white supremacy that still has a stranglehold on much of white Christianity," and now "you have this phrase and this movement that is forcing people essentially to take sides."[27] When I read some of the books coming out by evangelicals on the left, I see little daylight between their views and those of writers like Kendi, Coates, and DiAngelo.[28]

A good example is Daniel Hill's *White Lies*.[29] Hill is a successful church planter in downtown Chicago and a gifted storyteller. Hill's goal is to explain the nine lies of racism and how, through nine spiritual practices, White Christians can acknowledge their racism, discover ways to repent of it, and in the process have sight restored, seeing clearly for the first time the kingdom of God. A reader familiar with DiAngelo's *White Fragility* and Hill's *White Lies* will recognize a lot of similarities. Both cover similar themes, yet with different audiences in mind. While Hill is attempting to introduce the antiracism to his own evangelical tribe, he is providing a biblical grounding for it, one rooted in the Scriptures and the kingdom of God.

To make his case to his evangelical readers, he spends time in each chapter laying out biblical texts that he believes line up with the critical-race-theory view of reality. While he is careful on a number of occasions to say that there is nothing in the Bible that talks about White supremacy, he nonetheless goes on to show how well these texts sync with antiracism and provide the means for people to wake up from their racism, which is proven by anti-racism thought.[30] I conclude that he is trying to provide critical race theory with a biblical justification, in spite of the fact that it is wedded to meta-physical skepticism or that the Bible says nothing about it. I find this prob-lematic. Why is this?

INFLATION AND ACCOMMODATION

You may recall in chapter one J. Budziszewski argued that evangelicals, devoid of a public philosophy, often jump from the Scriptures to a political platform, inflating the Scripture to accommodate their political platform. Evangelicals on the left *and* right do this. Furthermore, you may recall that the only way to avoid these twin errors, inflation and accommodation, whether committed to the left or the right, is to have a well-thought-out doctrine of general revelation that contributes to a full-orbed political phi-losophy that equips one to analyze the current political reality. Yet this is what evangelicals often lack.

And here is the problem. What if the reified postmodernism of antiracism is wrong and we merge it with the Bible? What happens when we don't have a public philosophy built on general revelation and natural law—God's purpose and order implanted in his created world—to point this out? If the order left 3 position is wrong, we risk baptizing an erroneous view of reality and politics. What if this has happened with evangelicals like Hill? By taking for granted the antiracist view of reality, their reified postmodernism, he may have baptized a faulty view of America. And if he has, won't this lead the church and our nation in the wrong direction? Doesn't our first step, then, have to be this: to interrogate the narrative of antiracism and critical race theory (i.e., its once-upon-a-time story, its "germ theory") to make sure it stands up to history, reason, and general revelation? Would testing its narrative help us avoid the twin errors of inflation and accommodation, and help the church avoid going down the wrong road?

Here is where the rubber meets the road. On a number of occasions, Hill quotes Bryan Stevenson, the author of the bestselling book *Just Mercy*, as saying that the North won the Civil War but the South won the narrative war.[31] By this he means that while the Union Army may have won the war, the South, whose narrative goes back to the very founding documents of our country, actually won the only war that counts, the narrative war.[32] And this Southern narrative still empowers our system today. Hill accepts this contention.[33] Hill follows Stevenson's view, almost by extension, that while they had good intentions, the Civil War and the civil rights movement only attacked the symptoms of racism, leaving the cancer of racism in place, which is why we are just as racist and oppressive today as during the eras of slavery and Jim Crow.

But the Confederate view of America was counterfeit and the Civil War was fought to prove it, to ensure a different view of America, one which was in place from the very start of our nation, and the war was fought for a new birth of freedom, as Lincoln said. If this is true, which I contend, then what antiracism proponents have discovered (their new "germ theory") is in fact a counterfeit theory of America propagated by the South to defend slavery and the oligarchy of the slaveholders and which was roundly rejected by the North and the vast majority of American historians, including many on the left.[34] The Confederate narrative wasn't the true definition of the founding, as much as the South wanted people to believe it. It was fake. Pure revisionism. Yet, ironically, now the antiracism thinkers themselves *have* been persuaded by the false narrative and have bought the lie about America. Now, thinking they are opposing it, they have embraced it. At the same time, they have adopted a similar grounding as the racist South, that is, that all politics are about power, the struggle to get it and keep it.

Thus this false view not only perpetuates the wrong definition of America, taking us down the wrong road, but by baptizing reified postmodernism it has also cut it off from the very natural-law grounding of our founding documents that Abraham Lincoln, Frederick Douglass, and Martin Luther King Jr. appealed to in order to transform our society.[35] Thus, in the end, by rejecting the Union narrative of the founders and Abraham Lincoln, a narrative based on natural right, and instead adopting the Lost Cause narrative of the Confederacy as their view of America's founding, many antiracism thinkers (inside the church and out) have fundamentally misinterpreted our founding and our system, leading them to a faulty diagnosis and an erroneous prescription. And since this narrative of the Lost Cause is at the heart of the antiracist position of Kendi, Coates, DiAngelo, and the 1619 Project, they are all taking us down the wrong road, increasing racial division, and impeding improvement for our country, especially lower income minorities.[36]

OLD VITAL CENTER LIBERALS ISSUED WARNINGS

For over three decades a few vital-center liberals, who have risked being called racist or Uncle Toms by the establishment Left, have tried to sound the alarm. In the 1990s, as a member of the New York Commission on Education, Arthur Schlesinger saw the antiracism narrative taking shape in the battle over curriculum in New York City and vehemently objected, eventually venting his frustrations in his book *The Disuniting of America*.[37] Schlesinger saw that the version of the American past taught to late-twentieth-century schoolchildren was completely different from that taught to previous generations.[38]

Then, just after the 2016 presidential election, liberal professor Mark Lilla, author of *The Once and Future Liberal*, also tried to warn Democrats. Lilla lamented that his once great party had now become the party of identity politics, setting one group against another, fighting for recognition from the state and society, demanding rights, both economic and political, and not caring about the larger nation and the good for everyone.

And now, John McWhorter, who we looked at in the last chapter, a man who cares deeply about the Black community, especially the Black underclass trapped in our urban cores, and who knows that he opens himself up to the criticism of "self-hatred of being Black," nevertheless continues to sound the alarm through his writing and weekly podcasts. According to McWhorter, the self-image of Black America, built on victimology, segregation, and anti-intellectualism, leading to bad policies like affirmative action, have crippled black America.[39] And, according to McWhorter, White progressives who help push this victimology view on Blacks are complicit.

Why do White progressive liberals (order left 3) keep telling Blacks they are perpetual victims and that they need the help of welfare, doled out by the liberals, even though it makes things worse? It's simple, says McWhorter. It's a form of "atonement activism," one that makes White woke progressives feel superior and assuages their guilt at the same time.[40] When Blacks are kept in a state of victimhood, continually reminded about it and told that they can't get ahead because of it, it redeems White elites. This narrative, a system perfectly designed to keep Blacks down, is perfectly suited for the order left 3 to feel good about itself and at the same time stay in power.

WARNINGS GO UNHEEDED

But these warnings have gone unheeded. In fact, the order left 3 progressives have doubled down on their radical views. And this includes evangelicals who have baptized reified postmodernism and its critical-race-theory view of reality, including systemic racism and White Christian nationalism. In 2020 numerous books appeared with these same themes: Robert P. Jones, *White Too Long: The Legacy of White Supremacy in American Christianity*; Andrew Whitehead, *Taking America Back for God: Christian Nationalism in the United State*; and Kristin Kobes Du Mez, *Jesus and John Wayne: How White Evangelicals Corrupted a Faith and Fractured a Nation.*[41] As Robert P. Jones says, "the legacy of this unholy union still lives in the DNA of white Christianity today."[42] Jemar Tisby, writing in his review of *White Too Long*, argues that we are presented with a "stark choice," either "Hold onto white Christianity or hold onto Jesus. It cannot be both."[43] So we must acknowledge our complicity in systemic oppression, repent and work toward a new system, one of diversity, equity, and inclusion. But to get here, some may say we also need a new gospel, a new church, and ultimately a new nation.

But again we ask, what if this doubling down, this linking the cart of antiracism with the horse of the Bible, is taking us down the wrong road? What if order left 3 hasn't found the key that unlocks racism and White supremacy but in fact, by adopting the wrong narrative themselves, has actually been perpetuating racism and been complicit in the reified postmodern takeover of the nation? What if they are taking America down a road it may never get off, one that will mean the end of democracy, free speech, and tolerance, for centuries the hallmarks of classical liberalism? John McWhorter, once optimistic, is no longer so sanguine.

ANTIRACISM AS A NEW RELIGION

McWhorter is no longer so sanguine because the Far Left (order left 3) has been in the grip of a hysteria that he calls a new religion. It is not *like* a new religion but *is* a new religion, he contends. In his 2016 article "Antiracism, Our Flawed New Religion," McWhorter makes the case that antiracism "has a clergy, creed, and also even a conception of original sin."[44] In early 2021 he expands on this thesis in his *The Elect: The Threat to Progressive America from Anti-Black Antiracists*, where he makes many of the same points, while adding some new ones—that this new religion suspends "disbelief," especially when the facts of reality contradict it; that it is highly evangelistic, trying to convince and convert as many as they can; and that it is increasingly apocalyptic, preaching a Judgment Day, that Great Day when America finally owns up to its racism and fixes it, most likely through years of "psychological self-mortification combined with the political activism" of antiracist policies.[45]

And finally, says McWhorter, the progressive antiracists have a natural enemy, anyone who disagrees with their narrative. This new antiracism religion, placed beyond challenge or dissent, scares McWhorter, and he is frustrated it has taken over the Left, setting back race relations by decades. But now that it is upon us, now that the hysteria is reaching Salem witch trial –levels, he wonders if there is any turning back.[46] Will we step back from this abyss? It doesn't look like it. There is just too much at stake.

WHO BENEFITS?

The goal of this new religion isn't really antiracism, as hard as it is to believe. It's actually something much greater—the quest for power, influence, and control, the same thing that motivated the Confederate South, ironically. And while Blacks (and other minorities on the left) think they have the most power to gain by taking down White Christian men a notch, in the end, it is not Blacks or minorities who will primarily benefit. The real winner in all this racial division is the bipartisan ruling class, who are using antiracism to attack groups in society who oppose their oligarchic rule, many who are in the lower and middle classes (including many Hispanics, Asians, and Blacks) who still believe strongly in constitutional republicanism, and believe the words of the constitution that "all men are created equal." This is both a class war—the ruling elite against the middle and working classes—and a war of first principles: ruling class oligarchy versus constitutional republicanism.[47] The present bipartisan ruling class have made it clear what side they are on, and why they want to assure that oligarchy wins.

As reified postmodernism wipes away (under the guise of antiracism and antibigotry) natural-law and natural-right grounding and its concomitant view of human nature, biological sex and gender roles, and the original view of America, the ruling class and their antiracism clerisy (which includes some evangelicals) have adopted a new objective faith that is entirely more sinister. And as we will see in chapter ten, this new reality includes, shockingly, a new transhumanism, which is the prelude to a brave new world and eventually life everlasting. They want a golden age beyond race that will eventually not only deny all races but also biological sex and gender as well as all distinctions among sovereign nations.[48] But for now, until the time is right and science has delivered the requisite breakthroughs, they are using race as a ruse, as a Trojan horse, a wedge to divide. And our ruling class oligarchs could not care less what color a "human" robot is going to be or what "race" our consciousness will take once it is uploaded into the cloud. By then we will be in this brave new world and we won't care. But by then it will be too late to wake up.

IN SUM

- We see that for the radical Left the greatest threat to our democracy comes from White Christian nationalism and its merger with violent militia groups.

- Order left 3 represents the third phase of postmodernism, where the radical Left has reified their once skeptical views on objective truth, now accepting critical race theory as objectively true and the theory of everything that provides the diagnosis of what ails America and the prescription for what could transform the nation.

- Antiracism is now a faith, accepted with the certitude of dogmatic religion.

- Many evangelicals have accepted parts of this new faith of critical race theory and have attempted to justify it with a biblical grounding.

- But since the critical race theory and its adherents have adopted a faulty view of America, one built on a shaky grounding, they are leading the nation into racial division, hurting minorities, and opening the door for the ruling oligarchic elites to solidify their hold on power.

7

FREEDOM RIGHT 2

LIBERTARIANS AND THE QUEST FOR OPEN BORDERS

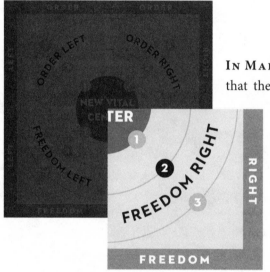

IN MARCH 2021, Axios announced that the Biden administration "confronts [a] mounting humanitarian crisis at the border," as "shelters are overflowing. Border crossings are rising. Border patrol facilities are overwhelmed . . . and the number of migrant children crossing the US border without their parents this year is likely to far exceed the previous record."[1] CCN's Paul Reyes reported "the news from the southern border is alarming,"[2] adding "the number of migrant children detained at the border has tripled in the last two weeks," forcing the Biden administration to rely "on existing models for holding—or, as some advocates would say, imprisoning—children."[3] Yet, in the midst of the growing flood of people crossing the border, a problem even media outlets like Axios and CCN are beginning to admit is out of control, the Biden administration refused to use the word *crisis*, instead claiming they were managing a "challenge."[4] Why were they so adamant to avoid using the word *crisis*? Well, on the one hand their reluctance is because they want to avoid the charge of hypocrisy, that is, having to admit that they are detaining migrant children at the same facility for which the Trump administration was excoriated.[5] "This is not kids being kept in cages," insisted White House

Press Secretary Jen Psaki, in spite of the fact that there was no tangible difference.[6] Yet, on the other hand, the Biden administration's reluctance to use the word *crisis* makes perfect policy sense. After all, throughout the presidential campaign Biden promised he would reverse most of Trump's immigration and border policies, which had slowed illegal immigration to historic lows.

Once in office, Biden signed six executive orders reversing Trump's policies and began changing hundreds of other rules and regulations. Realizing the situation was more favorable, migrants began crashing the border, almost 180,000 arriving in the first two months of 2021, more than double those arriving in the first two months in 2020. Once the warm spring months arrive, some predicted the numbers would double, with an estimated two and half million people crossing the border this year alone, pouring into our cities, increasing homelessness and unemployment, and overwhelming our health care systems.[7]

But this "destabilizing migration" is not a crisis for the Biden administration. They have welcomed it; they have invited the migrants. In fact, it is part of the plan; they want them to keep coming, effectively opening the borders, and in the process fundamentally transforming our nation into something entirely different.[8]

While one would expect the Democrats to rejoice over what's happening at the border, framing it as a struggle between compassionate Democrats and immoral Republicans, what is not so well known is that former President Trump's views on immigration have not represented those of the mainstream Republican Party, which for decades has been the pro-immigration party, taking its cues from its free-trade libertarian wing that believes immigration and the free markets go hand in hand and that a steady supply of cheap labor is good for everyone. Just how much Trump challenged the Republican establishment was seen when, in his first year, he tried to codify into law his views on immigration and the border, and the Republican establishment led by Republican Speaker Paul Ryan blocked his efforts. To understand just how far Trump stood outside of the mainstream *uniparty* in Washington, DC, on immigration policies, we need to understand that the Republican Party has become a house divided. Prior to Trump, it was libertarians that shaped the Republican party's views on immigration and open borders. For decades, it has been libertarians who have had an oversized impact on the thinking of Wall Street, the mainstream Republican establishment, and even the Democratic party.

As evidence of the oversized impact of libertarianism, Fox's Tucker Carlson, in his book *Ship of Fools: How A Selfish Ruling Class Is Bringing America to the Brink of Revolution*, points out that until Obama, the Democrats were the pro-working class and anti-open borders party.[9]

In fact, Carlson quotes President Clinton's 1995 State of the Union address, which sounds more like former president Trump than the current position of the Democratic Party:

> All Americans, not only in the states most heavily affected, but in every place
> in this country, are rightly disturbed by the large numbers of illegal aliens
> entering our country. . . . That's why our administration has moved aggres-
> sively to secure our borders. . . . It is wrong and ultimately self-defeating for
> a nation of immigrants to permit the kind of abuse of our immigration laws
> we have seen in recent years, and we must do more to stop it.[10]

As late as 2006, the *New York Times* said there were downsides to immigration. That same year Senators Hillary Clinton and Barack Obama voted for the border fence. "That was last gasp of a dying consensus," writes Carlson.[11] By 2008 the Democratic Party had abandoned any concerns about immigration and adopted the full libertarian view. "The Democratic Party now endorsed unrestrained mass immigration."[12]

The change of position on the Democratic side was so swift that Bernie Sanders struggled to keep up. In 2016 Sanders said to Vox's Ezra Klein that open borders were a "Koch brothers proposal," "a right-wing proposal," "that says essentially that there is no United States. . . . If you believe in a nation-state, in a country called the United States . . . you have an obligation, in my view, to do everything we can to help poor people. And open borders would make everyone poorer."[13] For this heresy Sanders was quickly castigated, called a bigot and racist. He quickly changed his mind and adopted the open borders view, now the de facto view of Democrats.

Carlson is right. For decades it was free-market libertarians on Wall Street and the Republican Congress who championed mass immigration and open borders, and only lately were they joined by Democrats. So, by

2016 when Trump took office, he challenged *both* parties, who by then were equally committed to open borders.

REPUBLICANS ARE A HOUSE DIVIDED

If Bernie Sanders was slow in realizing what had happened in his own party, one can forgive Republican voters for not catching on to what Trump was doing in the Republican Party. By early 2020, Tucker Carlson thought it was time to spell it out. In a rather shocking monologue, he drew a line in the sand, going after pro-immigration libertarians in the Republican Party. After defending the Koch brothers against left-wing attacks for years, Carlson turned on them, accusing them of working with Democrat megadonor George Soros and being "libertarian ideologues."[14] In a 2012 *Forbes* article, Laurie Bennet wrote, "The Kochs Aren't the Only Funders of Cato," claiming that Soros gives money to Cato.[15] Knowing this connection, Carlson went after the Koch brothers. Undoubtedly, for many viewers of *Fox News*, this was the first time they heard about libertarians and their pro-Democrat positions on immigration. It must have come as some shock.

But it should not have. After all, it has been libertarians and some free-market conservatives who for years have connected the growth of the market with increased immigration, and for some that means totally open borders. The libertarians' views on immigration now reign in DC's uniparty, even though they are an extremely small faction in the Republican Party. They are responsible for making immigration not only a major litmus test on economics and politics but in the culture war as well. Who are these libertarians, what do they believe, and why have I placed them in freedom right 2 quadrant? Let's consider their views.

BLEEDING-HEART LIBERTARIANS

One of the more helpful introductions to the basics of libertarianism is Professor Jason Brennan's *Libertarianism: What Everyone Needs to Know*.[16] According to Brennan, most people don't really understand libertarianism. Typically, what people have in mind are the "hard libertarians," most characterized by thinkers like Ayn Rand and Murray Rothbard, whose views we will examine in freedom right 3, chapter eight.[17] For Brennan, hard libertarians often go by the names *minarchists* and *anarchists*, thinkers who hold either to the barest conception of the *minimal government* paid by taxes—police, military, courts—or *no government*. Hard libertarians only care about property rights, not the poor.

For Brennan, "bleeding-heart libertarianism" is the correct term. Unlike hard libertarians, Brennan says bleeding-heart libertarians are all-in when it comes to caring about social justice. He may be against a huge welfare state, but he is for "welfarism."[18] Yet his criticism of egalitarian public policy aside, Brennan does *not* call himself a conservative. He stresses that "conservatives and libertarians are ideological foes."[19] For Brennan, conservatives (see chapters nine and ten) and libertarians are ideological foes because conservatives trample on civil liberties, calling for government involvement in education, creation of civic virtue, and promotion of Christianity. Libertarians, especially bleeding-heart libertarians, have an expansive view of civil liberties; they want the government to stay out of the virtue business. They want radical tolerance of all lifestyles, radical voluntarism, and radical freedom. Practically speaking, they adopt many of the liberal social policies of the Far Left—gay marriage, abortion on demand, full rights for LGBTQ community, and the legalization of drugs and prostitution.[20]

Brennan acknowledges that "conservative critics believe libertarianism would break down the social fabric. They think libertarianism would lead to widespread sexual promiscuity, sexual perversion, licentiousness, sacrilege, and drug use. They believe a libertarian culture would destroy traditional values."[21] While Brennan disagrees, he doesn't seem to care if traditional culture is eroded; he is no friend of Christianity or traditional religion. He and other "Beltway Libertarians" are mostly secular, with a high percentage of atheists and socially liberal members in their ranks, meaning they have more in common with the progressive Left than they do with social conservatives or Trump nationalists.

We are on familiar ground here; we've seen much of this narrative before. Brennan's bleeding-heart libertarianism sounds an awful lot like freedom left 2—that is, the voluntaristic self that must be left alone to choose the procedural republic that refuses to define the "good," one that brackets out religion, rejecting the natural law found in the Declaration of Independence, instead relying on secular pragmatism. Like freedom left 2, Brennan's narrative wants "radical tolerance" and "radical freedom" and "radical civil liberties,"

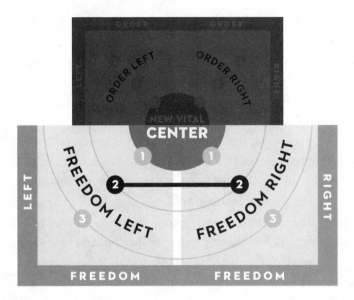

believing that these commitments will not lead to a culture war but to "radical peace."[22] In this sense, freedom left 2 and freedom right 2 merge.

Bleeding Heart Libertarians and Open Immigration

Brennan and other freedom right 2 libertarians build their commitment to open immigration on this grounding of radical choice.[23] For bleeding-heart libertarians, open immigration is based on their view of human autonomy and what Brennan calls the "live and let live" philosophy of libertarianism. Brennan summarizes this commitment well:

> Libertarians also support free immigration. They believe people have a right to cross borders as they see fit. They hold a Mexican has the same right to live in the United States as a native-born American . . . they hold that . . . governments may not forbid citizens from leaving a country, nor may governments forbid citizens from entering.[24]

In practice this means that immigration should be unlimited, the flow only controlled by the immigrants themselves or by those who want to hire them or rent property to them, both sides making rational economic decisions. Unlimited immigration would be best for everyone, increasing the economic pie and making the world freer.[25]

THE LIBERTARIAN BREAKAWAY

Trump pushed back on these mass-immigration and open-border views, contending they would bring crime, drugs, and unwanted people into the country and erode our working class. In the end this would destroy our nation's unique culture. The uniparty in DC and the libertarians on Wall Street reacted strongly, opposing him at every turn.

While it appears that the Trump presidency engendered this conflict, a major shift in both parties had been taking place for over a decade. Around 2010 a number of Republicans began railing against the downsides of globalization and mass immigration, trying to show the world that these policies have robbed jobs from our working class and hollowed out so many Midwest towns, in effect putting corporate shareholder profit ahead of real people. As this clarion call picked up speed, Wall Street libertarians got irritated and began to wonder if they were in the wrong party. Ten years ago, *New York Times* columnist Thomas Friedman picked up on this shift, claiming he knew the exact moment during the Obama presidency when Wall Street Republicans decided their party was no longer on their side and was preventing them from getting rich, putting all kinds of barriers in their way. "In principle," he wrote in the *New York Times*, "they have left the party, leaving behind not a pragmatic coalition but a group of ideological naysayers."[26] And as Lee Smith adds, "In the more than ten years since Friedman's column was published, the disenchanted elite . . . has further impoverished American workers while enriching themselves."[27]

This complete shift of loyalty was made clear in the 2020 election, as once solidly Republican Wall Street backed Biden and his commitment to mass immigration and cheap labor.[28] It has become even clearer as big business has fully supported woke capitalism and the Davos plan for globalization (see chapter eight), demonstrating how these Wall Street libertarians have much in common with the order left quadrant.[29]

Around the same time that Friedman noticed the shift taking place, Cato's Brink Lindsey was feeling the same tension and attempted to build bridges with the Left, calling his new fusionism *liberaltarian*.[30] For Lindsey, if the Republican Party was moving to an anti-mass-immigration policy, then maybe libertarians needed a new party or at least new allies. So, many of them, now going under the never-Trump banner, felt they had no choice but to abandon the Republican Party and to vote in 2020 for Biden, a candidate who, *despite his rhetoric* to the contrary, is *effectively* pro-open borders and mass immigration.[31]

Today, some of these libertarians like Lindsay have left the Cato Institute and have found a congenial home in the left-of-center Niskanen Center. The natural allies of these never-Trump libertarians are *no longer* social conservatives or Trump economic nationalists, who they contend have been captured by selfish nationalism, unhinged populism, and racial bigotry. "The right today," argues Lindsey, "is a fundamentally illiberal and authoritarian movement," and for this reason all libertarians should "break ranks and stand on our own." For Lindsey, libertarians should no longer frame their arguments in conservative terms but should seek areas of commonality with the progressive Left "on personal freedom, civil liberties, and foreign policy issues."[32]

Once upon a Time

In demonstrating the natural fusion between libertarians and the progressive Left, we are now ready to see clearly the bleeding-heart libertarians' "once upon a time" story. As we see in the figure earlier in this chapter, many of these bleeding-heart libertarians are philosophically linked to freedom left 2, with its secular pragmatism and view of personal freedom. Moreover, they also share natural affinities with order left 2, that is, a common commitment to social justice and what Brennan calls "welfarism." And with their commitment to left libertarian social and moral issues, what Ross Douthat calls "woke capitalism," they also have much in common with the goals of critical race theory in order left 3, which is why they are so comfortable with many in the Democratic Party, regardless of whether they have switched their party affiliation.

Going deeper, like progressives on the left, freedom right 2 libertarians have no desire to return to a mythic golden era grounded on our founding documents, natural law, and divine law but would welcome starting over instead, building only on economic and personal freedom and a minimal view of the state.

When we look at these libertarians, we see that they are at best ambivalent about the founding documents and at worst hostile to them. For Brennan, "the US Constitution is just paper . . . there is nothing magic about the US Constitution."[33] To the extent it limits government and protects individual freedom, he supports it. He can take it or leave it; it all depends. The guiding norm is not the Constitution, but philosophical freedom and liberty.

Other libertarians have taken the argument even further. In his essay "Did the Constitution Betray the Revolution?" Jeffrey Rogers Hummel and William Marina answer yes![34] Another libertarian, Nikolai Wenzel, agrees with Hummel and Marina, contending that "In many ways, the Constitution was a 'repudiation of 1776' and betrayed the Revolution."[35] For Wenzel, "there is no such thing as 'the' American founding."[36]

It is clear that for libertarians like Brennan, Lindsey, and Wenzel there is little desire to return to the spirit of the founding documents and certainly no desire to retrieve them from the past, being as compromised as they were. There is no vital center to return to because it never really existed, at least not long enough to make a difference. American's golden era was short-lived, maybe lasting ten years.[37] If we are ever going to experience a new golden age, these thinkers believe, we will need to create a new nation based on libertarian principles that promote total individual freedom and include beliefs in open borders and mass immigration, together ushering in a new era of peace and prosperity.

EVANGELICAL LIBERTARIANS

When I began this chapter, I must admit I didn't know of any evangelical libertarians.[38] While I knew social and religious conservatives who held to free-market economic principles, like those at the Acton Institute, I couldn't understand how evangelicals could be consistent libertarians, aligning themselves with a group that by and large is antagonistic to Christianity and rejects any authority that would transcend the autonomous, voluntaristic self.[39] After all, libertarianism was the party of Ayn Rand, who despised Christianity.[40] But after some digging, I came across an article by Kevin Vallier on the Bleeding Heart Libertarian website. Vallier is a Christian who says there are four or five Christians who frequently wrote for the *Bleeding Heart Libertarian* blog.[41]

Vallier, associate professor of philosophy at Bowling Green State University, admits, "Many of my sophisticated Christian friends think it is obvious that one cannot be a Christian and a libertarian. . . . [For them] radical individualism and celebration of profit making . . . is incompatible with Christian tradition."[42] If Vallier is speaking of Christians on the left, he wants to build a bridge to these progressive evangelicals through a kind of Christian liberaltarianism. Thus, Vallier attempts to find areas of common concern with his evangelical friends on the leftover issues like "poverty relief," "opposing crony capitalism," and "immigration reform."

One area he avoids when talking to his friends on the evangelical left is strong "support for capitalism" because he "found political Christians [on the left] tend to be ambivalent [about capitalism], as opposed to Christian conservatives who put their ideology ahead of the gospel."[43] Like others in the bleeding-heart libertarian camp, Vallier sees most conservatives as enemies, and if bleeding-heart libertarians are going to expand their base, it will have to appeal to evangelicals on the left, not conservatives.

As I continued to dig, I eventually came across two books, *Called to Freedom: Why You Can Be Christian and Libertarian* and *Faith Seeking Freedom: Libertarian Christian Answers to Tough Questions*, that, unlike Vallier, are attempting to build a bridge to fellow libertarians and religious conservatives.[44] Knowing conservatives are often skeptical about the libertarian view of secular reason and its alignment with the Left's social policy, they make the case that one can be a Christian *and* a libertarian.

In the case of *Faith Seeking Freedom*, Norman Horn, Doug Stuart, Kerry Baldwin, and Dick Clark, all connected to the Libertarian Christian Institute, contend that Christianity and libertarianism are not only compatible but that libertarianism is the most biblical political and economic view available. These authors ground their concept of liberty in the Bible, contending that both "libertarianism and the teachings of Christ demand that we respect one another, do no harm to each other, assist our fellows in distress, celebrate free will and diversity, and interact in peace."[45] They admit that the Bible doesn't necessarily take a position on politics, writing that "God doesn't give us an operations manual for providing the service of civil justice,"[46] but they nonetheless are confident that libertarianism is "the best expression of Christian political thought because it most aligns with God-given norms expressed in scripture and evidenced in nature."[47]

These writers connect a number of Bible verses with libertarianism. They believe one of the most important groundings for libertarianism, its principle of nonaggression, can be found in Romans 13, a text that other traditions ironically employ to argue for strong governments. For the authors of *Faith Seeking Freedom*, the Bible affirms the libertarian view; this is all that is needed. In making this epistemological jump they don't take on the philosophical secularism of thinkers in their camp, being satisfied to contend that the Bible is pro-liberty, sidestepping the fact that the vast majority of libertarians would reject any view of liberty rooted in the divine commands of God, norms that would obstruct the total freedom of the individual.[48]

That major disagreement aside and in spite of how much they would disagree with freedom right 2 libertarians, especially their affinity with the social and moral policies of the Left and their continued commitment to the welfare state (although more trimmed down than the progressive Left), the authors of *Faith Seeking Freedom* believe that the libertarian views on immigration and open borders are biblical.[49] Because they believe the individual should be left "free to live your life as your conscience leads you" and the state is not able to compel virtue or their conception of the good," they believe borders should be left open, free of government violence.[50]

In their chapter on immigration, the authors quote Jason Brennan, saying that when innocent people want to interact economically, "justice does not ordinarily allow other people to set up barriers between them."[51] Combining this nonaggression principle with pro-immigration views found in the Bible (using many of the same verses as evangelicals on the left), they argue that the Bible is pro-open borders and shuns state interference, they call it legalized violence.[52] And while the Left favors more government intervention to reach its immigration goals, these libertarian Christians would prefer a state that withered away completely, including welfare support, border police, and the military, replaced by private governance, security, charity, and courts. Even though that day may be far off, they still agree with bleeding-heart libertarians and those on the left that want open borders and mass immigration.

RIGHT-WING CRITICS OF LIBERTARIANISM

While a number of historians have put libertarians at the center of the conservative movement, contending that they sparked the pushback against big government liberalism, a number of conservative thinkers have disagreed, seeing libertarianism as a virus within the conservative movement.[53] Furthermore, while a number of these early critics are now dead, they would not have been surprised that libertarians have built bridges with the Left or that many have abandoned the Republican Party, including many on Wall Street.

In fact, Russell Kirk disliked libertarians so much that he called them "chirping sectaries" who didn't belong in the conservative movement and were pulling the movement away from its true foundations.[54] To Kirk, libertarians are heirs of the Cartesian French Enlightenment with its high view of human perfection; that is, reason alone would lead to human flourishing and would eventually end superstition and religious wars, allowing people to live in tolerance. Kirk rejected the view that humans could be perfected through rationality. And he rejected a public philosophy grounded on pure self-interest, atomistic individualism devoid of a higher authority, and a view that ultimately rejects the founders' view of a stable government built on the separation of power, federalism, and civic virtue.

I am convinced that an alliance between Christians and freedom right 2 libertarians is ultimately incompatible, no matter how hard they attempt to ground it in the Bible. Since the grounding for bleeding-heart libertarians is based on individualism, the unencumbered self, pragmatic or utilitarian reason, it is incompatible with a belief in a higher authority found in revelation or timeless natural law. And even though most Christian libertarians don't admit this, most libertarians *do*.[55] In fact, Brennan quotes the 2008 survey of *Liberty* magazine that found only 38 percent of libertarians believed in God. "*Reason*, a more popular libertarian magazine," says Brennan, "is avowedly atheistic. Its motto is 'free minds and free markets.'"[56] They are not fans of the America's Anglo-Protestant past. Nor are they fans of those who revere the original Constitution.

While Kirk was dismantling the political philosophy of libertarianism, Professor Walter Berns undressed their economics. Berns believed libertarians had succumbed to a crass economic materialism. In "The Need for Public Authority," Berns wrote,

> While I happily support the application of the libertarian principle of self-interest to economic activities—because I think that Adam Smith was right, and because it seems clear to me that capitalism is the only economic system ever devised by the wit of man that puts men to work and guarantees that men will in fact *work*—I cannot support the extension of that principle into other areas.[57]

For Berns, libertarians go wrong when they base their anti-state views on the thought of Thomas Hobbes.

According to Berns, Hobbes was the first liberal thinker to posit a "private realm" outside of the realm of the state, a place of liberty. Berns calls Hobbes "the first libertarian," the first thinker who said "that government may be founded on an anti-religious basis" and entirely on the first principle of "self-preservation."[58] But, whereas Hobbes saw this new private realm of liberty leading to "the war of all against all," engendering a life that is "solitary, poor, nasty, brutish, and short," and thus needing a strong state (the Leviathan) to keep the order, modern libertarians reduce Hobbes's view to a "minimal" or "night watchman" view of the state. "The state that leaves men alone" is how Bern's summarizes this kind of libertarians, and they see this as a good thing. This is a government that doesn't involve itself in teaching public virtue, forming "the character of its citizens" or a common public philosophy built on a higher law. Such a government attempts to remain neutral and not support one good over another.[59]

But when this night watchman view of the state is pushed to the extreme, argued Berns, it results in the call for the total elimination of the state and its police force. "They are Hobbesians without Leviathan," says Berns. "They would substitute private police forces. But why, on the basis of their own principles," asks Berns, "should the private police forces, however well paid they are, protect their employers?"[60] What assurance can libertarians give us that private police forces won't just grab power for themselves and place us right back into "a state of war of everyman against everyman"? What assurance can they give us that making self-interest the highest governing principle of our society won't lead to the postmodern breakdown of truth (freedom left 3) and the rise of a new despotism (order left 3)? For Berns, they can't. Thus they have opened the door to more forms of extremism and anti-democratic practices, this time on the right.

Over the years Kirk and Berns have not been alone in critiquing libertarianism and warning the conservative movement about its shortcomings, particularly its philosophical and economic grounding and its views on open immigration. Others have pointed out that it will ultimately destroy our nation's culture and traditions. Tucker Carlson reveals how these views erode what we have in common and weaken our nation.[61] If immigration keeps bringing in people who don't have anything in common with us and sometimes downright hate us, how can we have the national unity so necessary to hold our republic together?

Maybe that is the point. Joel Kotkin thinks that far from it being a bad thing that the middle class is fleeing California, "some California secessionists even suggest that it's a good thing to export our native middle class in order to make room for more energetic immigrants," a subtle reference to the radial-replacement view held by some on the far left.[62] Moreover, in her book *Open Society Inc.: Who's Funding America's Destruction?* first-generation Filipina Michelle Malkin claims that open-border policies are now pushed by George Soros and his Open Society with one goal in mind: to destabilize and then destroy our country.[63]

And the ultimate warning came from Hans-Hermann Hoppe, himself a libertarian, who warned pro-open border libertarians that, whether they are aware of it or not, they are "useful idiots [for the far Left] on their march toward totalitarian social control."[64]

WARNINGS GO UNHEEDED

Libertarians have rejected these critiques and warnings. In fact, over the past decade, as the bad news of globalization and open immigration has piled up, freedom right 2 libertarians have doubled down, clinging to their economic, political, and cultural views and going after Trump Republicans and social conservatives, calling them nationalists, bigots, and racists. Bryan Caplan's *Open Borders*, a book that refuses to admit negative consequences to immigration, continues to make the case that mass immigration can be defended economically and morally.[65]

In early 2020 the Libertarian Party platform proclaimed that "one of the proudest positions that we have in this party is our open border plank."[66] Party member and major donor Adam Kokesh added, "If being American means anything about standing up to unjust authority and employing civil disobedience, I would dare say most who come here illegally are *more* American than the average apathetic American today."[67] Along with the doubling down on economics and politics, the open-borders crowd continues to downplay the cultural change of the nation and welcomes it.

Javier Hidalgo captures their not-so-subtle views well, "Sure immigration brings about cultural change. Deal with it."[68] There is simply no going back.

Undoubtedly, some of this doubling down can be chalked up to cheerleading in order to not feed the Trumpian nationalist beast, strengthening the case against mass immigration and open borders. However, amid this cheerleading some are getting nervous, fearing that "Biden's generous immigration policies could turn out to backfire."[69] Fareed Zakaria, a spokesperson for the Wall Street billionaire class, in a rare moment of candor, warned that at the heart of the border crisis in early 2021 the real tragedy "is that this border crisis . . . could hinder Biden's efforts to achieve comprehensive reform of the whole system . . . [and] there is a much larger group that includes those who have skills the United States needs."[70] Zakaria said out loud what normally is only said in private—that the real reason for immigration is to promote economic growth.

WHO BENEFITS?

Here we return to our question: *cui bono*? As Tucker Carlson contends in his *Ship of Fools*, our bipartisan ruling elites love immigration because it provides housekeepers, nannies, and gardeners—enhancing the elites' personal lives; it provides highly skilled workers for their businesses, increasing their wealth. And with the demographic shift, it provides the votes they need to stay in power.[71]

Yet, as the ruling class gets richer and richer, more and more powerful, the working and middle classes suffer. The working poor in our cities, including Blacks and Hispanics and the middle class in our rust belt states, bear the brunt of these policies through higher taxes, lower wages, crime-ridden schools, and an overburdened health care system.[72]

Is it any wonder that Republicans made strides with Hispanic voters in Texas in 2020?[73] Is it any wonder that Donald Trump improved his standing with Black male voters during the 2016 election, in spite of some of the things he said on race?[74] Finally, is it any surprise that Middle America, which has seen its wages decrease by 40 percent over the past few decades and its towns and their inhabitants succumb to "deaths of despair," blames the plutocrats on Wall Street and the clerisy class in Washington and in the media?[75] It's perfectly rational. They have seen the truth before the rest of the country.

A FINAL WARNING

Now we can see that at the heart of the battle over immigration and open borders is the struggle between oligarchy and constitutional democracy, between the rule of the few and the rule of the people. In a profoundly insightful article in the *Claremont Review of Books*, Christopher Caldwell contends that the real reason behind mass immigration is not its compassion toward the less fortunate (though he admits they do benefit from jobs in the United States) but rather that open borders increase the ruling class's oligarchic monopoly on power. "When economists talk about 'gains' from immigration to the receiving country," says Caldwell, "they are including the $50 billion dollars that accrues to the oligarchs, making 'an extraordinary transfer of income and wealth.'"[76]

So while native capitalists get richer, native workers, who unfortunately have lost their jobs, get poorer, resulting in a huge transfer of wealth from "the poor to the rich, from workers to financiers," a kind of Robin Hood in reverse, producing tremendous inequality.[77] Caldwell concludes, if "immigration suppressed real wages of workers, and transfers much of their wealth to elites, then liberalized immigration is a policy that cannot be carried out without simultaneous injuries to democracy."[78] That is, it engenders oligarchy not democracy.

By flooding our borders with new arrivals, we are not only seeing the transfer of wealth from the poor to the rich but are witnessing the transfer of democratic power from the serfs to the oligarchs, solidifying the new alliance of big business and big government. This is what Michael Yon meant by "a destabilizing migration" that threatens our national sovereignty.[79] With this destabilization we are witnessing the destruction of our constitutional republic, the eventual obliteration of its native population and culture and laying down the foundation for the Great Reset.[80] And if our borders fall and the huge demographic and cultural shift takes place, we will have lost completely our republic, our government of the people, for the people, and by the people, replaced by an oligarchy ruled by a technological elite, who, in consortium with other world elites, will install a new global governance model.

For this travesty we can thank the libertarians on Wall Street and in the halls of Congress. And once this dark winter is upon us, dissent will be met by cancellation or maybe worse. Contemplating this grim future, I am reminded of Whittaker Chamber's famous book review of Ayn Rand's *Atlas Shrugged* in 1957, titled "Big Sister Is Watching You," where he hauntingly penned, "From almost any page [of the novel] a voice can be heard . . . commanding: 'To a gas chamber—go!'"[81]

To this grim reality we now turn.

IN SUM

- We have seen that both the mainstream Democratic and Republican parties, influenced by libertarianism, are pro-immigration and pro-open borders. President Trump's views on immigration challenged both political parties.

- Freedom right 2 libertarianism is similar to the freedom left 2 position—affirming the voluntaristic self, the procedural republic, the bracketing out of religion, the rejection the natural law found in the Declaration of Independence, instead relying on secular pragmatism and a vision of social justice similar to the radical progressive view of order left 3.

- For libertarians, if America had a golden age, it was short-lived and completely betrayed by the Constitution. There is no going back, only forward to a new era, a time when personal freedom, protection of civil liberties, market capitalism, and open borders are all affirmed, ushering in peace and prosperity.

- For libertarians like Jason Brennan, open immigration is built on the view of human autonomy and the *live and let live* philosophy of libertarianism, which means that individuals have a right to free movement, to live where they want, and that nations have no right to stop them.

- A small group of libertarian Christians also believe in mass immigration and open borders but ground their libertarianism not in secularism but in the Bible.

- Conservatives criticize libertarians for grounding their views in Enlightenment rationality and the politics of Thomas Hobbes, which by removing any transcendent or natural-law grounding weakens the role of the state in encouraging virtuous citizens and opens the door to politics built on power alone.

- A minority but growing chorus of voices on the right rejects open borders, arguing it will harm the working and middle classes and weaken national sovereignty.

- Ultimately, open borders and mass immigration favor the bipartisan ruling class, engendering inequality and a transfer of wealth from the poor to the rich, increasing their power and their control over society.

8

FREEDOM RIGHT 3

RADICAL LIBERTARIANS, THE END OF THE STATE, AND THE RISE OF UTOPIAN TECHNOCRACY

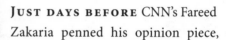

JUST DAYS BEFORE CNN's Fareed Zakaria penned his opinion piece, which we looked at above, warning that the crisis at the border could threaten comprehensive immigration reform, he had interviewed Eric Schmidt, the former CEO and chairman of Google. Schmidt, part of the fifteen-member bipartisan National Security Commission on Artificial Intelligence (NSCAI), had just released its final report on artificial intelligence. The conclusions were sobering: "America is not prepared to defend or compete in the AI area." According to the report, "it is this reality that demands comprehensive, whole-of-nation action," if we are going to "win the broader technology competition for the sake of our prosperity, security and welfare." The government must spend much more money on solving the problem. And along with a bigger financial commitment, it must do something just as important: improve US immigration. According to the report, the government must increase the number of highly skilled immigrants allowed into the country through the H-B1 visa process, the temporary worker program.[1]

It may be that the NSCAI report and the interview with Schmidt may have been on Zakaria's mind when he wrote his opinion piece on the crisis at the border. While Zakaria, who admits in the interview he is an unpaid consultant for Schmidt Futures, clearly wants high-tech companies to have the ability to secure more cheap labor, he undoubtedly also wants them to win the AI competition. And while I don't doubt Schmidt and Zakaria are concerned about China's growing global dominance, something every American should be worried about, I wonder what they mean by "win." Does winning mean mimicking whatever China does? For example, since China is working on superhuman soldiers, does that mean we should too? Or does winning mean creating "smart cities," combined with a "social credit system," capable of spying on the population through supersurveillance technologies, in effect creating digital gulags?[2] Or does winning mean beating China to a world where babies are genetically enhanced, where humans are merged with computers, and where we achieve a transhuman future?

Listening to Zakaria's interview with Schmidt it is not clear. But knowing that Silicon Valley and investors on Wall Street have been collaborating for years with companies owned by the Chinese Communist Party (CCP) doesn't inspire confidence.[3] Honestly, it is hard not to be cynical about the intentions of NSCAI. Recently, Project Veritas captured on secret video a high-level Facebook executive, Benny Thomas, revealing that the real goal of Facebook and its AI program is transhumanism, that is, designing a new type of superhuman that will render normal humans dispensable, worth no more than ants at a picnic.[4] So, again, what does winning mean? And once we have won, how do we know we haven't really lost?

This NSCAI report raises other concerns. Returning to the call for more skilled immigration, this raises alarms and prompts important questions. For example, when they talk about this kind of highly skilled immigrants, do they mean the kind that will prevent our Gen Z children from getting STEM jobs? Or do they mean the kind of immigration where high-tech companies underpay foreign workers, work them long hours, and deny them any legal right to protest poor labor conditions? It is hard to trust Schmidt and Zakaria's motives, especially when we know these same high-tech companies have offshored millions of manufacturing jobs to China.[5]

All of this raises the question that if we are falling behind China in the AI race, isn't it possible that our government and big tech, working together, are to blame?

FREE TRADE, GLOBALIZATION, AND CHINA

For the past fifty years our government has encouraged our business community to form joint ventures with Chinese businesses, believing it would grow a vibrant Chinese middle class who eventually would clamor for more democracy, forcing the Chinese Communist Party (CCP) to liberalize. To this end, American businesses were encouraged to go after the huge Chinese market. As joint ventures were formed, American businesses realized that labor was much cheaper in China, so they began shuttering their factories and shipping their jobs to China.[6] Over time, as China industrialized, it began dumping billions of cheap consumer goods onto the US market, a boon for consumers but a bust for the remaining US-based manufacturing companies. To stay competitive these small manufacturing businesses also had to ship their manufacturing jobs overseas. By one estimate, US manufacturing closed 57,000 factories and in the process devastated the local economies and communities of these small manufacturing towns.[7]

By the late 1990s, with offshoring in full swing and China's economy booming, the Clinton administration (with the full support of the Republican Congress) believed it was time to allow China into the company of other civilized countries and join the World Trade Organization.[8] In his 1999 speech promoting this idea, Clinton assured the United States and other international members that allowing China to join would lead to a fully democratic country.[9] This heady idea had bipartisan support in Congress and on Wall Street, an economic theory known as *globalization*. But two decades later, we know it hasn't worked out the way Clinton promised. In fact, while China's economy now rivals the US economy, their politics have become less democratic, and the CCP has tightened its draconian grip on the Chinese population, making any transition to democracy seem highly unlikely.[10] And furthermore, at the same time the CCP was telling the world that they supported free trade, they were protecting their own markets, stealing our high-tech intellectual property, manipulating their currency, abusing their work force, and colonizing vital natural resources and entire countries in Africa.[11]

We have to ask ourselves why we thought allowing China into the global economy was a good idea. Why were we under the impression that free trade and a growing economy would liberalize communist China? And why did we think that as we waited for this liberalization to happen, American companies wouldn't trade short-term gain (making profits in China) for long-term losses (giving away our intellectual property)?[12]

BIG TECH HAS NO GROUNDING

Over the last half of the twentieth century, America lost its grounding, its moral compass, which in the past would have guided our business decisions and provided more than just profit motivation to shape our free market. But with only the bottom line to guide US business leaders, they easily went astray, so often putting short-term riches ahead of long-term democratic health.

Oren Cass, a conservative critic of libertarianism, contends that "the free market is a wonderful thing, but we don't serve it—it serves us."[13] And "having a successful system of market capitalism isn't simply a matter of getting everything else out of the way," a belief now shared by both Republicans and Democrats. What started at mid-century as an economic philosophy on the right didn't stay there. "Republicans," claims Cass, "essentially trained a generation of Democrats to become what we now call neoliberal," committed to the principles of globalization, including free trade, deregulation, lower corporate taxes, weakening of US labor, and open borders. And, for Cass, embracing a philosophy that "places almost absolute priority on free markets to the exclusion of a lot of other things that are really important to human flourishing and a prosperous nation" isn't conservative, its libertarian.[14] And understanding its origins and impact is important if we are going to understand how free-trade fundamentalism took over both parties and in the process empowered China to become our number one threat.[15]

This is the story of the radical libertarians and freedom right 3, which "usually begins with Ayn Rand."[16]

IT USUALLY BEGINS WITH AYN RAND

While libertarian thought can be traced back to the 1930s and 1940s and its reaction to the welfare state, it wasn't until Russian immigrant Ayn Rand, a refugee to America, brought it to the attention of the world with her bestselling 1943 novel *The Fountainhead*. Fourteen years later when she wrote her follow-up novel *Atlas Shrugged*, another bestseller, she was the undisputed spokesperson for "the virtue of selfishness."[17] Since its first appearance in 1957, *Atlas Shrugged* has appeared on numerous top one hundred lists, and in 2009 Modern Library ranked it the number one best novel published in the English language. It continues to sell hundreds of thousands of copies each year.[18]

While her notoriety has ebbed and flowed over the years, today, almost four decades after her death in 1982, "fans of Ayn Rand include some 'Atlases' of the arts," says Marilyn Moore. Apple's Steve Jobs, *Shark Tank* hosts Mark Cuban and Kevin O'Leary, Uber founder Travis Kalanick, and PayPal founder Peter Thiel point to Ayn Rand as an inspiration. Added to the list is former Speaker of the House Paul Ryan, President Trump, and a number of his early cabinet officials. For many, says Brian Doherty, reading Rand is a "guilty pleasure."[19] And in the words of Jennifer Burns, Rand became the "ultimate gateway drug to life on the right." And, I would add, eventually for many on the left, particularly in Silicon Valley and on Wall Street.

In *Goddess of the Market: Ayn Rand and the American Right*, biographer Jennifer Burns claims that Rand was "among the first to identify the problem of the modern state's often terrifying power and make it an issue of popular concern."[20] Rand witnessed firsthand the power of collectivism in her native Russia and how it ruined her family's way of life. As she observed politics in America, she saw the same thing happening under FDR's New Deal. The common theme between communism and the New Deal was the misguided desire to eliminate poverty, and Rand became fascinated with "the failure of good intentions."[21] Rand believed the best way to counter the erroneous narrative of altruism was to propose a different narrative, a different morality built on rational self-interested individuals.

Rand held "that man exists for his own sake, that the pursuit of his own happiness is his highest moral purpose, that he must not sacrifice himself to others, nor sacrifice others to himself."[22] According to George H. Nash, the historian of the modern conservative movement, Rand contended that "anything that denigrated man's rationality, total self-reliance, and freedom was deemed evil."[23] For Rand rationality was the cardinal virtue. The way to happiness is through reason. Relying heavily on Aristotle, Rand called this grounding "objectivism," the ability of the human mind to observe the objective facts of existence and think one's way to the good life. Rand loved capitalism and the free market because she saw it as the closest to the embodiment of her moral philosophy of rational self-interest. She saw the rise of the welfare state, a form of collectivism, and its stress on altruism as a direct threat to capitalism and the elevation of the rational individual pursuing productive work.

For Brian Doherty, author of the monumental history of the libertarian movement, *Radicals for Capitalism*, Rand's critique of the welfare state and the rise of collectivism in America and the need to defend the virtues of capitalism were spot-on for most conservatives. Doherty contends, "Her daring, root-and-branch assault on the postwar liberal welfare state consensus made her beloved even among a rising generation of young conservatives."[24] Or, as they started to call themselves, libertarians.

While conservatives thrilled at her moral defense of capitalism and her ferocious attacks on big government, "not all conservatives were pleased by *Atlas Shrugged*," Nash adds.[25] They recoiled at her hatred of Christianity and her refusal to see it as the grounding of individual rights and the foundation of the American republic.[26] For Rand, all rights were founded on objective existence and rationality apart from God, any higher revelation, or any founding document. In place of God, "she offered rational self-interest and the dollar sign, the symbol of 'free trade and, therefore, of a free mind.' . . . Aggressiveness, egoism, energy, rationality, self-respect, the virtue of selfishness—these were some of values she enthroned," concluded Nash.[27] These are the virtues present in her novels' heroes, virtues that sounded more like Nietzsche than Christ.

While Rand credited Aristotle for her view of reason, her critics maintain that she actually held to a more modern view of reason, one that sounded the themes of the French Enlightenment—reason over revelation, the individual over society, rationality over tradition, rights over responsibilities. In the end she made liberty the highest ideological priority. At its center was atheism. According to Jennifer Burns, "although Objectivism appeared a way to escape religion, it was more often a substitute, offering a similar regimentation and moralism." It was a way to discard traditional religion without feeling "lost in a nihilistic, meaningless universe."[28]

ONCE UPON A TIME

Already in this too-brief overview, we can see all the telltale signs of modern libertarianism. First, we notice that Rand's thought has much in common with freedom right 2 (and freedom left 2), stressing the rejection of religious ethics and tradition, affirming a voluntarist and unencumbered view of the individual, claiming the right over the good, and calling for a minimal, procedural republic that leaves individuals alone to pursue their own vision of happiness. She approved of the Declaration of Independence as a libertarian document yet was ambivalent toward the Constitution, arguing that America's golden age had been betrayed by collectivism first enshrined in the Constitution, a document that opened the door to mixed government, egalitarian government meddling, and the eventual collectivism of the New Deal.

What we need is a second founding, a new commitment to liberty built on the right of individual selfishness, the right to private property, and right of the individual to be left alone, unencumbered by Christianity or any other outside authority. It is a world reimagined on the basis of the heroic virtues of selfish rationality and productivity, where heroic figures, like her fictional Rick Riordan and John Galt, live free of all governmental restraint, instead ruled by their own rational selfish need in a utopian world she calls Galt's Gulch, where only the most productive, the most rational, and the most capable reside.

In Rand's once-upon-a-time narrative, what role does the state play in the new golden age? If her fictional Galt's Gulch has done away with government, does that mean we should abolish it too? Or should we allow government some role? Rand never called for the abolishment of government, preferring a minimal government that kept the peace and protected order. Yet, according to Jennifer Burns, even though Rand scoffed at anarchism, saying it would never work, Rand had in "*Atlas Shrugged* indelibly etched the idea of a stateless capitalist utopia into the right-wing psyche. . . . Rand's fiction suggested that an alternative world was within reach. Once imagined, Galt's Gulch could never be forgotten."[29] And for this reason some of her followers saw "anarchism as the logical next step."[30]

ANARCHO-CAPITALISM

In his now-famous "Open Letter to Ayn Rand," Roy Childs Jr., a Rand admirer, accuses her of inconsistency, claiming that her view of rational individualism must logically result not in a minimal state that protects these rights but in anarcho-capitalism: "Your political philosophy cannot be maintained without contradiction, that, in fact, you are advocating the maintenance of an institution—the state—which is a moral evil," argues Childs. Since all governments must use force to maintain law and order, Childs continues, and since coercion was forbidden in objectivism and libertarian thought, then the state must be abolished. "Your approach to the matter is not yet radical, not yet fundamental: it is the existence of the state itself which must be challenged by the new radicals. It must be understood the state is an unnecessary evil."[31] Indeed, if at the heart of the state is force and coercion, then it must be opposed—abolished.

This letter opened the possibility of challenging Rand, splitting the movement into two warring camps. The anarchists, like Childs, say we must abolish the state. Others, following Rand, are not willing to get rid of the state entirely and still believe in a minimal state. Called the minarchists, these "minimal state" or "night watchman" libertarians contend that humans can't live without some form of the state to protect individual rights and create an environment of trust and "objective laws" that makes capitalism possible. So while they want to dismantle the entire welfare state and safety net, they nevertheless want to retain a government with minimal functions— police, military, and courts. Anarchists, on the other hand, didn't want even this minimal level of state involvement.[32] But in some ways it was an intra-family debate, both groups wanting the destruction of the welfare state.

Doherty traces the genealogy of anarchism, from Rand's novels to Childs open letter to economist Murray Rothbard to think tank head Lew Rockwell, all thinkers who believed the only logical conclusion of libertarians was the complete end of the state. Like Childs, once Rothbard and Rockwell accepted the nonaggression principle (NAP) as the key to liberty, abolishing the state entirely was the next logical step. Rothbard's *For a New Liberty: The Libertarian Manifesto* and Rockwell's *Against the State: An Anarcho-Capitalist Manifesto* laid out the principles of anarchist libertarianism, an argument that hasn't changed much since Rand.

In 2012 thirty years after Rand's death, Yaron Brook and Don Watkins picked up the mantle in their *The Free Market Revolution: How Ayn Rand's Ideas Can End Big Government*, attempting to resurrect her thought for a new generation. Wanting to make sure Rand gets the credit for a moral defense of capitalism, including the free market built on the rational self-interested individual, Brooks and Watkins wax eloquent about the liberating powers of her thought. Yet, unlike Rand, the authors don't hesitate to tread where Rand feared, calling for the abolition of all entitlement programs, the abolition of all government controls on business, the privatization of all property (including public lands), and the absolute restoration of free trade.[33] Only then can we experience a "free market revolution" led by capitalism and its commitment to rational selfishness.

Evangelicals in the Radical Libertarian Camp

Over the years both Rothbard and Rockwell attempted to find allies in their fight against big-government progressives, including neoconservatives and beltway libertarians, whom they accused of favoring big government and adopting the social policies of the Left.[34] In the late 1960s, Rothbard attempted to find allies on the left.[35] But this fell apart over the radical Left's hatred of capitalism. Then in the 1990s libertarians tried to find allies with paleocons like Patrick Buchanan (see order right 3), but this too fell apart over trade protectionism.[36] While they could never find common ground with paleocons over economics, they continued to partner on conservative social issues and in the process attracted a small group of evangelicals and conservative Catholics who were attracted to its combination of anti-statism, personal freedom and liberty, and the rejection of left libertarian positions on legalized drugs, abortion, and the LGBTQ agenda.

Many of these evangelical libertarians are gathered around the Libertarian Christian Institute, which "exists to make the Christian case for a free society" and "persuade Christians that the political expression of our faith inclines us toward the principles of individual liberty and the free markets."[37] Through their website, journal articles, blog, and podcasts, they demonstrate how the libertarian nonaggression principle, its anti-state views, and its commitment to individual liberty, voluntary associations, and the free market line up with Christianity. What sets this group apart from secular libertarians is its commitment to demonstrating how the Bible, church history, and theology support libertarianism. At the heart of this defense is changing the church's mind about the state. For two thousand years Western Christianity has believed the state is ordained by God (Romans 13) and that Christians should "render to Caesar the things that are Caesar's" (Matthew 22:21). But, for these Christian libertarians, the historic church has gotten it wrong: the Bible teaches the "state is evil," that the state promotes violence, and that Christians committed to nonviolence should have nothing to do with it.[38]

GREG BOYD AND ANABAPTIST LIBERTARIANS

To biblically justify their anti-state views, Christian libertarians often refer to *The Myth of a Christian Nation: How the Quest for Political Power Is Destroying the Church* by Greg Boyd, a pastor in Minnesota.[39] Because this is the kind of book title that progressive Christians in the godless-Constitution, freedom left 2 quadrant would find interesting, I was confused why a group on the right would recommend it. In fact, Boyd's own congregation was initially confused as well.[40]

Boyd's book fits well into anarcho-Christian views of the church, the state, and politics. Boyd and his defense of pacifism in the Bible gives Christian libertarians the theological resources to support their views on the nonaggression principle, their anti-statist views, and a countercultural view of the church. After reading this book, I searched online for "anarcho-Christian" and "Christian anarchy" and found an entire world that I didn't know existed on the right—an alliance between libertarians and pacifists holding anarcho-Christian views on politics and the state, retreating from all concern about political involvement, and focusing on the church as "resident alien," creating a subculture of communities off the grid. Like others in the freedom right 3 position, they also reject the state *in toto*, look down on the founding fathers, reject the US Constitution as morally compromised, and refuse to see the American project as noble and worth preserving. Sounding more like progressives in the order left 3 quadrant, these anarcho-evangelical libertarians also look to a new golden age, one not built on the past but entirely new, maybe even revolutionary.

In saying the state is evil, beyond salvaging, and thus putting all the focus on the private realm, maybe they are unaware of the vacuum they open up or that their anti-statist views can be so easily highjacked by the counterculture, which may one day merge with libertarian thought and have no trouble replacing the state with corporate monopolies, often more restrictive than the state.

LIBERTARIANS AND THE CALIFORNIA IDEOLOGY

When libertarianism was coming of age in the sixties and seventies, Christian libertarians were not the only group attracted to these anti-state, utopian views. As Doherty tells the story, in the 1950s a group of wealthy businessmen in California supported the work of Spiritual Mobilization, an organization dedicated to teaching pastors about the free market and libertarian principles.[41] Despite its success in training pastors in economics, some of these businessmen, many of them church goers, started feeling that libertarianism didn't speak to their deepest longings and need for meaning and purpose. So, surprisingly, they began dabbling in the current new age philosophies of the day, seeking the guidance of gurus and holding conferences in northern California, near the center of the counterculture and the *Whole Earth Catalog* crowd.[42] These conferences brought together libertarians with the new information-technology industry forming in Silicon Valley.

With their countercultural views from the sixties and their desire to defeat the oppressive system, it made sense that this new high-tech industry would find libertarianism attractive. They were drawn to libertarianism's low-tax, low-regulation, and antilabor views. By the early nineties, according to Doherty, this group "came to be known as the digerati . . . who saw in a digital high-tech future a world in which government had little or no place."[43]

Over time the merger of these ideologies took on more extreme views, a more utopian slant, calling themselves Extropians. Doherty concludes, "Advocating a richer, freer, more powerful human future, the Extropians, are a product of the libertarian movement; their ideas about liberated humans warping their minds and bodies through technology of all varieties, living forever, blasting off to the stars, or downloading themselves to computers."[44] Or as Richard Barbrook and Andy Cameron write in "The California Ideology," this "new faith has emerged from a bizarre fusion of the cultural bohemianism of San Francisco with the high-tech industries of Silicon Valley," infused with libertarian economics and the backing of Wall Street's commitment to free trade, deregulation, and low taxes.[45] In "the digital utopia, everybody will be both hip and rich." According to the authors, a commitment to free market economics and "the 'post human' philosophies of the West Coast's Extropian cult" were being combined.[46]

Once these two philosophies merged, the California ideology was guided by nothing more than personal fulfillment and "a profound faith in the emancipatory potential of the new information technology." According to Doherty, "whatever humanity can invent the technology to do, let's go for it."[47] The goal is not just libertarian escape from governments, it is also "full human liberation." In fact, what these titans of high-tech have in mind is ultimately liberation from creation, God's built-in order of the world, instead providing their own path to immortal life, using technology as the spaceship.

Interestingly, when Doherty concludes his history of libertarianism, he doesn't wrap it up with a summary of its economics but rather a discussion of these high-tech visionaries, connecting these purveyors of the California ideology with Mr. Libertarian himself, Murray Rothbard. Writing to libertarians who often got discouraged by their small numbers, Rothbard said they "should remain of good cheer. The eventual victory of liberty is inevitable, because only liberty is functional for modern man. . . . Reality, and therefore history, *is* on our side."[48] For, as both Doherty and the authors of "California Ideology" point out, this techno-libertarianism was celebrated and pushed by both the Left and the Right, the Democrats and the Republicans in DC and Wall Street, and they saw China as one of its major trading partners.

This hybrid ideology, the merger of libertarianism and techno-utopianism, fueled two public policy fronts at the same time—globalization and trade with China, and the wild foray into AI and a transhuman future. But, while technology has delivered so many wonderful breakthroughs, making our lives easier, healthier, and more enjoyable, this new ideology has had some great downsides, not the least of which is making the lives of millions of workers in the United States and China less livable. We have thirty years of data to prove it.[49] And on some level these high-tech plutocrats must know this. How do they live with the contradiction?

California ideology and its faith in a utopian future continues to help big tech and Wall Street overlook and rationalize the damage they are doing.

Barbrook and Cameron concluded in 1995 that "in the late twentieth century, technology is once again being used to reinforce the difference between the masters and the slaves, . . . [the] deepening of social segregation, . . . [and] a deeply pessimistic and repressive vison of the future," which is every bit true today.[50] Regardless of the downsides and the bumps along the way to their new utopia, they satisfy themselves knowing that one day, at the end of the ride, our species will have achieved immortality.[51]

For years social and religious conservatives saw these bipartisan libertarian high-tech companies as allies in their fight against big government liberals, approved their call for lower taxes and less regulation, and their desire to help liberalize China, but they often had no idea of the downsides of globalization and technological breakthroughs and seemed oblivious that these downsides would attack and attenuate the very things they cherished— mediating institutions, strong families, vibrant small towns, and religious authority capable of shaping citizens of virtue. All of these priorities were actually undermined by the California ideology. "Libertarians," observes Cass, have been "obsessed with liberty to the exclusion of other values," and in the process these other values have lost out.

But it's not as if they weren't warned.[52]

Multiple Warnings

In fact, just four years after Clinton's World Trade Organization speech announcing China had joined the international community, Harvard economist Dani Rodrik challenged the reigning belief in free trade globalization in *Has Globalization Gone Too Far?*[53] While recognizing the positives of free trade, like cheap consumer goods, he pointed to its serious downsides, like the major fall in the real value of wages, the offshoring of manufacturing jobs leading to more economic inequality in the country and tremendous "social disintegration," and a radical distrust in the ruling elites and our democratic institutions. Prioritizing global trade over domestic democratic institutions and national sovereignty has seriously imperiled our nation. Two decades later, Rodrik concluded, "I think globalization has contributed to tearing our societies apart" and "that by fetishizing globalization and exaggerating its benefits and understating its downsides, we have essentially privileged and prioritized a set of powerful interests."[54]

In 2004 Harvard's Samuel P. Huntington agreed that "powerful interests" were rigging the system, making the case that globalization had opened the door to less democratic control and more global governance, led by CEOs of multinational elites who are not guided by "nationalism" but "cosmopolitanism."[55] In his article "Dead Souls: The Denationalization of the American Elite," he contends that these "dead souls," what are often called "Davos Men," have "little need for national loyalty, view national boundaries as obstacles," and "see national governments as residues from the past."[56] The state's "only useful function is to facilitate the elite's global operation." Although he felt that this ruling elite was still small, he feared it was "growing among America's business, professional, intellectual and academic elites" and that left unchallenged it would continue to weaken our society, break down our democratic institutions, and alienate the American population, once they realize they have no say in politics or the forces governing their lives.

A decade and half later, more conservative voices were joining the voices of naysayers. Writing in the *New York Times*, conservative columnist Ross Douthat warned of the rise of "woke capital," claiming our business elites, as a way to paper over the downsides of globalization, cynically joined the side of social justice, buying protection and avoiding criticism through their virtue signaling.[57]

But others didn't see the adoption of far-left social issues as just a public relations cover. Not discounting their potential cynicism completely, Ben Weingarten posits that these plutocrats actually believe "woke capitalism's" major tenets, which we saw in our discussion of the California ideology, and believe they have found a way to combine their new woke commitments with the tools of corporate monopoly, creating what he calls a "woke theocracy," penetrating every major institution in our country.[58] As an example of their new woke theocracy, Weingarten shows how new woke regulatory burdens, what are called ESGs—environment, social, and governance—are placed on small businesses to weaken them or even put them out of business, which benefits the large high-tech companies, strengthens their monopolistic control, and provides an advantage to CCP-owned companies, many of which are in partnership with woke capital.[59]

All these unfair business practices are cloaked behind a "mask of virtue." It's a brilliant system that allows them to conduct war from the top, crushing competition and destroying the middle class at the same time.[60] But it is not just the middle class who gets squeezed from the top. Joel Kotkin claims this new high-tech neofeudalism has been terrible for minorities, widening the inequality gap and creating, in the words of Michael Lind, a new class war.[61]

But that is not the end to the warnings. As the digital censorship of big tech has become more aggressive, critics have been raising red flags about the danger technology poses to our lives. Pointing to the success of books like *Homo Deus*, *The Singularity*, and *Code Breaker*, critics warn of a growing optimism for genetic-engineered human enhancements and a new enthusiasm for transhumanism, Silicon Valley's "suicide pill" for humankind, which will a eventually end in posthumanism, a "dystopian nightmare."[62] In his essay "Transhumanism, The New Religion of the Coming Technocracy," Mark E. Jeftovic, argues "there are an abundance of well-respected thinkers who believe this [transhumanism] is possible, including well known tech entrepreneurs Ray Kurzweil, PayPal founder Peter Thiel, Google Ventures founder Bill Maris" and bestselling author Yuval Noah Harari, who believes that "in the twenty-first century, humans are likely to make a serious bid for immortality."[63] But if we are to transcend our mortality, we must embrace, in the words of Julian Savulescu, the unstoppable "radical technological power," and this means downgrading and ultimately altering our commitments to democracy and our moral nature.[64] Yet in this new dystopian future, one that will create tremendous inequality, only those who obey the rules set up by the small group of techno-utopian elites and get a high score on the social credit system will get the chance to have their minds "uploaded into an everlasting paradise."[65] Alexander Thomas concludes, the "socially moribund masses may thus be forced to serve the technoscientific super-project of Humanity 2.0, which uses the ideology of market fundamentalism in its quest for perpetual progress and maximum productivity."[66] No wonder Michael Rectenwald says we are facing a new digital gulag.[67]

If the threats to our citizens, our nation, and the very idea of human life is not enough, voices like Peter Navarro, Steven Mosher, and Michael Pillsbury, three "China Hawks," have been warning of China's threat and how big tech, backed by US government money, our nation's elite universities, and US capital markets, have willingly partnered with the CCP not only to get rich but in the process to strengthen global governance, further rigging the system in their favor.[68] And after thirty years of collaboration, libertarian fellow-traveler Tanner Greer claims it is hard to distinguish the California ideology from the CCP's authoritarian governance model, what they themselves call a "community of common destiny for mankind," where the international community now sees Beijing's model of state-controlled capitalism as superior to Western electoral democracy and capable of leading the world to a new era of peace, cooperation, and prosperity.[69] And maybe for our high-tech leaders this will lead to a chance for a new utopian future.

This openness to the CCP's authoritarian model of global governance has inspired the new agreements in Europe and the new calls for cooperation with China.[70] After all, working with China is the best way to insure free trade and continued globalization, defeating the populist nationalism of the past four years from ever raising its head again. Yet, in one final irony, as the high-tech plutocrats exploited libertarian views, using these antinational sovereignty views "to transfer assets to China," they have been "firmly captured in Beijing's sovereign grip and forced to surrender control of enterprises and technology to a power that has a nationalist agenda that will eventually displace them both at home and abroad."[71]

So, after thirty years of dire warnings, have libertarians woken up?

WARNINGS GO UNHEEDED

Thirty years of warnings continue to go unheeded by the libertarians. In fact, far from provoking soul searching in libertarian circles, they have pushed back, seeing most of these warnings as attacks on free-market capitalism, on globalization and the merits of technological advance.

Back in 2000, when the attack on globalization was mainly coming from those on the left, in "Globalization Under Fire" Hans F. Sennholz contended that in the face of these "radical critics" of capitalism we must keep "explaining the meaning of trade and the benefits of globalization by insisting that a peaceful and prosperous world requires more open market and economic development" and "does not call for a return to economic nationalism and international confrontation."[72]

By 2006, when conservative voices were joining the globalism naysayers, causing some in the radical libertarian camp to waver in their market-fundamentalism faith, Robert Murphy, also writing for the Mises Institute website, reminds his readers that "for some time now [the Mises Institute] has come out squarely in favor of free trade and has opposed the new attacks on trade and 'globalization.'"[73] Dismissing all the downsides to globalization, he concludes, "Most of these warnings fall apart."[74] Or as John Tamny, in "Blaming Globalization for Our Society's Problems Is Just Another Version of Victim Mentality," writes, "as opposed to relatively impoverished Americans being too exposed to globalization," the truth is that they have not been "exposed enough to the globalization . . . freedom works. *Always*."[75]

Two decades later, when they began realizing that globalized free trade had been hijacked by the global governance of the Left, libertarians like Ryan McMaken still argued that we should not get rid of global free trade but in fact push for more of it, claiming that that if we could just get governments and all international regulation out of the way, the world would prosper.[76] Ignoring the need for international rules and guidelines and for some court to punish those who cheat or break their contracts, his belief in market fundamentalism is unbounded.

But if they have dismissed all warnings of the downsides of free trade and globalization, I would think they would moderate their views at least when it comes to China and the threat it poses. And given that they agree that the neoliberal view that free trade with China was a mistake and has not worked out as planned, one would think they would want to get tough on China. Yet, even after laying out an argument against the CCP, Daniel Drezner rejects the pendulum swing to economic nationalism, saying the worst thing we could do is "close off the US market to China."[77] So after telling us for sixteen pages how globalization hasn't liberalized China, that free trade has actually strengthened Chinese authoritarianism mainly because we didn't pursue the policy with libertarian purity, our response shouldn't be to limit free trade with China or adopt a national economic policy but to pursue free trade the *right way*, calling on "US policy makers to restore their faith in the free enterprise system . . . and worry less about the Middle Kingdom."[78] A better example in the faith of market fundamentalism in the face of criticism could not be found.

Finally, with all the proof that big tech has been working with the CCP, that they pose a threat to our basic liberties, that they are committed to a utopian transhumanism, libertarians continue to defend high-tech.[79] Rachel Bovard summarizes well the libertarian position: "Any action by the government against tech companies even modifying laws that govern them—would be antithetical to the principle of small government and to liberty itself."[80] So they must be opposed.

FINAL WARNING: A NEW KIND OF CORPORATE SOCIALISM

Bovard observes that these pro-high-tech libertarians have narrowed down the concept of freedom "to sidestep a growing threat from mega-corporate power that rivals—and in some cases, arguably supersedes—that of the government . . . in a style of libertarianism so reductive that it seamlessly evolves into a corporatism that flips the American experiment on its head."[81] Now, instead of living under a constitutional republic, we live under a new oligarchy supported by libertarians on the left (freedom left 2) and on the right (freedom right 2), where "priority is given to the rights and liberties of corporate America to set the terms for how we, as a free people, will live together—over and above free expressions, preferences, and independent choices exercised by Americans themselves, for whom this entire system was in fact built."[82] Instead, we have the bipartisan ruling plutocratic oligarchs, inspired by their libertarian techno-utopians views, telling us that they will dictate what we believe and how we should act.[83]

While libertarians like to tell us they oppose collectivism, big government, both left-leaning libertarians (freedom right 2) and right-leaning libertarians (freedom right 3) have actually sold us a different kind of collectivism, a kind of corporate socialism, a new oligarchy. In the words of Joel Kotkin, this is neofeudalism: the bipartisan ruling class is in control and everyone else is a serf. Or, in the words of Michael Rectenwald, it's the "Google Archipelago," a new kind of world incorporation, in which monopolistic corporations take the place of governments, a digital global governance that will eventually include every resident on the earth.[84]

In the end, through a fantasy of free trade and technological utopianism we have been sold the lie of elite corporate superiority and everyone else's inferiority. It's a Galt's Gulch fiction that threatens the sovereignty of our constitutional republic and the nature of the human race. And we have, in part, our uniparty libertarians to thank for it.

IN SUM

- We have seen that the NSCAI report warns the United States is falling behind China in AI, and the consequences could be dire. It calls for more government investment, more high-tech immigration, and a whole nation effort to win the AI war.

- It is hard not to be cynical at the call for more government money and immigration when high-tech companies already have too much power and control over the American population and have helped China grow into the superpower it is today.

- Since ruling elites were committed to libertarianism, they pursued globalization, believing it would democratize China and in the process benefit America's economic growth. Many libertarian Christians have shared these beliefs, and so have high-tech Californians who have combined libertarianism and techno-utopianism into a set of beliefs called the "California Ideology."

- As China has become more authoritarian, America's working and middle class have suffered, and China is now our number one global threat.

- Over the past thirty years, critics have been raising alarms about the downsides of globalization for American workers, how it has empowered the China crisis, and how it is leading to a transhumanism and posthuman future.

- These warnings have been rejected by radical libertarians, and they have doubled down on their singular commitment to liberty, free trade, globalization, and the optimism of high-tech genetic engineering and a brighter future for the human race.

- Ultimately, this narrow view of liberty and free trade has opened the door to the monopolistic high-tech corporations, who, along with weak governments, rig the system in their favor, moving us in the direction of a new type of oligarchy, often called "neo-feudalism," "world incorporation," the "Google Archipelago," or "the Great Reset."

9

ORDER RIGHT 2

POISON PILL CONSERVATIVES

"**Globalization**," "The Great Reset," "techno-utopians," and a digital "Google Archipelago" are all terms from chapter eight that I realize sound so con-spiratorial, almost crazy, like the "smoking man" or the "deep state" is behind it all. And there are some on the left who accuse the Right, even the most moderate of conservatives, of being crazy, angry, afraid, looking for a scapegoat and coming up with the most wing-nut conspiracy theories. So when someone on the right points out what the elites are really up to, how they are using concepts like critical race theory to divide people, or that the globalists are using open borders for their own advantage, someone like journalist David Neiwert, who studies and writes about right-wing extremist groups, throws every conservative into the same basket of conspiracy nuts, of having been "red pilled," not only losing touch with reality but posing a threat to our democracy.[1]

Yet, people are now catching on to these ruling elite tactics, seeing clearly how politicians and CEOs are colluding to get their way, control the population, and increase their corporatocracy. While there may be no conspiracies, there are also no coincidences either, and when enough Americans start to connect the dots, they begin to wake up from their trusting slumber.[2] In fact, large-scale political awakenings (what we might call populism) happen when enough people start connecting these dots, begin to realize that they are not being told the truth—that something deeper is going on— and that the system is rigged. To explain this rigging they come up with a theory of conspiracy. See a crime, come up with a theory, find the facts, and indict the guilty. It's just criminology 101.[3] Once they see who is guilty, they want to hold them responsible. And when this happens, it can be quite a shock for the ruling elites, especially if they are in the Republican party. One Republican who found out the hard way is Governor Kristi Noem.

As one of a few governors that never locked down her state during the pandemic, Noem had become a rising star in the Republican Party, on everyone's short list for potential Republican presidential nominees for 2024. In late March 2020, just two weeks after Governor Noem tweeted her support for House Bill 1271, a law that would outlaw transgender women (biological men) participating in any women's sport in South Dakota, she shocked her constituency by vetoing it, creating a national firestorm. To quell her critics, she appeared on *Tucker Carlson Tonight* to make her case.[4] With the emotion of the day clearly visible in her eyes, she stressed her commitment to protecting women's sports but felt this bill would invite legal challenges from the NCAA, litigation she didn't think they could win. Carlson pushed back: "This is thousands of years of common sense and tradition," he said. "Girls play girls' sports. Boys play boys' sports. If you care so much about the issue, why not instead say, 'Bring it on, NCAA, I'm a national figure, go ahead and try us, I will fight you in the court of public opinion and defend principle.' Why not just do that?" Carlson challenged Noem. When she pushed back, saying, "Tucker, you're preaching my sermon. That's just what I did today," he immediately shot back, "you vetoed the bill. . . . You caved to the NCAA."

Frustrated that Tucker wasn't buying her excuse, she did what the Left likes to do—shame her critics with the charge of conspiracy theorist. She claimed she would not be "bullied by right-wing cancel culture." But trying to knock him off the scent of the trail wasn't going to work this time. She couldn't get away with it. People had connected the dots.

Rod Dreher, one of the most-read conservative bloggers, connected the dots. "These Republican politicians like Noem have to learn there will be a price to be paid if they side with Big Business over their voters," wrote Dreher. Like a detective coming up with a theory at the crime scene, you can sense his aha moment: "Whaddaya know," says Dreher, "it turns out that one of Governor Noem's closest political associates is also the state's most powerful lobbyist for the Chamber of Commerce." But Dreher goes on. As he connects the dots, the coincidences, he realizes it is more than just Republican big business, represented by the South Dakota Chamber of Commerce, that she is working with. Included in the collusion is "Amazon, the censorious Big Tech behemoth," which threated to pull its plan to build a fulfilment center in Sioux Falls, the board of regents representing a big university, and left-wing advocacy groups, many representing big pharma and big finance.[5]

For Dreher, we are witnessing a full-court press by our ruling elite to normalize transgenderism and convince more and more of our young people to embrace their gender dysphoria. In his essay "The Queering of Young America," Dreher writes that "the sky really is falling. . . . We are getting much closer to the time I wrote about in *The Benedict Option*, when faithful Christians and others who dissent from the new ideology are going to have to make decisions about whether or not they can continue working in their particular jobs . . . you should know that time is running out."[6] For if you object to what is going on, you will be regarded "as no better than a Klansman if you hold to the traditional teachings, not only about homo-sexuality, but transgenderism." Even "radical feminists," contends Dreher, "who deny that male-to-female transgenders are women will be held by the same contempt in the law as a fundamentalist preacher."[7]

For Dreher, and here he is quoting Southern Baptist ethicist Andrew Walker, we are living through a "metaphysical revolution," "the de-conversion of the West," "the final displacement of a Christian account of the universe by a wholly secularized one." As Walker says, "the self is the sole lens of reference for all moral guidance, making the tenets of natural law and divine revelation moot, mere objects of religious fascination rather than universal appreciation." It is nothing less, says Walker, than "an assault on the Christian imagination," replacing it with an entirely different imagination, one where biological binary sex is no longer important. The results are nothing short of "dire and calamitous."[8]

Many thought that Noem understood this. But it appears she was just giving lip service to conservative social policy, leaving female student athletes in her state to ask how she could prioritize a tiny slice of the population over the vast majority of the population, and in the process ignore, in fact override, important creational norms, the biological binary of men and women woven into the very creational order.[9] In this sense Noem, like so many on the left and an increasing number of libertarians on the right, is just going along with the drift of culture, one being pushed and funded by our ruling elites. In the case of Noem, these ruling elites, many of them Republicans, helped her conspire to overthrow HR 1217, a bill that would have put an end to the transgender and transhuman revolution that is being foisted on South Dakota, even though a majority of the people don't want it.[10] But as the local Republican state legislators found out, in this case the conspiracy against creational norms was just too powerful. Citizens in South Dakota are left wondering if they will ever be able to stop it.

But what can be done? It is this question more than anything that leads to the debates and the conflicts on the right.

THE BENEDICT OPTION

In his book *The New Right*, Michael Malice says that the Right strongly agrees on what has gone wrong and who is to blame—radical progressivism and the overthrow of constitutional republicanism. But while they agree on what the problem is and share a common enemy, the Right, says Malice, differ over what to do about it, both in the present and the future, differing over what comes after the collapse. Should conservatives fight to save America, or should they let it collapse, even giving it a shove if necessary? And once it collapses, what comes next? For Malice it is how a person answers the "what's next" question that determines the difference on the right, and it also determines where one falls within in the order right quadrant.

Dreher is a good example of the order right 2 position. Few writers can describe the conservative declension narrative more pointedly or vividly than this gifted storyteller. Because he describes the crisis so well, he has garnered a huge following in conservative and evangelical circles. Yet as much as Dreher agrees with the Right on who is to blame for our nation's current predicament, unlike most of the conservative movement he doesn't think politics is much of solution. Rather than waste our time trying to turn things around, we need to face its inevitable collapse, prepare for the suffering that is surely to come our way, and wait out the dark ages.

In his two bestselling books *The Benedict Option* and *Live Not by Lies*, Dreher describes this dark age as Christians living in a post-Christian world and Americans living under a new soft totalitarianism, respectively. "Christians who hold to biblical teaching about sex and marriage have the same status in culture, and increasingly in law, as racists," he writes, and combined with the surveillance state (another major theme of his books and blog), Christians face a future of bullying, intimidation, lost jobs, and suffering, a future that is "inevitable."[11] But, rather than waste a lot of time fighting a fight we can't and won't win, we need to retreat from the present hostile culture, spend our time building parallel institutions that can sustain and strengthen us, and then, when the time is right, rebuild society.

Despite the success of his books and his blog, Dreher receives a lot of pushback. He is open about this criticism and often shares it with his readers, and his answers go a long way toward explaining why he is in the order right 2 position. Generally, pushback, some friendly and some hostile, comes in two areas: how Christians should respond to the dark ages, and what his plan for the future looks like.

While many critics might agree with his declension analysis, they often call him out for being too pessimistic and without hope.[12] When Dreher concludes "that the best way to fight the flood is to . . . stop fighting the flood," critics demur.[13] We need to keep fighting the flood; retreat is not an option, they say. "Some people have expressed to me," Dreher confesses on his blog, "publicly and privately, frustration with both *The Benedict Option* and *Live Not by Lies,* saying that both are counsels of defeat."[14]

In response, Dreher points to the experience of Christians in the old Soviet Union in the twentieth century. Once they realized that the Communist Party couldn't be stopped, they concluded that to fight it would have been a waste of time. Instead, they faced reality and got to work building communities of faith, support structures to withstand the persecution, train a future generation of leaders, wait out the regime, and be ready to rebuild the larger society when the time was right. "In a similar way, in these two books of mine," Dreher tells his readers,

I am trying to prepare the small-o orthodox churches, families, and individuals to live in a world of intensifying adversity for people who believe the things traditional Christians do. . . . *The Benedict Option* is not focused much on persecution, but rather on the plain fact that we live in a world in which traditional Christianity is fast fading from our culture, in the same way that Roman paganism dissolved in the fourth century.[15]

Moreover, he explains, *Live Not by Lies* is very much focused on persecution, and "there is nothing in it that directs people not to fight politically and otherwise to protect our religious liberties, and so forth." That means, he concludes, "we are facing something like the Red Army, with regard to the power of invasive technologies and the ideological capture of elite institutions by zealots who have no interest in tolerating those who disagree." These are "forces that cannot be stopped by politics alone." While Dreher believes "that ultimately they will be turned back," "in the short term and in the near long term, the orthodox Christians, as well as Orthodox Jews, traditional Muslims, and other religious and social conservatives, are going to have to develop the skills to live under occupation, so to speak."[16]

So on the one hand Dreher has a positive message for Christians—build alternative communities to prepare them to suffer, and build parallel institutions to train them for leadership when the time is right. But on the other hand, under present circumstances, he doesn't seem to think much can be done to change the trajectory of the present regime.

But even Dreher questions his own pessimism. "I write angry, despairing blog posts," he says.

I don't know what else I can do. I'm feeling quite powerless and futile. I'm feeling about the country the way many of my Catholic friends are feeling about their Church: like the decadence is so deep, and the leadership class so rotten, that there's nothing to do but burrow in and build shelters for my family and my friends, so we can withstand the coming collapse, and preserve enough of what's good to seed the rebirth.[17]

Dreher admits, "This despair feels wrong. I'm a Christian; I'm supposed to hope. And I do have hope, in that I believe God will not abandon us. But we as a people have abandoned Him, that much is certain. And hope that's not based on a realistic assessment of where we are is Pollyanna optimism."[18]

DREHER'S RADICAL POLITICS

Dreher's feeling of despair, paired with his call for a strategic retreat, caught the attention of most of the evangelical critics of *The Benedict Option*. Yet Dreher admits he was surprised by this reaction; what is so controversial about telling evangelicals that they have lost the cultural battle and the best way to respond is building strong Christian communities?[19] And moreover, while so many critics, especially evangelicals, focused on his pessimism and his "Christ against culture" response to our present dark ages, what really surprised him is that they completely missed the most controversial part of his thesis—that America is post-Christian and that the erosion of the Christian West began well before the founding of America, and therefore there is no going back, no golden age to retrieve.

To clarify what he means by this, Dreher went on *The Briefing*, the daily podcast of Southern Baptist Al Mohler, and argued that "my argument in the book is this [post-Christian reality] has been going on for centuries. We've been building this increasing secularization for centuries, and we're just now living out the fruits of things that happened in this culture in the Enlightenment."[20] And at the heart of the Enlightenment, Dreher told Mohler, is the view that in America "the purpose of government is to liberate the autonomous individual," and this faulty view, erroneously embedded in American founding documents, like a poison pill, has now come to fruition.

Evangelicals spent much of their time discussing his strategy for the church's survival and influence and barely noticed his radical proposition— that the American founding was thoroughly modern, a product of the Enlightenment, and far from calling America back to it, we need to abandon it and move on. "I have been living in a weird neutral space," comments Dreher, "between those [conservatives] who want to defend liberal democracy, and those who have no faith in it anymore."[21] But as much as Dreher appreciates aspects of our liberal democracy, he finds it hard to defend, particularly since it is mostly to blame for the predicament we find ourselves in.

Here we see clearly one of the telltale signs of the order right 2 position that most evangelical critics completely missed. To understand this key piece of Dreher's narrative, we need to understand exactly what he means. When he is suggesting that our founding is part of the problem, Dreher is following the thinking of Notre Dame professor Patrick Deneen, the political philosopher who best articulates the order right 2 position.

THE POISON PILL THEORY

In *Why Liberalism Failed*, one of the most discussed books in 2017, hailed as a modern classic by thinkers and journalists on the right and left, Deneen spells out his provocative argument.[22] Deneen contends,

> Liberalism has failed—not because it fell short, but because it was true to itself. It has failed because it has succeeded. As liberalism has "become more fully itself," as its inner logic has become more evident and its self-contradictions manifest, it has generated pathologies that are at once deformations of its claims yet realizations of liberal ideology. [23]

This is what has become known as the "poison pill" or "seeds of own destruction" thesis.

Laying out a genealogy that has become increasingly popular among postliberal Catholic theologians, political philosophers, and many evangelicals, Deneen contends that

> a political philosophy conceived some 500 years ago, and put into effect at the birth of the United States nearly 250 years later, was a wager that political society could be grounded on a different footing. It conceived humans as rights-bearing individuals who could fashion and pursue for themselves their own version of the good life.[24]

The best way to promote this good life, according to our founders, was "by a limited government devoted to 'securing rights,' along with a free-market economic system that gave space for individual initiative and ambition."[25]

But for Deneen, the poison pill leading to the present crisis was saying that the rights of individuals in the American founding were connected *not* to "nature's God" but rather to radical individualism. According to him, "to call for the cures of liberalism's ills by applying more liberal measures is tantamount to throwing gas on a raging fire. It will only deepen our political, social, and economic, and moral crisis."[26] Moreover, what we are in the middle of may be "an increasingly systemic failure, due to the bankruptcy of its underlying political philosophy, of the political system we have largely taken for granted. The fabric of beliefs that gave rise to the nearly 250-year

American constitutional experiment may be nearing an end."[27] What we need "is liberation from liberalism itself."[28]

Ironically, Deneen's searing critique of American liberalism, whether championed by classical liberals or progressive liberals (for Deneen they are the same, part of the same uniparty in Washington) is identical to the freedom left 2 position, which sees the Constitution and the founding as secular, unsupported by natural law or religion. But while freedom left 2 celebrates this secularism, Deneen excoriates it. In the end they both see this secularism as the only accurate description of America. Moreover, while progressive evangelicals like Randall Balmer affirm the godless constitution as protecting religious liberty, Deneen suggests, "if the American [secular liberal] proposition is not only hostile to Christianity but in fact the product of its denial," then Christians cannot support it.[29] Christians, then, if they are going to be faithful and help turn things around in this country, are left with only one option.

"I increasingly fear," concludes Deneen, "that Americans will have to break with America, and seek to re-found the nation on better truth." For Deneen, these better truths must be found "explicitly in departure from the philosophic principles that animated its liberal founding . . . to build a new civilization worthy of preservation."[30] In other words, the plan for renewal cannot include a return to a golden age, a return to the principles of the founding, because these principles have been corrupted from the start. In fact, it is these founding principles contaminated by liberalism that have engendered the mess we are presently in. Rather, the way forward must be breaking from liberalism and creating something entirely new; what that is, however, he never really says.

EVANGELICALS AND THE POISON PILL THEORY OF AMERICA

If evangelicals by and large missed the radicalism of the poison pill in Dreher, they didn't miss it with Deneen, and many resonated with his critique of liberalism. Two of the most well-known evangelicals who appreciated Deneen's argument are Al Mohler and David Koyzis. When Deneen appeared on the *Daily Briefing* podcast, Mohler, the host, expressed multiple times during the discussion his appreciation for Deneen's book, going out of his way to show his agreement with Deneen's thesis that liberalism contained the seeds of its own destruction, and that its failure, which we are living through now, was inevitable.[31] Consider this summarizing statement by Mohler:

> We have two supposedly different branches of this liberalism, a classic liberalism now associated with American conservatives and a progressive liberalism now associated with American political liberals. You're [Deneen] putting an ax to the base of the tree that holds them both, at least in arguing that we . . . can now see that collapse of that great liberal experiment.[32]

Similarly, political scientist David Koyzis, who recently updated his highly successful book *Political Visions and Illusions*, decided to include Deneen's argument in his new edition, showing how liberalism's commitment to individualism contributes to its idolatry and eventually its demise.[33] And while most evangelicals missed Dreher's radical reliance on the poison pill theory of liberalism, Koyzis, a trained political philosopher, caught it.[34]

ONCE UPON A TIME

So here we have the once-upon-a-time narrative of order right 2. America had no golden era. The founding principles had been corrupted by Enlightenment rationalism, a movement that preceded America by a century. That means that if a golden age existed, it existed well before America was founded; in fact well before the modern era began, prior to the Protestant Reformation and the Enlightenment it spawned. Our present discontents, then, stem from the culmination of five hundred years of Enlightenment liberalism now coming to full fruition. "The past can instruct but there can be no return and no 'restoration,'" writes Deneen.[35] We are reaping what we sowed, and this whirlwind can't be stopped by political activity; it is much deeper, more profound, and most likely unstoppable.

Therefore, the only logical response, the only wise plan for renewal is to retreat from the corrosive effects of modernity, build strong families and institutions to help us through the inevitable suffering, patiently endure until the system collapses, and then help American rebuild itself again, this time on a grounding not contaminated by liberalism. While Deneen takes pains to say he is not calling for violent revolution, he *is* calling for a new system, a radically new reality that breaks cleanly and totally from modernity and thus has no intention of going back to the founders' principles.

"A better course," he posits, "will consist in smaller, local forms of resistance: practices more than theories, the building of resilient new cultures against the anticulture of liberalism." This will entail the "cultivation of cultures of community, care, self-sacrifice, and small-scale democracy—a better practice might arise, and from it, ultimately, perhaps a better theory."[36]

That, in a nutshell, is the order right 2 position. By saying that America has been compromised by modernity, it is really saying that America is bad and that something entirely new is needed. Understanding this syllogism will help us see how a conservative position ends up sounding so much like the once-upon-a-time narrative of many on the progressive left and at the same time sounds different from the traditional conservative position, which wants to defend America's founding. And it will help us comprehend how it can lead to pessimism, quietism, and even extremism, whether that is the intention of this position or not. To grasp this reality, we must dig deeper.

WHAT REALLY SEPARATES CONSERVATIVES

While many thought Deneen's thesis was new and insightful, providing an aha moment, it actually wasn't new at all. In fact, I first encountered the poison pill thesis at Georgetown in the writings of Leo Strauss, who had been talking and writing about it seventy years ago.[37]

Strauss (1899–1973), who was Jewish, had fled Nazi Germany in 1932, settled in the United States in 1937, and was hired by the University of Chicago in 1949 to teach classics, becoming one of the most influential conservative political theorists in the country.[38] According to Deneen, Strauss "was animated by one overarching question: how could fascism have happened."[39] To find the answer, says Deneen, Strauss dug deep into the history of Western political thought, claiming he found the answer in the modern rejection of ancient political philosophy and a new attempt to ground the moral and political life on a radically different foundation, not the foundation of what is naturally right or just and the ideal city, but instead on the selfish interests of humans and their individual rights, a rejection of the idea of the *good* and an affirmation of the lonely self.[40]

In other words, Strauss contended there was a rupture between the ancients and the moderns who rejected the natural-law grounding and wisdom of the ancients. For Strauss this rupture was a betrayal of the West and eventually led to totalitarianism in the form of fascism and communism. Once he spotted this rupture between the ancients and the moderns (caused by Machiavelli and followed by Hobbes and Locke), he then divided the modern period into three distinct periods called "the three waves of modernity."

In the first wave, ushered in by Machiavelli, modern political philosophy rejects the ancients' desire to "imagine republics and principalities," rejects any standard or foundation found in the "ideal city" and instead bases politics in the corrupted nature of humans, self-interest, and the defense of human rights. This modern view shaped the founding of America and can, claims Strauss, be found in the Declaration of Independence and the Constitution.[41]

The second wave can be found in Rousseau, who rejected the idea found both in the ancients and the first-wave moderns that humans had a fixed nature, whether noble or base, and instead thought that human nature could be changed. Humans were shaped by history, and history was moving in a direction where humans would be free, not by claiming their rights but by breaking free of the state and religion and tradition, giving up their rights, and finding their meaning and happiness in the "general will." For Strauss, the political fruit of this thinking is communism and progressivism.[42]

Strauss's third wave was summarized by Deneen as, "an intensification of Rousseau's claims against a human nature, one that insisted we are less the products of 'history' than our own self-fashioning." This wave is best articulated by Friedrich Nietzsche and furthered by many existentialists and eventually postmodernists.[43]

For our purposes, Strauss's second wave would fit best in our freedom left 2 (built on an unencumbered self, a strong administrative welfare state and the bracketing out of religion) and his third wave would fit in our freedom left 3, eventually engendering order left 3 or utopian socialism. Within the conservative movement there is very little controversy over the second and third waves, and conservatives have made use of them over the years to condemn all forms of progressivism.

The big question for us, a question at the heart of the controversy in conservatism, is where to place the first wave on the schematic. If the second and third waves line up with freedom left 2 and 3, as I contend they do, it would seem logical to put the first wave in freedom left 1, inside what I will describe in part three as the new vital center. But scholars like Deneen argue that trying to restore the vital center is actually doubling down on the first wave of modernity, which will make matters worse. That is, if the first wave is actually part of the second wave, or at least only slightly different, it would really share the freedom left 2 position. Thus, if this is true, all three waves are bad, all three have contributed to the rupture, and all three should be resisted, which is exactly what poison-pill conservatives do.

But not so fast. Not all conservatives read Strauss the way poison-pill conservatives do. It is true that Strauss believed modernism was bad. And it is true that he believed America was founded after the modern period began and thus was modern. Thus Strauss's syllogism goes like this:

1. Modernity is bad.

2. The American system is modern.

3. Therefore, the American system is bad.

But did Strauss really believe that America is bad, as Deneen concludes?

Here is where it gets interesting. Because he escaped fascism in Germany in the 1930s and America adopted him, some believe Strauss couldn't bring himself to say that America was *that* bad.[44] Thus, University of Notre Dame professors Catherine Zuckert and Michael Zuckert contend some scholars see Strauss's syllogism this way:

1. Modernity is bad.

2. America is modern.

3. America is good.

Obviously, this seems contradictory. If America is modern and modern is bad, how can America still be good? According to the Zuckerts, while Strauss contended that America is modern and wasn't as good as the ancients, he wasn't willing to say America was entirely bad, particularly in light of the fascism and communism of the twentieth century. While America was modern, he felt that it still retained enough of classical influence (natural rights) that it was better than the alternatives in modernity: progressive liberalism and postmodernism, which end in totalitarianism and fascism.

This is how many of his students heard and read him: appreciating America and in fact defending it and the foundation it was built on. And here we see the genus of the division within the conservative movement.

It is why Dreher mentioned that he feels caught between those on the right who defend America and those who have given up on it. Dreher and Deneen are, in fact, standing between two different interpretations of the Straussian syllogism. While I have placed the spot on which they both stand in the number 2 position, they lean away from the new vital center, because, ultimately, Dreher and Deneen express the Straussian syllogism this way:

1. America is modern (founded and grounded in the first wave of liberalism).

2. Modernity (all three waves of liberalism) is bad.

3. America is terminally ill (and not able to be saved in its present form).

Thus, for scholars like Deneen and Dreher, to defend America as good, the way order right 1 conservatives do, is a fool's errand, a futile doubling down on the same poison pill (containing all three waves of modernity), making our situation worse not better. And since all three waves are bad there is only one choice: break from the modern and break from America. Or, as we saw earlier, "Americans will have to break with America," concludes Deneen, "and seek to re-found the nation on better truth."[45]

Here we see the huge gap that has opened up on the right, between those in order right 1, who want to defend and save America, and those in the more extreme order right 3, some who hear this call to "break with America" as a call to illiberalism at best and violent revolution at worst.[46]

CONSERVATIVE PUSH BACK

While Deneen's poison-pill thesis has been celebrated by many religious conservatives, including evangelicals like Mohler and Koyzis, it has been rejected by a number of conservatives (who stand in the order right 1 position) who want to defend the American project.[47]

For Robert Reilly, a good representative of the order right 1 position, the major problem with poison-pill conservatives is that they are wrong about the Straussian syllogism. Since they contend all three waves are modern, they have to conclude that America is modern and thus bad. It also means that there is no difference between the classical liberalism of conservatism and progressive liberalism of the Left. But for Reilly this is wrong and is built on a faulty understanding of the first wave of modernity, which doesn't belong on the modern side of the rupture but rather on the ancient side and is thus worth defending.[48]

For Reilly, who represents the "West Coast Straussian" camp, a group of thinkers that *don't* believe America was founded on the wrong side of the rupture and who enthusiastically defend America's founding, the telltale sign that someone is following the poison pill theory is their negative view of John Locke—one that holds that Locke built on the foundation of Machiavelli, whose thought is the reason America has been compromised since the start.[49] In fact, one could say that Locke is the poison pill. This view of Locke is what I call the "bad-Locke view." In the bad-Locke view, since Locke was modern and since the founders built on his thought, America too is modern and thus bad. West Coast Straussians like Reilly disagree. They make the case that while America is indeed Lockean, Locke stood in continuity with the ancients, and thus American liberalism was actually in continuity with the ancients and thus is *good*.[50]

Commenting on Deneen's *Why Liberalism Failed*, Reilly says that for Deneen to pull off his view of America (that it was founded in the first wave of modernity), he has to first misinterpret Locke and then misquote James Madison, making them out to be first- and second-wave modernist thinkers who support an unencumbered self, the procedural republic, the bracketing off of religion, and the celebration of moral diversity.[51] Thus Locke and Madison are ultimately responsible for all the bad in America today. For Reilly this is an outrageous claim, and one not backed up by historical documents. This reading of Locke and Madison, argues Reilly, highly influenced by a misinterpretation of Strauss, contends that

1. Hobbes and Locke are the same.

2. The American founding is Lockean.

3. Therefore, the American founding is Hobbesian.[52]

Thus Madison and Jefferson are closet Hobbesians, which Reilly believes is flatly wrong. And if Deneen gets this genealogy wrong, as Reilly posits he does, then it is easy to see why Deneen misinterprets the Declaration of Independence and the Constitution, doing so in light of the three waves of modernity. Furthermore, with this view of liberalism, it isn't hard to see why Deneen thinks America is doomed.

Reilly has pinpointed the bad-Locke theory, a view of Locke that has been ascendant in Straussian circles for decades. In some ways, how one sees Locke is a litmus test for how one sees Strauss and his views on the founding. If one adopts the bad-Locke view, that is, his thinking is in continuity with Hobbes and not the classical tradition, it is a short step to repudiating the founding and calling for the end of America as we know it. Ironically, while freedom left 2 embraces the bad-Locke view as the true view of America's founding, poison-pill conservatives agree with them, though they do so to repudiate this corrosive liberalism.

Here we get to the crux of the matter for thinkers like Reilly. If Deneen's *description* of our present discontent falls apart, that is, his belief that the three waves of modernity have corrupted our nation, then so does his *prescription*, that we need to create an entirely new system that transcends American liberalism and the founding. He is taking us down the wrong road. Even more dire, with his faulty description and prescription he has done something worse: he "corrupts our youth." In getting Locke, Madison, and the founding wrong (just like freedom left 2 does), according to Reilly, a poison-pill conservativism "demoralizes our youth and disarms us in the face of our enemies, who are further empowered by their disavowal of the founding. . . . Students feel they no longer have a country they can love and should wish to serve."[53] According to Reilly this is madness and "a suicidal blunder to denigrate the founding in this way." And it leads to, sadly, an entire generation who "automatically exclude themselves from the public arena by conceding it to their opponents, thereby accelerating the very decline they decry."[54] And, although Reilly doesn't say it, the poison-pill theory may not just lead to resignation but, for those who see that we have no choice, to violence.

Poison-Pill Conservatives Respond

As one can imagine, Deneen rejects the view that he and others like Dreher are corrupting the youth.[55] He is doing no such thing. Rather, what he wants is young people to be honest about the corrupting influences of liberalism (all three waves) in our founding and move beyond it; only then can we fix America. In a long response to Reilly, he defends his Lockean view of the founding, rejecting the West Coast Straussian view as nothing but revisionism. For Deneen, Strauss is perfectly clear—America was built on Locke, is thus modern, and even if it had some redeeming features at the start, it is well past this time now. Only something entirely new, something radical, something built on premodern sources, will save our country. In the end it is disagreements on the Straussian syllogism and how one views America that lead to the split in conservative circles.

CUI BONO?

In Dreher's blog post "Our War of Religion," he mentions how woke indoctrination is taking place at an elite prep school in Los Angeles and how the parents resent that their children are being told that "America is a bad country."[56] While Dreher disapproves of this woke message, I wonder, in light of how he and Deneen fill out the Straussian syllogism, how he is able to disagree with the progressive message that America is evil. After all, he comes to the same conclusion. Poison-pill conservatives and progressives agree on the same thing: America is bad. And I wonder how these parents would respond to poison-pill conservatives if they knew these conservatives' views on America. I am not sure they would agree.

These parents of prep-school children, undoubtedly both Republicans and Democrats, seem to know intuitively that something is *not* right with the message that America is bad. For them, in spite of its weaknesses, America *is* still good. And while they are not political philosophers, may know nothing of the debate over Locke and even less about the Straussian syllogism, they intuitively know, it seems, that America is not racist and is not all bad. They may not realize, like the Midwest populists that are furious at Governor Noem, that the ruling elites are taking over our country, are redefining it as something bad, and are silencing anyone who dissents. But these same Americans would agree, if they knew what the poison-pill conservatives were really saying, that this view is indeed demoralizing and corrupting our youth. In fact, they might fear it corrupts their own children, weakening their love for America and their willingness to defend it.

People are waking up, and the popular uprising is happening. People are on to the ruling elite, the collusion of woke corporations with big government, and their attempt to control the population, to steal their freedom and their right to assembly. Call it whatever you want—collusion, conspiracy, or just the alignment of the ruling elites behind their oligarchic narrative and aspirations, but it is the same thing. There are no coincidences. And people are angry, losing their patience.

While the poison-pill conservatives recognize this anger, they are careful not to call for violence to overcome the stranglehold these new overlords have over the population, instead arguing for peaceful methods. But these same peaceful methods are not always shared by some in the order right 3 camp, a group that, unlike Dreher, know exactly what needs to be done, and have, at times, not hesitated to call for a right-wing counter-takeover of the system, using the same illiberal tactics of the Left, if necessary.

It is to that narrative we now turn.

IN SUM

- People on the right are starting to connect the dots, seeing the alignment of the ruling elites, composed of politicians and woke capital on both sides of the political aisle.

- While those on the right agree on the problem and who is to blame (the loss of our constitutional republic and the radical progressive elites), they differ substantially over what is to be done and what is next. The "what is next" question divides those on the right and separates them into the three positions in the order right quadrant.

- Rod Dreher and Patrick Deneen, as examples of the order right 2 position, contend that America has been compromised from the start by the poison pill of liberalism, and the more liberal we become the worse off we get.

- The once-upon-a-time narrative for order right 2 contends there was no golden age, America is reaping what it sowed from the beginning, and the plan for renewal can't include a return to the founding. Instead, we must start over, re-found our nation, creating something entirely new.

- Some conservatives push back, saying this poison pill is based on a faulty reading of the founding, particularly an erroneous interpretation of John Locke. Because of this error, they believe America is bad. By concluding this they are demoralizing and corrupting our youth.

- As more and more people reject this view of America as bad and gain the courage to resist the ruling elites who want to discredit America so they can turn it into something different, a popular uprising is in the works; the only question is whether it will be peaceful or not.

10

ORDER RIGHT 3

THE ILLIBERAL NEW RIGHT

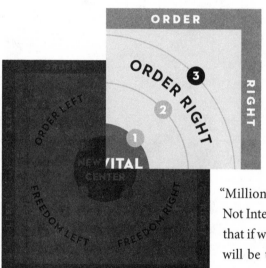

NO SOONER HAD THE VIDEO gone viral on social media of the Polish Canadian pastor pushing police officers out of his church, than the *New York Times* published "Millions of White Evangelicals Do Not Intend to Get Vaccinated," arguing that if we don't reach herd immunity, it will be the fault of evangelical Christians. According to Elizabeth Dias and Ruth Graham, the vaccine hesitancy of evangelicals is "rooted in a mix of religious faith and a longstanding wariness of mainstream science, and is fueled by broader cultural distrust of institution and gravitation to online conspiracy theories."[1]

For many on the right, the article is really saying that evangelicalism is anti-science, ignorant, racist, and a conspiratorial cult, and when it says they must be given "information that they can understand from people they trust," it really means information from experts that the *New York Times* approves.[2] Obviously, with an experimental vaccine, one that doesn't have a long track record to assess, common sense dictates caution. Yet instead of understanding this hesitancy, instead of answering some straightforward questions, some accuse evangelicals of conspiratorial thinking.[3] And in the face of this vaccine skepticism, the *New York Times* article warns that "a public education campaign alone may not be enough,"[4] And this could include vaccine passports administered by big business, a door-to-door pressure campaign, or social media cancellation for those who don't comply.[5] No wonder paranoia is growing. Many evangelicals see the elites colluding against them, and when they push back, they get blamed for being the crazy ones. But by the time the truth comes out, contend many evangelicals on the right, it is too late—the media has already moved on, looking for the next story to advance their narrative.[6]

Given this situation, it is easy to see why for those on the right the time for civil dialogue and winning rational arguments is over. Many on the right believe the American republic is gone, dead, buried.[7] As Michael Malice said, the real differences now (in the order right quadrant) are not over the diagnosis but over the prescription, debates over *what's next*. Conservatives like Rod Dreher and Patrick Deneen believe that the only response to the end of the republic and the silencing of people on the right is to build strong communities of faith, weather the suffering that is imminent, wait for this new regime to collapse, and then work to rebuild it. But those in order right 3 are not interested in such a passive approach to politics. They have lost patience. They don't want to retreat, they want to fight. They don't want to merely build their own communities, but they want to take back the entire country. The time for talking, winning arguments, and politics as usual is over.

Those in the order right 3 position, the New Right, believe the complete takeover of our country by the bipartisan ruling elites and their dystopian methods of control, the total shutdown of speech, leaves them with little choice: since they have been boxed into a corner, they have to take America back by illiberal means if necessary.[8] As Malice says, the New Right has arrived at a place where there are only two choices: either secede and form two countries or just seize power through a civil war or some illiberal takeover, and then impose a new order on the country, a new order guided by a standard other than progressive liberalism. How did the Right, once the bastion of law and order, once the party that decried the Left's illiberal ways, get to this point? That is the story of order right 3. We can place blame on those who fall in this position, but blame also stems from how the ruling elite have worked hard to shut down free speech.[9] If you only tell your political opponents to sit down and shut up, don't be surprised if they rebel, sometimes violently.

THE GENEALOGY OF ORDER RIGHT 3

I'm old enough to remember that in the 1990s *First Things* magazine held a symposium for a group of conservatives, including some evangelicals like Prison Fellowship's Chuck Colson, who were so alarmed by the Supreme Court and its rulings, particularly in the areas of abortion, marriage, and gender, that they thought the only option might be civil disobedience. At the time this call for civil disobedience for some conservatives was so scandalous, antidemocratic, and dangerous that a few members of the *First Things* advisory board resigned in protest, believing the symposium had gone too far by proposing things that are out of bounds for conservatives.[10]

Fast forward thirty years and calls for civil disobedience seem almost quaint, especially after a summer of violent street protests. Things have gotten so bad that when those on the far right propose civil disobedience or even a military takeover, hardly anyone on the right bats an eye. And as the Right pushes back, the ruling elites push back even harder. As this continues to happen, the "Overton window" (i.e., acceptable political speech) continues to shift, becoming more extreme, more apocalyptic, more revolutionary, creating a new cottage industry of pundits and practitioners.[11] Malice observes that many of these more extreme actors on the right have one thing in common: they own books by Pat Buchanan (even though he never called for violence) and see reading him as a rite of passage in New Right circles.

PAT BUCHANAN AND THE SHIFTING OF THE OVERTON WINDOW

Long before Donald Trump, three-time presidential candidate and author Patrick J. Buchanan first roused the right for battle. At the 1992 Republican National Convention, Buchanan made history by delivering his famous "Culture War" speech.[12] "This election," he told the convention audience,

> is about more than who gets what. It is about who we are. It is about what we believe, and what we stand for as Americans. There is a religious war going on in this country for the soul of America. It is a cultural war, as critical to the kind of nation we will one day be as was the Cold War itself. . . . We must take back our culture, and take back our country.[13]

On the campaign trial Buchanan took on the ruling elites, the uniparty in Washington, hammering home the same themes day after day—if

America doesn't halt the deleterious effects of globalization, multiculturalism, moral permissiveness, and the loss of religion by defending its borders
from illegal immigration, putting America first in economics and foreign
policy, shrinking the ever-expanding "nanny state," then nothing will stop
America's slide toward national suicide. After his failed campaigns he turned
out six bestselling books on the same themes—attempting through each to
alert the country to the culture war, sounding the alarm that we may lose
our country, and rousing the public to act before it is too late.

Buchanan's is a classic declension narrative, one many on the right share.
We are losing the culture, the people, the religion, the way of life that once
characterized America, and the enemies of America are progressive elites
on the left and the right. In many ways Buchanan shares the poison-pill
theory of America. He has rejected the golden era of the founding documents, accusing the founders of putting the country on the road to ruin by
smuggling in French Enlightenment reason.[14] He argues in *Day of Reckoning*
that the Declaration of Independence, regardless of its lofty sentiments that
"all men are created equal," is nothing more than "war propaganda."[15]

For Buchanan, the Declaration started America's slow death march, a
steady decline carried forward by Lincoln, propelled by the progressives in
the 1920s, and then accelerated by the neocons in the 1980s. But where
Buchanan differs from Deneen and Dreher, who want to return to a more
Catholic premodern source for our grounding, Buchanan argues that if
America ever had a golden era, it can still be found in America: not during
or after the founding but in the years before the Revolution. America's true
grounding is found in the period *between* the settlement in Jamestown in
1611 and July 3, 1776.[16] It is in this era that he thinks we can find the genius
of America, what defines it, and what should form our attachment and our
patriotism. We learn this from the first 150 years after people from England
landed on our shores.

In *State of Emergency*, Buchanan defines patriotism as "a passionate attachment to one's own country—its land, its people, its past, its heroes, literature, language, traditions, culture, and customs. This is a traditionalist
view of a nation."[17] To the extent that this history and this culture still exist
in America, Buchanan claims, America will exist as a nation and will continue to be good. If America loses its unique and exceptional history, culture,

and tradition, then it will no longer exist. By claiming "this is a traditionalist view of a nation," Buchanan is staking out his own ground in the conservative movement and offering different criteria, a different grounding for deciding whether America is still good. Whereas Deneen and Dreher judge America with the yardstick of wisdom and reason from ancient sources, Buchanan's yardstick is different. He finds America's grounding in culture and history and tradition.

Buchanan's yardstick is found in what James Ceaser calls "customary history," the idea that America's grounding, its standard for right and wrong, the glue that holds the nation together, the narrative that shapes it is *not* mainly intellectual (e.g., the Bible, natural law, or even natural rights) but rather is found in America's past, in its culture and religion and people. To make his case Buchanan appeals to the founder John Jay, who, writing in *Federalist Paper* No. 2, wrote that America is made up of "one united people—a people descended from the same ancestors, speaking the same language, professing the same religion, attached to the same principles of government, very similar in their manners and customs."[18] And Buchanan contends that "to be a nation, a people must *believe* they are a nation, and that they share a common ancestry, history, and destiny. Whatever ethnic group to which we may belong, we Americans must see ourselves as of a unique and common nationality—in order to remain a nation."[19] Moreover, Buchanan seems to be saying that as long as immigrants *believe* in our nation's history and founders, they can become Americans. They can be assimilated. And if we lose our commitment to culture, history, and tradition, America will lose its grounding, its identity, and if America should lose "her ethnic core and become a nation of nations, America will not survive."[20]

By 2011 Buchanan was losing patience with conservatives, not convinced they were listening. In frustration he seemed to cross a red line when he wrote that America is grounded in "blood and soil," that is, a shared ethnicity and common racial background, pushing the Overton window too far right, even for some conservatives. In his 2011 book, *Suicide of a Superpower*, Buchanan included a chapter titled "The End of White America"— arguing that the destruction of White Christian culture was being pushed by the progressive Left, who favor a dangerous immigration policy that not only wants to dilute the culture and history of our British ancestors but more importantly the very White people in general who carry this culture and history. For many critics he went too far. MSNBC, a news outlet committed to multiculturalism, open borders, and the growth of the welfare state, fired Buchanan, who had worked for them as an on-air pundit. Others on the right were also critical and attempted to kick him out of the conservative camp.

This didn't stop Buchanan, who kept speaking out. And over the last decade his pessimism about America has only increased. He seems to have given up hope, in spite of the fact that conservatives have taken over many of his talking points.[21] Now past the point of no return, Buchanan argues that America is fatally "balkanized," divided into multi-tribes and multi-nations that can no longer avoid a new civil war (i.e., hot war). Taking a radical step, Buchanan contends that there is only one solution: allow states like California and the states in the South to break away, to secede. Tribalism and ethnic sectarianism are on the rise in the world, and without a strong state or a common ethnic heritage to hold the nation together (no creed or proposition or constitution will do the job), America will break apart, he argues, returning it to a nation of "blood and soil."[22]

A number of writers followed Buchanan, thinkers like Ann Coulter and Michelle Malkin, who also have been banished from Conservative Inc. circles.[23] While it may be acceptable and within mainstream conservative policy positions to point out the harmful effects of unlimited immigration on our economy, on blue-color workers, on the cultural homogeneity of the country, on the need for a culture, history, and tradition (a "customary history") that unifies us as Americans, it is not acceptable to link these positions to race and ethnicity. To do that is outside of the Overton window.

As they were banished from Conservative Inc., many of them have settled into the order right 3 position and gathered more people around them. They were banished but never went away, and in many ways mainstream forces on the right have moved closer because of their shift of the Overton window. Yet the Overton window continues to shift. Consider a recent monologue by Tucker Carlson at Fox News, where Carlson dared to voice a once-taboo subject that the Left wants to "replace White voters" and that race and ethnicity matter to the kind of country we have.[24] But while Carlson is *not* calling for a White ethno-state, obviously, preferring a kind of civic nationalism instead, others on the right believe America must return to a Whites-only nation.

THE RISE OF THE ALT-RIGHT

According to alt-right expert George Hawley, the alt-right continues to shift the Overton window. By taking customary history and reducing it to one thing, race, they are moving well beyond mainstream conservatism. A conservative himself, Hawley says a realistic immigration policy, rejecting open borders, and caring about the proper assimilation of immigrants are not alt-right positions. In fact, members of both parties shared these same views just ten years ago. But what the alt-right is doing is much more radical.[25] In "its mildest elements" the alt-right calls "for open and explicitly white identity politics." In its most extreme forms it is

> committed to white nationalism, ultimately seeking the creation of one or more racially pure white ethno-states in North America. . . . The Alt-Right is not just a more racist version of American conservatism, [but rather] views all of politics through a racial lens, and it has little interest in political and policy questions that do not have an obvious racial edge.[26]

And yet Hawley believes "the connection between President Trump and the Alt-Right is often overstated—the Alt-Right's ultimate goals are more radical and revolutionary than anything on Trump's policy agenda."[27] As Hawley points out, every plank in Trump's immigration policy was shared by members of the Democratic Party just ten years ago, including a border wall.

What critics from the left may find hard to believe is that soon after the 2016 election the alt-right broke from Trump, contending that his immigration policies were still within the old Overton window, were still within the bounds of conservative policy conversation. Attacking Trump and other conservatives, the alt-right accuses them of not being radical enough, of selling out to big business that likes cheap labor, of being afraid to name the real problem in our country (non-White immigration) for fear of being called racist. So to achieve what they want they continue to push the Overton window further right, including calling for a White ethno-state and suggesting that Blacks do the same.

KILL ALL NORMIES

By embracing White identity politics, calling for a White version of multicultural separatism, and utilizing the tactics of fascist control (its own form of right-wing political correctness), the alt-right, according to Hawley, has become a mirror image of the radical Left, composed of groups like antifa and other Black separatist groups. Angela Nagel agrees, and in *Kill All Normies: Online Culture Wars from 4chan and Tumbler to Trump and the Alt-Right*, a dark and depressing look into the world of the online alt-right culture, she demonstrates how the alt-right mirrors the alt-left, not only in substance (identitarian politics) but also in tactics (cancel culture politics), and in fact the alt-right often utilize the cancel-culture tactics in more effective ways than the Left.[28] Journalist Jacob Siegel contends the alt-right's "mix of shock-and-meme culture" is really just "another form of the left-wing identity politics that they [the alt-right] have claimed to despise."[29]

Along with the shock-and-meme cancel culture, I would add their willingness to use violence, whether that is to take on Antifa in the streets (e.g., the Proud Boys) or take back the country (e.g., the Oath Keepers). And in their willingness to brook violence they mirror the Far Left, which promotes violence as a legitimate form of protest. In the end we see that the alt-right has become the alt-left and vice versa. And as we saw with Stanley Fish (freedom left 3), politics has now become just *power* politics, a kind of survival of the fittest, winner-take-all, civility-be-damned grasp for control, unmoored from any transcendent grounding.

FROM POISON PILL TO CATHOLIC ILLIBERALISM

For religious conservatives it was the poison-pill thesis that first moved the Overton window, and, although Deneen really didn't provide much guidance for *what's next*, he opened up space for other thinkers to do so, thinkers who are not hesitant to propose radical solutions.

A friend of mine at the Claremont Institute told me he is amazed at how many Ivy League–educated Catholics (those who are willing to see our grounding in more intellectual terms, like natural law) are so frustrated by the far Left takeover of the political system that they are now themselves calling for illiberal solutions.

A more radical shift recently going on in Catholic circles can be seen in the discussion at the University of Notre Dame in fall 2018.[30] Deneen, the moderator, sat between two Catholic speakers. On one side sat Notre Dame professor Philip Muñoz, representing an older orthodox Catholicism, one that had reconciled Catholicism with the American founding and classical liberalism. On the other side of Deneen sat Harvard's Adrian Vermeule, representing the more radical traditional Catholics, often called "Rad Trads," a group that "rejects the view that Catholicism and liberal democracy are fundamentally compatible."[31] According to Rod Dreher, who was live-blogging the event, Deneen (and Dreher would include himself) "sits uneasily between liberalism and integralism," perfectly illustrating the three positions in the order right quadrant—Muñoz in order right 1, Vermeule in order right 3, and Deneen (and Dreher) in order right 2, right in the middle.[32]

While all three participants debated the true nature of liberalism (whether there ever was a good version of it or not) and whether it is now finally dead (i.e., beyond saving), the real takeaway for our purposes were the solutions proposed. Muñoz, not giving up on our republic, wants to win back true liberalism (first wave) from the progressives who highjacked it (second and third waves). But for Rad Trads like Vermeule, the republic is dead, has always been dead, and it is now time to move on. And while he can appreciate Dreher's Benedict Option or Deneen's call for more localism, Vermeule believes these options are too mild, not radical enough. It is time to envision something new.

A RETURN TO CHURCH AND STATE

The something new for Rad Trads is a return to the church as ultimate authority. While Vermeule and other Rad Trads agree that we must return to a more Catholic version of natural law (pre-natural-rights thinking), he also claims we need something much more shocking, more radical: we need to return to the church as *the* authority that interprets the true reality of natural law. And this can only happen if church and state are brought back together, with the church guiding the union. This contention that America needs a marriage between church and state as partners in promoting the good is often called *integralism*, which desires a return "to something like High Medieval Christendom."[33] According to Edmund Waldstein, for radical Catholics like Vermeule, "it makes no sense to distinguish Church and State as separate spheres at all; rather there was one single kingdom in which spiritual and temporal authorities operated. . . . Integralists want an ordered relation of the temporal and spiritual power in the deliberate pursuit of the good for the human project."[34]

Integralism is not just an academic discussion but is also growing in popularity with younger Catholics who have lost patience with liberalism, the secularization of society, and are willing to go to the extreme to fix it. So they are beginning to explore "the 'nonliberal' elements of their religious traditions."[35]

Integralists see the Far Left becoming more and more extreme, applying an iron grip to their power and silencing any dissenting speech. To counter this they believe they also need to become extreme, offering young Catholics "an invitation to boldness. . . . To participate in this no-longer-neutral public square, the Catholic tradition must be prepared to speak its own voice," which rejects America's founding and the principles it was grounded on.[36] It's time to seize the day, to seize control, to return authority to the church. It's time for something new, something radical. But how can this be accomplished?

For Vermeule, conservatives must "co-opt and transform the decaying regime from within its own core. . . . The vast bureaucracy created by liberalism . . . may . . . be turned to new ends, becoming the great instrument with which to restore a substantive politics of the good."[37] What this will mean for non-Christians or non-Catholics he does not say, but I doubt they will like it. What we need, claims Vermeule, is a new "epic theory" that will chart a "new departure in political thinking."[38] He is not prepared to fully lay out this "epic theory" but hopes someone younger will take up the task.[39]

THE PROTESTANT TEMPTATION

If Catholic integralism remains mostly an intellectual movement at this time, we are seeing more extreme Protestant versions of order right 3 breaking into the public realm. These blur faith and politics, confidently identifying God's cause in history with America's mission in the world. That America's survival is at the heart of God's plan for the world was at the heart of the Jericho Rally on the National Mall in Washington, DC, in early December 2020, a rally to call on God's name to "stop the steal," judge those who had betrayed the republic, and to save America before it was too late, even using the military if necessary.

Since it's not uncommon for a political rally to be a big-tent affair, bringing together diverse elements of a party for a common goal, it may be unfair to attack it for its inconsistencies and contradictions. The goal was a common political outcome, and almost everyone who wanted this was invited, regardless of differences. Realizing this should make critics more charitable and take much of its rhetoric with a grain of salt. But to some, the rhetoric of the Jericho Rally proved just one thing: that the Right has become authoritarian and unified in one thing—to set up a Taliban-like theocracy. Ultimately, they pose an existential threat.

But even though some of these same types of people were involved in the January 6, 2021, Capitol riot, John McWhorter does not believe they constitute a threat. As he contends, these groups are so small and have almost no institutional, cultural, or political power that they, in spite of the bad optics of the Capitol riots (and it did look bad), pose almost no threat to the survival of the US government.[40] By best guesses, these right-wing militia groups, White nationalist organizations, QAnon conspirators, and religious dominionists add up to between ten thousand members on the low end or one hundred thousand on the high end, a statistically small number. If the media keep inflating this danger, calling it the number one existential danger the country faces and using it as an excuse to target all people on the right, these numbers undoubtedly will continue to swell.[41]

But not only will it increase the extremism on the right, it is also intellectually dishonest and unfair. As Jewish writer Stanley Kurtz wrote a few years ago,

> The notion that conservative Christians want to reinstate slavery and rule by genocide is not just crazy, it's downright dangerous. The most disturbing part [is] the attempt to link Christian conservatives with Hitler and fascism. Once we acknowledge the similarity between conservative Christians and fascists . . . we can confront Christian evil by setting aside the "old polite rules of democracy."[42]

Yet this "dystopian political program" of the reconstructionism movement is "utterly marginal," claims Kurtz, and is led by an "extremist sect [that] has absolutely no traction with anyone of significance."[43] Some evangelicals agree. Writing in *Christianity Today*,[44] Robert Gagnon and Edith Humphrey contend the dominionist Christian takeover "has become a bogeyman," using "conspiratorial nonsense, . . . political paranoia, . . . [and] guilt by association."[45] And *Washington Post* columnist Michael Gerson, someone whose opposition to Donald Trump is well-known, says "thin charges of dominionism are just another attempt to discredit opponents rather than answer them."[46]

But having made the point that the hysteria and conspiracy theories that surround Christians in politics is both unfair and dangerous, and that the number of Protestants that hold theocratic views are small, it doesn't mean that the theocratic temptation doesn't exist on the right or that it isn't held by some, regardless of how small the groups are. As Kurtz is willing to admit, "there is, in fact, a fringe Christian group of 'Dominionists' or 'reconstructionists,' who really would like to see an American theocracy, and a return to the death penalty for blasphemy, adultery, sodomy, and witchcraft."[47] And it is important to take them seriously. But this is rarely done.

At the heart of these fringe groups is the belief that since the republic is dead, Christians must get out of their holy huddles and take back the seven mountains—politics, the media, business, arts and entertainment, education, family, and religion—covering all the areas of the world that have succumbed to secularism. But for many this means little more than getting involved in life outside the church.

Sara Diamond, who has written a couple books on seven-mountain dominionism, contends that for most of these Christians, whom she calls the "soft dominionists," this means that they need to influence politics, be salt and light, and return America to a foundation in which our laws are rooted in God's Word, in "nature's God" as Jefferson wrote in the Declaration.[48] It really isn't that radical at all. It's the "hard dominionists" (those calling for total Christian reconstruction) who Diamond says are calling the shots in the movement and are at the heart of the effort to take over the government.

Yet as scary as she makes these people out to be, and the media tells us they pose an existential threat to America, authors like Diamond can't demonstrate that these groups have any institutional or political power or serious influence over the White House, Congress, or the conservative movement in general. So they remain, for the most part, a boogeyman that the Left can tar the Right with, notwithstanding the bad optics and the foolishness of the extremists on January 6, 2021.

ORDER RIGHT CHALLENGES THEIR OWN

Just because the Left uses these groups as boogeymen, with conspiracy theories swirling around them, it doesn't mean their views aren't a dead end for people on the right. And there have been plenty of voices on the right warning Christians of this temptation, calling them out on their use of apocalyptic language that borders on calling for violence and their association with more extreme voices in the movement.[49]

In fact, a few years ago Rod Dreher was one of the first on the right to condemn Patrick Buchanan, the hero for many in the order right 3 position, for crossing the red line on race. When Buchanan was unwilling to condemn the White nationalism present at the Charlottesville rally and attacked the most famous phrase of the Declaration, "All men are created equal," Dreher pushed back, arguing that Buchanan repudiates not only the founding principle of our constitutional order but also a core teaching of the Christian faith, which holds that all humans are created in the image of God.[50] For Dreher, what Buchanan wrote "is abhorrent, and must be rejected in the strongest terms by conservatives. If this is where the Right is going, it can go right off that racist cliff without me."[51] Pushing back strongly against Buchanan's stress on race, Dreher concludes, "It grieves me to see a conservative writer and thinker I have long admired, even if I did not always agree with him, descend to the gutter like this. . . . He has crossed a bright red line. No, no, *no!* Conservatives, this is not us."[52]

This is a good place to pause for a moment return to our discussion of public philosophy and the importance of grounding, which will help us see the danger in what Buchanan is doing. Once we ground public life in customary history, in effect baptizing the history and traditions of a nation, regardless of whether it was just or not, it is easy to baptize race and let it be the foundation to build a nation on. The danger of customary history shorn of any connection to nature, reason, or biblical revelation, which hold it together, is that it can succumb to stressing one part of a nation's history over other parts. And for the alt-right, customary history is reduced to ethnicity and race. In the process it begins to resemble the race identitarianism of the Left.

One thinker who sees this danger clearly is prolific author and professor Paul Gottfried, who himself coined the term *alt-right*. While he favors a more robust customary history that includes tradition and culture, he nevertheless sees its weakness (unlike Buchanan), and would thus reject this slide into ethno-nationalism on the far right. Speaking of Richard Spencer, one of the organizers of the Unite the Right rally in Charlottesville and one of his former students, Gottfried concluded that "as somebody whose family barely escaped from the Nazis in the '30s, I don't want to be associated with people who are pro-Nazi. . . . I just do not want to be in the same camp with white nationalists. . . . Whenever I look at Richard, I see my ideas coming back in a garbled form."[53] For Gottfried, customary history doesn't have to be reduced to race and ethnicity. Once race and ethnicity are held up as the defining characteristic of America's past, the next step is radicalism, which must be rejected.

While some conservatives like Gottfried have warned of the dangers of customary history and its slide into radical identitarian White politics, they have also found fault with religious thinkers who believe the poison-pill view must be taken to its logical conclusion, usually meaning the elimination of our present system and a return to the integration of church and state (integralism) and even, under the right circumstances, a return to monarchy.

Consider the pushback from Sohrab Ahmari, who, as an immigrant and a recent Catholic convert, shares some sympathy with the Rad Trad declension narrative but still worries that it has taken the poison-pill theory too far. When Rad Trads say "that liberalism itself [is] another form of totalitarianism all along [and], therefore, that no amount of conservative course correction can set right what is wrong with the system" or that "liberalism isn't all that different from Communism, that both are totalitarian children of the Enlightenment," this is a dismaying ideological turn, argues Ahmari.[54]

But for Ahmari the alternatives of life under other regimes in other countries is so much worse. Once we go down the path of illiberalism, cautions Ahmari, we will

> lose the legal guarantees that protect the Church, however imperfectly, against capricious rulers and popular majorities. And if public opinion in the West is turning increasingly secular, indeed anti-Christian, as social conservatives complain and surveys seem to confirm, is it really a good idea to militate in favor of a more illiberal order rather than defend tooth and nail liberal principles of freedom of conscience?[55]

He also admits that "the two illiberalisms [radical Left and radical Right] enjoy a remarkable complementarity and even cross-pollinate each other."

Along with voices on the right cautioning against illiberalism among Rad Trad Catholics, others have challenged evangelical Christians on the right who also have adopted illiberal positions and in the process look more and more like the Far Left. Like Amari, Dreher sees this left-right congruence happening in Protestant far right movements and has been highly critical of it. In fact, he was so worried about it that he spent hours live blogging the Jericho March, pointing out some of its more worrisome and extreme elements.[56]

Dreher reminded those following along that while he is a fellow believer and shares much of the same declension narrative, he nonetheless is concerned with the rhetoric of many of the speakers at the march, contending that if followed it could destroy the last vestiges of democratic institutions, "causing things to get worse" and unleashing an even more totalitarian situation.[57] In his live comments Dreher argued that much of the rhetoric was not only dangerous but theologically confused, inflating biblical verses into rigid political positions, causing them to "conflate Trump politics with religion." But what worried him the most was how so many speakers based their convictions in private dreams, visions, and impressions, putting their views beyond challenge and falsification. For Dreher, this is dangerous.

As Dreher watched, he "began to think that all of this is the right-wing Christian version of Critical Race Theory," of which he has spent "the past few years documenting this destructive insanity." But now he is seeing something similarly irrational happening on the right. As he says, "I wish I could add a new chapter about how we conservatives are allowing ourselves to be conquered by the same kind of unreality." Dreher fears that while the Right is "not totalitarian," he has no doubts "that a significant portion of the Right would accept an *authoritarian* regime, though not a totalitarian one." For Dreher, people on the right have become so alienated by the Left that they "are willing to believe ideology over truth," and they "are willing to smash any institutions for the sake of seeing their idea of justice triumph."[58]

We are witnessing the Overton window getting pushed further to the right. What began with the poison-pill theory undermining belief in the goodness of the American system, has now contributed to many Rad Trads and evangelicals despairing of any gradual movement back to the founding and adopting their own form of illiberalism in spite of their contention that they differ from the Left.

At the heart of the problem is that the radical Right inflated its faulty grounding. For Buchanan, but more so those who followed him, this means customary history inflated into race and ethnicity alone. For integralists this means the church as authority inflated into church and state and in some cases a return to monarchy. For some evangelicals, particularly some in the charismatic and Pentecostal churches, this means personal revelation inflated to prove God's approval of America. When Christians lack the right public philosophy and are confused about grounding, it is extremely easy to inflate *their* Bible into *their* politics. We have seen this on the far left, and now we see it on the far right. To the extent that this inflation endorses armed insurrection or military coups and tribunals to punish political enemies, the Right must reject them. Moreover, to the extent this inflation on the right returns to the Lost Cause narrative of racial superiority, it must be condemned. To the extent that biblical inflation leads to the call for a new church-state alliance or theocracy or new authoritarian government, it must be rejected as just another form of oligarchy, this time by the Right, and it must be denounced.

No Time for Theological Quibbles

For many in the order right 3 position these criticisms are just theological niceties, mere distractions, excuses for inaction, ways to appease the ruling class—all things we don't have time for, especially when America's survival is at stake. They believe they are at war, don't have time to engage in endless speculation, and need to remain unified against a common enemy—the bipartisan ruling elites. And to win this war everyone on their side is welcome.

While I certainly am sympathetic to the need for action and that the ruling elites pose an existential danger to our country, I disagree with the view that we can put off the development of a sound grounding and public philosophy. The fact that we are in a culture war makes this development even more urgent.

Without the right public philosophy, Christians are at risk of unbiblical inflation, and this kind of inflation comes with accommodation. For evangelicals of the Right this accommodation can mean getting swept up by the tide of illiberalism on the far right. Put otherwise, without the proper grounding and public philosophy, the Bible is inflated, politics becomes distorted, and evangelicals are easily co-opted by the wrong ideologies. And for many in order right 3 this has happened, dangerously aligning themselves with less-than-savory characters and groups, excusing the alliance for political purposes. To the extent evangelicals on the right do this, they open themselves up to critics who attack them for believing crazy conspiracies that can't stand up to scrutiny.

SAYING OUT LOUD WHAT USED TO BE SAID IN PRIVATE

Yet, just when it seems possible that the far Right may have been overwhelmed by crazy conspiracy theories, which, along with the accusation of racism, is now the most common way to ridicule, silence, and control the Right, the ruling elite say out loud what they used to say in private, producing another big "I told you so" moment for the far Right and making it harder to moderate their beliefs.

In the same week the *New York Times* article blamed conservative evangelicals for not believing science, not trusting the experts and doing their part to reach herd immunity and instead believing conspiracy theories, James O'Keefe's Project Veritas released another shocking undercover video, this time of a CNN executive, Charlie Chester, bragging that "no one ever says those things out loud but it's obvious." Chester said that CNN conspires with the ruling elites to push their narrative, that CNN is a propaganda network, that it doesn't believe in "neutral news," and that its ultimate goal is to take down political opponents, using fabricated stories built around fake anonymous sources. And Chester even admitted that now that Covid-19 has reached a saturation point and people are tired of hearing them talk about it, CNN will switch the topic to the environment crisis, applying their propaganda in similar ways, keeping the campaign of fear going. For as Chester confessed, "If it bleeds, it leads."[59]

What did O'Keefe get for his groundbreaking journalism, exposing the collusion of Big Media with Big Government, Big Tech, and Big Pharma? As a reward, Twitter, coming to the defense of Big Media and showing how the ruling elites conspire, pulled out its high-tech guillotine and chopped off O'Keefe's Twitter head, banning him from their platform permanently and severing him from his one million followers.[60] And the ruling elites wonder why so many on the right are paranoid and believe in conspiracy theories. It's because they keep admitting it, producing a collective "I told you so" from many on the right, even from those who reject the illiberalism of the far right and instead want to return to a new vital center.

In Sum

- The New Right is prepared to end the America project. Since it is dead, we need something new.

- For many on the New Right, particularly those like Pat Buchanan who want to build something new on the grounding of customary history (i.e., the traditions, culture, and original ethnicity of America), it means reclaiming America's past, which is found in Jamestown, long before America's founding.

- Some in the New Right, pushing this view of customary history and the Overton window too far, want to prioritize ethnicity as the ultimate grounding, which would guide all immigration and public policy.

- Catholic integralists, while rejecting a grounding on customary history and ethnicity, also reject a return to the US founding documents (because of the poison pill), instead wanting to ground America on the authority of the Catholic Church, arguing for a new church-state alliance.

- Many charismatic and Pentecostal Protestants believe that only a takeover of the seven mountains, a hard dominionism, can rescue America, and if this requires a military takeover, the indictment and conviction of the guilty by military tribunals, or other illiberal methods, then so be it.

- The illiberalism of these three groups is dangerous and could lead to an authoritarianism worse than what we have now. All three groups suffer from a type of inflation—White ethno-state proponents inflate ethnicity to the overarching grounding, integralists inflate their view of church authority in the Bible to the necessity of a new church-state alliance, and hard dominionists inflate the cultural mandate to mean Christians need to run society, including the government.

- Finally, these illiberal groups have much in common. In fact, they are the mirror image of the illiberal alt-left.

Having concluded a survey of the eight polarized positions (chapters three through ten), where do we go from here?

PART THREE

FORMING THE NEW VITAL CENTER

THE RETURN OF THE STRONG GODS

No one summarizes better the cold civil war and our present polarization than R. R. Reno, who, in his new book *The Return of the Strong Gods*, places the blame for the "return of the strong gods" (extremism on the right) at the feet of the globalist ruling elites.[1] Extremism exists because the ruling elite exist. It grows because they grow. For the past seventy years, Reno contends, these bipartisan ruling elites have pushed an open-society agenda (one we saw most clearly in freedom left 2 and freedom right 2), which has brought moral and cultural disintegration, political and spiritual homelessness, and working and middle-class suffering. These deleterious consequences, says Reno, have led to the return of the strong gods of religion, tradition, patriotism, and national sovereignty (order right), all aspects of life that human beings, communities, and nations can't live without and need in order to find safety, purpose, and unity. But instead of listening to American citizens, particularly those most affected by this open society globalism, our global elites have overreacted and in their impatience, anger, and contempt have pushed normal people into extreme positions, leaving them little choice.

In giving people only one choice—embrace the open society and reject your strong gods or else—the elites have sparked a reactionary pushback, a populist uprising for which they are mainly responsible. Since the ruling elites no longer allow even dialogue about the strong gods, the Right (particularly order right 3) believes they must resort to illiberal means to fight back. Moreover, when those on the right see the ruling elites condone and celebrate left-wing violence, calling it healthy political protest, the Far Right adopts the same tactics.

So, for Reno, if the strong gods have returned, and it appears they have, the responsibility can be laid at the feet of our ruling elites. And the more they suppress freedom of speech and discussion, even of healthy strong gods (see chapters eleven through fourteen), the more the Right pushes back, forcing the Overton window further from a vital center. This makes sense. When people are barred from talking about strong gods, they gravitate to the most extreme versions of these gods, and in the process they begin to mirror the all-or-nothing extremism of the Left.

As we saw in part two of this book, we have seen how each of the eight polarized positions is guilty of moving the Overton window, taking one aspect of the vital center and pushing it further out in each quadrant. But at the same time there has been another force at work in each quadrant, as if a centrifugal force were pulling each quadrant further from the vital center. This force is the ruling elites of both parties. They shove the open society in everyone's faces, force ordinary Americans to push back, and when they do, ruling elites blame them for their extreme reaction and then clamp back down even harder, starting the cycle all over again. We are seeing this cycle repeat itself again with mandatory vaccines and vaccine passports.

As the ruling elite stoke this mutual antagonism, attacking America from below and from above, the ruling elites are teaching Americans to dislike, distrust, and divide from each other. In the process the ruling elite get more powerful. We divide; they unify. We are weakened; they are strengthened. Yet to the extent evangelicals of the right call for illiberal solutions, they too are playing along with the script. And to the extent progressive evangelicals attack all conservatives (especially evangelicals) as White Christian nationalists, racist, and selfish, they too play along, being manipulated by the political theater of the ruling class. Like a boa constrictor squeezing the life out of its victim, the ruling elites are using the Far Left and Far Right to crush the vital center, squeezing the life out of the American project and putting an end to our constitutional republicanism. Both the Left and the Right are being played as fools by bipartisan ruling elites. Or as Joel Kotkin claims, both sides are oblivious that "our covid era oligarchs are fitting us for neo feudalism."[2]

REDISCOVERING THE TRUE STRONG GODS

While Reno recognizes the danger of radicalism on the right, he says that the return of the strong gods was inevitable. People need meaning, and the strong gods provide it in ways that the open society, open borders, free trade, corporate capitalism, crass materialism, cheap consumer goods, and the lure of a posthuman future never could. These leave people empty, spiritually and culturally homeless. But for Reno, adopting *false* strong gods, many of which have been offered on the far right and far left, will never meet our deepest needs. What we need are the *true* strong gods. He says false strong gods can only be conquered by the true strong gods. Only the true strong gods can meet our deepest needs and end polarization and the reign of the oligarchic elites.

If this is true, then we need to reject the false strong gods and return to the true ones. We need to reject all eight polarized positions on the quadrant graph and discover a different way forward. We need to turn to the true strong gods. We need to rediscover the proper grounding; in the process we will build a new public philosophy that will protect us from spinning off into extremes, wake us up from the manipulation of the ruling elites, and in the end give us a chance to reclaim our constitutional republic. I only hope it is not too late.

11

THE NEW VITAL CENTER

THE AMERICAN SYNTHESIS AND THE FOUR SOULS

BY SPRING 2021, with President Trump no longer in office, the Republican Party was attempting to define what they stood for in a post-Trump world, at least until he decided whether he would run for president again. While the power in the party still resided with those most compromised by the DC uniparty and who rarely challenged the ruling oligarchic elites, there were hints of a new America First Caucus being formed in the House that was committed to policies that challenged the bipartisan status quo.[1] Yet, before the official announcement and rollout, someone leaked a draft of their policy statement covering fourteen topics—among others, fixing our electoral systems, reforming immigration, reining in globalization, and ending the pandemic lockdowns.[2]

While this document contained enough policy statements to anger the uniparty Republicans, especially for its positions on high tech, China, and free trade, it was the section on immigration reform that raised the ire of Republican minority leader Kevin McCarthy. "America is built on the idea that we are all created equal, and success is earned through honest, hard work," McCarthy wrote on Twitter soon after the platform was leaked. "It isn't built on identity, race, or religion. The Republican Party is the party of Lincoln [and] the party of more opportunity for all American's—not nativist dog whistles," he wrote, as if his words had been lifted right from Far Left talking points.[3]

Why such a strong reaction? Likely McCarthy was responding to the section on immigration reform where the platform "recognizes that our country is more than a mass of consumers or a series of abstract ideas. . . . America is a nation with a border, and a culture, strengthened by a common respect for uniquely Anglo-Saxon political traditions," and for this reason mass immigration must be curtailed because it threatens "the long-term existential future of America as a unique country with a unique culture and a unique identity."[4] It was the phrase "Anglo-Saxon political traditions" that elicited McCarthy's Twitter rebuke and sent the Democratic media into overdrive, accusing the America First Caucus of racism, nativism, and of pushing the "white replacement theory" of far Right conspiracy theory demagogues.[5] This led another Republican, Congressman Adam Kinzinger, to call for the immediate stripping of committee positions from any Republican involved in this caucus.[6]

To McCarthy and Kinzinger, the America First Caucus platform had crossed a red line, misunderstood where the Overton window stood inside the Republican Party, and was being rebuked. Were they wrong, and, if so, why? Moreover, was this conflict just over language of grounding ("Anglo-Saxon political traditions" versus "the party of more opportunity"), or was this just an easy way to attack the AFC platform, dismiss its policies and the challenge it posed to the Republican Washington establishment, especially its cozy relationship with big tech, China, and free trade?

Above, I mentioned the need to discover the right "strong gods," the right principles and traditions on which to ground our nation, giving us the glue to hold a polarized people together and providing the resources for a new vital center (i.e., a strong constitutional republic) capable of returning the power to govern to the America people. The dustup over the America First Caucus platform raises many of the fundamental issues at the heart of the polarization described over the past ten chapters, illustrating well the chasm that separates the ruling elites who want oligarchy from the populist working and middle classes who want constitutional republicanism, which gives them the power to rule.

We saw in chapter ten how policy positions built on customary history (divorced from a transcendent norm) can easily slide into an ethnic nationalism and a new kind of authoritarian illiberalism. After looking at the order right 3 position, we are now able to see some of the possible pitfalls at the heart of the America First platform. It is not possible to know the full extent of its grounding (i.e., what they mean by "Anglo-Saxon political traditions"[7]), but we can conclude that if these political principles and their grounding are only found in customary history, that is America's "unique country," "unique culture," and "unique identity," and is not balanced in nature (whether that be natural law or divine revelation or a combination), then it very well can be co-opted into ethnic nationalism, becoming nativistic. But if they mean more by the phrase "Anglo-Saxon political traditions," which may well include the natural-law traditions, then it is little more than political theater to accuse them of racism, nativism, and xenophobia. Moreover, we see in Rep. McCarthy's reaction other words for the kind of liberty at the heart of beltway libertarianism (freedom right 2) and the unencumbered self (freedom left 2): he claims America is grounded on "opportunity" (or what the platform rejected as "abstract ideas") and transcends "identity, race, or religion." Once again what we see in this dustup is a microcosm of our cold civil war, the clashing polarization of the extremes. Furthermore, we see that this conflict is ultimately over America's grounding, which demonstrates that our leaders are still stuck in polarized positions, outside of the vital center, with no intention or ability to move beyond the political theater.

But another way of understanding this dustup around the America First Caucus is to see it as a replay of the perennial debate between *creed* ("party of more opportunity") and *culture* ("Anglo-Saxon political traditions"), which has been going on for hundreds of years in America. Political philosophers like James Ceaser also call this creed/culture clash the conflict between history and nature/reason.[8] So, for example, look at Abraham Lincoln (whom McCarthy referenced, albeit wrongly). At the time Lincoln entered politics, this customary history and nature/reason debate was at the heart of Whig Party politics, a conflict between those Whigs who wanted to ground our nation on customary history (culture) and those who wanted to ground our nation on nature/reason, that is, a transcendent norm, whether natural law or some kind of right reason or divine revelation. Eventually this debate would split the party, similar to what is happening now in the Republican Party. But Lincoln attempted to hold the two positions together in synthesis, and in so doing articulated a grounding and public philosophy similar to what I call the four souls of the new vital center (the four position 1s), avoiding the possible pitfalls of the America First Caucus and McCarthy's beltway libertarian reaction (as well as the Far Left's overreaction).

Until we get beyond this dispute and rediscover what Lincoln himself rediscovered, that our founders synthesized these two concepts—which became the grounding for our republic and the glue that held us together for the first 150 years—we will never move beyond our cold civil war and will stay locked in dueling authoritarianisms. The ruling oligarchs welcome this war, as it gives the best chance to destroy the legitimacy of our original republic and for the revolutionary creation of a new system.

CREED OR CULTURE: THE CASE OF SAMUEL P. HUNTINGTON

The uniparty wants to accuse populist Republicans, like those in the America First Caucus, of being racist and nativist. One of their own, the renowned Harvard professor Samuel P. Huntington, "an old-fashioned Democrat" and the most famous foreign-policy expert of the past fifty years, who himself called for a recovery of America's unique culture in the aftermath of the 9/11 tragedy. In his 2004 book *Who Are We?* Huntington sounded the alarm about the amount and speed of cultural change in America. "Without national debate or conscious decision," he wrote, "America is being transformed into what could be a very different society from what has been."[9]

According to Huntington, a self-described patriot, if America loses its cultural inheritance, the loss of its principles, the creed, won't be far behind. "A nation may, as America does, have a creed, but its soul is defined by the common history, traditions, culture, heroes and villains, victories and defeats, enshrined in its 'mythic chords of memory.'"[10] For Huntington, "This would mean a recommitment to America as a deeply religious and primarily Christian country . . . adhering to Anglo-Protestant values, speaking English, maintaining its European cultural heritage, and committed to the principles of the Creed."[11]

Just as the ruling elites pounced all over the America First Caucus platform, Huntington's fellow Democrats attacked him, especially his reference to

"Anglo-Protestant values," rejecting the view that this culture takes precedence over creed.[12] For his critics, talk of this kind of culture can only be a code word for one thing: racism or ethnic nationalism. But Huntington rejects ethnic nationalism (as do many in the national populist movement), which believes what unites America is a common ethnic or racial background. For Huntington this ship has sailed. America is too ethnically diverse to go back. Yet Huntington rejects multiculturalism as an "abstract idea" that minimizes America's unique culture. For Huntington it is our distinct American culture that gave birth to our creed, and without the culture the creed will die.

While he contends that we need both culture and creed, he seems to prioritize America's unique culture, saying, "the Creed is unlikely to retain its salience if Americans abandon the Anglo-Protestant culture in which it has been rooted," a sentiment that finds its echo in the America First phrase "Anglo-Saxon political traditions."[13] We are losing this culture, says Huntington, and this culture gave rise to the creed in the first place. For Huntington, the American creed "with its principles of liberty, equality, individualism, representative government, and private property," grew out of a unique culture.[14] The similarities of language between Huntington and the America First Caucus are stunning.

The heart of the cold civil war is a conflict between creed and culture, over which one should be paramount, both extremes rejecting any attempt to hold creed and culture together. For the most part the polarization in our country can be seen in the fact that each side believes it knows which of the two choices is correct and attempts to impose their view on the rest of the country, forcing everyone who disagrees to conform and accept their version of unity. Yet when one side stresses creed or culture to the exclusion of the other, we get what Damon Linker of *The Week* observes, "Each side seeks a degree of national unity and homogeneity that would require the other side's erasure or expulsion from the political community." What this comes down to, argues Linker, is "that the effort to attain national unity and homogeneity has the paradoxical effect of increasing disunity and political antagonism."[15] The only way to avoid this mutual exclusion and polarization is to find a way to hold creed and culture together.[16] Is this possible? Can we ever find national unity again?

The Interpretive Key That Unlocks Our Polarization

In his *Designing a Polity*, Ceaser surveys American history and demonstrates that from the very beginning America was in search of a foundation (grounding), "a first principle that explains or justifies a general political orientation."[17] Ceaser explains that at the Continental Congress in 1774, two years before the Declaration, the colonies tried to find a grounding that could justify breaking away from Britain. "We very deliberately considered and debated," reflected John Adams, "whether we should recur to the law of nature" and combine it with the historical foundations of tradition like "common law" and "the charters" or the "rights of British subjects."[18]

According to Ceaser, Adams and other founders like Jay and Jefferson and Madison eventually combined nature and history. While it wasn't revolutionary to appeal to their rights as British citizens, it was radical to combine it with the concept of nature, appealing for the first time to the concept of natural law as justification for their rebellion against the king and as a grounding for their political life together. This began, says Ceaser, a back-and-forth contest between nature (where "right is found in a permanent or eternal standard discovered by philosophical, or scientific, investigation") and history (where "right is known from something that occurs in time, whether from what is old or ancestral (Customary History) or from where knowledge is going (Philosophy of History)."[19] As Ceaser shows so well, these two positions became the foundations for each political party right up to the present. Sometimes a party relied on only one grounding, nature or history, creed or culture, and sometimes a party combined them.

What is fascinating for our purposes is that nature and history are at the heart of the dispute between creed and culture. Those who take nature/reason as their grounding tend to end up in the creed camp, and those who rely on history/tradition tend to land in the culture camp. And it tracks fairly well with our quadrant system. On the *order* half of the graph, both quadrants look to some form of history. So for example, those in order right 2 and 3 tend to look to customary history (truth is located in tradition, that which is old) or the history and tradition of the Catholic Church. On the other hand, those in order left 2 and 3 tend to look to a philosophy of history (truth comes from discerning the forward trajectory of history, the "law of progress," thus progressivism). The same holds for the *freedom* half of the graph. Here the two quadrants tend to depend on nature/reason. Those in the freedom left quadrant look to natural rights (freedom left 2) or applied postmodernism (freedom left 3), both appealing to something in the structure of reality that can be discerned through pragmatic reason. Those in the freedom right quadrant look to a type of nature called "spontaneous order" ("invisible hand" drawn from natural law; the system of natural liberty) stemming from the nature of reality.

CULTURE ⬌ **CREED**
(HISTORY/TRADITION)　　　　　　　　　　(NATURE/REASON)

Figure 11.1. The distance between culture and creed

Even more interesting is that when one party depends solely on one grounding and rejects a synthesis, they tend toward the extreme (and in the process push the Overton window to the extreme). This confirms what I have been saying throughout. Returning to Ceaser and his survey of the Whig Party in the nineteenth century, he shows that when a party grounds their platform exclusively on history as their foundation and justification, it soon tumbles into historicism, making whatever reality existed in the past as the standard for the present or judging the good solely by the winds of the nation. For Ceaser this has led liberal progressives to rely on the march of history to slide into political correctness and utopian socialism (order left 3). In a similar way, traditionalists (those in the national populist camp today) who rely on history at the exclusion of nature/reason soon adopt their own kind of historicism, baptizing the nation as their own normative standard. We saw this tendency in Pat Buchanan and taken to the extreme in the alt-right, rejecting all races other than the White race that was here at the start, and wanting to return to an ethno-nationalist state. Moreover, a similar thing can be said about the Catholic integralists. Once they prioritize the traditions of the church (which has its own form of customary history) at the expense of nature/reason, they too become unbalanced and susceptible to illiberalism.

The same thing happens with those who hold to nature/reason without a balance in history and tradition. We saw how libertarians (freedom right 2) depend on secular instrumental reason, opening the door to radical libertarianism (freedom right 3). And we saw how secular natural rights as the grounding for the unencumbered self and procedural republic (freedom left 2) morphs into applied postmodernism (freedom left 3).

How do we avoid historicism on one side and rationalism on the other? By pushing to the center of our quadrant system, moving into the new vital center, creating a new synthesis.

A NEW SYNTHESIS AND THE RETURN OF THE WHIGS

It is no secret who Ceaser's heroes are—those thinkers and parties that best synthesized history *and* nature (creed *and* culture), particularly the Whigs.[20] In the 1830s and 1840s, while the Democrats grounded their platform in a philosophy of history (the voice of the people, leading to a defense of slavery), the Whig Party (which eventually became the antislavery Republican Party) emphasized tradition as the source of authority, praising the Founders as "Fathers."[21] Since the Founders themselves had relied on a foundation of nature ("nature's God") American Whigs did not initially oppose tradition to nature. They sought a synthesis.[22] This synthesis was to keep the foundation of nature from becoming rationalism, the kind of instrumental reason at the heart of the French Revolution and eventually modern liberalism (freedom left 2 and freedom right 2). By holding history and nature in tension it would save liberalism from tumbling into the second and third wave (Strauss) of late liberalism and retain the best of liberalism.

This synthesis, says Ceaser, "could encourage certain moral and political qualities, such as duties and nobility, that were undervalued in the philosophy of nature."[23] Put another way, the *Whig synthesis*, in attempting to correct liberalism with history, was trying to protect it from its worst extremes. But in the same way, a commitment to nature would protect history from its worst extreme, holding the two foundations together and in the end producing what the founders had wanted. Both Frederick Douglass in the 1890s and Martin Luther King Jr. in the 1960s appealed to this synthesis, calling America to a return to its original creed and to live up to its own culture that treated all human beings with dignity.[24]

Once the Whigs forged this synthesis, they had to fill their view of tradition with content and their view of reason with principles, which together would provide the grounding and the once-upon-a-time story, a narrative able to guide, temper, and direct the nation. How did they come up with the content and principles? Another essay by Ceaser spells it out, appealing to one of the greatest friends of America, whose writings provide one of the best illustrations of this Whig synthesis.

THE TWO-FOUNDING THESIS

To help my students understand this Whig synthesis between nature and history, I often assign them Tocqueville's *Democracy in America*, written at the height of Whig Party power in the 1830's, as well as Ceaser's ground-breaking essay "Alexis de Tocqueville and the Two-Founding Thesis," which better than any secondary source explains this synthesis.[25] In the essay, Ceaser contends that Tocqueville (who was vehemently antislavery) absorbed the Whig views and articulated them in his classic book, becoming its greatest spokesperson. At its simplest, following Whig teaching, Tocqueville claims that the "first founding," initiated with the arrival of the Pilgrims and Puritans and then established over their 150 years of governing, was just as important as the "second founding" of Jefferson, Adams, and Madison from 1776 to 1789. If the second founding represents their commitment to nature (natural rights connected to natural law; the Declaration of Independence) and principles of Enlightenment reason (liberal democracy and the Constitution), then the first founding represents their devotion to customary history (tradition, culture, language, and religion) as a guide.

For Tocqueville and the Whigs these "two foundings" are necessary to form the synthesis; both are needed to develop a "new political science," and both became the heart of a new foundation (grounding) for the American republic. Interestingly, in making his two-foundings case, he does not include Jamestown, a troublesome fact for those like Buchanan who see Jamestown as a kind of golden era, and the 1619 Project radical progressives who claim it represents America's true founding. While he recognized Jamestown as one of the "two principle offshoots" that grew up alongside each other,[26] Tocqueville scorned the South as a counterfeit (what Reno would call a "false strong god") and far from representing the true essence of America (tainted as it was by slavery). It was an oligarchy whose culture infected its leaders with laziness and cruelty and contaminated everything it touched and ruled, including the lower and middle classes.[27] Jamestown represented a rival viewpoint that existed on our continent from the start and to this day fights for supremacy.[28]

Tocqueville and Lincoln saw it for what it was: a perversion of America. For Tocqueville and Lincoln the essence of America was not found in Jamestown or the rest of the slaveholding South but in the Puritan North, the birthplace of constitutional republicanism, the cradle of American liberty, the best example of Whig philosophy, and the true essence of America.[29]

THE NEW SYNTHESIS BECOMES THE FOUR SOULS OF THE NEW VITAL CENTER

Having now laid out this synthesis between nature and history, a synthesis that can help us understand creed and culture and avoid the polarized extremes of each quadrant, I am now prepared to tell the story of the new vital center. This is a narrative that includes the first positions in each quadrant, showing how all four positions are needed to keep nature or history, creed or culture, from polarizing and in turn being co-opted by the ruling elites for their own power.

Each of the four souls can be found in the first position of each quadrant. While two are on the left and two on the right, they actually transcend the left-right category, allowing us to move beyond polarization. They are dynamic. Think of them as a circle or a gear continuously rotating, only stopping in a certain position when needed, to speak to a quadrant that is getting out of balance or starting to polarize, and pulling it back in to align with our democratic republic.

While each of the position 1s can be discussed as stand-alone positions, each one is in fact connected to the other three first positions. They form a dynamic, synthesized whole—each needing the other to stay in the new vital center and avoid polarization. There is no perfect theoretical model and the founders knew this, which is why they combined all four souls together. The key is knowing what part of the new vital center needs attention at any given time to keep the balance in our complex system.

Second, while it has been helpful to look at the liberal and conservative sides of the graph, when we get to the new vital center it is better to see these four positions as beyond the left-right spectrum and shared by all Americans. So while I will continue to use *left* and *right* to specify the part of the quadrant I am addressing, these positions are beyond left and right, pulling all quadrants toward the graph's center and toward unity. Finally, while in this chapter I lay out the historical genealogy, assigning one historical person to represent each soul, in chapter twelve I will provide current thinkers in each quadrant of the new vital center.

CONSTITUTIONAL SOUL (FREEDOM LEFT 1)

As in part two I will start with freedom left, with position 1—what I am calling the "constitutional soul."[30] The hero of this new vital center position is James Madison, the father of the US Constitution and coauthor of *The Federalist Papers*.[31] We owe much of what we think of the creed (that is, the correct view, not that of freedom left 2 and freedom right 2) to him. At the time of the second founding, Madison, a Calvinist trained at Princeton under John Witherspoon, had scrutinized history and decided that America shouldn't be a pure republic, as much as Madison admired the ancient republican's passion for the nation. As a Calvinist who understood well the depravity of individuals, Madison contended that ancient republics, comprising the "great body of the people" (*Federalist Paper* No. 39) speaking in one voice, often lacked a mechanism to constrain powerful leaders who, when losing patience with the deliberative procedures, would abandon these procedures and incite the people into a mob, which in turn would lead to disorder and tyranny.[32] Democracy, because it had no way to restrain powerful demagogues and the mobs they created, was the ruin of ancient republics.[33]

But Madison also realized that constitutionalism, built in part on British and Scottish liberalism, had its problems as well. He realized that it could coexist with a monarchy, as in England, and while it was able to check powerful leaders, it could also impede democracy, getting in the way of a people's right to self-government. In his helpful and brief introduction to Madison's thought, *The Political Philosophy of James Madison*, Garrett Ward

Sheldon shows how Madison's profound understanding of Reformed theology and common grace allowed him to brilliantly fuse British Enlightenment liberalism and civic republicanism. One side (republicanism), grounded in history and tradition, would be combined with the other side (liberal democracy), grounded in nature and reason, producing something new called a democratic republic. Together these two systems would be a "new order of the ages."[34]

But Madison also realized that the two models clashed at points. "Just as proponents of constitutional government had doubts about republicanism, so, too," comments Ceaser, "did many advocates of republicanism have reservations about constitutionalism."[35] In order to find a synthesis, each side would have to compromise. Each side had to make modifications for the new synthesis to work. In his *Liberal Democracy and Political Science*, Ceaser contends that Madison and the founders "understood that to combine constitutionalism and republicanism in one regime required a reworking of the pure form of each."[36] In order for constitutionalism to be combined with republicanism, each model had to make concessions, and it was Madison's Christianity, particularly his doctrine of human nature, that provided the insights for this compromise.[37]

For Madison, constitutionalism protects individual rights from arbitrary powers, nurtures limited government, and sets up safeguards so that majorities can't abuse minorities. And because it limited the self-government of the people, it created tension. So republicanism was suspicious, thinking that constitutionalism would eventually install a monarchy, thwarting the self-government of the republic. One way that Madison modified constitutionalism, which he grounded in nature/reason and not customary history (which would have supported a king) was to follow thinkers like John Locke (who influenced Thomas Jefferson) and put the stress on the equality of people.[38]

The key to understanding constitutionalism is found in the words of the Declaration of Independence, "We hold these truths to be self-evident, that all men are created equal."[39] Thus, unlike the British constitution where estates and nobility were protected, the American constitution gave rights equally to all people ("We the People") irrespective of class and satisfied the republican requirement for self-government. In the words of *The Federalist*

Papers, the "protection of the diversity in the faculties of men, from which the rights of property originate" was now the "first object of government."[40] Rights, founded in nature and the natural equality of all humans, now become enshrined in the Constitution and the Bill of Rights. While sovereignty rests with the people, it is expressed through a written constitution, where, in a large nation like the United States, the voice of the people is expressed through representatives, checks and balances are established, and the government is broken into three competing branches to protect minority rights from the tyranny of the majority. Thus government is set up to safeguard the fundamental rights of all people, allowing them to seek "life, liberty, and the pursuit of happiness."

This view of rights created tension almost immediately, particularly in the area of morality and virtue, two things at the heart of republicanism. But before we look at how this tension was resolved, let's look at how republicanism was modified to fit with constitutionalism.

REPUBLICAN SOUL (ORDER LEFT 1)

We now turn to order left 1, the republican soul. The hero in this quadrant is Thomas Jefferson (whom Abraham Lincoln appealed to in spite of Jefferson's hypocrisy—being against slavery in principle but holding slaves in practice), a friend and colleague of Madison.[41] Like Madison, Jefferson was also interested in the synthesis between classical liberal constitutionalism and republicanism. But, whereas Madison tended to tilt toward constitutionalism, Jefferson tilted toward republicanism and the importance of self-government and virtue among the people—more classical themes.

Some prominent historians of the twentieth century began making the case that civic republicanism, often thought to have been studied and rejected by the founders, in fact played a key role in the American system.[42] Stressing the "great body of the people," republicanism was grounded in a form of customary history in which "the people," ruled by a majority, are committed to the ancient ways of the republic. The majority has best access to this foundation, these ancient traditions and institutions, and the people become the guardians of the republic; written constitutions often get in the way. But Garrett Ward Sheldon claims that "Jefferson's understanding of freedom encompasses both the liberal Lockean ideas of individual freedom from government and interference [constitutionalism] and the classical notion to participate in the public deliberation which develop one's highest qualities and shape the laws under which one lives [republicanism]."[43] And the key to this synthesis is the character of the people.

For republicans like Jefferson, a constitution alone is not the best way to guarantee that justice is carried out but that the character of "the people" remains virtuous. "For republicans," writes Ceaser, "the most important factor that accounts for the health of the republic is not its political institutions but the mores [culture] of its people," and "without certain mores, a republic could not exist or endure."[44] In fact, if the people were to continue to make good decisions (based on what history teaches), they needed a virtuous people shaped by a certain culture of morality and that possess the right "habits of the heart." The greatest virtue is the willingness to sacrifice individual rights for the good of the republic. In order to nurture a virtuous citizenry, one incapable of corruption and descending into the rule of the mob, the character of the people had to be continuously shaped. "The city must be a 'school' that forms and molds a certain kind of human being."[45] It's a noble goal, and founders like Jefferson desired a virtuous citizenry to support public life, protecting it from corruption and decay and tyranny.

But Ceaser points out there was a problem with republicanism. "To foster and maintain virtue in a republic is no easy task. It requires . . . tight social controls that are in direct tension with the individual liberty sought under constitutional government."[46] Moreover, Ceaser contends that "closed society" is the best way to describe an ancient republic like Sparta. And there were many at the time of our founding that believed this kind of closed, tightly controlled society was necessary to promote liberty and to protect a self-governing people against the monarchy. Yet, for those on the constitutional side of the argument, thinkers like Madison and the coauthors of *The Federalist Papers*, "this kind of liberty for the city as a whole is purchased at the cost of liberty for the individual," whose rights could be trampled by the mob. "The liberty of the republic [against a monarch] is at odds with the modern conception of individual liberty [enshrined in constitutionalism]."[47] For republicanism to be joined with constitutionalism it had to be modified, to make concessions. And it did this in four ways. First, it allowed the constitution to act as the authority of the people in place of one man, one vote.

Second, it conceded to allowing elected representatives to represent the people. Third, it looked to constitutional structures to guard liberty in place of a virtuous citizenry. And finally, it awarded the individual more freedom to pursue personal ends in place of the "love of the republic." In modifying republicanism to fit a constitutional structure and modifying constitutionalism to synthesize with republicanism, the founders were able to combine the two systems, ameliorating the weaknesses of each. Like the Whigs, who combined customary history and nature/reason into a new synthesis, the founders were able to synthesize republicanism (based on history) and constitutionalism (grounded on nature/reason) into a new system. Both sides made concessions; both sides checked and balanced each other, keeping each from being pulled away from the new vital center.

But the new synthesis wasn't without tension. And this tension has been argued over for the past two hundred and twenty years. If both sides agreed that a virtuous citizenry is needed to guard liberty, that is, to keep the majority from devolving into corruption and abusing minority rights, then what, if *not* the republican's "school of virtue," would engender this? In other words, if the creed was built on a certain culture, what or who cultivated this culture? Is a new kind of citizenry possible in this new democratic republic? Or is the creed, the system of checks and balances and the mechanisms in the constitution, enough? Here the story gets even more interesting.

Middle Class Soul (Freedom Right 1)

Turning to freedom right 1, the middle class soul, the hero is Adam Smith, and his *The Wealth of Nations,* echoed in *The Federalist Papers*, which cares about virtue, but often in negative terms. What this means is that for freedom right 1, classical republican virtue, which often is high and lofty, so often outside the capabilities of the average human being, is rejected in favor of a "low" view of human nature, taking humans as they are and not based on some utopian vision. As Hoover Institute's Thomas Sowell says in his *A Conflict of Visions*, Adam Smith [and Madison] saw "the fundamental moral and social challenge was to make the best of possibilities which existed within that constraint" rather than waste energy trying to change human nature.[48] The goal, then, was to work with existing conditions and realities and devise a system that would be the most efficient within the constraints of human nature as it really existed. Sowell calls this the "constrained" vision.[49]

In a similar fashion to Smith's constrained vision, the "Madisonian system," best articulated in *The Federalist Papers*, holds that constitutionalism by itself channels people's lower passions ("ambition must be made to counteract ambition"), allowing a "policy of supplying, by opposite and rival interests, the defect of better motives." By allowing the "private interest of every individual" it will "be a sentinel over the public rights."[50]

Political philosopher Martin Diamond summarizes both Smith and Madison's position well in his fifty-year-old essay "Ethics and Politics: The American Way," saying this low view is based on a person "as he actually is" and not on a utopian view of what he could be. Unlike the classical era, when the republic was responsible to shape the character of the people, this new synthesis "could rely largely instead upon shrewd institutional arrangements of the powerful human passions and interests."

> Not to instruct and to transcend these passions and interests, but rather to channel and to use them. . . . Politics would now concentrate upon the "realistic" task of directing man's passions and interests toward the achievement of those solid goods this earth has to offer—self-preservation and the protection of those individual liberties which are an integral part of that preservation and which make it decent and agreeable.[51]

Based on the grounding of "spontaneous order"—a belief that built into the nature of things is an order that if left to itself would work itself out, provided no one tried to impose a particular order on it—individuals and groups produce order by their action but not by human design. It needs to be spontaneous. And the result is that when thousands of people interact on a daily basis, sometimes competing, other times cooperating, the *invisible hand* will ensure that the best order will result. The virtue produced may not be as lofty as that in republicanism, but it is still an improvement over the tyranny that can result in ancient republics.

But, according to Diamond, these virtues would not be shaped by the government but by commerce. Often called "commercial virtue" or "bourgeois virtues," they are not created by the republican school of virtue but by the capitalistic school of virtue. "In fact," says Diamond, "the American political order rises respectably high enough above the vulgar level of mere self-interest in the direction of virtue—if not to the highest reaches of the ancient perspective, still toward positive human decencies or excellences."[52] These excellences come about through commercial means. As Alexander Hamilton said, the commercial society inculcates "the assiduous merchant, the laborious husbandman, the active mechanic, and the industrious manufacturer."[53] Diamond concludes, "These may be put down as merely 'bourgeois virtues,' but they are virtues, or human excellences, nonetheless."[54]

In sum, then, the *constrained* vision of Adam Smith, which became the Madisonian system, believed the tension between republicanism and constitutionalism could be resolved by mixing "in republican ideas of participation and traditionalist themes of religiosity, community, spiritedness, blending these elements in a way that might allow them to form a workable whole." This synthesis, argues Ceaser, did not produce a perfect whole but one that gets us closer to an ideal.

In the real world this may be all that we can hope for, given the sinfulness of human beings. And besides, a perfect theoretical consistency between these three souls we have looked at so far is not possible, and "thus to insist on one principle," argues Ceaser, "as the sole foundation of liberal democratic society becomes an act of political prudence."[55]

Toward the end of "Ethics and Politics" even Diamond cracks open the door for the need for some active role of the republic in cultivating character. While he continues to argue that the founders' political order was based on the "human interests and passions" as we find them, not as we hope them to be, and while he believes the constitution is set up to manage these passions, to set one faction against another, he makes this startling concession:

> We must appreciate also that their political order presupposes certain enduring qualities that can and should be achieved in the American character ... *[that] the preservation of that foundation [culture] and at the same time the nurturing of the appropriate ethical excellences remains the compound political task of enlightened American statesmen and citizens.*[56]

For Diamond, both sides of the compound need to be nurtured. We make a mistake and the balanced system gets out of whack if stress is put only on raw passion and self-interest (as libertarians do in freedom right 2 and 3) without the balance of republican excellences. Diamond never got around to telling us how this compound could be maintained, as he passed away soon after writing "Ethics and Politics." But one thing is certain, if the synthesis was going to be maintained, if the tension is to be resolved, one other component was missing.

In sum, then, while Adam Smith's constrained vision, channeled into the Madisonian constitution, can develop certain kinds of low, bourgeoisie, middle class virtues, ones that need to be protected and nurtured against republican overreach (something we need to remember, with the rush to socialism among millennials), it is nonetheless still not enough (and is susceptible to be overrun by materialism and greed) to solve the tensions between the republican ideal and constitutionalism. It moves the ball closer, and this is important, but for us to move the ball further toward the goal, a new vital center, we need what order right 1 contributes to the whole, the statesman soul. And this will come about when statesmen and citizens, the political philosophers of our nation, help nurture the appropriate virtues for a constitutional republic.

STATESMAN SOUL (ORDER RIGHT 1)

What then, is the component that is missing? How do we seek, in Diamond's words, "the preservation of that foundation [a culture composed of virtuous citizens] and at the same time the nurturing of the appropriate ethical excellences"? In short, we need to adopt a view, argues Ceaser, that

> holds that liberal democracy demands constant superintendence, even if its basic political institutions have been wisely designed. . . . Its maintenance requires certain mores [habits of the heart] in citizens that do not flow automatically either from people's "natural" dispositions . . . or from the arrangement of the primary political institutions.[57]

The key is leadership. Statesmen. Something that is in short supply today.

Tocqueville seemingly agreed. "Self-interest well understood" is not enough. He called for secular and religious strategies for protecting the synthesis. While we will look at his religious strategy in chapter thirteen, here I will emphasize Tocqueville's secular strategy, one evangelicals can affirm in the category of natural revelation (or common grace), that is, the need for leaders of uncommon virtue and vision to step out of the pack and direct people's attention to something higher. Tocqueville calls for statesmen and "enlightened" citizens to lift "up souls" and keep "them pointed toward heaven."

> It is necessary that all those who are interested (whether religious or not) in the future of democratic societies, unite, and that all in concert make continual efforts to spread within those societies the taste for the infinite, the sentiment for the grand and the love of non-material pleasures.[58]

Leaders then, for Tocqueville, need to raise the ambitions of citizens above the here and now, above the tawdry pleasures of life, to something grander, something more spiritual, a type of earthly glory. If they don't do this, then materialism and crass self-interest will eventually ruin democracy, which we are witnessing today.

For those on order right 1, the statesman who best exemplifies wise leadership was Abraham Lincoln.[59] He embodies the statesman soul. He best held together the tensions at the heart of the American synthesis and did so without some of the baggage of Jefferson and Madison on the slavery question. Early in his political career, as a Whig, Lincoln attempted to hold history and nature in tension, while stressing history a bit more than nature/reason. We see this stress on history/culture in his Lyceum Address. In the face of violence that was sweeping the nation, Lincoln called his audience to "swear by the blood of the Revolution" and to revere "the laws of the country" in order to "be united with each other," and thus find unity in our common affections for our traditions and laws.[60] Like so many in the Whig party, he looked to Edmund Burke and his emphasis on history, tradition, prudence, and reason applied within that tradition.

But by the 1850s, as nature/reason were being eclipsed by those who looked exclusively to history to defend slavery, Lincoln leaned more on nature, the principles of the Declaration of Independence (self-evident truth gleaned through reason), and natural right/natural law to defend the equality of all humans, including Blacks. In fact, as Daniel Walker Howe says, the "Whiggish use of Burkean methods was leading them back to the Lockean principles of the Declaration of Independence."[61] History was teaching the Whigs and Lincoln to return to first principles, the principle that "all men are created equal" (Jefferson's phrase), the first things of the founding and to never give up the fight to realize them in society.

"Four score and seven years ago our fathers brought forth on this continent, a new nation, conceived in Liberty, and dedicated to the proposition that all men are created equal," Lincoln said in his address at Gettysburg, memorializing the loss of half a million Americans.[62] In the final part of his career, the period of the Civil War, he added sacred history to his foundations, realizing the need for a religious grounding beneath history and nature. In his Second Inaugural Address he appeals to the nation with the poetic words "with malice toward none; with charity for all; with firmness in the right, as God gives us to see the right, let us strive on to finish the work we are in."[63]

Lincoln adjusted the balance of his synthesis as the times dictated. When the nation was getting out of balance, for example stressing reason/nature (creed) too much, he pushed back with history (culture). And when it was stressing history (culture) too much, for example in the battle over slavery and equality, he countered with nature/reason and ultimately the Bible.

Order right 1, then, presents a view of the ideal leader, the statesman. It's about the need for wise and noble elites who pursue the common good and remind the other three souls what is at stake. As wise a leader, the statesman's soul recognizes the tension in our system and the need for *mores*, the habits of the heart, the kind of virtues that transcend bourgeois virtue. They recognize that "ways must be found to produce and cultivate the necessary mores."[64] Ceaser calls this task "superintendence," a kind of statesmanship that helps check and balance, guide and mold the three souls of republicanism, constitutionalism, and "self-interest properly understood." It is complex and requires knowledge, prudence, and wisdom, virtues that escape our uniparty politicians.

"The task of superintendence," claims Ceaser, "cannot be fully institutionalized or written into a constitution or a set of laws. It is a variable enterprise that requires an ongoing adjustment and readaption of secondary institutions and of intellectual strategies in such realms as religion, art, and education."[65] And this calls for statesmen and citizens, tutors who take up the call for a "new political science" to superintend the compound. In some ways, order right 1 is the call for leaders trained in old-school political science (i.e., the art of political education) to constantly remind the other three quadrants of the need for balance, to warn them when they are polarizing, and to inspire the entire democratic republic vision to grandeur. Wise statesmen and citizens are needed for the ongoing training and shaping of our citizens, strengthening their understanding of the Constitution (creed) and helping the society develop the kind of republican character (culture) that over time inculcates the republican virtues that shape the liberal democratic citizen (mores) and maintain our union. Order right 1 is the tutor for the other three souls.

For example, wise statesmen realize that the political and economic system doesn't run for long on autopilot, requiring no superintendence, as freedom left 2 and freedom right 2 argue. But it also doesn't require total control of the economy and the political realm, as progressives in order left 2 and 3 demand, collapsing any distinction between politics and society. The statesman soul wants a third way, a new vital center, a wise balance of creed and culture, reason and tradition, freedom and cultivation, order and liberty, a system that realizes that while the state-society distinction is not the last word (freedom left 2) the two have to be carefully balanced in order to avoid overreach.

In *The Federalist Papers*, Hamilton wrote that this form of government is "complex and skillfully contrived" and thus needs the wisdom of statesmen to maintain the complexity, statesmen who possess the requisite knowledge. This wisdom is the knowledge of political science, one that understands how the system is balanced, what forces threaten it, and what is needed for continual restoration. That is, in the words of Hamilton, "the means by which the excellences of republican government can be retained and its imperfections lessened and avoided."[66] Likewise, Tocqueville called for "a new political science" to instruct and tutor liberal democracy.[67] Order right 1 takes up this task, the wisdom and knowledge to properly tutor democracy, which includes the new vital center. It does this in six ways.

How the Wise Statesman Tutors Democracy

First, the statesman soul constantly reminds the other three souls that the American project is grounded on both reason and tradition, history and nature, creed and culture. It continually pushes back against the enemies of this historical synthesis who have the tendency to emphasize one side over the other, pushing to extremes: for example, history/tradition leading to the alt-right (order right 3) or woke radicalism (order left 3) on the one hand, or nature/rationalism leading to applied postmodernism (freedom left 3) or radical libertarianism (freedom right 3), on the other. It knows when to correct one quadrant for straying outside of its limits, a negative function. But it discerns when to balance a quadrant getting out of kilter with the attributes of another quadrant, the positive function.

Second, the statesman soul reminds our democratic republic that over time America has become its own unique tradition that since the Pilgrim landing has combined the best of British liberalism and ancient civic republicanism. It defends natural rights rooted in natural law but also draws on the republican standard of virtue and excellence, allowing us and calling us to a standard by which to criticize consumer and sexual vulgarity in our culture.

Next, the statesman soul teaches that wise laws are needed to shape a culture of virtue and excellence. The statesman soul teaches that all political arrangements (i.e., the laws) are arranged with the goal of shaping mores. There are no neutral laws, no such thing as a procedural republic, no reality of an encumbered self. All individuals are encumbered; it's just a matter of what encumbers them and what shapes them. So the statesman rejects the antiperfectionism of freedom left 2 that doesn't believe the *good* exists, but the statesman isn't in favor of the heavy-handedness (perfectionism) of the ancient republics either. Instead, our democratic republic favors *soft perfectionism*, a view that sees our constitution and government playing "a legitimate but indirect or subsidiary role in fostering and protecting the conditions in which individuals pursue their own perfection ('the pursuit of happiness,' as the Declaration puts it)."[68] In other words, "the law cannot make people moral" by itself (perfectionism), "but it can effect the conditions in which human beings make themselves moral" (soft perfectionism), and, in the end, promote human flourishing.[69]

Fourth, the wise statesman teaches that "secondary political and social institutions" help "promote helpful habits and practices."[70] The statesman reminds the new vital center that, like the law (which instructs and tutors), local government, mediating structures, and the family are "schools of democracy" (Tocqueville). The goal is not to grow the shaping power of the government but to keep it small so that the natural associations and mediating structures in our society can grow. For humans are shaped as citizens and individuals in these associations and are taught to look beyond their own interest to something greater. Moreover, by taking part in local government, citizens learn and practice self-government, learning to take care of themselves (and not look to government for handouts). They also learn to get along with people with different views, a kind of school of civility and citizenship wrapped up in one. These mediating structures, "small platoons" as Burke called them, also provide a buffer that protects individuals and their associations from an encroaching welfare and administrative state.

Fifth, the statesman soul tutors the new vital center to take seriously the call found in the Declaration to "mutually pledge to each other our Lives, our Fortunes, and our sacred Honor," and to be committed to "devising intellectual and cultural strategies to foster supportive ideas, opinions, and beliefs," which elevate our republic beyond crass materialism and greed.[71] In other words, the wise statesman is committed to educating our society about our unique public philosophy, what it is grounded on, how the synthesis is structured, the kind of virtuous citizenry that is needed to sustain it, and what democratic grandeur looks like. Statesmen, cultural leaders, and pastors take seriously the charge of Abraham Lincoln, a hero and a saint for those in order right 1, who once said, "In this and like communities, public sentiment is everything. With public sentiment, nothing can fail; without it nothing can succeed. Consequently, he who molds public sentiment, goes deeper than he who enacts statutes or pronounces decisions."[72]

Finally, the statesman soul reminds the new vital center that America's unique balance of constitutionalism/individual rights (creed) and republicanism/excellences (culture) are the product of a certain people, history, and tradition, that is, the genius of the American people and our nation. Tocqueville reminds his readers that the Puritans of New England "left to their descendants the habits, the ideas, and the mores that are most fitting to lead to the flourishing of liberal democracy."[73] *The Federalist Papers* mention that "no other form of government [but a liberal democratic form] would be reconcilable with the genius of the people of America."[74] While the genius of a nation doesn't necessarily determine the structure of the government a country adopts, it does make the connection between the nation, the citizens of a nation, their unique culture, and what kind of government that culture can sustain.

SUMMARY

This, in a nutshell, is the new vital center, a synthesis of constitutionalism and republicanism balanced by higher and lower motives and guided by wise statesmen who recognize the need to cultivate virtue in citizens. The new vital center is grounded on history and nature, and creed and culture. It is confident in its origins but humble about its constant frailty. It is both confident in knowing truth but modest about how to apply it. It is generous but protective. It stresses freedom constrained by order.

Taken together, the four souls of the new vital center teach a healthy love of country, an instinctive patriotism, one that celebrates the heritage of the nation, promotes the bonds that unite us as a people, and holds a commitment to creed and culture.[75] Without this "instinctive patriotism" ("My country, 'tis of thee, sweet land of liberty" [76]), a nation lacks national enthusiasm, a kind of "spiritedness," a "higher idea of themselves and the humanity," in Tocqueville's words, and that without this "sacred flame," unity, strength, and flourishing would be impossible for America, as we are finding out the hard way.[77] How different the wise statesman is from our present ruling elites, who manipulate the eight polarized positions in order to denigrate America, divide its citizens, and ultimately overturn our constitutional republicanism, not only because it stands in the way of their monopolistic power but because, in their hearts, they are authoritarians, oligarchs. Ironically, they are strikingly similar to the oligarchs of the slaveholding plantations, who wanted to sit atop the class hierarchy.

The wise statesman of the new vital center inculcates a profound love of America, a renewed patriotism built on the history, tradition, grounding, and constitutionalism of our past—the glue, which provides the "mystic chords of memory," a new civic faith, capable of a rebirth of freedom (creed) and a rediscovery of national unity (culture), giving identity to American citizens. But some don't want this rebirth of freedom or this rediscovery of patriotism; some are threatened by it. And this is seen in the area of immigration, the section of the America First Caucus platform that created such a dustup. And it is to that topic we now turn.

12

PATRIOTIC CITIZENSHIP

THE SWEET OFFER FOR RESIDENT ALIENS AND ALIENATED RESIDENTS

THERE MAY BE NO BETTER EXAMPLE of the intentions and goals of the bipartisan ruling elites than their commitment to mass immigration and eventually open borders, proving that their quest for monopolistic power is of *one piece*; that is, it is here, with their transformation of the border and their commitment to letting in millions of illegal aliens, that their goals and intentions, which we have highlighted throughout this book—globalization, free trade, the China class, critical race theory, and twin insurgency, all come together in a powerful mix, demonstrating, without a shadow of doubt, their desire to transform America economically, politically, and culturally.

By May 2021 the border was *effectively* open for months, allowing the majority of migrants to stream across, thousands each day, arriving in historic numbers, including close to nineteen thousand children.[1] The "catch and return" policy of the Trump administration has been replaced with the "catch and bus" policy of the Biden administration, as the US government acts like a tourist agency, distributing these migrants to cities across the nation.[2] Each month, fewer and fewer migrants are being sent back and instead the current administration is finding excuses to let them stay, quietly and in the dead of night busing them to the interior of our country.[3]

While the mainstream press has been discouraged from reporting the crisis at the border, a few intrepid reporters have been embedded at the US-Mexican border for months, reporting on the humanitarian crisis.[4] There have been reports of terrorists blending in with the migrants and slipping across the border,[5] of the physical and sexual abuse of unaccompanied migrant children,[6] and of accelerated illegal activity of drug cartels in recent months.[7]

For our ruling elites, mass immigration and the quest for open borders may be the single most important and effective way to weaken national sovereignty and transform American society. Even more than the critical race theory that continues its long march through our institutions or the mass rioting in our streets destroying middle-class business, open borders is the most effective way to achieve globalization and bring on demographic, political, and cultural change.[8] Biden has made it one of his top priorities and the Republican leadership is mostly silent.

The nature of this bipartisan left-right coalition explains why both Republican and Democrat leaders attacked the America First Caucus platform, especially its views on immigration.[9] It also may explain why three days after the America First Caucus platform was leaked, the Biden Administration issued a directive: all immigration enforcement agencies were barred from using the terms *illegal alien* and *assimilation* when referring to the people flooding our border. Instead, they were to use the words *undocumented* and *integration*.[10] But while it seems like it is just a squabble over words, adopting words that are more sensitive to the migrant's plight, they are attempting to shift the way Americans perceive these migrants and how Americans should respond to them, which is to welcome them with open arms. Andrew R. Arthur, resident fellow at the bipartisan Center for Immigration Studies, concludes, "in the context of the proposed linguistic changes, aliens who enter illegally are not to blame (they are not even 'aliens' and their entry was not even 'illegal'), for they lack the documents, which *you* refused to give them."[11] Thus the directive can be seen as an attempt to seize the language and control the narrative of the debate of mass immigration and open borders.

In contrast to the Biden Administration's position on immigration, the America First Caucus platform holds a position affirming that the uniqueness and unity of our country is threatened by mass immigration, "particularly without institutional support for assimilation and the expansive welfare state to bail them out" when they can't make it on their own.[12] "America's borders must be defended," the platform continues, "and illegal immigration must be stopped without exception."[13] These are views that until recently were shared by Barack Obama and Bernie Sanders.[14] According to the AFC platform, the immigration situation has reached a crisis point, and thus we need a pause in immigration, which "is absolutely essential in assimilating the new arrivals," teaching them to "plunge head-first into mainstream American society," while at the same time rejecting those who "could not or refused to abandon their old loyalties." Yet the ruling class attacked the platform, belittling those who hold similar views. But the truth of the matter is that by February 2021, many Americans disapproved of Biden's approach to the crisis.[15]

The title of a recent book, *They're Not Listening: How the Elites Created the National Populist Revolution*, captures the frustration of those Americans well.[16] For the corporate global elites, President Biden was the Democratic candidate of choice, and he continues to get their support.[17] And for corporate CEOs, any talk of nationalism is a direct threat to what they want to achieve—open borders, cheap labor, massive demographic and cultural change, and the rule of the globalized elites. But there are those who believe in the new vital center and continue to push back, showing that a sovereign country has a moral right to defend its borders, protecting its own citizens.[18]

Some have shown how mass immigration forces wages down for our Black and Hispanic working class, harming Middle America.[19] Others point out how unchecked immigration impoverishes our health care system and educational system, making life for the working and middle classes difficult.[20] Still others demonstrate how mass immigration expands the welfare system, giving more power to the federal government and creating more dependency among our poor.[21] Some critics have pointed out that the goal of mass immigration is to replace White middle-class workers with cheaper workers from foreign countries.[22] Finally, critics have attempted to expose the goal of mass immigration—to weaken the electoral power of those who have been in the country for generations, effectively negating their electoral power and in the process transforming the nation into something radically different.[23]

In sum, what all these critics are exposing is the ruling elite strategy of twin insurgency. And here we see it at work once again—the "war from below" carried out by encouraging migrants to enter illegally, and the "war from above"—corporate America replacing America workers with cheap foreign labor, creating a permanent underclass, and in the process transforming America's unique culture that is so important to support constitutional republicanism and a new vital center. And who is most hurt? The working and middle classes squeezed from the top and the bottom.

Yet any attempt to point out the deleterious effects of mass immigration is met with a familiar refrain: racism and White supremacy. As the former Arizona state senator Alfredo Gutierrez, a Democrat, once said about immigration, "We call things racism just to get attention. We reduce complicated problems to racism, not because it's racism, but because it works," saying out loud what is often whispered in private—the best way to silence critics is to tar them with the ultimate pejorative: racist.[24]

This tarring of critics also goes on, perhaps more subtly, in evangelical circles, particularly from those on the progressive left. Calling for border enforcement, restrictions on immigration, limits to the number of immigrants (all within its rights as a sovereign nation protecting the rule of law and common good of its citizens), or job-place enforcement through an identity card, is charged with being unfair, harsh, un-Christian, and going against the Bible. When immigration is in the news, my social media is flooded by progressive evangelicals accusing immigration restrictionists of racism, xenophobia, and being un-Christian. In *The Immigration Crisis*, James Hoffmeier looks at every major passage in the Bible about aliens and concludes that progressive Christians are confusing the biblical terms for legal and illegal immigrants, leading them to erroneously think that the Bible endorses the same rights for illegal immigrants as legal aliens when it clearly doesn't.[25]

While it is often thought that most dissenters to mass immigration and open borders come from those on the right (like the American First Caucus), in fact there have been a number of courageous Democrats who over the years have spoken out, sounding the alarm that the United States has let in people whose "culture and values of their countries of origin differ substantially from those prevalent in America," substantially transforming the demographics of the country over the past seventy years.[26]

One of the most significant voices has been Jerry Kammer, a fellow at the bipartisan Center for Immigration Studies, who is a self-proclaimed liberal in favor of immigration restrictions and job-site enforcement. In his recent book *Losing Ground: How a Left-Right Coalition Blocked Immigration Reform and Provoked a Backlash That Elected Trump,* maybe the best book on the history of immigration policy over the past seventy years, Kammer demonstrates that the Democratic Party once was the biggest opponent of illegal immigration because it took jobs away from the working class and suppressed their wages.[27] But over the last decade the party has done an about-face. He says the Democratic Party, pushed by woke progressives, has drifted so far left on this issue that they have actually woken up on the libertarian right. And now the Democratic Party, like the libertarian Republicans, is part of the left-right coalition protecting mass immigration, turning its back on the working class. Kammer writes, "Unchecked immigration is a threat to our ability to hold together as a people, our ability to maintain the *Unum* while honoring the *Pluribus*."[28] Unsurprisingly, Kammer's message has been received uncharitably by his fellow members of the Left.

Because the demographic and cultural changes have been so devastating, we require an immigration pause in order to allow the country to properly assimilate all the newcomers, a position echoed in the AFC platform.

WHEN THE BATHWATER IS OVERFLOWING, TURN OFF THE WATER

If left-of-center voices like Kammer's are calling for a pause in immigration, there are voices on the right that want an immediate moratorium. Like Kammer, Ann Coulter sounds the alarm over the dramatic "demographic and cultural change" that has taken place and has been "devastating" to our nation.[29] Coulter points out that Whites, who in 1960 were 90 percent of the country, by 2050 will be the minority, "If this sort of drastic change were legally imposed on any group other than White Americans, it would be called genocide."[30] For Coulter, "The only thing that stands between America and oblivion is a total immigration moratorium."[31] If the bathwater is overflowing, you don't scurry about looking for a towel to mop it up, you turn off the water, she says.

As part of the growing populist backlash against immigration, voices on the right and the left are calling to "shut off the bathwater." While some like Kammer want a temporary pause followed by new restrictions at the border and strong enforcement at the workplace, others like Coulter want an immigration moratorium, maybe forever. But whether the pause is temporary or forever, these critics agree that something must be done soon. Therefore, attempting to shut off the bathwater, proponents have proposed a number of strategies, including building the border wall, enforcing employment compliance through E-Verify, ending chain migration and birthright citizenship, terminating the asylum program, and outlawing the H-1B visa program.

While I agree that an immediate pause is necessary and that we need to end all immigration laws that have put us in this crisis, there is something even more important that we must address—assimilating those immigrants who are already here. According to the Pew Foundation, since the passage of the 1965 Immigration and Nationality Act, "nearly 59 million immigrants have arrived in the United States."[32] These immigrants are not going anywhere. And if mass immigration is indeed weakening our *e pluribus unum*, as Kammer, Huntington, and other voices conclude, then it is vital that along with calling for a pause we also take seriously those who are already here.[33]

We can't limit our response to just turning off the bathwater. Along with the negative, pausing mass immigration, we need a positive, a once-upon-a-time narrative that inspires new immigrants as well as citizens. There must be both a *negative* project (a pause) and a *positive* project (a call to citizenship) for both immigrants *and* citizens. In the words of Duke University professor Noah Pickus, we need a positive project that lays out "a unified nation that embraces newcomers" and "requires making demands of immigrants and of Americans."[34] It is a plan to turn the resident alien into an enthusiastic American and transform the alienated resident into a true citizen.

But even this is not without problems. If there really are ninety million legal and illegal immigrants in the country, do we really want them to assimilate, asks Peter Skerry, especially if what they are assimilated *into* is a woke public philosophy, one that teaches immigrants to hate America, grab as much welfare money as possible, and never fully embrace the nation?[35] If this is the only option, the answer would have to be no. To assimilate them into a culture of dependence, victimhood, and anti-American sentiment would just perpetuate the problem and continue to divide America.

But thankfully in the new vital center there is another option: assimilating all immigrants and citizens into a fundamentally different and attractive narrative. As P. P. Claxton, a leader in the early Americanization movement in the 1920s, wrote, "Americanization is a process of education, of winning the mind and the heart through instruction and enlightenment. . . . It must depend . . . on the attractive power and the *sweet reasonableness* of the thing itself."[36] And the secret to this instruction is in the word *sweet*, what the new vital center calls the *sweet offer of assimilation*, a call to embrace the best of America, an invitation that still attracts millions of immigrants, Black, Brown, and White, from all over the world. It is to this sweet offer of assimilation, a call to full citizens, that we now turn, and in the process it will give us a better idea how the new vital center can restore unity in our country.

THE SWEET OFFER OF ASSIMILATION AND THE FOUR SOULS

A good place to begin fashioning a sweet offer of assimilation is David Miller's *Strangers in Our Midst: The Political Philosophy of Immigration*, where he outlines the available options for "integrating immigrants," and, I would add, alienated residents, including many Black Americans who see assimilation as a bad thing.[37] Miller contends there are generally three options, "social integration," "civic integration," and "cultural integration," and all three have been bitterly argued over by scholars and practitioners, and all three can be seen in the disputes between our quadrant positions. Generally, freedom right libertarians prefer social integration; freedom left liberals prefer civic integration, and order right conservatives defend cultural integration.

Miller argues there is truth in each option and that our best path forward isn't to cling to just one option, which distorts and leads to extremism, but to find a way to combine the best aspects of all three. As we are about to see, these three options of integration, along with the need to spread them with an evangelist's fervor, are similar to the four souls of the new vital center.

THE INVITATION INTO THE MIDDLE CLASS
SOUL (FREEDOM RIGHT 1)

Miller begins with the first option, "social integration," because he believes it is the least controversial of the three options, involving "not only creating a rich pattern of social interaction but also interaction of the right kind—involving friendly, respectful relationships between equals."[38] It may also be the easiest to gauge. Miller indicates we will know social integration has taken place when certain patterns of behavior take place, for example, when the new immigrant (and citizen) becomes socially integrated in how things are done here. This is not, however, an invitation to crass materialism (come here to get rich) or a globalized mass culture (where everyone dresses and looks the same) but an invitation to join our market economy as workers, bosses, and entrepreneurs and in the process be shaped by participation in the market. As Alexander Hamilton, himself an immigrant, wrote, "the established rules of morality and justice" on which America is grounded teach Americans that they

> are bound to keep their promises, to fulfill their engagements, to respect the rights of property which others have acquired under contracts with them. . . . Without this, there is no end of all distinct ideas of right and wrong, justice and injustice, in relation to society or government.

For Hamilton, without this moral and ethical behavior, which needs to be present and to be shaped, "there can be no such things as rights—no such thing . . . as liberty."[39] This is Tocqueville's "self-interest well understood." It is not a call to greed or selfishness but an understanding that in pursuing proper self-interest we are not only benefiting others but being shaped, becoming more virtuous, in the process.

No contemporary thinker captures the option of social integration better than Thomas Sowell, a Black economist at the Hoover Institute in Palo Alto, California.[40] Sowell contends that multiculturalism and its emphasis on group rights and victimhood have led Blacks and Mexican Americans to believe they are victims of racial discrimination, that America is an evil and exploitive place run by Whites, and that success is impossible for them. Further, they believe that the only way to get ahead is to extract wealth from the majority culture. According to Sowell, once a group starts to believe this, they become locked into a culture of dependency and victimhood, incapable of getting out.[41]

Rather than seeing themselves as victims dependent on government handouts, Sowell wants them to see America as a land of opportunity despite continued discrimination, a land that rewards hard work, thrift, prudence, and trust. In many of his forty-five books, Sowell makes the case that

Blacks and Hispanics must realize (as the Asian community already has) that the key is education, hard work, and developing the habits of social integration that engender success. In *Race and Culture*, Sowell highlights what is key for new immigrants: "Those aspects of culture which provide the material requirements of life itself—the specific skills, general work habits, saving propensities, and attitudes toward education and entrepreneurship—in short, what economists call 'human capital.'"[42]

In books like *Discrimination and Disparities* Sowell has spent a career debunking the notion that discrimination and racism are the main causes of economic disparities. He believes the best way to help racial and ethnic minorities is to invite them to acquire the right skills, habits, and attitudes, all things that for centuries have propelled new immigrants in this country into the middle and upper classes.[43] In one example, the nation's biggest charter school network dropped its slogan "Work hard. Be nice" because it "support[ed] the illusion of meritocracy."[44] Nothing could be more damaging to immigrants, according to Sowell.

Since possessing these personal qualities is so important for individual success, Sowell believes that our immigration policies should prioritize people who have these skills, habits, and attitudes, not only because they are so necessary for personal achievement but because immigrants who possess these characteristics can best contribute to our common national cultural identity. Sowell believes we need to look for people who possess enough of the right cultural habits when they come here, and when they do arrive they will develop more of these qualities as they participate in our moral economy.[45]

Finally, in rejecting the excuse of discrimination, Sowell believes the offer to immigrants and citizens is not the dead-end offer of welfare dependency and victimhood but "social integration" (to use David Miller's phrase) and the openness to the virtues of thrift, hard work, dedication, and trust, which are engendered by involvement in our market economy.[46] When these virtues are significantly cultivated, we can safely say an immigrant and a citizen have been socially integrated. For Sowell, commercial virtues or the middle-class soul come about by adopting and living into the right vision, not the cosmic vision of the anointed but a vision that sees capitalism as moral and ethical, as rooted in our constitutionalism, not in greed, and that can thrive only when the "moral sentiments" of a people are strong.[47] Here is the first part of our sweet offer to immigrants and citizens: come join, be a full participant in our deeply ethical economic system, and be changed in the process. When this offer is embraced, we will see immigrants and citizens become deeply "socially integrated."

The Invitation into the Constitutional Soul (Freedom Left 1)

The second part of the sweet offer is what Miller calls "civic integration," which fits with my label of the "constitutional soul." For Miller, civic integration happens when people come to "share a set of principles and norms that guide their social and political life."[48] For the new vital center, this entails a certain public philosophy, grounded in nature and history, and a view of constitutionalism.

One of the best exemplars of the constitutional soul is William Galston, who worked in the Clinton White House and is one of the few left-of-center thinkers who has not succumbed to a view of the creed redefined by the second and third-wave of liberalism (freedom left 2 and 3).[49] According to Galston, the constitutional soul is not neutral when it comes to questions of the good. Rather, the constitutional system of checks and balances, the separation of powers, federalism, and the rule of law were arranged by the founders not only to restrain factions and protect freedom but to cultivate virtue in our citizens. When we invite immigrants (and citizens) into the constitutional soul, we are not asking them to accept procedural neutrality or so-called American values of pragmatic relativism or even identitarianism, diversity, or the welfare state, but rather a view of the Constitution undergirded by the new vital center.

In his essay "Public Morality and Religion in the Liberal State," Galston contends that "certain traits of character are to be valued because they are needed to sustain liberal institutions." Arguing from the position of a "non-Lockean Locke" (an interpretation of Locke that does not place him in the "godless constitution" camp of freedom left 2), Galston sees in Locke's *Second Treatise* and his *Thoughts Concerning Education* a view of liberal democracy that requires virtues like civility, self-denial, industry, trust, and justice. "Moral virtue," contends Galston, "is more than individual self-restraint, it is also the display of due concern for the legitimate claims of others." But it is more than a procedural republic too. "Moral virtue is more than a system of rational demands we make on one another," a kind of "rights talk" that always devolves into group identity politics. Rather, "it requires . . . taking responsibility for oneself, and cultivating one's humanity while tempering one's passions and desires."[50]

This vision is diametrically opposed to freedom left 2 and freedom right 2, which are built on a kind of instrumental reason and the selfish utilitarian self, eroding our creed to nothing more than individuals and groups using the system to extract cash payments and gain political power. But the invitation into the constitutional soul understands that our system is built on a certain kind of individual with a definitive kind of character and that the system in turn helped to "encourage . . . the formation of good character."

For Galston, while religion plays a huge role in cultivating virtue, he is not willing to say that the Constitution is without the means to cultivate virtue. In fact, he believes that the "first wave of liberalism," far from carrying the seeds of its own destruction, far from promoting a neutral proceduralism, "contains within itself the resources it needs to declare and to defend a conception of the good life." That is, "it is unnecessary to import these virtues from the outside, for they are immanent in the liberal practice and theory." This means that if constitutionalism is going to be sustained, it must draw on all the resources it has within itself, doing the best it can in a fallen world. And when it comes to virtue, it must work toward "the traits of character that individuals must possess if they are to uphold liberal institutions and to pursue their good with these institutions."[51]

So the sweet offer of "civic integration" is not to group rights or utilitarian individualism (both pull the individual away from the new vital center) but to a robust view of the Constitution that says to the immigrant (and citizen) that our wonderful system won't last without citizens of character, "and that at some point the attenuation of individual virtue will create pathologies" that will destroy the system, which are on display in so many areas of our country. At the same time the system itself, when staying true to its original designs, "engenders a virtuous citizenry."[52] Acting as a "soft perfectionism," concludes Galston, the constitutional soul engenders

general virtues (courage, law-abidingness, loyalty), Virtues of Liberal Society (independence, self-sufficiency, self-restrain, family solidarity), Virtues of the

Liberal Economy (imagination, initiative, drive, determination, punctuality, reliability, civility, and adaptability) and the Virtues of Liberal Politics (citizenship, respecting the rights of others, moderate in their demands, willingness to sacrifice for the common good).[53]

Galston rejects the poison pill view of order right 2 that would lump the constitutional soul into the three waves of modernity, thus throwing out the baby with the bathwater. For Galston the constitutional soul was not a harbinger of progressive liberalism but, rather, it remains the best hope for restoring our country and for assimilating immigrants and citizens. For Galston and other thinkers of the freedom left 1 quadrant, the constitutional soul believes "daily life in the liberal polity is a powerful if tacit force for habituation to at least the minimal requirements of liberal virtue."[54] In other words, for the immigrant and the citizen, "the sort of things regularly expected of us at home, in school, and on the job shape us in the manner required for the operation of liberal institutions." Moreover, "while hardly models of moral perfection, citizens of modern liberal communities are at least adequately virtuous and not demonstrably less so than were citizens in the past."[55]

But, for the immigrant and the citizen alike, to "resist this civic education would be irrationally contradicting their own self-interest, rightly understood."[56] To attack the constitutional soul, to resists its shaping power, is to choose a life of "stealing and dealing," which always leads to a life of poverty and the impoverishment of the very real virtue needed to sustain the system, one built on honesty and trust. Without this trust, life becomes that much harder for the immigrant and citizen alike to succeed. And to the extent that our liberal democratic system tries to remain neutral, to "betray its own deepest and most defensible position," the immigrant and citizen, those who accept the sweet offer of the constitutional soul, will demand their government promote the "civic core." That is, they will ask their leaders to protect "those beliefs and habits needed to bolster the institutions that secure liberal rights," utilizing civic education, political speeches, and the rule of law. In sum, to do all it can to protect a notion of the good, a life built on liberal virtues that will lead to civic integration in the best possible way.[57]

THE INVITATION INTO THE CIVIC
REPUBLICAN SOUL (ORDER LEFT 1)

The third part of the sweet offer to immigrants and citizens is what David Miller describes as "cultural integration," which happens "when they share a common culture, which might mean having the same values and experiences or, on the other hand, having a common cultural identity."[58] As Miller rightly concludes, cultural integration is more controversial than social or civic integration because it is asking immigrants to not only accept an idea about America but to "abandon their own cultural matrix in order to assimilate" into America—in other words, exchanging one nationality for another and becoming fully American and doing so gladly. As they embrace being American, immigrants and citizens will embrace the unique culture and the habits of the heart (moral, ethical, and religious) at the core of the new vital center.

Integration is more than adopting a version of the Protestant work ethic or the principles and constitutional practices of our democracy while remaining Mexican or Indian or Swedish or African. It means becoming American (without the hyphen). This may not happen overnight, but it nonetheless is an invitation for immigrants and citizens alike to join our "common public institutions—social, educational, economic, political," and in doing this they slowly exchange one set of cultural and ethnic practices for another.[59] While it is okay to hold onto some elements of our ethnic past (food, songs, national sporting teams), it is necessary to adopt a thicker view of cultural integration, a more robust public side where the immigrant is integrated into our "feasts and holidays, artistic and literary icons, places of natural beauty, historical artifacts" and religious history.[60] As Miller says, "cultural integration matters because it allows immigrants to identify with that society more fully and to adopt its national identity as their own."[61] This will allow America "to solve collective action problems more effectively,"[62] to establish trust between groups that would not usually trust one another, creating a sense of oneness and solidarity with the nation. In other words, immigrants are going to want to embrace it. It's a good thing.

For this thicker view of cultural integration to happen, immigrants (and citizens) need to be clear about the invitation. What exactly are they being invited into? Is it more than a "brutal bargain" and attractive enough to put down their own country's flag and pick up the American one? Will this kind of cultural integration, a thicker integration than just believing that America is an idea, also benefit the immigrant as much as the nation?

While he is not addressing immigrants directly, Harvard's Michael Sandel is one of the best thinkers to make the sweet offer of the republican soul to immigrants. In his *Democracy's Discontent: America's Search for a Public Philosophy,* no one is more enthusiastic for a "republican political theory" than Sandel, probably the best-known of the civic republican thinkers. As Sandel summarizes, "if liberty [constitutionalism] cannot survive without virtue, and if virtue tends always to corruption [because of human nature], then the challenge for republican politics is to form or reform the moral character of citizens, to strengthen their attachment to the common good."[63]

Recognizing the tension in the founders' synthesis between constitutionalism and republicanism (see chapter eleven), Sandel says that the way to heal the tension is by recognizing that "the public life of a republic must serve a formative role, aimed at cultivating citizens of a certain kind."[64] This means that citizens and immigrants embrace this cultivating role of public life because without this our nation not only is lacking the kind of citizens it needs to sustain the synthesis—the new vital center—but it lacks the unity, the glue it needs to be strong. To accept the sweet offer to become Americanized, then, means allowing our institutions (civic, moral, religious, and political) to shape citizens and immigrants alike and in the end to become part of a family that also nurtures—a country worthy of the immigrant's love.

Part of the sweet offer is to accept what Sandel calls "republican political theory" (republican soul), and this includes the exciting invitation to self-rule, which immigrants from corrupt authoritarian and totalitarian societies have never experienced. "Sharing in self-rule involves . . . deliberating with fellow citizens about the common good and helping to shape the destiny of the political community."[65] But this deliberation "requires more than the capacity to choose one's ends and to respect other's rights to do the same"— in other words, to live and let live.[66] For this wouldn't take us much past the unencumbered self and the procedural republic of freedom left 2. Sandel calls immigrants and citizens alike to a thicker view of belonging where they are concerned for the whole, where there is a moral bond between all members of the community. It invites immigrants to bring their character and virtue (or at least the aspiration) into the group, working with the group to promote virtue in its members and the larger society, and to be open to a process that will shape them along the way.[67]

As immigrants or citizens willingly and enthusiastically join civic, religious, and political organizations, they will learn that their freedom must be balanced with obligation, that the pursuit of happiness is intrinsically wedded to the happiness of others, and that the more they live for others, the more happiness they will experience. They will realize that we understand ourselves as particular persons with rights and dignities by understanding that our self is embedded in "loyalties and responsibilities . . . as members of this family or city or nation or people, as bearers of that history, as citizens of this republic."[68]

The cultural integration that takes place through the republican soul happens, says Tocqueville, by "the slow and quiet action of society upon itself." By joining associations or "mediating structures" (e.g., the Rotary Club, the local church, neighborhood watch organizations) that stand between the government and the individual, immigrants and citizens learn self-government, and along with fellow citizens develop the habits of the heart. In Tocqueville's words, they "practice the art of government in the small sphere within [their] reach," not through coercion but through invitation, not through threat but through persuasion.[69] Once immigrants or citizens experience the joy of being part of the moral fabric of families, neighborhoods, or communities, they learn virtue, gain character, deepen in self-government, experience freedom balanced by obligation, and not only become the kind of persons needed for our democratic republic to work, but also in the process of cultural integration are transformed into citizens who love America.

In a sense, then, the sweet offer of the republican soul is an offer for immigrants and citizens to join our unique institutions that "include the townships, schools, religions, and virtue sustaining occupations that form the 'character of mind' and 'habits of the heart,'" according to Sandel, that "a democratic republic requires" and keep our nations "from dissolving into an undifferentiated whole" of separate groups.[70] So the invitation is more than a "brutal bargain" of begrudgingly trading one's cultural heritage for another cultural heritage (just to be successful in America); it is so much nobler. It is an invitation and a call for immigrants and citizens to join the

American project, to strengthen it, to fight for it, to shape it, to extend it into the future, to fully own and love our country and what it stands for in spite of its weaknesses.

The Invitation into the Statesmen Soul (Order Right 1)

According to David Miller, the three areas of integration—social, civic, and cultural—need to work together for real integration to happen. And at the heart of this threefold assimilation or integration is a kind of learning, an education of citizenship. But while Miller mentions the need to expand the citizenship test to include more cultural elements than simple facts about the principles and practices of our democracy, he doesn't go into much depth about the kind of education needed for thick integration. That's where our statesman soul can be helpful, laying out a program for the Americanization of citizens and immigrants.

In thinking about the Americanization of citizens and immigrants, no book is more helpful than Thomas West's magisterial *The Political Theory of the American Founding*.[71] For West, the founders embraced the natural law/natural rights grounding of constitutionalism (freedom left 1) that protected individual rights. But these rights also included obligation to others, and for individuals to understand this they needed to possess a certain amount of virtue or character (order left 1). For the founders these habits of the heart preceded the adoption of our constitution, but for the Constitution to survive, leaders in every area of the society, including parents, teachers, school principals, pastors, and elected officials, need to promote "the learning of liberty."[72] Primarily, the statesman's soul (order right 1) reminds immigrants and citizens that virtue must be at the heart of our constitutionalism. Laws alone, while helpful, are not enough to cultivate people of virtue.

Our founding statesmen, says West, saw "virtue as a condition of freedom and a requirement of the laws of nature."[73] West points to the Northwest Ordinance in 1787, ratified two years before the Constitution was signed, saying, "Religion, morality, and knowledge, being necessary to good government and the happiness of mankind, schools and the means of education shall forever be encouraged." The need for this continual education is at the heart of the statesman soul and the invitation to citizens and immigrants alike. From the Northwest Ordinance, says West, we learn that education has public (good government) and private (happiness) dimensions.

So the sweet offer to the immigrant and citizen is to embrace the genius of the original Constitution, support it, champion it, for it is the very thing that protects our rights and brings national unity. But education is more than civic; it also includes the habits of the heart. So the statesman is continually exhorting immigrants and citizens to the "learning of liberty," acquiring the knowledge, the habits, the virtue needed for good government and happiness. This knowledge must include religion and specifically Christianity. According to West, "no government that expects to provide security of natural rights can 'simply assume' that there is sufficient virtue," or assume that the present cultural habits are enough.[74]

For the statesman soul the need for the education of citizens and new immigrants never ceases. Citizenship education takes place first and foremost in the home, then in school, and later in university. Ideally, the healthy assimilation of immigrants and citizens happens through our national holidays, our seals and symbols, patriotic music like our national anthem, an appreciation of our national architecture, our shared common history, and public opinion. It also happens in our associational life. For the founders, "government made use of divine revelation, rational insight, laws with coercive force, and the promotion of a healthy 'law of private censure' in the minds of the citizens."[75]

Thus we see that the statesman soul's invitation to immigrants is an offer to enter into, be shaped by, and be integrated into Americanism. This means developing the virtues—justice, moderation, temperance, industry, frugality, and piety—needed for happiness and success as well as good government that protects one's rights and the pursuit of happiness in the first place. And once immigrants have become citizens, they are called to take up the mantle of the new vital center, teaching it to their children, their families, building schools and other institutions that support and promote the new vital center.

EMULATING THE NEW VITAL CENTER

Taking seriously this call to emulate the statesman soul with my own children, I sat down with them to watch a documentary on George Washington, a three-part series produced by the well-known presidential historian and progressive Democrat Doris Kearns Goodwin. In the first of three episodes, one of the historians asked this arresting question: "What makes this a Nation?" His answer: "Two things—The Constitution and George Washington."[76]

Throughout the documentary the historians, most on the political left, stress that while Washington was not perfect (they mention that he lied on occasion, that he had a fiery tempter, and had slaves —though he freed them upon his death), no one resolved and worked harder to overcome their weaknesses as did he.[77] Washington, better than any of the founders, exhibited the persona and civic virtues, the four souls (and what would become the Union Narrative) needed for statesmen in our democratic republic.

At the end of the third installment of the documentary, selections of his Farewell Address are read and discussed. I was amazed that his address was not mere advice for the new nation to stay out of foreign entanglements but a *sweet offer* of assimilation to citizens and immigrants alike. There may be no other historical document that captures so perfectly this invitation, what makes America special and why the four souls of the new vital center are needed to restore unity.

Washington's sweet offer, his invitation to "citizens, by birth or choice"— those that have "every inducement of sympathy and interest"—is an invitation to a "common country," a nation that has the ability "to concentrate your affections."[78] It's an invitation to love, cherish, and protect the nation in spite of its flaws and hypocrisy. In a sense, while the sweet offer may have four souls, it only has "one heart," the heart of patriotism, of a profound affection for our country, always wanting the best for it, always reforming it, always calling it back to the new vital center.

Listen to Washington's sweet offer of patriotic assimilation:

> The name of American, which belongs to you . . . must always exalt the just pride of patriotism more than any appellation derived from local discriminations. With slight shades of difference, you have the same religion, manners, habits, and political principles. You have in a common cause fought and triumphed together; the independence and liberty you possess are the work of joint counsels, and joint efforts of common dangers, sufferings, and successes.[79]

THE QUESTION OF RELIGION

As much as I appreciated the Goodwin documentary on Washington, I noticed one glaring omission: the documentary and its discussion of his

Farewell Address completely ignored his admonitions on religion and virtue, skipping right over Washington's clear advice that "of all the dispositions and habits which lead to political prosperity, *religion and morality are indispensable supports*."[80] In fact, by avoiding the topic of religion and virtue, the documentary did the very thing Washington so strongly advised against: it ignored the importance of religion.

Washington warned,

> In vain would that man claim the tribute of patriotism, who should labor to subvert these great pillars of human happiness, these firmest props of the duties of men and citizens. The mere politician, equally with the pious man, ought to respect and to cherish them. A volume could not trace all their connections with private and public felicity. Let it simply be asked: Where is the security for property, for reputation, for life, if the sense of *religious* obligation desert the oaths which are the instruments of investigation in courts of justice? And let us with caution indulge the supposition that *morality can be maintained without religion*. Whatever may be conceded to the influence of refined education on minds of peculiar structure, reason and experience both forbid us to expect that national morality can prevail in exclusion of *religious principle*.[81]

In Washington's own life and that of the country, religion and virtue are the "foundation of the fabric," the ultimate grounding of our four souls and that which makes our country so great. Undoubtedly, most of the historians in the documentary either didn't believe Washington was sincere when he said these things, that his comments were just religious rhetoric, or they decided to ignore his teaching because they disagree with him.[82] In either case, by ignoring his comments they clearly believe that we can have a strong nation without religion. Washington disagreed; without religion there would be no virtue, and without virtue there would be no liberty. Without liberty there is no republic. Without the republic, that is, one unified nation, there is no sweet offer to immigrants and citizens. And without the sweet offer, one grounded in natural and divine truth, there is no way to unify the nation, leaving us divided, polarized, and caught in a cold civil war. Since religion is so important for the new vital center and national unity, we must discuss it next. What we will discover is that the new vital center will unlock the secret of national renewal.

13

CHRISTIANITY

THE SECOND CONSTITUTION

UNDOUBTEDLY, THE UNITED STATES is at an inflection point. Will we discover the new vital center or continue to move toward oligarchy, where a small group of bipartisan technocratic elites rig the system politically, economically, and culturally to their advantage? At the end of his *New Class War*, Michael Lind observes that we will either return to what he calls democratic pluralism (which has many similarities to the new vital center) or continue down the path where neo-liberal technocratic elites consolidate their power.[1] If we choose the latter, we are heading to a massive crisis, he contends, one where the technocratic elites continue to crush the middle and working classes from the top, taking away all political, economic, and cultural power. In response, these marginalized classes, devoid of a voice, will lash out in populist uprisings, often looking to populist politicians who will help claw back some share of power, but with no guarantee of democratic pluralism. Sadly, according to Lind, the ruling elites are making the wrong choice; instead of listening to the populist uprising, instead of taking the concerns of the middle and working classes seriously, instead of finding ways to share power and move toward democratic pluralism, the technocratic ruling elites are responding in the worst possible way to the marginal classes, telling them to stay in their place.

For Lind, if the ruling elites continue down this scorched-earth path, society will devolve into chaos, a tiny technocratic elite will retreat behind the safety of their gated walls, and a huge, disenfranchised, and angry population will storm the gates. We will be a high-tech caste society.[2]

ALITO SOUNDS THE ALARM

Just days after the 2020 presidential election, Supreme Court Justice Samuel Alito delivered a speech to the Federalist Society, sounding the alarm over the loss of religious freedom in the country. After referencing the Covid-19 pandemic and the "previously unimaginable restrictions on individual liberty," Alito pointed out the obvious: "It pains me to say this, but in certain quarters, religious liberty is fast becoming a disfavored right."[3] As one example, Alito mentions the recent case in Nevada where the governor allowed casinos to operate but not churches. "So if you go to Nevada," said Justice Alito, "you can gamble, drink and attend all sorts of shows," but churches are limited to fifty people. Alito mentions a blog post by Harvard law professor Mark Tushnet, who wrote, "The culture wars are over. They lost. We won. The question now is how to deal with the losers in the culture wars." For Tushnet, "taking a hard line seemed to work reasonably well in Germany and Japan after 1945."[4] But, Alito asks, "is our country going to follow that course?" It certainly seems that way.

Nowhere is the ruling elite's deafness more apparent than in the reaction to Alito's speech. Mark Joseph Stern called it "a grievance-laden tirade."[5] Matt Forde accused him of promoting the "cultural hegemony for his particular vision of American life."[6] Katherine Stewart, author of *The Power Worshippers*, wrote that the speech presented a "false underlying narrative of religious persecution," "a deeply anti-democratic agenda," and "evidence of the drift in America's right flank toward a new authoritarian religious nationalism," once again demonstrating that even a sitting supreme court justice arguing on behalf of the first amendment can be accused of order right 3 authoritarianism.[7] According to Stewart, "these assaults on the separation of church and state are in fact part of a larger attack on democracy and the rule of law itself. Religious nationalism is the kind of thing that takes democracies down." She accuses Alito of using religious liberty cases to falsely claim Christians are being persecuted, claiming the secular Left is singling them out as "legally sanctioned objects of public contempt, so that they can turn around and persecute secularists, and in the process make the rights of religious believers paramount."[8]

Coming from a journalist in the clerisy class, the claim of being a victim is almost laughable. Clerisy class members like Stewart claim to be on the side of nonpartisan freedom, but they defend their version of freedom, the kind of naked public square that brackets out Christianity and gives them favored status. But while Michael Lind believes the battle in our culture is mainly over power, who has it and who exercises it, he seems to overlook the danger of these false strong gods.

At the heart of the cold civil war is a battle not just over power but over religious narratives, over whose grounding of America is going to prevail, the religion of the "elect" (John McWhorter's name for what Joel Kotkin calls the clerisy class) and woke capitalism, or the religion of the Judeo-Christian tradition and the new vital center.[9] Unlike Lind, Katherine Stewart understands this narrative battle, accusing Alito of taking sides in the religious battle by representing the religious claims of those "whose religion involves conservative or reactionary views" and simultaneously discriminating against those whose "religion calls for respecting the truth of the natural sciences, universal respect for people regardless of belief systems, a conviction that you are entitled to evidence-based, best-practice health care in maternal medical settings, and the rights of same-sex couples to get married."[10] I couldn't have said it better.

Alito also recognizes the true nature of the cold civil war. "During my 15 years on the court," he says at the end of his speech, "a lot of good work has been done to protect freedom of speech, religious liberty, and the structure of government created by the constitution."[11] For Alito, religious freedom and the structure of government created by the constitution go together. Protect one and you are protecting the other. Attack one and you are attacking the other. But he goes further. Even more than the constitution, he seems to say, religious liberty is the key. In his speech Alito quotes Learned Hand, who famously wrote, "Liberty lies in the hearts of men and women. When it dies there, no constitution, no law, no court can do much to help it."[12] And since this liberty is placed in the heart most acutely by religion, Christianity (and Judaism) must be protected. Because if we lose religion, we lose liberty, and if we lose liberty, we lose the republic. So both Stewart and Alito are making the same point: it comes down to narratives, to grounding, to religion.

JAMES HUNTER AND THE QUESTION OF AUTHORITY

Thirty years ago James Davison Hunter coined the term *culture wars*, arguing that the conflict at the heart of the cold civil war is really a conflict over authority, two rival views of grounding. In his 1990 essay "Religious Freedom and the Challenge of Modern Pluralism," Hunter demonstrated that underneath the original American project (the four souls) was the dominant culture of Christianity (Anglo-Protestantism), which supported our constitutional arrangement and continuously shaped people to be virtuous.[13] At the heart of this dominant culture has been a certain grounding, what Hunter calls "authority."

According to Hunter, over the past seventy years this dominant culture, a kind of "pan-Protestantism" (what Huntington calls Anglo-Protestantism and what the America First Caucus calls Anglo-Saxon political principles) has been eroded (by immigration, religious pluralism, and the rise of secularism) and has been replaced by a new dominant culture of progressive secularism.[14] Hunter pointed to the 1947 *Everson* case as the watershed moment.[15] According to Hunter, the secular progressives used their interpretation of the First Amendment to claim that religion was violating the non-establishment clause and needed to be privatized.[16] In short, secular progressives welcomed the naked public square.

But, Hunter claims, the square didn't stay naked—that was never the progressive Left's intention—but was filled with secularism, not a "diffuse moral ethos" but rather like a "religion." It has become its own pan-secularism, a new "quasi establishment" that acts like the dominant public philosophy or, as John McWhorter says (see chapter six), a new religion with its own creed, liturgy, and elected leaders shared by libertarians on both sides of the political spectrum. The ruling elite of this new dominant culture, contends Hunter, "share a strong interest in maintaining both the status quo and their own dominant position in it."[17] They have won; and the rest of us need to get over it. And for Hunter the courts have gone along with this, keeping Christianity out of the public square under the non-establishment clause.[18] That is why Catherine Stewart and the clerisy class reacted so strongly to Alito's speech, which to them represented the threat of a vibrant cultural Christianity returning, one that threatens their dominant culture, their established religion.

Since Hunter's essay, many have caught on to what those in dominant culture have been doing for decades. As Ceaser says, the progressives Left's interest in religious freedom over the years has been "a ruse." The real goal wasn't religious freedom for all but rather to "bracket out" Christianity, all the while smuggling back into the public square a new secular "non-foundationalism" that really is a foundation, a grounding. Ceasar continues,

> The result is that the Left today is characterized by the curious combination [blending freedom left 3, postmodernism, and order left 3, a cosmic vision] of a scrupulous denial of foundations together with a persistent affirmation of values, a position that might best be described as 'idealistic nonfoundationalism.'[19]

Or, as James Lindsay calls it, the applied postmodernism of critical theory, which has been applied to race, gender, and sexuality.[20]

Likewise for Hunter, this new "idealistic non-foundationalism" is very much a new "non-establishment" *establishment*, which, ironically and sadly, the courts have allowed. It is this double standard that has seemed so unfair to Christians over the past seventy years and even more so in the battles over race, gender, and sexuality, all of which Justice Alito high-lighted in his speech. Hunter and Ceaser make clear that this godless-constitution call for a neutral public square is a ploy to keep religious conservatives out of the public square so the elites' own religious narra-tives have no rival. The weaker conservative religions are, the stronger the elites' false strong gods become.

NOT JUST A VICTIM

But this weakened role of Christianity in our culture can't be blamed solely on the attack by secular libertarianism and applied postmodernism. Some of the cultural loss has been self-inflicted, as Joseph Bottum shows in *An Anxious Age: The Post-Protestant Ethic and the Spirit of America*.[21] According to Bottum, in the twentieth century American mainline Protestantism eroded from within, losing its prophetic role and blending into the sur-rounding culture like a chameleon, going from countercultural to mim-icking culture. Once it lost its countercultural prophetic role and became a mouthpiece for progressive causes, the mainline Protestants ceased helping our constitutional system maintain the tension in the democratic synthesis of the vital center.

Without a vibrant faith, it was only a matter of time before all four quadrants were centrifugally pulled away from the center. Some of the polarization was caused, says Bottum, by the erosion of mainline Christianity from within. And this continues to go on today in many segments of evangelicalism, on both the right and the left. Evangelicalism has more often than not eroded from within, succumbed to conformism, capitulating in the face of pressure by the ruling oligarchy, and in the process it has lost its important historical role—providing checks and balances in our system. As a result of this capitulation to culture, the false strong gods have run amok on both the left and the right, fueling polarization and the cold civil war.

AMERICA'S BROKEN COVENANT

Here is the problem: the capitulation of the church has engendered a crisis of faith in our system. Almost fifty years ago in *The Broken Covenant*, Robert Bellah contended that we are in the midst of the "third great crisis" in our nation's history. The first was the revolutionary war; the second was the Civil War. This third is a crisis of our "external covenant," the belief in our constitutional republic; and the crisis has been caused by those who attempt to delegitimize this covenant.

For Bellah the only answer to this crisis is religious revival; only a revived Christianity can renew the external covenant; only Christianity has the transcendent sources, divine law, to check the abuses of democracy. If the external covenant of constitutionalism (creed) is not continuously renewed by the "internal covenant" of Christianity (culture), it will collapse. The external covenant, as important as it is, "is never enough. . . . It is of the nature of a republic that its citizens love it, not merely obey it." For this to happen it must "become filled with meaning and devotion."[22] But this won't happen, says Bellah, without a "religious and ethical" revival. But the problem is "the external covenant has been betrayed by its most responsible servants," and most of them "do not even seem to understand what they have betrayed."[23] We have seen this betrayal throughout this book, on both the left and the right, inside the church and outside in the culture.

If we are going to get back to a new vital center, we need to return to the important place that Christianity once played for generations in reviving and sustaining the democratic project. Charles Taylor, a thinker on the left, writing in the same book that Hunter penned his thoughts about the "quasi establishment" of secularism, asks that if "civic freedom [the creed] cannot accommodate this bleeding of the public square of all significance," but in fact "requires strongly held common values [culture]," is it possible that religion can "be altogether absent from these?"[24] Taylor doesn't think so. Yet it now is. Still, Taylor is optimistic that America can get back to its original view of religious freedom and the role religion played in our democratic republic.

While Hunter affirms Taylor's contention that we need "a compelling story that binds a community in common purposes," Hunter doesn't share Taylor's optimism that we can retrieve it.[25] For Hunter the problem is that "the cultural logic that underwrote liberalism exists in fragments, and it is not likely to come together again in any coherent way."[26] In fact, Hunter despairs of any new vital center because "a common cultural logic is unlikely to return because there is no credible foundation on authority upon which to build it." Hunter asks whether "the cultural logic underwriting late-state democracy can be fixed." His response: "Maybe, but not easily and not anytime soon."[27]

But what would Hunter say about a revival of Christianity as Bellah argues? Can a renewed Christianity provide a renewed authority, a grounding on which to build a new vital center and a new dominant culture? Sadly, Hunter says no—for "religious faith has been thoroughly weaponized on behalf of partisan interests," and "in the civic or political realm, it speaks no universal truths."[28] He is right on both counts. Both the religious Right and progressive religious Left have aligned religion with their quadrant positions and have politicized Christianity. The progressive liberal evangelicals then accuse the religious Right of being "court evangelicals" for the Trump administration, and the religious Right accuses the progressive liberal evangelicals of being captive to the multicultural woke Left.[29] Both sides accuse the other of being anti-Christian.

Second, Hunter is correct that Christianity no longer speaks universal truths that can be embraced by both sides (or by all four souls of the new vital center). And if Christianity is only partisan, only used to defend one polarized position on the quadrant, how can it help us rediscover a new vital center? This is the question I have struggled with, and it eventually birthed a new insight and a change to my quadrant graph.

A NEW INSIGHT

How could religion, and more particularly, historic Christianity, so important for the renewal of the external covenant (the new vital center), meet Hunter's challenge to (1) speak to universal values (all four souls), and (2) avoid being politicized (siding with just one quadrant position)?

As I was researching this book, I assumed that Christianity would fit into order right quadrant, the place associated with the religious Right.[30] But over time I realized that there are Christians represented in all four quadrants. And if Christianity is not to be pigeonholed or politicized and thus easily dismissed, I had to find a way to link it to all four quadrants, meeting Hunter's challenge of a nonpoliticized view of Christianity, one that could be embraced by all four souls of the new vital center. Moreover, I had to do this in a way that avoided "inflationary tactics" (chapter one), which would mean keeping special revelation and general revelation held together.

As I was struggling with how general revelation/natural law (the grounding of the new vital center) and special revelation of Christianity fit together (providing universal values for all four quadrants), I came across this arresting passage in Ceaser's *Designing a Polity*: "For those of the faith, the adoption of the legal Constitution in no way abrogated" the importance of Christianity because "it has always been thought that there is a *second and unwritten constitution* meant to operate alongside of the legal one."[31] That's when it dawned on me: I didn't need to include religion in each of the four quadrants (souls) because "historically, religion, and more particularly Christianity acted as a secondary constitution" that provides the grounding for the grounding, as it were.[32]

Here was the key insight: *special revelation is the grounding under—that is, supporting—the grounding of general revelation discovered through the "right reason" of nature and history, culture and creed.* Just as special revelation builds on general revelation, so general revelation builds on special revelation.[33] God speaks through both and uses both to communicate. They are the same, but they are different. This reality, one known by the founders, led to this important and revolutionary insight: "Because these two constitutions were concerned with largely distinct matters," Ceaser points out, "there was no need to combine them into a single document—indeed, it would be harmful to the purposes of both realms ever to merge them."[34] In fact, the best way to keep Christianity and the state from unhealthy meddling in the other's business was to keep the two constitutions separate. But while they were parallel constitutions, both protected by the First Amendment; they were not divided, and they needed each other.

"The two constitutions," writes Ceaser, "existed together in the hearts and thoughts of many Americans and proved complimentary in practice."[35] In fact, America wouldn't be America if this faith tradition is "renounced and its faith survives here, at best, as merely one belief among many."[36] Concluding this explosive thought, Ceaser asks, "Would it be too strong to say that an America without faith is 'unconstitutional'?"[37] I think it would. The founders thought so. And if religion doesn't act as the second constitution, then my proposal for a new vital center would be no different than the mid-century vital center, which was built on pragmatic reason, which didn't hold. Why? Because it didn't have the grounding of special revelation, that is, Bellah's internal covenant or Hunter's authority to constantly renew it.

So with Ceaser's insight I took out my quadrant image, grabbed a Sharpie, and I drew a smaller circle inside the new vital center, still touching all four quadrants, the four souls. There is now an inner circle showing that religion—

Christianity—holds all four quadrants together and provides the authority they all need, something higher than secular reason or historical experience, for grounding our public philosophy. It also helps maintain the delicate balance, the built-in tension in the republican synthesis. Furthermore, it keeps the four souls from flying off into polarization or being manipulated by the ruling elite.

In returning to its historic role, religion recovers both its prophetic and its balancing functions. Alan Kahan calls this the checks and balances of religion.[38] Prophetic religion, when working properly, restrains (and calls back) the new vital center from polarizing into the second and third positions of the quadrants. But it also helps produce virtuous citizens, a kind of perpetual renewal (balances) of the internal covenant, who are so vital for the democratic republican synthesis to work.

RELIGIOUS AND MORAL REVIVAL

How do we convince our nation that the best grounding, the best way to protect religious freedom of all people and restore the synthesis at the heart of our democratic republic is by allowing historic Christianity to act as the undercurrent of our culture? I am under no illusion that this is going to be easy. For the animus toward Christianity has increased in recent years, not lessened, and many are clearly afraid of a resurgent Christian cultural witness. Nonetheless, as hard as it is to overcome their animus, if we are going to make the case that historic biblical religion is vital to our democracy, we need more than a negative case (fighting for religious liberty). We need a positive case, a sweet offer of religion, a kind of apologia for the importance of religion to protect the rights of all people and groups, one showing the salubrious role religion can and should play.

The first step in this sweet offer is to make the case that over the past two hundred fifty years, Christianity, or at least a faithful remnant of it, has renewed the external covenant when it was most in crisis. The ruling elites refuse to admit that over our long history the religious foundation, the "second constitution," has inspired the nation's first founding, the Revolutionary War, the Civil War, the end of slavery, the social reforms of the progressive era, and civil rights. While Christianity has not always been perfect and has much to repent of, it still provides the only transcendent foundation capable of checking and balancing our republican synthesis and doing so in a way that holds together the new vital center. The founding fathers at the time of the Revolutionary War, the abolitionists in the nineteenth century, Lincoln during the Civil War, and civil rights leaders of the 1960s all appealed to the Bible as the foundation of human dignity, human rights, religious freedom, and sustaining our common national bond.[39] If we are going to understand why they looked to religion in the midst of crisis and understand why it is part of the key to surviving our current crisis, our own cold civil war, we must understand why prophetic religion is so vital.

TOCQUEVILLE'S CHECKS AND BALANCES OF RELIGION

Carlos Lozada, writing in the *Washington Post*, penned an article titled "The Book Every New American Citizen—and Every Old One, Too—Should Read." Lozada says he marked his first year of US citizenship by reading Tocqueville's *Democracy in America*. As it "turns out, *Democracy in America* is an ideal book to read as a new citizen" because it "explains perfectly to a brand-new compatriot so much of the essential minutiae of life here, so much of what America is and was, so much of what it risks losing."[40] Tocqueville, better than any, captures our American DNA, how this cultural DNA was formed, and how we risk losing it. His book is part of the sweet offer to immigrants and citizens alike. But Tocqueville also captures something else—the importance of religion in America.[41] And if we are going to make a sweet offer for the importance of religion in America, there is no better guide than Tocqueville.[42]

Over the years as I have taught through *Democracy in America*, my students have been amazed by how a major political philosopher, one who stands in the classical liberal tradition, could so openly appreciate religion and its value for maintaining democracy. And while there are scholars who doubt his sincerity, the more I have read through *Democracy* over the years, I have become convinced that Tocqueville believed the truth of Christianity (even though he struggled with faith himself).[43] Not only did he believe it was true, but he was also convinced Christianity had to be the "second constitution," the "undercurrent," if democracy was to avoid its worst excesses and eventually devolve into despotism.

From the start, Tocqueville makes clear that while constitutional law is important, it isn't enough to protect democracy. "Self-interest rightly understood," while a step in the right direction, couldn't protect democracy and produce virtuous citizens on its own. And even patriotic piety, the love of country, isn't enough to inculcate the necessary virtue, the habits of the heart, the character necessary to help sustain our republic and prevent the majority from oppressing those in the minority. For Tocqueville the key to protecting our democratic republic from devolving into the tyranny of the majority or the rule of the elites is religion, and more specifically Christianity.[44]

THE IMPORTANCE OF RELIGION

Much like the secular enemies of religion today, Tocqueville was no stranger to secular attacks on religion. In fact, he took on many French secular Enlightenment thinkers who saw religion and the church as enemies. And he was not unaware of the potential excesses of religion. But after studying America extensively, he had to admit that "I have never been more convinced than today that it is only freedom . . . and religion that can, by combined effort, lift men above the quagmire where democratic equality naturally plunges them, as soon as one of these supports is lacking them."[45] On his nine-month visit to America, Tocqueville realized that in America "liberty sees in religion the companion of its struggles and triumphs, the cradle of its early years, the divine source of its rights. Liberty considers religion as the safeguard of mores, mores as the guarantee of laws and the pledge of its own duration."[46]

And it was this "duration," that is, the survival of democracy, that he was interested in. He realized that without religion as the foundation under the foundation, natural rights and history would become secularized and ultimately lead to tyranny. Religion was necessary, then, to moderate democracy's excesses. Religion did this by helping individuals and society to achieve a well-balanced soul. It was America's first founding. For Tocqueville, ultimately religion, and it alone, writes Kahan, "is the sovereign spiritual antidote to democracy's flaws."[47] "In America, it is religion that leads to enlightenment; it is the observance of divine laws that guides man to freedom."[48]

Initially Tocqueville found Americans' "patriotic love of religion" curious. He wondered how those who fought for freedom could still argue for a higher authority, which would bind or curtail freedom. How can divine law lead to liberty? It seemed like a contradiction. But what shocked Tocqueville was that in the United States the two were combined and were mutually supportive. Democracy in America then "is the product . . . of two perfectly distinct elements that elsewhere have often made war with each other, but which, in America, they have succeeded in incorporating somehow into one another and combining marvelously . . . the *spirit of religion* and the *spirit of freedom*."[49] So the more he interviewed clergy and elected officials, the more he realized that each side appreciates the other: "Religion sees in civil freedom a noble exercise of the faculties of man," an area of creation open to serving God.[50] "Americans mix Christianity and liberty so completely in their mind that it is nearly impossible to make them conceive of the one without the other."[51]

For these reasons, Americans have a profound patriotic affection for religion. And the reason they do so is simple: according to William Galston, "Free societies rest on public morality, and that morality cannot be broadly effective without religion. Public morality is essential to free societies."[52] And, moreover, continues Galston, Tocqueville wrote that

> when there is no authority in religion or in politics, men are soon frightened by the limitless independence with which they are faced. . . . With everything on the move in the realm of the mind, they want the material order at least to be firm and stable, and, as they cannot accept their ancient beliefs again, they hand themselves over to a master.[53]

Only religion gives individuals structure for their freedom. It is the law of perfect freedom.

Tocqueville knew that if we bracket out religion, real democratic freedom withers away, preparing the way for despotism. "I am led to think," wrote Tocqueville, "that if [man] has no faith he must obey, and if he is free, he must believe."[54] And here was his great insight:

> Despotism may be able to do without faith, but freedom cannot. Religion is much more needed in the republic they advocate than in the monarchy they attack, and in democratic republics most of all. How could society escape destruction if, when political ties are relaxed, moral ties are not tightened? And what can be done with a people master of itself if it is not subject to God?[55]

In sum, for Tocqueville religion as a second constitution was a companion to liberty; it taught individuals what true freedom was and at the same time protected the natural rights of constitutionalism, keeping it from secularization and the inevitable destruction of liberty. More than any other belief or institution, Christianity raised up the kind of people who respected the laws because they saw divine law behind them. In God's divine law they saw the culmination of their true freedom. Seeing how Christianity has been dismissed today, Tocqueville wouldn't be surprised at the oligarchic system of government; in fact, oligarchy is the logical result of dismissing Christianity. Without religion there is no liberty and without liberty there is no republic. Only religion can block the false strong gods, which so often lead to tyranny and authoritarianism, whether on the left or the right.

HABITS OF THE HEART

But even though Tocqueville stressed the importance of religion to sustain democracy, that didn't mean he thought government needed to impose it on society. For Tocqueville religion had its greatest impact on liberty and law indirectly by shaping *mores*, defined by Tocqueville as "the habits of the heart."[56] According to Tocqueville, the influence of religion in the United States is largely indirect, working through the opinions and attitudes of the people, shaping their habits, inculcating middle class virtues, teaching them to be free, independent from government control. While religion did not give Americans the taste for liberty, "it singularly facilitates their use thereof. . . . It is just when it is not speaking of freedom at all that [religion] best teaches Americans the art of being free."[57] And there is no better tutor for the art of being free than the church, when it is doing its job.

Christianity supports liberty in two ways, according to Tocqueville. First, on the individual level it teaches restraint, virtue, and trust in others. It teaches them that true freedom is in God. Moreover, it provides individuals something to live for beyond materialism and selfish ambition. It gives them hope in the eternal. As Alan S. Kahan says, "Christianity tells us . . . that you must prefer others to yourself in order to gain heaven; but Christianity also tells us that you must do good to your fellows out of love for God. That is a magnificent expression."[58] Here the church and its teaching is vital. In a sense, for Tocqueville the church not only preached salvation but was also an amazing "school for democracy."

Second, on the social level Christianity checks the excesses of the majority, reminding them not to use the instruments of government or the

economy for their well-being alone but to care about the minority, protecting them against injustice and reminding the state that a higher law
exists, and not to become obsessed with power. Only the higher authority
provided by religion inspires the majority to respect the constitutional
system.[59] But only with the checks does it balance democracy and maintain
the delicate synthesis of the new vital center.

Kahan summarizes the checks and balances of Christianity well:

> Religion limits and balances both thought and action. It checks people's ac-
> tions and thought through dogma and by imposing religious limits on their
> materialism and on the actions of the government and the majority may take.
> It balances democratic society's natural flaws, especially excessive materialism,
> by encouraging non-material desires and disinterested virtues. Because they
> are so great, religion is an indispensable support for freedom and greatness
> in democratic society.[60]

Thus for Tocqueville there were ultimately only two sources of authority
in democratic republic: either that of the majority (regardless of whether it
is right or wrong) or the authority of religion. And without religion there
was nothing to check the majority, whether on the right or left. Without the
authority of God, a higher law, it was only a matter of time before the majority would highjack the system for their own gains.

In the end we must choose between two authorities and two different
fates. "For me," predicted Tocqueville ominously, "I doubt that man can ever
bear complete religious independence, and full political liberty at the same
time; and I am led to think that, if he does not have faith, he must serve, and,
if he is free, he must believe."[61]

Thus, what we see is that Tocqueville provides a view of the second constitution that all four souls can embrace. And like the four souls of the new
vital center, he believes in three propositions that animate the new vital
center: the republic needs liberty (constitutionalism), liberty needs virtue
(civic republicanism), and virtue needs Christianity (higher authority).
Without Christianity as the first institution, individuals and mobs will throw
off even these protections to get what they want. Only the higher authority
will keep people from doing this and instead protect the system that gives
them so much freedom.[62]

At the end of her essay on Tocqueville, Notre Dame professor Catherine Zuckert makes this arresting statement: "If churchmen and democratic politicians would merely cease to attack each other politics and religion could mutually reinforce each other's strengths."[63] But they don't, and they can't. Because ultimately, religion is a threat to their narrative and their power. So they attack it mercilessly.

IS THE NEW VITAL CENTER JUST ANOTHER CALL FOR THEOCRACY?

Is the call for a revitalized religion and its fight for religious liberty just a ruse to set up a theocracy that would favor Christians over others? Isn't this what Stewart accused Justice Alito of doing, rigging the system to favor one religion over another? Tocqueville rejected the view that in favoring Christianity he wanted to set up a theocracy or a new church-state alliance. In fact, he contended that what made religion so effective in shaping mores and protecting democracy is that it is separate from the state, and won't be used to oppress other groups but in fact would protect all groups. By shaping the mores of both the individual and the society, wrote Tocqueville, "Religion, which never intervenes directly in the government of American society, should therefore be considered as first of their political institutions."[64] That is why I have drawn it on my quadrants illustration as a separate circle. But that doesn't mean church and state are enemies. Church and state must be separated, but not too far. For Tocqueville, Christianity must affect politics morally and ethically; it must provide the grounding under the grounding. But it must do this while remaining separate from partisan political allegiances. Only thus can it effectively help to check and balance democratic societies and support human greatness and freedom.

In discussing Tocqueville, Kahan helpfully puts it this way: "Religion and the state are like two adjoining houses which share a common wall, but have separate entrances. . . . each checking the other. The wall between religion and the state should be thin, however, so that the noise in one can be heard clearly in the other."[65]

James Ceaser also uses an architectural metaphor, this time not a wall but a foundation. While Tocqueville saw the genius of the First Amendment to keep the state out of religion and religion out of politics, a third way that was neither secular nor theocratic, Ceaser believes that Tocqueville was not in favor of the godless-constitution view of a neutral public square devoid of religious influence. Tocqueville, contends Ceaser, "does not claim, indeed his entire approach denies, that this principle [separation of church and state] can support a full or adequate understanding of liberal democracy."[66] For this separation is not the foundation of a liberal democratic edifice but rather—to continue the architecture metaphor—its first floor (or on our graph the inner circle of the new vital center). "But the entire structure rests on a deeper foundation, which must be the principal object of study."[67]

And when we inspect this foundation (the second constitution), we discover, argues Ceaser, that unlike the first floor there are no walls between the political on the one hand and the cultural, the religious, or the economic on the other. Instead, there is constant interaction among these spheres that respects no formal boundaries. And without this foundation under the first floor (under the four souls), the habits of the heart, the character of virtue, the first floor (the four souls) will crumble.

In practice this means that while Tocqueville supported the separation of church and state, it wasn't divided by a *high wall* incapable of being crossed but more of a *low wall* that both sides could jump back and forth from time to time, working together in mutual supportive fashion to create virtuous citizens. The formal principles were important but secondary. By limiting the state and the church, keeping each on their own side of the wall, together they promote the underlying culture so needed for constitutional republicanism. This is what Tocqueville meant by religion as the "first institution." He took a third way between the godless-constitution liberals and libertarians (who wanted to bracket out religion) and the religious Right of order right 3. He is willing to say that there is a prior foundation under the first floor of formal principles because "liberal democracy depends upon a certain political culture, which is a product not just of law but of philosophic and religious views, of habits and sentiments."[68]

Georgetown professor Joshua Mitchell sums up Tocqueville's view well: "The right relationship between religion and politics, then, is, on the one hand, that the two should be utterly separated and, on the other hand, that politics must be undergirded by religion." This means that "American democracy will not survive" if it mixes "politics and religion" the way the

French did, "but neither will it survive unless religion is the indirect support for politics. . . . Political freedom rests upon nonpolitical foundations. This is the cornerstone of Tocqueville's seemingly peculiar liberalism."[69] Or it is the cornerstone of the new vital center.

It's important to point out, lest you get nervous, that Tocqueville doesn't think statesmen should attempt to directly promote religion (which would increase the centralizing power of the state), but rather that they should do it by "quietly influencing the conditions that encourage and discourage certain activities over the long term"—exactly what the founders did with their Thanksgiving prayers, support of chaplains in Congress, and allowing states to support religion more directly, if desired. This is the role of the statesman soul not only in government but also in all realms of life, private and civic. Those who direct and shape society also shape the culture; this includes religious leaders, poets, scientists, film producers, social philosophers, historians, educators, and social scientists. At first blush this call to religious and cultural leaders seems paradoxical. For in one sense the state is saying to the private realm: You are free to pursue your own flourishing. But to the individual it is saying: You also need to promote the system of liberty that allows you this liberty in the first place, and you can do this by using your gifts of art, poetry, writing, speaking, philosophy, music, and theater to help sustain liberal democracy so you and future generations can flourish. You can do this by enthusiastically promoting the four souls, championing our constitutionalism, our heritage of civic republicanism, the bourgeois values that shape character and trust in the marketplace, and the need for an educational system that raises up future generations of citizens who have a healthy patriotism, deep gratitude for our nation, and desire to reform it based on the new vital center, and not some cosmic vision that will destroy the "best regime" created by humans.[70]

CAN THIS VISION OF CHRISTIANITY AND
DEMOCRACY IN AMERICA BE REVIVED?

After laying out Tocqueville's grand vision of Christianity and democracy, I am well aware that our bipartisan elites are not going to be convinced. For them any talk about reviving this view, any calls for religious freedom and reminders to respect the rights of association or the need to bring God back as the ultimate foundation will be met with anger. This is particularly true for those on the progressive left because they see such calls as a threat to the dominant secular version of authority and grounding. And here we are brought back to Hunter's pessimism. If religion is the key to protecting liberty and democracy, and if religion has to be allowed to play a role in the public square, influencing all four quadrants, how can this happen once the dominant culture rejects the idea?

Once the role of religion in shaping the habits of the heart has been supplanted and is pushed out of the public square, thus eliminating the very thing that can regenerate the culture in the first place, and once a new rival religion is now shaping mores, is there any way to turn back? For Galston, a Democrat, like Hunter and Bellah, we are a crossroads: "If, to be effective in a liberal society, moral norms need the underpinning of transcendent religious faith, then the dwindling of faith gradually erodes the practical foundations of that morality."[71] Without that morality, tolerance of other religious minorities will also fade away. While Christianity does teach moral boundaries, at the same time it teaches and inspires people to tolerate others with different views. Secularism is incapable of doing this. Once civility has eroded, it is hard to get back.

Here is the dilemma. Without the once-dominant culture of religious civility, how can we get past the cold civil war? And as the legacy culture, which is based on the new vital center, tries to make a comeback, the Far Left and Far Right will continue to react in anger, shaming, repressing, and punishing it, making it clear it is no longer welcome in the public square. Does this mean that Christians just give up and retreat into Benedict option communities? Are we without hope? Have we reached the "twilight of authority"? Is a hot civil war the only option? Many on the left and right think so.

Obviously, I don't think so or I wouldn't have written this book. But if our only hope is renewal of the external covenant, reinfusing the vision of the American founding with the internal or invisible covenant, then some kind of revival in morality, ethics, and public philosophy is our only hope. This means the church and Christians, those committed to the new vital center, have a very important job to do, and it is to that job we now turn.

CONCLUSION

THE HEROIC ROLE FOR THE CHURCH

In the first decade of the new millennium, elites were fond of using mockery to take down their opponents, a tactic President Trump also used. Whether it was President Obama in 2008 mocking rural working class voters or Hillary Clinton in 2016 calling Trump supporters the "basket of deplorables," the goal was always the same—mock and humiliate the working and middle classes, many of them religious, calling them uneducated, uncultured, and stupid, susceptible to the authoritarian personality, followers of cult leaders and conspiracy theories.

But at some point this mockery has turned into something more sinister and dangerous—a deep disgust, says Ilya Feoktistov, writing in the *The Federalist*. This disgust, according to George Orwell, author of *1984*, can be summed up in four words: "The lower classes smell."[1] As Orwell wrote, while "race-hatred, religious hatred, differences of education, of temperament, of intellect . . . can be got over . . .physical repulsion cannot."[2] And Feoktistov says, "It is when members of the in-group are 'brought up to believe that [members of the out-group] are dirty that harm is done,' Orwell wrote. Disgust, perhaps more so than fear or greed, appears to be the primary source of most of human conflict."[3]

This disgust has begun to creep into the elite's disdain for religious conservatives. Consider a recent column by erstwhile conservative Jennifer Rubin of the *Washington Post*, writing in response to vaccine hesitancy. While she begins describing vaccine-hesitant voters as "self-destructive, selfish, and potentially deceitful people," "the ornery holdouts," and "imperious to reason and facts," all ways of saying the same thing—they are stupid rubes—she then argues, maybe not even aware she is doing it, that they "remain a breeding ground for dangerous coronavirus."[4] Or consider Governor Andrew Cuomo, who, when the orthodox Jewish community in New York City refused to stop meeting in community worship, called a press conference to single them out and then presented a "redlined" map of the Jewish neighborhood, not only targeting them for more severe restrictions but making it clear that other residents should avoid these areas, as if they were a breeding ground for disease.[5] As Josh Blackman wrote, Governor Cuomo "demonstrated a hostility to Jews, without even recognizing it." "Regrettably," contends Blackman, Cuomo "played on [an] old, deeply rooted, and painful anti-Semitic trope: that Jews spread disease."[6]

About a decade ago, writing in *The Week*, Damon Linker tried to warn his progressive friends that their dislike of religion had morphed into an "irrational animus against religion in general and traditional forms of Christianity in particular." He told them that their desire "to eliminate Christianity's influence on and legacy within our world" demonstrates this animus. While he says his liberal friends are just defending a certain version of liberalism (the godless-constitution view, freedom left 2), it is this animus that leads them to "increasingly think and talk like a class of self-satisfied commissars enforcing a comprehensive, uniformly secular vision of the human good."[7]

But his warning went unheeded. And, it seems, with this shift to disgust we have crossed a Rubicon in the cold civil war. The question is whether the church, armed with the confidence of its convictions, the new vital center, and prophetic religion, can stand up to this disgust—not wither, not compromise, not succumb—and continue to fight for the new vital center for all people. Can the church rise to a new heroic role? And if so, does it even matter? Is it too late?

THE HEROIC ROLE FOR THE CHURCH

Conservative Christian podcaster Matt Walsh thinks it is too late. In his "It Is Time to Face the Facts: We Cannot Be United," Walsh says the divide is so great that there is "almost no common ground" and that "we are speaking different languages, both literally and metaphorically. We are a people divided by gaps that cannot be closed. There is no bridge that can connect the Left and the Right."[8] And, truth be told, there are those on the left who have come to the same conclusion; what other message are they sending when they tear down George Washington's statue? Everything that came before must be destroyed. There is no common bridge with those who honor the past, whether that past is historic Christianity or America's historic founding; there is no room to talk.

When we look at our present political climate, it is hard not to despair, to throw up our hands, and give up, to admit that secession or civil war are our only options—many have.[9] But I cannot abandon hope. I cannot throw in the towel for no other reason than I believe in the providence of God and the natural law foundation this country was built on. It is never too late to wake up from our national nightmare. It has happened before, and it can happen again.

Matt Walsh concludes his essay, "I don't know where we go from here, or how to fix it, or if it can be fixed at all, but I know that any path forward must begin with an honest assessment of the situation."[10] He is right. As I come to the end of this book, having provided an honest assessment (parts one and two), I still believe there is a solution (part three). And it is found in our grounding, our original founding documents, the new vital center, and our second constitution. Clearly, our democratic institutions are fraying, but they are not gone, not yet anyway. Until then we can fight to the very last minute. The church and Christianity, the best and maybe only sources of renewal, must be at the heart of this fight for the new vital center—the only foundation that can pull our republican democratic project back from the brink.

Therefore, I have one final courageous plea: the church has to become the church again for it to regain *the* public philosophy that can renew our republic. The church and its leaders must stand up and be heard, for the sake of all people.

FIRST STEP: RENEWAL WITHIN

For the church and Christianity to be part of the solution, they must first renew themselves in order to overcome the present accommodation to the reigning culture and to regain their true essence. How? First, the church must recover its gospel, its teaching on salvation, and its robust exhortations to live out the faith in all areas of life. It must resist (if it is not already too late) the fate of the liberal mainline church of the twentieth century, which has gone the way of accommodation, aping the reigning culture. Second, along with reclaiming its supernatural message, the church must also gain a public philosophy, one rooted in the new vital center. Through the gospel *and* its public philosophy, through special revelation and general revelation, its understanding that the "spirit of liberty" and the "spirit of religion" must go hand in hand, we can revive our republic.

In our present crisis the church, though a small remnant, is almost alone in holding to a transcendent grounding that maintains the link between natural rights and natural law/divine revelation. The church has the resources to stand against the prevailing culture, the non-establishment establishment that now reigns, and push back against its dehumanizing teachings. When it is living up to its potential, the church can truly model the best association, the best community, the best shaper of mores, because only the church has the source of transcendent hope, the message to satisfy human beings' deepest longings and to form an identity that frees up people to serve others.

Therefore, the church is best able to inculcate citizenship, inspire both the "resident alien" and the "alienated resident," teaching them how to hold together freedom and responsibility, liberty and civic responsibility, and a love of country without idolatrous nationalism.

A THIRD GREAT AWAKENING

None of this will happen if the church itself doesn't experience a revival, giving the church the confidence to see that its *internal covenant*, built on divine law, is necessary to renew the *external covenant*, built on general revelation. Only these two held together—the spirit of liberty and the spirit of religion—can keep our nation from sliding into despotism, authoritarianism, and the false strong gods. As Robert Bellah said four decades ago,

"No one has changed a great nation without appealing to its soul, without stimulating a national idealism."[11] Because "religion is the key to culture," he contends,

> We certainly need a new "Great Awakening." The inward reform of conversion, the renewal of an inward covenant among the remnant that remains faithful to the hope for rebirth, is more necessary than it has ever been in America. The great experiment may fail utterly, and such failure will have dark consequences not only for Americans but for all the world. We do not know what the future holds and we must give up the illusion that we control it, for we know that it depends not only on our action but on grace. While recognizing the reality of death, we may return finally to Winthrop's biblical injunction: Let us choose life.[12]

While I may disagree with Bellah on exactly what this "great awakening" looks like and the society it will produce, I agree with him that without a revival in the church, without the church regaining its life-giving gospel and embracing the public philosophy of the new vital center, rooted as it is in general revelation, there is little chance to renew the external covenant that holds our democratic republic together.[13]

Notre Dame University's Vincent Phillip Muñoz agrees: "Politics affects culture, of course, but culture shapes, limits, and sometimes directs politics. Cultural renewal, including a revival of traditional religion, is an essential facet of political renewal."[14]

AN EXCITING ROLE FOR THE CHURCH

The history of revival teaches us that even though God is the author of these great awakenings, the church doesn't simply sit around awaiting the breath of the Spirit to revive the church; the church must actively pray, prepare, and work for revival.[15]

Thus, in the midst of cultural decay and our hopeful waiting for a better day, there still remains an important role for the church to play. As I laid out in my book *Deep Church*, it starts with rediscovering the twofold nature of the church: institution and organism. First, the church as *institution* is called to be a distinct association, a community marked by Word and sacrament, a fellowship that weekly models a new reality, that shapes people through its communal practices, and that constantly reminds individuals of their sin, need for salvation, and the necessity for grace to inspire lives of virtue, character, and faithful presence. The church is an association of both checks and balances. The church and its message check the idols in our lives and culture, pushing back, taking "every thought captive" (2 Corinthians 10:5), and exposing the darkness, whether coming from the far right or far left. But along with the checking function (being light) of the church, it also balances (being salt). By being salt, the church adds flavor to our culture and our politics—by creating truth, beauty, and goodness in all areas of our culture, by training citizens of virtue, by educating the population, by extolling Christians to serve the common good, and by upholding the new vital center. As Tocqueville writes, religion is one of the main supports of democracy, teaching the habits of the heart needed in each individual for our democratic republic to thrive. Edmund Burke likened the church to a "little platoon," a model of associational life that profoundly affects the individual, protecting them against the encroachment of the ever-growing administrative state, but also shaping the individual to be a contributor to the common good of society.[16] And to destroy these little platoons, these mediating institutions, is to destroy the foundation needed to sustain constitutional republics.

Moreover, the church creates leaders who take seriously their role as statesmen, but not as politicians. Statesmen trained in and through the teaching ministry of the church, animated by principle and not party, fight for the separation of church and state (to protect the church from the state and the state from the church), but at the same time they never see the separation of the state and religion.[17] These leaders see the church as vital in shaping the character of its people, to think and live differently, to push back, to be countercultural. The church inculcates new vital center people, citizens of both heaven and earth, shaped by both divine revelation and general revelation, divine grace and common grace. As Jason Willock says, in the past the church was "a mediating institution that both conditioned men for ethical participation in the public affairs and provided an outlet for yearning that politics of the liberal sort [order left 3) could never satisfy."[18]

CHURCH AS ORGANISM

But along with being a unique institution, the church is also an *organism*, that is, the church is also dispersed.[19] Along with transforming individuals through Word and sacrament, shaping them into a unique community of the new vital center, it also supports, exhorts, and trains them in their individual callings.[20] Along with sending its members into the world to be salt and light, it also teaches them about "self-interest well understood" (freedom right 1), covenantal reciprocity (freedom left 1), the need to see our new freedom in Christ as also a call to obligation (order left 1), and to speak boldly yet humbly into our culture as a statesman (order right 1).

The church as organism trains its members in the new vital center. On the one hand the church teaches and trains members when to say *stop* to our culture (check). On the other hand it trains them when to say *go* (balance). In political life, knowing when to say go means affirming America, protecting its best and improving its worst; standing with the union narrative and continuing to call America to live up to its highest ideals. The church as balance is the church that supports healthy, godly patriotism.

Faithful Americans can and should be patriotic citizens and champions of the American principles that animated the American founding, what I call the new vital center. While there is still a long way to go before we live up to our founding ideals, counsels Muñoz, "our founding principles, rightly understood, remain the surest available means to help us restore a decent and just political order."[21]

Because we embrace the renewing function of the church, that the church's internal covenant can help renew the outer covenant of the new vital center, we can humbly but confidently agree with Lincoln scholar Harry Jaffa that America, despite all its faults, still remains the best regime.[22]

It means we can affirm with David F. Forte that our founders were "noble sinners" who somehow, by the grace of God, formed a more perfect union.[23]

We can affirm with Leo Strauss that not all modernity is bad and that far from rejecting America, we can affirm that America, despite its flaws, is still good. This is patriotism. This is our civic faith. This is *the* public philosophy we must embrace.

JUST ANOTHER CIVIC RELIGION?

Some religious critics will push back: Isn't this just another civil religion, another form of national idolatry?[24] Secular progressives will say it's just another call to theocracy. Libertarians will contend it endangers our political freedom; it's too perfectionist. Even those in the theonomy camp will condemn the new vital center as not being biblical enough.

Do these critiques hit the mark? Does new vital center patriotism, its civic faith, mean I am presenting just another form of religious nationalism or theocracy, or a watered-down civil religion, no more helpful than a myth?

All of this criticism would be true if I didn't have the inner circle, the second constitution. Having the inner circle protects the boundary between church and state, eliminating the theocratic temptation. The second constitution guards against making the nation the final source of authority, instead basing natural rights not on the general will but on the grounding of natural law backed by divine revelation. Finally, the "spirit of religion" is not a watered-down useful myth but a living, breathing faith tradition with the power to renew individuals and the external covenant. It can ground the new vital center. And it protects us from the use of inflationary tactics, the very thing that leads to the polarization of religion and its abuse in the first place, a tactic of both the religious Left and religious Right.

The only way to prevent these inflationary stances is to hold both divine revelation and general revelation—the new vital center (general revelation and common grace) combined with revelation (Christianity as a second constitution). When we do this, we are meeting Budziszewski's challenge of a full-orbed political philosophy or what Ceaser calls the public philosophy. Holding to both constitutions, special revelation and general revelation, we can reject inflationary tactics whether on the Christian right or left. We can instead choose the new vital center, which protects our constitutional republic and fights against the polarization in the four quadrants.

The Father of Our Nation

In June 2020, rioters in Portland tore down the statue of George Washington, once recognized as the father of our country by the majority of those on the right *and* the left. Around that time, I picked up Michael Novak's *Washington's God: Religion, Liberty, and the Father of our Country*, and was reminded of Washington's "Thanksgiving Prayer of 1789." Reading it again, I couldn't believe how different his views on America were from those of the rioters, bringing in stark relief the two completely different narratives, two utterly different views on what America is. Washington's prayer was meant for all Americans, but as I read it I also saw it as an appeal to Christians and the church to take our calling of citizenship and civic friendship seriously.[25] I read it as a call to Christians to resist polarization, to push back on the destruction of our founding and our country, and to see again that it is the best possible regime.

For Christians, Washington's prayer is a call to remember what our founders established in the four souls and to remember the genius behind our long-lasting union that has persisted for over two hundred years and has been a beacon and magnet for lonely and freedom-loving souls from around the world. It is a call to unity, to friendship, to mutual citizenship, to the support of middle class values, so "that we may then unite," implores Washington,

> in most humbly offering our prayers and supplications to the great Lord and Ruler of Nations and beseech him to pardon our national and other transgressions—to enable us all, whether in public or private stations, to perform our several and relative duties properly and punctually—to render our national government a blessing to all the people, by constantly being a Government of wise, just, and constitutional laws, discreetly and faithfully executed and obeyed—to protect and guide all Sovereigns and Nations (especially such as have shewn kindness unto us) and to bless them with good government, peace, and concord—To promote the knowledge and practice of true religion and virtue, and the increase of science among them and us—and generally to grant unto all Mankind such a degree of temporal prosperity as he alone knows to be best.[26]

It is a stirring prayer, a true prayer, one grounded on both the *first* constitution and the *second* constitution. It is a prayer by the father of our nation, the very one whose statue the rioters tore down. It is a prayer about the very best of America, what America was and what America can be. It is a prayer of blessing.

As I read the prayer on a warm spring afternoon and thought of our present cold civil war, I was deeply saddened. But at the same time, I was once again inspired; inspired to get back to work, inspired to fight, to not give up, to not lose hope. Indeed the hour is late. But not too late to affirm the words of the Declaration of Independence, "with a firm reliance on the protection of Providence, we mutually pledge to each other our Lives, our Fortunes, and our sacred Honor."

Let us pray it is not too late. Let us pray, in God's good governance, that we can rescue our republic. And as we "raise a glass to freedom," may God help us.

ACKNOWLEDGMENTS

I AM GRATEFUL TO A MYRIAD OF PEOPLE who have helped me formulate a public philosophy, that is, the New Vital Center. Thirty years ago after spending a weekend at the ancestral home of Russel Kirk, studying Edmund Burke with other graduate students and scholars, listening to Russell tell late-night ghost stories, he was kind enough to introduce me, a seminary student at the time, to George Carey at Georgetown, which turned out to be providential. To this day, tucked inside my copy of Kirk's *The Conservative Mind* is his letter to me undoubtedly typed on his Remington electric typewriter, encouraging me to reach out to Professor Carey. After meeting with Professor Carey on a wintery December day at Georgetown, he invited me to study with him. Not only was Professor Carey instrumental in getting me into Georgetown but he inspired me to love *The Federalist Papers*, which was his expertise, and eventually became my dissertation advisor. I owe a debt of gratitude to Professor Carey, and I will forever be grateful to Russell for the introduction.

I am also grateful for Georgetown professor Father James Schall, who taught me Plato and Aristotle and who allowed me to write papers comparing classical philosophy with reformational thinkers like John Calvin and Martin Luther. Even back then, I was in search for the right grounding for public philosophy. I am grateful to Walter Berns, whose class on Alexis de Tocqueville's *Democracy in America* set me on the path to study, ponder, and teach this classic work on America, which I have been doing for the past thirty years.

Ever since I began this project three years ago, the scholars who write for the *Claremont Review of Books* have been a steady and helpful influence, as I have attempted to understand the academic landscape and correctly place authors in the distinct quadrants. For decades this small publication has been doing its part in defending constitutional republicanism, and I am grateful for their labors.

The discovery of J. Budziszewski's chapter, "Evangelicals in the Public Square," proved formative, helping me see clearly why evangelicals have never been able to develop a coherent public philosophy.[1] His numerous books on Natural Law have been invaluable in filling the gap, demonstrating so clearly how reason and revelation must go together.[2]

I am grateful to the work of James Ceaser for helping me understand the Founders' synthesis, and his view that the founders saw Christianity as a second constitution helped me further clarify the new vital center.

I want to thank Al Hsu, who has been my editor at IVP on all three of my books. He is a true professional and always a joy to work with.

Finally, I want to thank my wife, Michelle, who stayed up most school nights helping our girls, Lindsay and Meghan, with their homework, allowing me to be asleep by 9:30 p.m. so I could be up at 4 a.m. to write. Without her sacrifice every night (after her own long day of work) I couldn't have completed this project. Michelle also served as a sounding board for all the ideas in this book and was a constant encouragement on days that I got discouraged. I am deeply thankful for her unwavering support of my vocation as a writer.

NOTES

FOREWORD

[1]Patrick Joseph Buchanan, "Culture War Speech: Address to the Republican Convention (17 August 1992)," Voices of Democracy: U. S. Oratory Project, University of Maryland, https://voicesofdemocracy.umd.edu/buchanan-culture-war-speech-speech-text/.

INTRODUCTION

[1]Angelo M. Codevilla, "The Cold Civil War: Statecraft in a Divided Country," *Claremont Review of Books*, Spring 2017, https://claremountreviewofbooks.com/the-cold-civil-war/.

[2]Jonathan Haidt, *The Righteous Mind: Why Good People Are Divided by Politics and Religion* (New York: Vintage Books, 2012), 319.

[3]Jonathan Haidt, *Can't We All Disagree More Constructively?* (New York: Vintage Books, 2016), 1.

[4]Stephen Hawkins, Daniel Yudkin, Miriam Juan-Torres, and Tim Dixon, "Hidden Tribes: A Study of America's Polarized Landscape," More in Common, October 2018, 136, https://hiddentribes.us/media/qfpekz4g/hidden_tribes_report.pdf.

[5]Bari Weiss, "Resignation Letter," www.bariweiss.com/resignation-letter.

[6]Bari Weiss, "The Great Unraveling," January 12, 2021, https://bariweiss.substack.com/p/the-great-unraveling.

[7]Weiss, "The Great Unraveling."

[8]2021 Joseph R. Biden Jr. Executive Orders, Federal Register, www.federalregister.gov/presidential-documents/executive-orders/joe-biden/2021.

[9]The orders included, among other things, support for transgender biological males in women's sports, making abortion on demand easier, reversing Trump's border and immigration policies, terminating the construction of the border wall, ending the 1776 Commission in favor of the policies for "racial equity," rejoining the Paris Climate Agreement, terminating the Keystone XL pipeline, and moving toward the eventual elimination of all fracking. While I believe presidential politics are important, my goal, while difficult in our hyper-polarized environment is to transcend party politics as much as possible and focus on principles more than party. I will mention Biden and Trump occasionally but my loyalty lies with constitutional republicanism, over against the oligarchy of the ruling class, and this means I will be critical of both parties, particularly in our two houses of Congress.

[10]Joseph R. Biden, Inaugural Address, January 20, 2021, www.whitehouse.gov/briefing room/speeches-remarks/2021/01/20/.

[11]But while anyone who acted violently that day should be prosecuted they should also get due process and be treated fairly. As I worked on the final edits of this manuscript in July 2021, many of those arrested were still languishing in a DC prison, awaiting trial, and not receiving due process. See Julie Kelley, "Man in Pelosi's Office Discusses Jail Conditions for January 6 Detainees," American Greatness, May 25, 2021, https://amgreatness .com/2021/05/25/man-in-pelosis-office-discusses-jail-conditions-for-january-6-detainees/.

[12]I recognize that there is a place for violent revolution, as we experienced in our independence from Great Britain. Yet, while there is a need to have a philosophical discussion on revolution and violence, I will not take up this discussion in this book, other than to say that vigilante violence is wrong. However, saying that doesn't mean that every principle held by a group that calls for violence is wrong. Sometimes they might be right on the diagnosis and wrong on the solution. We can have discussions about the beliefs, agreeing with some even when we reject solutions as misguided.

[13]Jordan Davidson, "John Brennan: Biden Intelligence Agencies to Investigate Pro-Trump 'Bigots' and 'Libertarians,'" *The Federalist*, January 21, 2021, https://thefederalist.com /2021/01/21/john-brennan-biden-intelligence-agencies-to-investigate-pro-trump -bigots-and-libertarians/.

[14]Brennan was wrong. While this manuscript was being prepared for publication in August 2021, the FBI finally concluded that there was no proof of an organized plot of insurrection on January 6, 2021. See Jonathan Turley, "The FBI Comes Up Empty Handed in its Search for a January 6th Plot," *The Hill*, August 11, 2021, https://thehill.com/opinion /judiciary/568842-the-fbi-comes-up-empty-handed-in-its-search-for-a-jan-6-plot.

[15]To understand how those on the right interpret January 6, 2021, and what has transpired with the prisoners in the months following their arrests, see Lee Smith, "America's New Political Prisoners: Insurrectionists, White Supremacists, and Domestic Muslim Terrorists Are All the Same People–Us," Tablet, June 30, 2021, https://tabletmag.com/sections /news/articles/lee-smith-insurrectionists-january-6.

[16]Glenn Greenwald, *Tucker Carlson Tonight*, January 20, 2021. To see the complicity of the bipartisan ruling elite in the aftermath of the Capitol riot, see Ryan J. Reilly, "After Hundreds of Arrests in Sprawling Capitol Hunt, The FBI Just Made A Pretty Big Mistake," *Huffington Post*, May 7, 2021, www.huffpost.com/entry/60930634e4b0c15313fbe48f; also see Glenn Greenwald, "The US Intelligence Community, Flouting Laws, is Increasingly Involving Itself in Domestic Politics," Glenn Greenwald, https://greenwald.substack .com/; and Victor Davis Hanson, "The Bleak Biden Way," American Greatness, May 2, 2021, https://amgreatness.com/2021/05/02/the-bleak-biden-way/.

[17]*Tucker Carlson Tonight*, January 20, 2021, https://www.youtube.com/watch?v=nPU0 axNkEK0.

[18]*Tucker Carlson Tonight*, January 20, 2021.

[19]Ben Stein, "In Class Warfare, Guess Which Class Is Winning," *New York Times*, November 26, 2006, www.nytimes.com/2006/11/26/business/yourmoney/26every.html.

[20]Angelo M. Codevilla, *The Ruling Class: How They Corrupted America and What We Can Do About It* (New York: Beaufort Books, 2010).

[21]Oligarchy is defined as a small group of people who control the main political, economic, and political institutions of the country, rigging the system for their own benefit. To see how it contrasts with constitutional republicanism, see Leslie G. Rubin, *America, Aristotle, and the Politics of a Middle Class* (Waco: Baylor University Press, 2018).

[22]Joel Kotkin, *The Coming of Neo Feudalism: A Warning to the Global Middle Class* (New York: Encounter Books, 2020).

[23]Michael Lind, *The New Class War: Saving Democracy from the Managerial Elite* (New York: Portfolio, 2020).

[24]Robert J. Bunker and Pamela Ligouri, eds, *Plutocratic Insurgency Reader* (Bloomington: Xlibris, 2019).

[25]Emma Colton, "Rahm Emanuel Reprises 'Never Let a Crisis Go to Waste' Catchphrase Amid Coronavirus Pandemic," *Washington Examiner*, March 24, 2020, www.washingtonexaminer.com/news/rahm-emanuel-reprises-never-let-a-crisis-go-to-waste-catchphrase-amid-coronavirus-pandemic.

[26]Sarah Cammarata, "Biden promises wealthy donors he would not 'demonize' the rich," June 19, 2019, Politico, https://www.politico.com/story/2019/06/19/biden-wealthy-donors-1369957.

[27]Eric Levitz, "Biden 2020: Change That Wall Street Liberals Can Believe In?" *Intelligencer*, September 8, 2020, https://nymag.com/intelligencer/2020/09/biden-2020-agenda-wall-street-silicon-valley-progressives.html.

[28]Levitz, "Biden 2020."

[29]See Chrystia Freeland, *Plutocrats: The Rise of the Super-Rich and the Fall of Everyone Else* (NY: Penguin Books, 2013); Jacob S. Hacker and Paul Pierson, *Winner-Take-All Politics: How Washington Made the Rich Richer—and Turned its Back on the Middle Class* (New York: Simon and Schuster, 2011); Jeff Faux, *The Servant Economy: Where America's Elite is Sending the Middle Class* (Hoboken, NJ: Wiley, 2012); Robert G. Kaiser, *So Damn Much Money: The Triumph of Lobbying and the Corruption of American Government* (New York: Knopf, 2009); Peter Schweizer, *Throw Them All Out: How Politicians and Their Friends Get Rich Off Insider Stock Tips, Land Deals, and Cronyism that Would Send the Rest of Us to Prison* (New York: Houghton Mifflin Harcourt, 2011).

[30]Nils Gilman, "The Twin Insurgency—Facing Plutocrats and Criminals," chap. 3 in *Plutocratic Insurgency Reader*, ed. Robert J. Bunker and Pamela Ligouri Bunker (Bloomington, IN: Xlibris, 2019).

[31]For the ways that Trump's anti-oligarchic rhetoric didn't always match his actions, falling woefully short at times, and how Trump actually inadvertently empowered the ruling class (even as they attacked him), see Angelo Codevilla, "What Is Trump to Us?," American Greatness, July 6, 2021, https://amgreatness.com/2021/07/06/what-is-trump-to-us/.

[32]Joel Kotkin, "The Pandemic Road to Serfdom," *The American Mind*, May 1, 2020, https://americanmind.org/salvo/the-pandemic-road-to-serfdom/.

[33]Niall McCarthy, "US Billionaires Added 1 Trillion to Their Collective Wealth Since the Start of the Pandemic," *Forbes*, November 27, 2020, www.forbes.com/sites/niallmc carthy/2020/11/27/us-billionaires-added-1-trillion-to-their-collective-wealth-since -the-start-of-the-pandemic-infographic/?sh=54aa736d66ce; Peter Eaves and Steve Lohr, "Big Tech Domination of Business Reaches New Heights," *New York Times*, August 19, 2020, www.nytimes.com/2020/08/19/technology/big-tech-business-domination.html.

[34]Kotkin, "The Pandemic Road to Serfdom."

[35]Anne Spraders and Lance Lambert, "Nearly 100,000 Establishments That Temporarily Shut Down Due to the Pandemic Are Now out of Business," *Fortune*, September 28, 2020, htttps://fortune.com/2020/09/28/covid-business-shut-down-closed/.

[36]John Hayward, "7 Ways Governments Used the Coronavirus Pandemic to Crush Human Rights," Breitbart, December 25, 2020, www.breitbart.com/national-security/2020/12/25 /hayward-7-ways-governments-used-the-coronavirus-pandemic-to-crush-human-rights/.

[37]Joy Pullman, "Big Corporate Uses Capitol Riots to Push Communist-Style Social Credit System on Americans," *The Federalist*, January 11, 2021, https://thefederalist.com/2021/01/11 /big-corporate-uses-capitol-riots-to-push-communist-style-social-credit-system-on -americans/.

[38]If we are ever going to avoid a civil war, political violence must be rejected at all times, regardless of whether you agree with the philosophy of the group doing the violence. We have to support protest and dissent of all kinds, on the left and the right, but reject riots, violence, and insurrection of any kind.

[39]Angelo Codevilla, *The Ruling Class: How They Corrupted America and What We Can Do About It* (New York: Beaufort Books, 2010), 69.

[40]Codevilla, *The Ruling Class*, 73.

[41]James Davison Hunter, *Culture Wars: The Struggle to Define America* (New York: Basic Books, 1991).

[42]Hunter, *Culture Wars*, 50.

[43]Hawkins et al., "Hidden Tribes," 137.

[44]Hawkins et al., "Hidden Tribes," 137-38.

[45]Hawkins et al., "Hidden Tribes," 138.

[46]For a helpful book explaining why the middle class is so important in maintaining a constitutional democracy, see Leslie G. Rubin, *America, Aristotle, and the Politics of a Middle Class* (Waco, Baylor University Press, 2018).

[47]For an example on the left, see Lee Drutman, "We Need Political Parties. But Their Rabid Partisanship Could Destroy American Democracy," Vox, September 5, 2017, www.vox.com/the-big-idea/2017/9/5/16227700/; For pessimism on the right, see Angelo Codevilla, "Revolution 2020," *The American Mind*, September 23, 2020, https://american mind.org/salvo/revolution-2020/.

[48]In fact, the American Mind website ran a series of articles after the 2020 Election, asking

the question, "Should We Split?"; You can access the articles here: https://americanmind
.org/feature/will-we-split/.

[49]Charles Kesler, "America's Cold Civil War," *Imprimis* 47, no. 10 (October 2018): 8.

[50]Alexis de Tocqueville, *Democracy in America*, translated and edited by Harvey C. Mansfield and Delba Winthrop (Chicago: University of Chicago Press, 2000), 7.

[51]Tocqueville, *Democracy in America*, 7.

[52]Tocqueville, *Democracy in America*, 15.

1. The Evangelical Dilemma and the Search for Public Philosophy

[1]Ryan Burge, "The Growing Divide Within American Evangelicals," Religion Unplugged, December 15, 2020, https://religionunplugged.com/news/2020/12/15/the-growing -divide-within-american-evangelicalism; Joe Carter, "Why Evangelicals Are (Still) Divided over Trump," The Gospel Coalition, October 29, 2020, www.thegospelcoalition .org/article/why-evangelicals-are-still-divided-over-trump/.

[2]Kevyn Burger, "The Political Divide Is Threatening Relationships Among Family, Friends, and Co-Workers," *The Star Tribune*, January 23, 2021, www.startribune.com/the -political-divide-is-threatening-relationships-among-family-friends-and-co-workers /600013687/.

[3]Bill Bishop, *The Big Sort: Why the Clustering of Like-Minded America Is Tearing Us Apart* (New York: Houghton Mifflin Company, 2008).

[4]Matt Taibbi, *Hate Inc.: How Today Media Makes Us Despise One Another* (New York: OR Books, 2021).

[5]Kevin Roose, "How the Biden Administration Can Help Solve Our Reality Crisis," *New York Times*, February 2, 2021, www.nytimes.com/2021/02/02/technology/biden-reality -crisis-misinformation.html.

[6]"Roy Austin Joins Facebook as VP of Civil Rights," https://about.fb.com/news/2021/01 /roy-austin-facebook-vp-civil-rights/.

[7]See the documentary the *Creepy Line: Google and Facebook Censorship Manipulation Undermine Democracy*, directed by M. A. Taylor (Seattle: Amazon Prime Videos, 2018).

[8]Dana Kennedy, "CA Podcaster Gets Visit from Police After 'Lightly' Criticizing AOC on Twitter," *New York Post*, April 10, 2021, https://nypost.com/2021/04/10/ca-podcaster -gets-visit-from-police-after-aoc-tweet/.

[9]Phil Stewart and Idrees Ali, "Pentagon, Stumped by Extremism in Ranks, Orders Stand-Down in Next 60 Days," Reuters, February 3, 2021, www.reuters.com/article/idUSKBN 2A335W.

[10]Jesse T. Jackson, "Godspeak Calvary Chapel Fined $3,000 for Holding Indoor Worship," Church Leaders, August 21, 2020, https://churchleaders.com/news/381075-godspeak -calvary-chapel-fined-3000-for-holding-indoor-gatherings.html.

[11]J. Budziszewski, "Evangelicals in the Public Square," *Evangelicals in the Public Square: Four Formative Voices*, ed. J. Budziszewski (Grand Rapids, MI: Baker Academic, 2019), 16, italics added.

[12]Budziszewski, "Evangelicals in the Public Square," 17.

[13]Budziszewski, "Evangelicals in the Public Square," 18.

[14]Budziszewski, "Evangelicals in the Public Square," 18.

[15]Budziszewski, "Evangelicals in the Public Square," 18-19, italics original.

[16]Tremper Longman, *The Bible and the Ballot: Using Scripture in Political Decisions* (Grand Rapids, MI: Eerdmans, 2020); Jonathan Leeman, *How the Nations Rage: Rethinking Faith and Politics in a Divided Age* (Nashville, TN: Thomas Nelson, 2018).

[17]Carl R. Trueman, "Evangelicals and Race Theory," *First Things*, February 2021, www .firstthings.com/article/2021/02/evangelicals-and-race-theory; see Voddie T. Baucham Jr., *Fault Lines: The Social Justice Movement and Evangelicalism's Looming Catastrophe* (Washington, DC: Salem Books, 2021).

[18]John Fea, *Was America Founded as a Christian Nation?* (Louisville, KY: Westminster John Knox Press, 2016); Mark David Hall, *Did America Have a Christian Founding?* (Nashville, TN: Thomas Nelson, 2019).

[19]For the challenge to biblical authority in the late nineteenth century, see Mark A. Noll, *The Civil War as a Theological Crisis* (Chapel Hill: University of North Carolina Press, 2015).

[20]Budziszewski, *Evangelicals in the Public Square*, 21.

[21]Budziszewski, *Evangelicals in the Public Square*, 23, italics added.

[22]Budziszewski, *Evangelicals in the Public Square*, 23-27.

[23]Budziszewski, *Evangelicals in the Public Square*, 27.

[24]Budziszewski, *Evangelicals in the Public Square*, 28-29.

[25]Budziszewski, *Evangelicals in the Public Square*, 30.

[26]Two examples of inflationary tactics from each side might include: Jerry Falwell, *Listen, America!* (New York: Doubleday, 1980) and Daniel Block, "Is Trump Our Cyrus? The Old Testament Case for Yes and No," *Christianity Today*, October 29, 2018.

[27]Budziszewski, *Evangelicals in the Public Square*, 30.

[28]Budziszewski, *Evangelicals in the Public Square*, 31.

[29]Also see J. Budziszewski, *Written on the Heart: The Case for Natural Law* (Downers Grove, IL: IVP Academic, 1997); For a discussion of natural law in Reformed Protestant circles see Stephen J. Grabill, *Rediscovering the Natural Law in Reformed Theological Ethics* (Grand Rapids, MI: Eerdmans, 2006).

[30]J. Budziszewski, *The Line Through the Heart: Natural Law as Fact, Theory, and Sign of Contradiction* (Wilmington, DE: ISI Books, 2009), 10.

[31]Albert M. Wolters, *Creation Regained: Biblical Basics for a Reformational Worldview* (Grand Rapids, MI: Eerdmans, 2005).

[32]Budziszewski, *The Line Through the Heart*, chap. 1.

[33]Budziszewski, *Evangelicals in the Public Square*, 31.

[34]Budziszewski, *Evangelicals in the Public Square*, 31.

[35]Budziszewski, *The Line Through the Heart*, 23-40.

[36]A good introduction to his thought is *Abraham Kuyper: A Centennial Reader*, James D. Bratt, ed. (Grand Rapids, MI: Eerdmans, 1998), especially "Common Grace," pages 165-210.

[37]Richard Mouw, *He Shines in All That's Fair: Culture and Common Grace* (Grand Rapids, MI: Eerdmans, 2002); Nicholas Wolterstorff, *Understanding Liberal Democracy: Essays in Political Philosophy* (Oxford: Oxford University Press, 2012); *Political Order and the Plural Structure of Society* James W. Skillen, Rockne McCarthy, eds. (Scholars Press, 1991), George Marsden, *Understanding Fundamentalism* (Grand Rapids, MI: Eerdmans, 1990); H. Evan Runner, *Scriptural Religion and Political Task* (Toronto: Wedge Publishing Foundation, 1974). Overall, from the neo-Kuyperian tradition, I learned a great deal about the church's responsibility to transform culture, how to critique the Enlightenment's commitment to reason over revelation, how to diagnose the dangers of expressive individualism in our modern liberal tradition, and the proper role of the different spheres of society. But that tradition wasn't without weakness, which I came to realize much later. Many in this camp were deeply ambivalent about America's founding, often the result of being first generation immigrants from Holland. But some of the ambivalence came from their view that America was too rooted in Enlightenment thinking, particularly Thomas Jefferson, and missed the role that the Scottish Enlightenment played. Because neo-Kuyperians were often ambivalent about America's founding and were critical of the influence of the Enlightenment on our founding, I too often took a critical stance toward the main currents of ancient and modern political thought, a stance where I stood outside our tradition as a critic. It took me a number of years after Fuller to correct my faulty thinking.

[38]As it turned out, Georgetown in the 1990s proved to be a great place to study political philosophy and understand public philosophy. Along with George Carey, who taught me *The Federalist Papers* and had written extensively on issues in public philosophy, I was exposed to thoughtful thinkers on both sides of the political spectrum. From those on the left, I studied the history of classical liberalism under Gerald Mara and Marxism under Bruce Douglass. On the right, Walter Berns, the famous Constitutional scholar, who once voted for Adlai Stevenson, taught me about Tocqueville (and introduced me to the idea of *civic republicanism*) and Father James Schall taught me Plato, Aristotle, and Aquinas, deepening my appreciation for classical and medieval political thought. I also had professors who saw political science as purely secular, devoid of normative considerations, a topic that could be studied scientifically using social science tools, and in the end had more to do with postmodern power struggle than with justice.

[39]George Carey, "On The Degeneration of Public Philosophy in America: Problems and Prospects" in E. Robert Stratham Jr., ed., *Public Philosophy and Political Science* (New York: Lexington Books, 2002), 44.

[40]Carey, "On The Degeneration of Public Philosophy," 45.

[41]James Ceaser, "What Is the Public Philosophy?," in *Public Philosophy and Political Science: Crisis and Reflection,* E. Robert Stratham Jr., ed. (New York: Lexington Books, 2002).

[42]Ceaser, "What Is the Public Philosophy?" 17.

[43]Ceaser, "What Is the Public Philosophy?," 17.

[44]Ceaser, "What Is the Public Philosophy?," 17.

[45]Ceaser, "What Is the Public Philosophy?," 17.

[46]Ceaser, "What Is the Public Philosophy?," 18.

[47]Within the church over the past twenty years, this theme of justification or grounding has been called "public theology"—often defined as the relationship of God's people—the church—to the state. As James K. A. Smith contends, a Christian political theology asks the question "in what ways—and to what extent—can the 'peculiar people' that is the church live in common with citizens of the earthly city?," James K. A. Smith, *Awaiting the King: Reforming Public Theology* (Grand Rapids, MI: Baker Academic, 2017), 6.

Thus, in many ways public philosophy and political theology share similar terrain; they deal, in part, with questions of grounding. While public theology is mainly about how the church as a unique people of God relates to the secular world, drawing from God's direction for politics in the Bible and natural revelation, with the stress usually on the Scriptures first, public philosophy looks more from the vantage point of public life and its relation to the moral and spiritual realm, dealing with issues of separation of church and state and the role of virtue in sustaining the political system. Yet both public philosophy and public theology examine how humans get along, form and maintain a common life together, and determine the ultimate authority in life, the grounding.

[48]Along with seeking answers to questions about the parts of political life and about human nature, God, the common good, the ends of society, and how we ground our life together, my quest for understanding the concept of public philosophy—how our crisis in America is over rival-first principles—my time at Georgetown wasn't just an exercise in cultural and political anthropology, that is, understanding what goes into the concept. While this was important, I also wanted to come away with a public philosophy that could unify America again and be the social glue that bonds America together. So while the term *public philosophy* is a concept that can encompass many different versions of political philosophy, whether progressive or conservative, I follow Walter Lippmann (see chap. two) by putting *the* in front of *public philosophy*, as in *the* public philosophy of our nation's founders, a public philosophy rooted in Western civilization, grounded in something deeper than pragmatic progressivism, a "civic faith," a glue that binds Americans together and that has been in crisis since the 1960s. In other words, the quest to find a public philosophy, a general concept that guides people's thinking about politics and the common life together, will take on a more peculiar meaning in the context of America. It will be defined as the common glue that holds America together and allows us to transfer power peacefully every four years. But this public philosophy, one more about recovering the past than reinventing the future, is also so disputed today. In fact, as we begin mapping the different versions of public

philosophy, we will see that all of them are reacting either against or for the original founding. This becomes a certain litmus test for our study. What does each thinker believe about our founding? Is the founding part of our grounding, and can it be recovered? Or was the founding hopelessly compromised and the only way forward is to repudiate it and adopt something entirely new? As I look for a new vital center, I too will take a certain position toward the founding.

[49]While not everyone on the far left thinks America is evil, I will demonstrate in chapters three through seven how many on the far left have become more and more radical over the past seventy years.

[50]Jim Belcher, *Deep Church: A Third Way Between Emerging and Traditional* (Downers Grove, IL: InterVarsity Press, 2009).

[51]While this doesn't include everyone on the right, I will show in chapters nine and ten, that a group of thinkers have become more extreme and more illiberal over the last few decades.

2. The End of the Vital Center

[1]Jeet Heer, "The Right is Giving Up on Democracy," *New Republic*, October 24, 2016, https://newrepublic.com/article/138019/. For two good representative books on the threat of this anti-democratic sentiment, and what became a cottage industry of articles and books for four years, see Timothy Synder, *On Tyranny: Lessons from the Twentieth Century* (New York: Tim Duggan Books, 2012) and Ann Applebaum, *Twilight of Democracy: The Seductive Lure of Authoritarianism* (New York: Doubleday, 2020).

[2]Mike Allen, "Institutionalizing Trumpism," Axios, May 7, 2021, www.axios.com/institutionalizing-trumpism-1289f127-ff6e-4edd-aa34-7a6982d1984b.html.

[3]Michael Gerson, "Trumpism Is American Fascism," *Washington Post*, February 1, 2021, www.washingtonpost.com/c410f662-64b2-11eb-8c64-9595888caa15_story.html.

[4]Chris Hayes, "The Republican Party Is Radicalizing Against Democracy," the *Atlantic*, February 8, 2021, www.theatlantic.com/ideas/archive/2021/02/republican-party-radicalizing-against-democracy/617959/.

[5]John Daniel Davidson, "Why the Left Still Can't Understand Trump's Appeal," *The Federalist*, February 10, 2021, https://thefederalist.com/2021/02/10/why-the-left-still-cant-understand-trumps-appeal/.

[6]Davidson, "Why the Left Still Can't Understand Trump's Appeal."

[7]Seth Barron, "What Is 'Our' Democracy?," *The American Mind*, February 11, 2021, https://americanmind.org/salvo/what-is-our-democracy/.

[8]Yuval Levin, *The Fractured Republic: Renewing America's Social Contract in the Age of Individualism* (New York: Basic Books, 2016) 3.

[9]Levin, *The Fractured Republic*, 3.

[10]Levin, *The Fractured Republic*, 156.

[11]George M. Marsden, *The Twilight of the American Enlightenment: The 1950s and the Crisis of Liberal Belief* (New York: Basic Books, 2014), 20.

[12]Marsden, *Twilight of the American Enlightenment*, 59.

[13]Arthur M. Schlesinger Jr., *The Vital Center: The Politics of Freedom* (Boston: Houghton Mifflin Company, 1949).

[14]Marsden, *Twilight of the American Enlightenment*, 57.

[15]Marsden, *Twilight of the American Enlightenment*, 57. Quoted material is from Schlesinger's *The Vital Center: The Politics of Freedom* (Boston: Houghton Mifflin Company, 1949).

[16]While we will see how the Right contributed to the loss of the vital center (see chaps. seven through ten) this chapter is about how the progressive Left successfully led an attack on the vital center. That they did so and were so successful is a story shared by historians on the left and the right. While the Left celebrates the destruction of the vital center and the Right bemoans it, nonetheless, they both agree that the Left was the most vocal, the most powerful, and the most successful. To make this clear, I rely mainly on voices on the left—like Hartman, Marsden and Schlesinger—to tell the story.

[17]Arthur M. Schlesinger Jr., *The Vital Center: The Politics of Freedom* (Boston: Houghton Mifflin Company, 1949), 8.

[18]In his second chapter, "the Failure of the Right" Schlesinger warned that the Right had become too aligned with the business community, "the property of the plutocracy." *The Vital Center*, 25.

[19]Andrew Hartman, *A War for the Soul of America: A History of the Culture Wars*, 2nd ed. (Chicago: University of Chicago Press, 2019), 2.

[20]Roger Kimball, *The Long March: How the Cultural Revolution of the 1960s Changed America* (San Francisco: Encounter Books, 2000), 41.

[21]Hartman, *War for the Soul of America*, 12.

[22]Hartman, *War for the Soul of America*, 12.

[23]Theodore Roszak, "Youth and the Great Refusal," the *Nation*, 1968, quoted by Hartman, *A War for the Soul of the Nation*, 14.

[24]Kristin Kobes Du Mez, *Jesus and John Wayne: How White Evangelicals Corrupted a Faith and Fractured a Nation* (New York: Liveright Publishing, 2020).

[25]Hartman, *War for the Soul of America*, 71.

[26]Christopher Caldwell, "Can There Ever Be a Working-Class Republican Party? The Party of the Country Club Tries to Embrace a New Egalitarian Economic Agenda," *The New Republic*, Feb. 8, 2021, https://newrepublic.com/article/161113/.

[27]While this chapter is mainly focusing on how the radical Left attacked the vital center, in chapters seven through ten I will tell the story of how some on the right, particularly libertarians, also helped radically transform America in the areas of economics, politics, and culture. To see how radical forces on the right and the left transformed America from a constitutional republic to an oligarchy, see Lee Smith, "The Thirty Tyrants: The Deal That the American Elite Chose to Make with China Has a Precedent in the History of Athens and Sparta," *Tablet*, February 4, 2021; Thomas Freidman, "Our One-Party Democracy," *New York Times*, September 8, 2009, www.nytimes.com/2009/09/09/opinion/09friedman.html.

[28]James Davison Hunter, *Culture Wars: The Struggle to Define America: Making Sense of the Battles over the Family, Art, Education, Law, and Politics* (New York: Basic Books, 1991), 42.

[29]Hunter, *Culture Wars*, 43.

[30]Hunter, *Culture Wars*, 43. Italics original.

[31]Hunter, *Culture Wars*, 44.

[32]Hunter, Culture Wars, 43.

[33]Chris Hayes, "The Republican Party Is Radicalizing Against Democracy," the *Atlantic*, February 8, 2021, www.theatlantic.com/ideas/archive/2021/02/republican-party-radical izing-against-democracy/617959/.

[34]Barry Rubin, *Silent Revolution: How the Left Rose to Political and Cultural Dominance* (New York: HarperCollins, 2014).

[35]Marsden, *The Twilight of the American Enlightenment*, xvi.

[36]Marsden, *The Twilight of the American Enlightenment*, xvi.

[37]Marsden, *The Twilight of the American Enlightenment*, xxi.

[38]Marsden, *The Twilight of the American Enlightenment*, xxi.

[39]Marsden, *The Twilight of the American Enlightenment*, 60.

[40]Marsden, *The Twilight of the American Enlightenment*, 60.

[41]Marsden, *The Twilight of the American Enlightenment*, 62.

[42]Marsden, *The Twilight of the American Enlightenment*, 130.

[43]Marsden, *The Twilight of the American Enlightenment*, 130.

[44]Marsden, *The Twilight of the American Enlightenment*, 130.

[45]Arthur M. Schlesinger Jr., *The Disuniting of America: Reflections on a Multicultural Society* (New York: W. W. Norton, 1998), 13.

[46]Schlesinger, *Disuniting of America*, 20.

[47]Schlesinger, *Disuniting of America*, 49.

[48]Mark Lila, *The Once and Future Liberal: After Identity Politics* (San Francisco: Harper Paperbacks, 2019).

[49]Schlesinger, *Disuniting of America*, 23.

[50]Schlesinger, *Disuniting of America*, 124.

[51]Schlesinger, *Disuniting of America*, 118.

[52]Schlesinger, *Disuniting of America*, 141.

[53]Schlesinger, *Disuniting of America*, 142.

[54]President Biden's 2021 Fourth of July speech is a good example of reducing America's uniqueness to an idea: "I've long said that America is unique, unlike every other nation on earth, we are founded on an idea," Rev, www.rev.com/blog/transcript/joe-biden-july -4-2021-independence-day-speech-transcript.

[55]Robert N. Bellah, *The Broken Covenant: American Civil Religion in Time of Trial* (New York: The Seabury Press, 1975), 142.

⁵⁶Bellah, *The Broken Covenant*, 143.

⁵⁷Bellah, *The Broken Covenant*, ix.

⁵⁸Bellah, *The Broken Covenant*, xvi.

⁵⁹Bellah, *The Broken Covenant*, 142.

⁶⁰Bellah, *The Broken Covenant*, 142.

⁶¹Bellah, *The Broken Covenant*, 142.

⁶²Yuval Levin, *The Fractured Republic: Renewing America's Social Contract in the Age of Individualism* (New York: Basic Book, 2016), 46-66.

⁶³Matt Walsh, "It is Time to Face the Facts: We Cannot Be United," The Daily Wire, June 12, 2020, www.dailywire.com/news/walsh-it-is-time-to-face-the-facts-we-cannot-be-united.

⁶⁴Kurt Schlichter, "Should We Just Let It Burn?" Townhall, April 29, 2021, https://townhall.com/columnists/kurtschlichter/2021/04/29/should-we-just-let-it-burn-n2588663.

⁶⁵See Victor Davis Hanson, "The World Goes on While America Sleeps," American Greatness, February 10, 2021, https://amgreatness.com/2021/02/10/the-world-goes-on-while-america-sleeps/.

Part Two: Mapping Our Differences: The Quadrant Framework System

¹See chapter four, "Living Narratives," in Christian Smith, *Moral Believing Animals* (New York: Oxford University Press, 2003).

²Jason Willick, "A Center That Can Hold," *National Affairs*, summer 2018, www.nationalaffairs.com/publications/detail/a-center-that-can-hold.

3. Freedom Left 2: The Theory of the Godless Constitution

¹Philip Wegmann, "Religious Litmus Tests Are Becoming All the Rage on the Left," *Washington Examiner*, September 6, 2017, www.washingtonexaminer.com/religious-litmus-tests-are-becoming-all-the-rage-on-the-left; Aaron Blake, "Did Dianne Feinstein Accuse a Judicial Nominee of Being Too Christian?," *Washington Post*, September 7, 2017, www.washingtonpost.com/news/the-fix/wp/2017/09/07/did-a-democratic-senator-just-accuse-a-judicial-nominee-of-being-too-christian/.

²They had to retract this story. The inspiration was another Catholic group, not the People of Praise.

³Julie Zauzmer, "The Story behind Amy Coney Barrett's Little-Known Christian Group People of Praise," *Washington Post*, September 28, 2020, www.washingtonpost.com/religion/2020/09/28/people-of-praise-amy-coney-barrett/; Kristin Kobes Du Mez, "Trump Pick Amy Coney Barrett's Christian 'Handmaid' History Matters," *Think*, October 10, 2020, www.nbcnews.com/think/ncna1242770.

⁴Adrian Vermeule, "Beyond Originalism," the *Atlantic*, March 31, 2020, www.theatlantic.com/ideas/archive/2020/03/common-good-constitutionalism/609037/.

[5]Peter Hammond Schwartz, "Originalism Is Dead. Long Live Catholic Natural Law," *New Republic*, February 3, 2021, https://newrepublic.com/article/161162/.

[6]Schwartz, "Originalism Is Dead."

[7]Schwartz, "Originalism Is Dead," 11.

[8]Schwartz, "Originalism Is Dead," 12.

[9]Schwartz, "Originalism Is Dead," 12.

[10]Schwartz, "Originalism Is Dead," 14.

[11]Schwartz, "Originalism Is Dead," 14.

[12]Schwartz, "Originalism Is Dead," 22.

[13]While I think what he is doing is unfair, I agree with him that there exist post liberal thinkers in the Catholic Church, and I will focus on them when we get to order left 2 and 3. But I will make the case that there are NNL thinkers who are not post-liberal.

[14]Michael Sandel, *Democracy's Discontent: America in Search of a Public Philosophy* (Cambridge, MA: Belknap Press of Harvard University Press, 1996).

[15]John Dewey, *Liberalism and Social Action* (New York: Prometheus, 1999), 58.

[16]Commencement Address at Howard University, June 4, 1965, http://constitutionreader.com/reader.engz?doc=constitution&chapter=OEBPS/Text/ch122.xhtml.

[17]Sandel, *Democracy's Discontent*, 281.

[18]Sandel, *Democracy's Discontent*, 279.

[19]West Virginia State Board of Education v. Barnette, 319 U.S. 624 (1943) quoted in Michael Sandel, *Democracy's Discontent*, 279.

[20]Sandel, *Democracy's Discontent*, 279.

[21]Everson v. Board of Education of Ewing Township, 330 US 1 (1947); Wallace v. Jaffree, 472 US 38, 52-53 (1985).

[22]For one of the best treatments of this view, see Andrew L. Seidel, *The Founding Myth: Why Christian Nationalism is Un-American* (New York: Sterling Publishing, 2019).

[23]Isaac Kramnick and R. Laurence Moore, *The Godless Constitution: A Moral Defense of the Secular State* (New York: W.W. Norton & Company, 2005).

[24]Kramnick and Moore, *Godless Constitution*, 75.

[25]Richard John Neuhaus, *The Naked Public Square: Religion and Democracy in America* (Grand Rapids, MI: Eerdmans, 1984).

[26]Kramnick and Moore, *Godless Constitution*, 174.

[27]Randall Balmer, *Thy Kingdom Come: How the Religious Right Distorts the Faith and Threatens America: An Evangelical's Lament* (New York: Basic Books, 2006).

[28]Balmer, *Thy Kingdom Come*, ix.

[29]Balmer, *Thy Kingdom Come*, ix.

[30]Balmer, *Thy Kingdom Come*, 35-69.

[31]Balmer, *Thy Kingdom Come*, 64.

[32]Balmer, *Thy Kingdom Come*, 66.

[33]Balmer, *Thy Kingdom Come*, 64.

[34]Balmer, *Thy Kingdom Come*, 65.

[35]Balmer, *Thy Kingdom Come*, 185.

[36]Ironically, points out *New York Times* columnist Ross Douthat, just before Balmer's chapter on real Baptists, he "celebrates Victorian evangelicals for taking on 'the task of reforming society according to the standards of godliness,' and seeking 'generally to make the world a better place.'" What this can only mean, says Douthat, is that a Christian is "allowed to mix religion and politics in support of sweeping social reforms—but only if those reforms are safely identified with the political Left, and with the interests of the Democratic party." Ross Douthat, "Theocracy, Theocracy, Theocracy," *First Things*, August-September 2006, www.firstthings.com/article/2006/08/.

[37]George Yancey and David Williamson, *What Motivates Cultural Progressives? Understanding Opposition to the Political and Christian Right* (Waco, TX: Baylor University Press, 2012), 159. Yancey and Williamson set out to confirm that cultural progressives (what we call Freedom Left 2 position) do indeed share a distinct narrative. Through a major research project consisting of interviews, surveys, and review of the literature, they concluded that cultural progressives held a very well-thought-out narrative that consists of a beginning, a middle, and an end that tracks identically with what we have been laying out. But what surprised them was the clarity for which the progressive Left defined its enemy—calling the religious Right a new "Taliban," and, to save America from theocracy, progressives must fight against Christianity in the public sphere, pointing out its backwardness and its resistance to progress, continuing to reaffirm a secular state, affirming the view of the founding that kept religion out of the public realm, maintaining a neutral public square, and warning people about the danger of a theocracy.

[38]Yancey and Williamson, *What Motivates Cultural Progressives?*, 159.

[39]Yancey and Williamson, *What Motivates Cultural Progressives?*, 159.

[40]For more examples of this view, see Steven K. Green, *Inventing Christian America* (Oxford: Oxford University Press, 2015); John Fea, *Was America Founded as a Christian Nation?* (Louisville, TN: Westminster John Knox, 2016): Katherine Stewart, *The Power Worshippers: Inside the Dangerous Rise of Religious Nationalism* (New York: Bloomsbury Publishing, 2020); Ben How, *The Immoral Majority: Why Evangelicals Chose Political Power Over Christian Values* (New York: Broadside Books, 2019).

[41]R. Bruce Douglass and Gerald M. Mara, "The Search for a Defensible Good: The Emerging Dilemma of Liberalism," in *Liberalism and the Good*, ed. R. Bruce Douglass, Gerald M. Mara, and Henry S. Richardson (New York: Routledge, 1990).

[42]Douglass and Mara, "The Search for a Defensible Good," 255.

[43]Douglass and Mara, "The Search for a Defensible Good," 265-66. Italics original.

[44]Sandel, *Democracy's Discontent*, 274-315.

[45]Michael J. Sandel, *Public Philosophy: Essays on Morality in Politics* (Boston: Harvard University Press, 2005), 157.

[46]Sandel, *Public Philosophy*, 157.

[47]Sandel, *Public Philosophy*, 162.

[48]Sandel, *Public Philosophy*, 162.

[49]Sandel, *Democracy's Discontent*, 4.

[50]See Robert N. Bellah, *Habits of the Heart: Individualism and Commitment in American Life* (Berkeley: University of California Press, 1985), 55-166.

[51]Sandel, *Public Philosophy*, 172.

[52]Sandel, *Public Philosophy*, 172.

[53]See Mary Ann Glendon, *Rights Talk: The Impoverishment of Political Discourse* (New York: Free Press, 1991), where she demonstrates how our society is now addicted to individual rights over any conception of the common good.

[54]For an explanation on how this happened, see Sandel's chapter eight, "Liberalism and the Keynesian Revolution in his *Democracy's Discontent*, 250-73.

[55]Randall Balmer, *Solemn Reverence: The Separation of Church and State in American Life* (Lebanon, NH: Truth to Power, 2021).

[56]Balmer, *Solemn Reverence*, 35.

[57]We will look at the radical Right and the theocratic temptation when we cover order right 3.

[58]See Daniel L. Dreisbach, *Thomas Jefferson and the Wall of Separation Between Church and State* (New York: New York University Press, 2002); and Thomas West, *The Political Theory of the American Founding: Natural Rights, Public Philosophy, and the Moral Conditions of Freedom* (Cambridge , UK: Cambridge University Press, 2017).

[59]For a good overview of Madison's view on church and state, one that differs from Balmer's interpretation, see Garrett Ward Sheldon, *The Political Philosophy of James Madison* (Baltimore: Johns Hopkins University Press, 2001).

[60]Charles Taylor, "Religion in a Free Society," in *Articles of Faith, Articles of Peace: The Religious Liberty Clauses and the American Public Philosophy*, ed. James Davison Hunter and Os Guinness (Washington, DC: Brookings Institute, 1990), 103.

[61]Taylor, "Religion in a Free Society," 103.

[62]Taylor, "Religion in a Free Society," 104.

[63]Taylor, "Religion in a Free Society," 104.

[64]Taylor, "Religion in a Free Society," 104.

[65]Randall Balmer, "The Pope Spoke Out. What About You, Amy Coney Barrett?" *Los Angeles Times*, October 22, 2020, www.latimes.com/opinion/story/2020-10-22/pope-francis-amy-coney-barrett-same-sex-unions.

[66]While it came out after my manuscript went to the publisher, it appears his newest book, *Bad Faith: Race and the Rise of the Religious Right* (Grand Rapids, MI: Eerdmans, 2021) is just another example of Balmer lumping all religious conservatives in the same mythic theonomic camp, painting them all as illiberal, and ignoring the radicalism on the Left.

4. Freedom Left 3: From Open Society to Closed Society

[1]Christopher F. Rufo, "Gone Crazy: A New York Public School Principal Calls on White Parents to 'Subvert White Authority,'" *City Journal*, February 18, 2021, www.city-journal .org/east-side-community-school-tells-parents-to-become-white-traitors/.

[2]Rufo, "Gone Crazy."

[3]Christopher F. Rufo, "Failure Factory: Buffalo's School District Tells Students That 'All White People Play a Part in Perpetuating Systemic Racism'—While Presiding over Miserable Student Outcomes," *City Journal*, February 23, 2021, www.city-journal.org/buffalo -public-schools-critical-race-theory-curriculum/.

[4]Max Eden, "There Is No Apolitical Classroom," *City Journal*, June 19, 2020, www.city -journal.org/rise-of-woke-schools/; Also, after month of denying CRT was officially taught in our nation's schools, in July 2021, the National Education Association (NEA), declared that teaching critical race theory in K-12 schools is a major priority and that the NEA "Convey[s] its support" for teachers under attack by parents opposing CRT. Christopher R. Rufo, "Embracing Critical Theory, Teacher's Union Says They—Not Parent—Control What Kids Learn," *New York Post*, July 5, 2021, https://nypost .com/2021/07/05/embracing-critical-theory-teachers-union-says-they-control-what -kids-learn/.

[5]Max Eden, "There Is No Apolitical Classroom."

[6]Angela Davis, quoted in Eden, "There Is No Apolitical Classroom."

[7]Eden, "There Is No Apolitical Classroom."

[8]Eden, "There Is No Apolitical Classroom."

[9]"There Is No Apolitical Classroom: Resources for Teaching in These Times," National Council of Teachers of English, August 15, 2017.

[10]Max Eden, "Critical Race Theory in American Classrooms," *City Journal*, September 18, 2020, www.city-journal.org/critical-race-theory-in-american-classrooms/.

[11]Eden, "Critical Race Theory in American Classrooms."

[12]Tristan Justice, "Parents Vote to Stop Critical Race Insanity in Texas's Top School District," *The Federalist*, May 3, 2021, https://thefederalist.com/2021/05/03/parents-vote-to -stop-critical-race-insanity-in-texass-top-school-district/.

[13]Jon Levine, "Half of New York Times Employees Feel They Can't Speak Freely: Survey," *New York Post*, February 13, 2021, https://nypost.com/2021/02/13/new-york-times-em ployees-feel-they-cant-speak-freely-survey/.

[14]Paul Bond, "'Woke' Christians Are Eroding Donald Trump's Base and Dividing the Evangelical Church," *Newsweek*, October 1, 2020, www.newsweek.com/1534720.

[15]Aysha Khan, "Jim Wallis Replaced as *Sojourners* Editor After Controversy over Article on Catholic Racism," Religion News, August 14, 2020, https://religionnews.com /2020/08/14/.

[16]Bond, "'Woke' Christians."

[17]Mark Wingfield, "Houston Pastor Quits Southwestern and SBC over Seminary Presidents' Statement on Race," *Baptist News*, December 17, 2020, https://baptistnews.com /article/houston-pastor-quits-southwestern-and-sbc-over-seminary-presidents -statement-on-race/.

[18]Erick-Woods Erickson, "Warnings in the PCA: Conservative Christians Are Dabbling in Marxism," ewerickson.substack, September 12, 2020, https://ewerickson.substack .com/p/warnings-in-the-pca; Anthony Bradley, "Critical Race Theory Isn't a Threat for Presbyterians," *Mere Orthodoxy*, February 3, 2021, https://mereorthodoxy.com/critical -race-theory-presbyterian-church-in-america/.

[19]Rod Dreher, "Postmodernism Destroyed His Church," *The American Conservative*, December 10, 2019, www.theamericanconservative.com/dreher/how-postmodernism -destroyed-his-evangelical-church/.

[20]J. D. Hall, quoted in Bond, "'Woke' Christians."

[21]James Lindsay, "Eight Big Reasons Critical Race Theory Is Terrible for Dealing with Racism," *New Discourses*, June 12, 2020, https://newdiscourses.com/2020/06/reasons -critical-race-theory-terrible-dealing-racism/.

[22]See Valerie Hobbs, "Is Critical Race Theory a Religion?," *Christianity Today*, January 18, 2021, www.christianitytoday.com/scot-mcknight/2021/january/is-critical-race-theory -religion-responding-to-carl-trueman.html; Jemar Tisby believes that Christian nationalism is creating the conflict and is way more dangerous to America than the Far Left.

[23]Robin J. DiAngelo, *White Fragility: Why It's So Hard for White People to Talk About Racism* (Boston, MA: Beacon Press, 2018); Andrew L Whitehead, *Taking America Back for God: Christian Nationalism in the United States* (Oxford: Oxford University Press, 2020); Kristin Kobes Du Mez, *Jesus and John Wayne: How White Evangelicals Corrupted a Faith and Fractured a Nation* (New York: Liveright Publishing, 2020).

[24]Christopher Butler, *Postmodernism: A Very Short Introduction* (Oxford: Oxford University Press, 2002), 13.

[25]Butler, *Postmodernism*, 15.

[26]Charles Taylor, *Malaise of Modernity* (Toronto: House of Anansi Press, 1998).

[27]Christopher Lash, *The Revolt of the Elites and the Betrayal of Democracy* (New York: W.W. Norton, 1996); and Phillip Rieff, *The Triumph of the Therapeutic: Uses of Faith After Freud* (Wilmington, DE: Intercollegiate Studies Institute, 2006).

[28]Butler, *Postmodernism*, 11, 16.

[29]Butler, *Postmodernism*, 60.

[30]Butler, *Postmodernism*, 60.

[31]Butler, *Postmodernism*, 60.

[32]Helen Pluckrose and James A. Lindsay, *Cynical Theories* (Durham, NC: Pitchstone Publishing, 2020). Another helpful overview is Stephen Eric Bronner, *Critical Theory: A Very Short Introduction* (Oxford: Oxford University Press, 2012).

[33]Pluckrose and Lindsay, *Cynical Theories*, 111.

[34]Richard Delgado and Jean Stefancic, *Critical Race Theory: An Introduction* (New York: New York University Press, 2017).

[35]Jim Belcher, *Deep Church* (Downers Grove, IL: InterVarsity Press, 2009), 71-90.

[36]D. A. Carson, *Becoming Conversant in the Emerging Church: Understanding the Movement and Its Implications* (Grand Rapids, MI: Zondervan, 2009).

[37]Timothy Keller, *Generous Justice* (New York: Viking, 2010); Brian McLaren, *The Justice Project* (Grand Rapids, MI: Baker Books, 2009); Shane Claiborne and Chris Haw, *Jesus for President: Politics for Ordinary Radicals* (Grand Rapids, MI: Zondervan, 2008).

[38]Jemar Tisby, *How to Fight Racism: Courageous Christianity and the Journey Toward Racial Justice* (Grand Rapids, MI: Zondervan, 2021).

[39]For an alternative more balanced view of America's history of slavery and racism, see Yale's David Brion Davis, who has written over a half dozen of the best histories of international and American slavery. See *The Problem of Slavery in the Age of Emancipation* (New York: Alfred A. Knopf, 2014); and *Inhuman Bondage: The Rise and Fall of Slavery in the New World* (Oxford: Oxford University Press, 2008). Regarding current levels of discrimination and how far we have come as a society, see Eugene Robinson, *Disintegration: The Splintering of Black America* (New York: Anchor, 2011).

[40]See Tisby, *How to Fight Racism.*

[41]Jonathan Lehman, "Identity Politics and the Death of Christian Unity," 9 Marks, April 15, 2020, www.9marks.org/article/identity-politics-and-the-death-of-christian-unity, and David French, "On the Use and Abuse of Critical Race Theory in American Christianity," *The Dispatch*, September 13, 2020, https://frenchpress.thedispatch.com/p/on-the-use-and-abuse-of-critical.

[42]The most prominent are Helen Pluckrose and James A. Lindsay, *Cynical Theories* (Durham, NC: Pitchstone Publishing, 2020); Greg Lukianoff and Jonathan Haidt, *The Coddling of the American Mind: How Good Intentions and Bad Ideas Are Setting Up a Generation for Failure* (New York: Penguin, 2018); Sam Harris, *Making Sense* podcast, #217, "The New Religion of Anti-Racism."

[43]Karen E. Fields and Barbara J. Fields, *Racecraft: The Soul of Inequity in American Life* (New York: Verso, 2014).

[44]See Lindsay, "Eight Big Reasons," 2-3.

[45]Lukianoff and Haidt, *Coddling of the American Mind*, 70.

[46]But at least they are being honest. Princeton professor Stanley Fish, a postmodernist, admits that while the defenders of the godless-constitution view of the First Amendment continue to trumpet liberalism as the best way to avoid theocracy, the best way to maintain neutrality in the public square, he claims their tactics are, in fact, a ruse. "It's a great move in which liberalism, in the form of academic freedom, gets to display its generosity while at the same time cutting the heart out of the views to which that generosity is extended." Progressive are not for neutrality, contends Fish, but "in actuality they are trying to impose one point of view—their own—on those who disagree with them." Stanley Fish, *The Trouble with Principle* (Cambridge, MA: Harvard University Press, 1999), 41.

Exposing the contradiction and hypocrisy at the heart of this liberal procedural view, Alan Wolfe contends that "an ideology ostensibly dedicated to fairness thus becomes inherently unfair, forcing its opponents" to appear unfair, partial, and unjust. The game is rigged against them from the start." Alan Wolfe, *The Future of Liberalism* (New York: Knopf, 2009), 141. Moreover, Wolfe argues that what Fish is claiming is that you will "immediately discover that its presumed neutrality is at best a sham and at worst a clever ploy." (Wolfe, 141). Fish says that liberals should drop the ploy, abandon the scam, and be honest and say, "the presence of Marxists on campus is beneficial to education and the presence of bigots and racists is not, and that's all there is to it." (Fish, 89).

[47]Molly Ball, "The Secret History of the Shadow Campaign That Saved the 2020 Election," *Time*, February 3, 2021.

[48]Lukianoff and Haidt, *Coddling of the American Mind*, 64-65. See also Stephen Eric Bonner, *Critical Theory: A Very Short Introduction* (Oxford: Oxford University Press, 2017); and Bradley Campbell and Jason Manning, *The Rise of Victimhood: Microaggressions, Safe Spaces, and the New Culture Wars* (Cham, Switzerland: Palgrave Macmillan, 2018), 224.

[49]Lukianoff and Haidt, *Coddling of the American Mind*, 66. Marcuse, a member of the critical theory Frankfurt School, rejected tolerance and free speech, arguing that they favor the dominant class, and called for shutting down free speech as a way of wrestling power away from the dominant culture. He called for a "liberating tolerance," says Haidt and Lukianoff, one that favors the disadvantaged and discriminates against the dominant class. What liberating tolerance meant in practice for Marcuse "would mean intolerance against movements from the Right, and toleration of movements from the Left."

[50]For a prophetic prediction on how our liberal democracy would move from an open society to a closed society, see Wilmore Kendall, "The Open Society and Its Fallacies,"

[51]Lindsay, "Eight Big Reasons," 8.

[52]Dana Kennedy, "CA Podcaster Gets Visit from Police After 'Lightly' Criticizing AOC on Twitter," New York Post, April, 10, 2021, https://nypost.com/2021/04/10/ca-podcaster-gets-visit-from-police-after-aoc-tweet/.

[53]Sarah Repucci and Amy Slipowitz, *Special Report 2020: Democracy Under Lockdown*, Freedom House, https://freedomhouse.org/report/special-report/2020/democracy-under-lockdown.

[54]"Woman Refuses to Wear Mask in Texas, Again, Gets Arrested," Associated Press, March 17, 2021.

[55]Bill Hutchinson, "New Jersey Gym Owners Arrested After Repeatedly Defying COVID Shutdown Orders," ABC News, July 27, 2020, https://abcnews.go.com/US/jersey-gym-owners-arrested-repeatedly-defying-covid-shutdown/story?id+72008020.

[56]Ryan Lovelace, "Big Tech Companies Insist Spying on Users, Government Is Inadvertent," *Washington Times*, August 2, 2020, www.washingtontimes.com/news/2020/aug/2/big-tech-companies-insist-spying-on-users-governme/.

[57]Andy Ngo, *Unmasked: Inside Antifa's Radical Plan to Destroy Democracy* (Nashville, TN: Center Street, 2021).

[58]Lindsay, "Eight Big Reasons," 6.

[59]Andrew Sullivan, "A Glimpse at the Intersectional Left's Political Endgame," *Intelligencer*, November 15, 2019, 8-9.

[60]*Tucker Carlson Tonight*, February 22, 2021, www.foxnews.com/transcipt/naomi-wolf -sounds-alarm-at-growing-power-of-autocratic-tyrants; Naomi Wolf, a democrat, has been warning America about the growth of the national security state for over fifteen years. See her book *The End of America: Letters of Warning to a Young Patriot* (Hartford, VT: Chelsea Green Publishing, 2007).

[61]Chip Walter, *Immortality, Inc.: Renegade Science, Silicon Valley Billions, and the Quest to Live Forever*, (Washington, DC: National Geographic, 2020); Yuval Noah Harari, *Homo Deus: A Brief History of Tomorrow* (New York: Harper Perennial, 2018); and Franklin Foer, *World Without Mind: The Existential Threat of Big Tech* (New York: Penguin, 2017).

5. Order Left 2: The Rise of the Welfare State
and the Great Society

[1]For a perspective on how this happened, see Andy Ngo, *Unmasked: Inside Antifa's Radical Plan to Destroy Democracy* (New York: Center Street, 2021).

[2]Travis Campbell, "Black Lives Matter's Effect on Police Lethal Use-of-Force," SSRN, January 15, 2021 https://papers.ssrn.com/sol3/papers.cfm?abstract_id=3767097; Jerusalem Demsas, "The Effects of Black Lives Matter Protests," Vox, April 9, 2021, www .vox.com/22360290/black-lives-matter-protest-crime-ferguson-effects-murder; Jennifer A. Kingson, "Exclusive: $1 Billion-Plus Riot Damage is Most Expensive in Insurance History," Axios, September 16, 2020, www.axios.com/276c9bcc-a455-4067 -b06a-66f9db4cea9c.html.

[3]Tim Harris, "CNN's Chris Cuomo: Who Says Protests Are Supposed To Be Polite and Peaceful?," Real Clear Politics, June 4, 2020, www.realclearpolitics.com/video/2020 /06/04/cnns_chris_cuomo_who_says_protests_are_supposed.html.

[4]Josh Kraushaar, https://twitter.com/hotlinejosh/status/1267498902544101376?lang=en.

[5]Kamala Harris, on Stephen Colbert's *The Late Show*, June 18, 2020.

[6]Nathan Layne, "One City 'Ready to Explode' as US Murder Rates Surge in Pandemic," *Reuters*, June 25, 2021, www.usnews.com/news/top-news/articles/2021-06-25/one-city -ready-to-explode-as-us-murder-rates-surge-in-pandemic.

[7]David Bernstein, "Gaslighting Last Summer's Riots and the Law Enforcement Response," *Reason*, January 11, 2021, https://reason.com/volokh/2021/01/11/gaslighting -last-summers-riots-and-the-law-enforcement-response/.

[8]Heather MacDonald, *The War on Cops* (New York: Encounter Books, 2016).

[9]"Liberal Cities, Radical Mayhem: Democratic Mayors and Governors Seem Unable to Stop the Destruction of Their Own Cities," Editorial Board, June 2, 2020, *Wall Street Journal*, www.wsj.com/articles/liberal-cities-radical-mayhem-11591140986; Marc A. Thiessen, "Biden Can't Blame Trump for the Anarchy in Democrat-Run Cities," *Washington Post*, September 1, 2020, www.washingtonpost.com/opinions/2020/09/01/biden-cant-blame-trump-anarchy-democrat-run-cities/.

[10]Marc Thiessen, "Maybe Trump Shouldn't Save the Democrat-Run Cities Besieged by Violence," *Washington Post*, July 16, 2020, www.washingtonpost.com/opinions/2020/07/16/maybe-trump-shouldnt-save-democrat-run-cities-besieged-by-violence/.

[11]Benjamin Wallace-Wells, "Baltimore After Freddie Gray: A Laboratory of Urban Violence," Intelligencer, November 30, 2015, https://nymag.com/intelligencer/2015/11/baltimore-after-freddie-gray.html, www.nytimes.com/2019/03/12/magazine/baltimore-tragedy-crime.html.

[12]See Crystal Wright, *Con Job: How Democrats Gave Us Crime, Sanctuary Cities, Abortion Profiteering, and Racial Division* (Washington, DC: Regnery Publishing, 2016), chap. 3.

[13]Alec MacGillis, "The Tragedy of Baltimore," *New York Times*, March 12, 2019, www.nytimes.com/2019/03/12/magazine/baltimore-tragedy-crime.html.

[14]Tim Harris, "Bob Woodson: Democrats Blame Racism to Deflect Attention from Failures of Cities They've Run for 50 Years," Real Clear Politics, June 3, 2020, www.realclearpolitics.com/video/2020/06/03/.

[15]For video link to video interview with Bob Woodson, see Harris, "Bob Woodson: Democrats Blame Racism."

[16]Michael Sandel, *Democracy's Discontent: America in Search of a Public Philosophy* (Cambridge, MA: Belknap Press of Harvard University Press, 1996), 278.

[17]See Sandel, *Democracy's Discontent*, 280, where Sandel mentions the Court's decision, *Everson v. Board of Education of Ewing Township*, 330 US 1 (1947) as a watershed moment.

[18]Sandel, *Democracy's Discontent*, 280.

[19]Sandel, *Democracy's Discontent*, 280.

[20]Sandel, *Democracy's Discontent*, 280-82.

[21]Sandel, *Democracy's Discontent*, 281.

[22]Johnson, "Address at Swarthmore College," June 8, 1964, in *Public Papers*, 1963-64, vol. 1, 757, quoted in Sandel, *Democracy's Discontent*, 284.

[23]Sandel, *Democracy's Discontent*, 284.

[24]Johnson, "Remarks Before the National Convention," August 27, 1964, *Public Papers*, 1963-1964, vol. 2, 1012-13, quoted in Sandel, *Democracy's Discontent*, 284.

[25]Sandel, *Democracy's Discontent*, 284.

[26]Johnson, "Remarks Before the National Convention."

[27]Sandel, *Democracy's Discontent*, 285-89.

[28]Sandel, "The Procedural Republic and the Unencumbered Self," *Political Theory*, 12:1 (1984), 81-96.

[29]Ron Sider, *Rich Christians in an Age of Hunger* (Nashville, TN: Thomas Nelson, 2015); Tony Campolo, *Red Letter Christians: A Citizens Guide to Faith and Politics* (Raleigh, NC: Regal, 2008); Jim Wallis, *God's Politics: A New Vision for Faith and Politics in America* (San Francisco: HarperSanFrancisco, 2005).

[30]Jonathan Wilson-Hartgrove, *Revolution of Values: Reclaiming Public Faith for the Common Good* (Downers Grove, IL: InterVarsity Press, 2019); *Reconstructing the Gospel: Finding Freedom from Slaveholder Religion* (Downers Grove, IL: InterVarsity Press, 2018).

[31]Wilson-Hartgrove, *Revolution of Values*, 163; 19; 156; 168-69; 53; 7; and 170 respectively.

[32]Wilson-Hartgrove, *Revolution of Values*, 167. His narrative skips right over the Civil War, our national fight to end slavery, to end the oligarchy of the South, and take steps in Reconstruction to install a constitutional republic in the southern states. And like his jumping over the Civil War, he also has the tendency to jump from the Jim Crow era (a horrible chapter in American history) and over the seventy years of racial progress in our country (like electing our nation's first Back president and the tremendous growth of the Black middle and super-rich classes), conflating the past with the present and contending that we are just as racist as we have ever been. This connecting of the Jim Crow past with present racism is a common tactic of the progressive Left, conflating the worst atrocities of the past—like chaining people to the cargo holds of slave ships— is equal to requiring I.D. for voting. Not only are these attempts at conflation not true but they devalue the suffering that took place under slavery and Jim Crow.

[33]Wilson-Hartgrove, *Revolution of Values*, 160.

[34]Wilson-Hartgrove, *Revolution of Values*, 171.

[35]Wilson-Hartgrove, *Revolution of Values*, 160.

[36]Wilson-Hartgrove, *Revolution of Values*, 112.

[37]Wilson-Hartgrove, *Revolution of Values*, 26, 28.

[38]Wilson-Hartgrove, *Revolution of Values*, 39-40.

[39]Wilson-Hartgrove, *Revolution of Values*, 112, 42-43.

[40]Wilson-Hartgrove, *Revolution of Values, 153-73.*

[41]Wilson-Hartgrove, *Revolution of Values*, 7.

[42]Louis Woodhill, "The War on Poverty Wasn't a Failure—It was a Catastrophe," *Forbes*, March 19, 2014, www.forbes.com/sites/louiswoodhill/2014/03/19/the-war-on-poverty -wasnt-a-failure-it-was-a-catastrophe/?sh=527283006f49; Charles Murray, *Losing Ground: American Social Policy, 1950-1980* (New York: Basic Books, 2015).

[43]For those curious to explore the Black dissent (often called *Uncle Toms, traitors*, or *not really Black*) against the monolithic Black establishment, see Shelby Steel, *White Guilt: How Blacks and Whites Together Destroyed the Promise of the Civil Rights Era* (New York: Harper Collins, 2009); Thomas Sowell, *Black Rednecks and White Liberals* (New York: Encounter Books, 2005); Jason Riley, *Please Stop Helping Us* (New York: Encounter Books, 2014); Candace Owens, *Black Out: How Black America Can Make Its Second Escape from the Democrat Plantation* (New York: Threshold Editions, 2020) and

Glenn Loury, *One by One from the Inside Out: Essays and Reviews on Race and Responsibility in America* (New York: Free Press, 1995).

[44]John McWhorter, *Winning the Race: Beyond the Crisis in Black America* (New York: Gotham, 2005). See also John McWhorter, *Losing the Race: Self-Sabotage in Black America* (New York: Free Press, 2000).

[45]See especially chapters two and three of McWhorter's *Winning the Race* for his critique of these common excuses for Black poverty.

[46]McWhorter, *Winning the Race*, 376.

[47]McWhorter, *Winning the Race*, 377.

[48]For the story of how Black welfare dependency increased dramatically, see McWhorter, *Winning the Race*, 114-51.

[49]McWhorter, *Winning the Race*, 392.

[50]McWhorter, *Winning the Race*, 75.

[51]For a description of this tragedy, see McWhorter, *Winning the Race*, 376-92.

[52]See chapter four, "Why Are You Talking About Blacks on Welfare?" in McWhorter, *Winning the Race*; for the impact of the 1960s on the white underclass, see Charles Murray's *Coming Apart: The State of White America, 1960-2010* (New York: Crown Forum, 2021).

[53]"Feds Deny Minnesota Request for Aid to Rebuild After Unrest," Associated Press, July 11, 2020, www.usatoday.com/story/news/politics/2020/07/12/george-floyd-feds-deny -minnesota-request-aid-rebuild/5423569002/.

[54]Wilson-Hartgrove, *Revolution of Values*, 55.

[55]For an account of how the Democrat party resisted Reconstruction, see Forrest A. Nabors, *From Oligarchy to Republicanism: The Great Task of Reconstruction* (Columbia: University of Missouri Press, 2017;) For the story on how the Democrat Party continued to support racial segregation until the mid-1960's, see Bruce Bartlett, *Wrong on Race: The Democratic Party's Buried Past* (New York: St. Martin's Press, 2008).

[56]For one of the most in-depth studies of the Republican Party during Reconstruction, see Forrest A. Nabors, *From Oligarchy to Republicanism: The Great Task of Reconstruction* (Columbia: University of Missouri Press, 2017).

[57]See Bruce Bartlett, *Wrong on Race: The Democratic Party's Buried Past* (New York: St. Martin's Press, 2008), 166-68.

[58]For the account on how the Democrat party enticed Blacks with welfare benefits (something they historically resisted), see McWhorter, *Winning the Race*, 376-92.

[59]McWhorter, *Winning the Race*, 114-50.

[60]This doesn't mean the Republican Party is free of the ruling class or innocent when it comes to enslaving the Black, Brown, and White underclass; as we will see when we cover freedom right 2 and 3, this class war has infected the Republican Party as well. And over the years the Republican Party has been home to many enemies of constitutional republicanism, giving them cover for their oligarchic policies. So there is no pure party. I am just trying to correct Wilson-Hartgrove's description of the two parties and his attribution of oligarchy to the Republican Party.

[61]If any narrative is enslaving the poor along with the working and middle classes, it is not Christian nationalists (which for the most part want to return to our Constitution, the grounding of natural law, and the protection of minorities). We will look at Christian nationalism in chapters ten and eleven, trying to understand when it supports constitutional republicanism and when it slides into illiberalism.

[62]Joel Kotkin, "What Do the Oligarchs Have in Mind for Us?" *Quillette*, June 19, 2019, https://quillette.com/2019/06/19/what-do-the-oligarchs-have-in-mind-for-us.

[63]Astra Taylor, "Reclaiming the Future: On the Growing Appeal of Socialism in an Age of Inequality," *New Republic*, May 17, 2019, https://newrepublic.com/article/153804.

6. Order Left 3: The Reified Postmodernism of Antiracism

[1]Rebecca Sagar and Brie Loskota, "White Christian Nationalism and the Next Wave of Political Violence," *The Hill*, February 2, 2021, https://thehill.com/opinion/civil-rights/539530-white-christian-nationalism-and-the-next-wave-of-political-violence.

[2]Brian Naylor and Ryan Lucas, "Wray Stresses Role of Right-Wing Extremism in Hearing About January 6 Riot," NPR, March 2, 2021, www.npr.org/2021/03/02/972539274/.

[3]"Remarks by President Biden Commemorating the One Hundredth Anniversary of the Tulsa Race Massacre," the White House, June 1, 2021, https://whitehouse.gov/briefing-room/speeches-remarks/2021/06/02/remarks-by-president-biden-commemorating-the-100th-anniversary-of-the-tulsa-race-massacre/.

[4]Christopher F. Rufo, "State-Enforced Racial Segregation—by Progressives," *New York Post*, October 18, 2020, https://nypost.com/2020/10/18/state-enforced-racial-segregation-by-progressives/.

[5]Rufo, "State-Enforced Racial Segregation."

[6]Helen Pluckrose and James Lindsay, "Social Justice Scholarship and Thought," chap. 8 in *Cynical Theories: How Activist Scholarship Made Everything About Race, Gender, and Identity—and Why This Harms Everyone* (Durham, NC: Pitchstone, 2020).

[7]Pluckrose and Lindsay, *Cynical Theories*, 182, italics original.

[8]Pluckrose and Lindsay, *Cynical Theories*, 182.

[9]Pluckrose and Lindsay, *Cynical Theories*, 182.

[10]Pluckrose and Lindsay, *Cynical Theories*, 182.

[11]Pluckrose and Lindsay, *Cynical Theories*, 183, italics added.

[12]Pluckrose and Lindsay, *Cynical Theories*, 183.

[13]Ibram X. Kendi, *How to Be an Antiracist* (London: Oneworld Publications, 2019). See also Ta-Nehisi Coates's *Between the World and Me* (London: Oneworld Publicans, 2015); Robin DiAngelo, *White Fragility: Why It Is So Hard for White People to Talk About Racism* (Boston: Beacon Press, 2020); and Michael Eric Dyson, *Long Time Coming: Reckoning with Race in America* (New York: St. Martin's, 2020).

[14]Kendi, *How to Be an Antiracist*, 13-23.

[15]Kendi, *How to Be an Antiracist*, 13.

[16]Kendi, *How to Be an Antiracist*, 19.

[17]Kendi, *How to Be an Antiracist*, 24-34; Here Kendi argues a point very similar to the *New York Times* 1619 Project, which contends the Revolutionary War was fought to maintain slavery and that our country was founded on racism. For a good overview of the 1619 Project and some of the pushback from liberal historians, see Adam Serwer, "Historians Clash with the 1619 Project," the *Atlantic*, December 23, 2019, www.the atlantic.com/ideas/archive/2019/12/historians-clash-1619-project/604093/.

[18]Aja Romano, "The 'Controversy' over Journalist Sarah Jeong Joining the *New York Times*, explained," Vox, August 3, 2018, www.vox.com/2018/8/3/17644704/sarah-jeong -new-york-times-tweets-backlash-racism.

[19]Libby Watson, "The *New York Times* Really Fucked This One Up," Splinter, August 2, 2018, https://splinternews.com/1828061129.

[20]Watson, "The *New York Times* Really Fucked This One Up."

[21]Zach Beauchamp, "In Defense of Sarah Jeong," Vox, August 3, 2018, www.vox.com /policy-and-politics/2018/8/3/17648566/.

[22]For two recent examples, see Alex Morey, "FIRE Warns University of Illinois at Chicago Over Investigation into Law Professor's Exam Question," FIRE, January 22, 2021, www .thefire.org/fire-warns-university-of-illinois; Bari Weiss, "Whistleblower at Smith College Resigns Over Racism," bariweiss.substack.com, February 19, 2021, https://bariweiss .substack.com/p/whistleblower-at-smith-college-resigns.

[23]George Orwell, *Nineteen Eight-Four* (New York: Harcourt, Inc., 1949), 10.

[24]Denny Burke, "Can We Eat the Meat and Spit Out the Bones of CRT?" Denyburk.com, www.dennyburke.com/can-we-eat-the-meat-and-spit-out-the-bnes-with-crt/.

[25]Neil Shenvi, Twitter, @neilshenvi, February 26, 2021, https://twitter.com/neilshenvi /status/1365308240691666951.

[26]Eliza Griswold, "How Black Lives Matter Is Changing the Church," *New Yorker*, August 30, 2020, www.newyorker.com/news/on-religion/how-black-lives-matter-is-changing -the-church.

[27]Jemar Tisby, quoted in Griswold, "How Black Lives Matter," www.newyorker.com /news/on-religion/how-black-lives-matter-is-changing-the-church.

[28]A few examples of evangelicals who seem to have embraced antiracism are Latasha Morrison, *Be the Bridge: Pursuing God's Heart for Racial Reconciliation* (Colorado Springs, CO: WaterBrook, 2019); Daniel Hill, *White Awake: An Honest Look at What It Means to Be White* (Downers Grove, IL: InterVarsity Press, 2017); Jemar Tisby, *How to Fight Racism: Courageous Christianity and the Journey Toward Racial Justice* (Grand Rapids, MI: Zondervan, 2021).

[29]Daniel Hill, *White Lies: Nine Ways to Expose and Resist the Racial Systems That Divide Us* (Grand Rapids, MI: Zondervan, 2020). I am aware that not everyone who calls themselves a progressive evangelical fits into order left 3. By focusing on one book, I am attempting to help readers spot the telltale signs of those who can fit more or less into

this quadrant position. To this end I have chosen Hill's book as an example, but not the only one, of an evangelical whom I place in this position.

[30]Hill, *White Lies*.

[31]See chapter four, "Attack the Narrative," in *White Lies*, Daniel Hill, 77-104. Also see David Morgan, "Bryan Stevenson: 'The North Won the Civil War, but the South Won the Narrative War' on the History of Racism" CBS News, June 24, 2019, www.cbsnews .com/news/bryan-stevenson-we-are-all-complicit-in-our-countrys-history-of-racism/.

[32]To understand the false narrative of the Confederate South and their rejection of a natural-right grounding found in the Constitution, no book has been more helpful to me than Harry Jaffa, *A New Birth of Freedom: Abraham Lincoln and the Coming Civil War* (Boston: Rowan & Littlefield, 2000).

[33]See chapter four, "Attack the Narrative," in *White Lies*, Daniel Hill, 77-104.

[34]For one of the best examples of the historians on the left who reject the Confederate narrative as the true definition of the American founding, see Sean Wilentz, *No Property in Man: Slavery and Antislavery at the Nation's Founding* (Boston: Harvard University Press, 2019).

[35]Ironically, in attempting this wholesale exchange, that is, the antiracism narrative adopting the Lost Cause narrative, siding with John C. Calhoun over Abraham Lincoln—thus taking on Calhoun's views that our nation was conceived in slavery, that the Constitution was a scam to support slavery, and that natural rights were nothing but a legal fiction on which to ground our political life together—they are at the very same time rejecting the philosophical and religious grounding of the founders and, unlike Lincoln and Martin Luther King Jr., have nothing to appeal back to. Moreover, while it is true that Calhoun uses his narrative to support slavery and the antiracism narrative uses it to oppose it, they both hold the same view of America' founding and its rejection of natural rights.

[36]See Joel Kotkin, "Woke Politics Are a Disaster for Minorities," *The American Mind*, January 25, 2021, https://americanmind.org/memo/woke-politics-are-a-disaster-for -minorities/.

[37]Arthur M. Schlesinger Jr., *The Disuniting of America: Reflections on a Multicultural Society* (New York: W. W. Norton & Company, 1991).

[38]See Andrew Hartman, *A War for the Soul of America: A History of the Culture Wars*, 2nd ed. (Chicago: University of Chicago Press, 2019), 262-65.

[39]John McWhorter, *Losing the Race: Self-Sabotage in Black America* (New York: Free Press, 2000), see chapters one through four, 1-163.

[40]John McWhorter, "Atonement as Activism," *American Interest*, May 24, 2018, www .the-american-interest.com/2018/05/24/atonement-as-activism/.

[41]Robert P. Jones, *White Too Long: The Legacy of White Supremacy in American Christi- anity* (New York: Simon & Schuster, 2020); Andrew L. Whitehead and Samuel L. Perry, *Taking America Back for God: Christian Nationalism in the United States* (Oxford:

Oxford University Press, 2020); and Kristen Kobes Du Mez, *Jesus and John Wayne: How White Evangelicals Corrupted a Faith and Fractured a Nation* (New York: Liveright, 2020).

[42]Robert P. Jones, "Racism Among White Christians Is Higher Than Among the Nonreligious. That's No Coincidence," *Think*, July 27, 2020, www.nbcnews.com/think /ncna1235045.

[43]Jemar Tisby, "Is the White Church Inherently Racist?" *New York Times*, August 18, 2020, www.nytimes.com/2020/08-18/books/review/white-too-long-robert-p-jones.html; also see Carl Trueman, "Evangelicals and Race Theory," *First Things*, February 2020, 7.

[44]John McWhorter, "Antiracism, Our Flawed New Religion," *Daily Beast*, July 27, 2015, www.thedailybeast.com/antiracism-our-flawed-new-religion.

[45]John McWhorter, *The Elect*, https://johnmcwhorter.substack.com/p/the-elect-the -threat-to-a-progressive. While not scheduled for publication until 2022, he is making the first few chapters available to subscribers on Substack.

[46]McWhorter, *The Elect*.

[47]For an interesting discussion on how the conflict between oligarchy and constitutional republicanism goes back to the first American settlers in Jamestown and Plymouth and how two distinct cultures, political philosophies, and religious outlooks could be found in the North and the South, see James C. Cobb, *Away Down South: A History of Southern Identity* (Oxford: Oxford University Press, 2005); Ritchie Devon Watson Jr., *Normans and Saxons: Southern Race Mythology and the Intellectual History of the American Civil War* (Baton Rouge: Louisiana State University Press, 2008); D. H. Fisher, *Albion's Seed: Four British Folkways in America* (Oxford: Oxford University Press USA, 1989).

[48]Perhaps this is why Amazon.com banned Ryan T. Anderson's book *When Harry Became Sally: Responding to the Transgender Moment* (New York: Encounter Books, 2018).

7. Freedom Right 2: Libertarians and the Quest for Open Borders

[1]Stef W. Kight, "Biden Confronts Humanitarian Crisis at the Border," Axios, March 5, 2021, www.axios.com/1948f056-15a1-4a63-bf4d-1f3f7e846b69.html.

[2]Paul A. Reyes, "The Southern Border Is Biden's Biggest Test Yet," CNN, March 12, 2021, www.cnn.com/2021/03/12/opinions/unaccompanied-minors-biden-test-southern -border-reyes/index.html.

[3]Reyes, "The Southern Border Is Biden's Biggest Test Yet."

[4]Joe Concha, "Team Biden Offers Alternative Reality on Border Crisis with No Plan to Fix It," *The Hill*, March 8, 2020, https://thehill.com/opinion/immigration/542043-team -biden-offers-alternative-reality-on-border-crisis-with-no-plan-to.

[5]Concha, "Team Biden Offers Alternative Reality."

[6]Concha, "Team Biden Offers Alternative Reality."

[7]According to Melissa Chinchilla's report "Stemming the Rise of Latino Homeless: Lessons from Los Angeles County," roughly half of the fifty-five thousand homeless in

Los Angeles are Hispanic, many of them recent immigrants, who can't find housing or jobs. Latino Policy and Politics Initiative, https://latino.ucla.edu/wp-content/uploads /2019/01/Stemming-the-rise-of-Latino-Homelessness-2-1.pdf; Todd Bensman, "New Influx of Covid-19 Patients Floods U.S. Border State Hospitals: But Who Are They? Reporters Don't Want to Know," Center for Immigration Studies, June 10, 2020, https:// cis.org/Bensman/New-Influx-Covid19-Patients-Floods-US-Border-State-Hospitals.

[8]Ashley Parker, Nick Miroff, Sean Sullivan and Tyler Pager, "'No End in Sight:' Inside the Biden Administration's Failure to Contain the Border Surge," *Washington Post*, March 20, 2021, www.washingtonpost.com/21824e94-8818-11eb-8a8b-5cf82c3dffe4_story.html.

[9]Tucker Carlson, *Ship of Fools: How a Selfish Ruling Class Is Bringing America to the Brink of Revolution* (New York: Free Press, 2019).

[10]Carlson, *Ship of Fools*, 65.

[11]Carlson, *Ship of Fools*, 67.

[12]Carlson, *Ship of Fools*, 67.

[13]Bernie Sanders, quoted in Park MacDougald, "Why Do Libertarians and the Left Have Such Similar Views on Immigration?" *New York*, December 12, 2018, https://nymag.com /intelligencer/2018/12/why-are-libertarians-and-the-left-both-for-open-immigration.html.

[14]*Tucker Carlson Tonight*, June 19, 2019, http://youtu.be/8lgekVVqwkk. A quick Google search shows that Soros, who through his Open Society organization, a major funder of left-wing open-border groups, has also been a major funder for the Cato Institute, a major libertarian think tank in DC, founded by Charles Koch.

[15]Lauri Bennett, "The Kochs Aren't the Only Funders of Cato," *Forbes*, March 13, 2012, www .forbes.com/sites/lauriebennett/2012/03/13/the-kochs-arent-the-only-funders-of-cato/.

[16]Jason Brennan, *Libertarianism: What Everyone Needs to Know* (New York: Oxford University Press, 2012), 10.

[17]For the best history of libertarianism and its different camps see Brian Doherty, *Radicals for Capitalism: A Freewheeling History of the Modern American Libertarian Movement* (New York: Public Affairs, 2007).

[18]While Brennan accepts the lofty goals of the progressive Left, particularly its social and moral agenda, he disagrees on the means to achieve these ends. He shares their ideal— that economic institutions should benefit the poor—but he disagrees with the way to achieve this.

[19]Brennan, *Libertarianism*, 14.

[20]The irony, however, is that the order left 3 progressive Democrats no longer want government to be neutral or to protect civil liberties but want it to be decidedly woke. We will look at "woke capitalism" more in chapter eight.

[21]Brennan, *Libertarianism*, 23.

[22]Brennan, *Libertarianism*, 3-4.

[23]Peter Margulies, "The Libertarian Case for Immigration (and Against Trump)," *Lawfare Book Review*, July 16, 2020; Zoey Poll, "The Case for Open Borders," *New Yorker*, February 20, 2020.

[24]Brennan, *Libertarianism*, 38.

[25]Jason Brennan, "In Praise of Open Borders," *Bleeding Heart Libertarians*, March 17, 2014, https://bleedingheartlibertarians.com/2014/03/in-praise-of-open-borders.

[26]Thomas Freidman, "Our One-Party Democracy," *New York Times*, September 8, 2009, www.nytimes.com/2009/09/09/opinion/09friedman.html.

[27]Lee Smith, "The Thirty Tyrants," *Tablet*, February 3, 2021, 2.

[28]Stuart Anderson, "A Biden Immigration Policy: New Hope for Immigrants and Business," *Forbes*, November 8, 2020, www.forbes.com/sites/stuartanderson/2020/11/08/a-biden-immigration-policy-new-hope-for-immigrants-and-businesses/?sh=680b90637842.

[29]Ross Douthat, "The Rise of Woke Capitalism," *New York Times*, February 28, 2018, www.nytimes.com/2018/02/28/opinion/corporate-america-activism.html.

[30]Brink Lindsey, "Right Is Wrong," in Brink Lindsey, Jonah Goldberg, and Matt Kibbe, "Where Do Libertarians Belong? A *Reason* Debate," *Reason*, August-September 2010, https://reason.com/2010/07/12/where-do-libertarians-belong-3. See also Brink Lindsey, "Why Libertarians and Conservatives Should Stop Opposing the Welfare State," *Niskanen Center*, August 9, 2017, www.niskanencenter.org/libertarians-conservatives-stop-opposing-welfare-state.

[31]Michael Borone, "Team Biden Knows Its Open-Borders Plan Is Unpopular—So Why Do It?" *New York Post*, March 12, 2021, https://nypost.com/2021/03/12/team-biden-knows-its-open-borders-plan-is-unpopular-so-why-do-it/; Victor Joecks, "What If Open Borders Is Biden's Plan?," Las Vegas Review-Journal, June 12, 2021, www.reviewjournal.com/opinion/opinion-columns/victor-joecks/victor-joecks-what-if-open-borders-is-bidens-plan-2377133/.

[32]Brink Lindsey, "Right Is Wrong," 3.

[33]Brennan, *Libertarianism*, 73.

[34]Jeffrey Rogers Hummel, William F. Marina, "Did the Constitution Betray the Revolution?," Independent Institute, January 1, 1981.

[35]Nathan W. Schlueter and Nikolai G. Wenzel, *Selfish Libertarians and Socialist Conservatives? The Foundations of the Libertarian-Conservative Debate* (Palo Alto, CA: Stanford University Press, 2017), 95.

[36]Schlueter and Wenzel, *Selfish Libertarians*, 93.

[37]Gordon Wood, *The Creation of the American Republic 1776-1787* (Chapel Hill: University of North Carolina Press, 1969), 319-21.

[38]I am grateful to a phone conversation with C. J. Engel, an evangelical who runs the *Reformed Libertarian* website, for confirming that there are indeed Christian libertarians and also for explaining the often confusing genealogy of libertarianism and the myriad factions within it.

[39]Since most of the writers at the Acton Institute are committed Catholics and believe in the existence of natural law, I don't consider them philosophical libertarians. Most of them fit much better in the New Vital Center, which I will lay out in part three.

[40]While we will look at Ayn Rand in chapter eight, readers might like to consult "Objectivism, Anarcho-Capitalism, and the Effects of the Psychedelics on Faith and Freedom," ch. 5 in Doherty's *Radicals for Capitalism* for a good overview of her thought.

[41]The blog is no longer active as of 2021.

[42]Kevin Vallier, "Christian Pacifism but Not Christian Libertarianism," *Bleeding Heart Libertarians*, April 30, 2014, https://bleedingheartlibertarians.com/2014/04/christian-pacifism.

[43]Vallier, "Christian Pacifism."

[44]Elise Daniel, ed., *Called to Freedom: Why You Can Be Christian and Libertarian* (Eugene, OR: Wipf & Stock, 2017); and Norman Horn, Doug Stuart, Kerry Baldwin, and Dick Clark, *Faith Seeking Freedom: Libertarian Christian Answers to Tough Questions* (St. Louis: Libertarian Christian Institute Press, 2020).

[45]Horn, Stuart, Baldwin, and Clark, *Faith Seeking Freedom*, 5.

[46]Horn, Stuart, Baldwin, and Clark, *Faith Seeking Freedom*, 14.

[47]Horn, Stuart, Baldwin, and Clark, *Faith Seeking Freedom*, 15.

[48]For a list of all the resources on Romans 13 produced by the Libertarian Institute, see Doug Stuart, "Romans 13 for Dummies," June 16, 2018, https://libertarianchristians.com/2018/06/16/romans-13-for-dummies/.

[49]See Horn, et al., *Faith Seeking Freedom*, 83, for their discussion on immigration. Also, the most well-known critique of immigration and open borders from a libertarian comes from Hans-Hermann Hoppe, "The Case for Free Trade and Restricted Immigration," *Journal of Libertarian Studies*, July 30, 2014.

[50]Horn, Stuart, Baldwin, and Clark, *Faith Seeking Freedom*, 21.

[51]Horn, Stuart, Baldwin, and Clark, *Faith Seeking Freedom*, 83.

[52]See Horn, Stuart, Baldwin, and Clark, "What About Immigration?" in *Faith Seeking Freedom*, 83-89.

[53]For positive accounts of the early libertarian movement, see George Nash, *The Conservative Intellectual Movement in America* (Wilmington, DE: ISI Books, 1996); Lee Edwards, *Educating for Liberty: The First Half Century of the Intercollegiate Studies Institute* (Washington, DC: Regnery, 2003); Justin Raimondo, *Reclaiming the American Right: The Lost Legacy of the Conservative Movement* (Wilmington, DE: ISI Books, 2008); and Murray N. Rothbard, *The Betrayal of the American Right* (Auburn, AL: Ludwig Von Mises Institute, 2007).

[54]Russell Kirk, "Libertarians: Chirping Sectaries," essay accessed at https://mikechurch.com/epic-paleocons-vs-libertarians-in-russell-kirks-chirping-sectaries/.

[55]For a long, thought-out defense of atheism from the Ayn Rand Institute, see Onkar Ghate, "America Needs a Second Revolution to Save Its First," *New Ideal*, September 17, 2018, https://newideal.aynrand.org/america-needs-a-second-revolution-to-save-its-first.

[56]Brennan, *Libertarianism*, 51.

[57]Walter Berns, "The Need for Public Authority," in *Freedom and Virtue: The Conservative/Libertarian Debate*, ed. George Carey (Wilmington, DE: ISI Books, 2004), 58-59.

[58]Berns, "Need for Public Authority," 59.

[59]Berns, "Need for Public Authority," 62.

[60]Berns, "Need for Public Authority," 63.

[61]See Tucker Carlson's speech at the National Conservatism conference in 2019, https:// nationalconservatism.org/natcon-dc-2019/presenters/tucker-carlson/.

[62]Joel Kotkin, "A New Way Forward on Immigration," *Orange County Register*, August 22, 2017, www.ocregister.com/2017/08/20/a-new-way-forward-on-trade-and-immigration/.

[63]Michelle Malkin, *Open Borders Inc.: Who's funding America's Destruction?* (Washington, DC: Regnery, 2019).

[64]Hans-Hermann Hoppe, "The Case for Free Trade and Restricted Immigration," *Journal of Libertarian Studies*, July 30, 2014, https://mises.org/library/case-free-trade-and -restricted-immigration-0.

[65]Bryan Caplan and Zach Weinersmith, *Open Borders: The Science and Ethics of Immigration* (New York: First Second Books, 2019).

[66]Matt Welch, "Libertarian Presidential Candidates Champion Open Borders," *Reason*, February 26, 2020, https://reason.com/2020/02/26/libertarian-presidential-candidates -champion-open-borders/.

[67]Welch, "Libertarian Presidential Candidates," italics added.

[68]Javier Hidalgo, "The Libertarian Case for Open Borders," *Washington Post*, September 20, 2017, www.washingtonpost.com/news/volokh-conspiracy/wp/2017/09/20/the-lib ertarian-case-for-open-borders.

[69]Fareed Zakaria, "Biden's Generous Immigration Policies Could Turn Out to Backfire," *Washington Post*, March 11, 2021, www.washingtonpost.com/ded049ac-82a9-11eb-81db -b02f0398f49a_story.html.

[70]Zakaria, "Biden's Generous Immigration Policies."

[71]Carlson, *Ship of Fools*, 59-82.

[72]Carlson, *Ship of Fools*, 59-82.

[73]Dylan Scott, "Why Democrats Hopes Were Dashed in Texas," Vox, November 4, 2020, www.vox.com/21549000/texas-election-results-trump-biden-hispanic-vote.

[74]Maggie Fitzgerald, "Black and Hispanic Unemployment is at a Record Low," CNBC, October 4, 2019, www.cnbc.com/2019/10/04/black-and-hispanic-unemployment-is-at -a-record-low.html; Sean Collins, "Trump Made Gains with Black Voters in Some States. Here's Why," Vox, November 4, 2020, www.vox.com/2020/11/4/21537966/trump -black-voters-exit-polls.

[75]Anne Case and Angus Deaton, *Deaths of Despair and the Future of Capitalism* (Princeton, NJ: Princeton University Press, 2020).

[76]Christopher Caldwell, "Immigration's Hidden Costs," *Claremont Review of Books*, Fall 2016, 50.

[77]Caldwell cites George J. Borjas: "The earnings of the North's native workforce will drop by almost 40 percent, while Southern workers will more than double their earnings." Caldwell, "Immigration's Hidden Costs," 50.

[78]Caldwell, "Immigration's Hidden Costs," 50.

[79]Michael Yon, *War Room Pandemic*, episode 794; www.pandemic.warrroom.org; Also see Todd Bensman, "Congress and Journalists Report on Historic Surge of 'Extra-Continental' Migrants Now Pouring Through Panama to U.S. Border," Center for Immigration Studies, June 2, 2021, https://cis.org/Bensman/Congressman-and-Journalists-Report-Historic-Surge-ExtraContinental-Migrants-Now-Pouring.

[80]We will look at the Great Reset in chapter eight.

[81]Whittaker Chambers, "Big Sister Is Watching You," *National Review*, December 28, 1957, www.nationalreview.com/2005/01/big-sister-watching-you-whittaker-chambers/.

8. Freedom Right 3: Radical Libertarians, the End of the State, and the Rise of Utopian Technocracy

[1]Jonathan Ponciano, "Google Billionaire Eric Schmidt Warns of 'National Emergency' if China Overtakes US in AI Research," *Forbes*, March 7, 2021, www.forbes.com/sites/jonathanponciano/2021/03/07/google-billionaire-eric-schmidt-warns-of-national-emergency-if-china-overtakes-us-in-ai-tech/. See also "The Final Report," National Security Commission on Artificial Intelligence, at www.nscai.gov/2021-final-report.

[2]For a discussion of AI and smart cities, see Michael Rectenwald, *Google Archipelago: The Digital Gulag and the Simulation of Freedom* (Nashville, TN: World Encounter Institute, 2019).

[3]Miranda Devine, "US Companies Riddled with Members of Chinese Communist Party," *New York Post*, December 13, 2020, https://nypost.com/2020/12/13/us-companies-riddled-with-members-of-chinese-communist-party/; Varun Hukeri, "American Companies Used to Collaborate with the Nazis. Now They're Working with the Chinese Communist Party," Daily Caller, July 22, 2020, https://dailycaller.com/2020/07/22/companies-chinese-communist-party-nazi-germany-collaborators-uighur-camps-forced-labor/.

[4]Jordan Davidson, "Facebook Executive Caught on Secret Recording Warns About Big Tech's Power: 'They Must Be Stopped,'" *The Federalist*, March 16, 2021, https://thefederalist.com/2021/03/16/facebook-executive-caught-on-secret-recording-warns-about-big-techs-power-they-must-be-stopped/.

[5]Cathalijne Adams, "U.S. Job Loss to China Swells to 3.7 Million," Alliance for American Manufacturing, January 30, 2020, http://americanmanufacturing.org/blog/u-s-a-job-loss-to-china-swells-to3-7-million/; also see Chapter four, "Death to America's Manufacturing Base: Why We Done Play (or Work) in Peoria Anymore" in Peter Navarro, *Death by China: Confronting the Dragon—A Global Call for Action* (Upper Saddle River, NJ: Prentice Hall, 2011), 49-66.

[6]Cody Cain, "No, Mr. President: China Didn't Steal our Jobs. Corporate America Gave Them Away," *Salon*, May 27, 2019, www.salon.com/2019/05/27/no-mr-president-china-didnt-steal-our-jobs-corporate-america-gave-them-away/; Tom Hamburger, "Romney's

Bain Capital Invested in Companies That Moved Jobs Overseas," *The Washington Post*, June 21, 2012, www.washingtonpost.com/business/economy/romneys-bain-capital-in vested-in-companies-that-moved-jobs-overseas/2012/06/21/gJQAsD9ptV_story.html.

[7]See the documentary *Death by China: One Lost Job at a Time*, directed by Peter Navarro (Seattle: Amazon Prime Videos, 2013).

[8]Bob Davis, "When the World Opened the Gates to China," *Wall Street Journal*, January 27, 2018, www.wsj.com/articles/when-the-world-opened-the-gates-of-china-1532701482.

[9]See "President Bill Clinton's 1999 International Trade Speech," www.c-span.org/video /?153935-1/international-trade-speech.

[10]Any criticism I have of China is not about the Chinese people, who are victims, but the Communist Chinese Party and its leaders. See Steven W. Mosher, *Bully of Asia: Why China's Dream Is the New Threat to World Order* (Washington, DC: Regnery, 2017).

[11]Peter Navarro, *Death by China: Confronting the Dragon—A Global Call to Action* (Hoboken, NJ: Pearson FT Press, 2011); and Clive Hamilton, *Hidden Hand Exposing How the Chinese Communist Party Is Reshaping the World* (London: Oneworld, 2020); Clyde Prestowitz, *The World Turned Upside Down: America, China, and the Struggle for Global Leadership* (New Haven, CT: Yale University Press, 2021).

[12]Ben Weingarten, "Americans Need to Stop Funding the Chinese Gulag," *The Federalist*, November 19, 2019, https://thefederalist.com/2019/11/19/americans-need-to-stop -funding-the-chinese-gulag/; and Ben Weingarten, "How China Exploits Commerce to Curb-Stomp the United States," *The Federalist*, February 5, 2021, https://thefederalist .com/2021/02/05/how-china-exploits-commerce-to-curb-stomp-the-united-states/. On how China exploits our bipartisan ruling elite, see Peter Schweitzer, *Secret Empires How the American Political Elite Hides Corruption and Enriches Family and Friends* (New York: HarperCollins, 2019).

[13]Oren Cass, *Pitchfork Economics* podcast, December 1, 2020, https://pitchforkeconomics .com/episode/restoring-conservative-economics-with-oren-cass/; for more of his crit icism of libertarianism and how it has been adopted by both Republicans and Demo crats, see Oren Cass, "A New Conservatism," *Foreign Affairs*, March-April 2020, www .foreignaffairs.com/articles/united-states/2021-02-12/new-conservatism-free-market.

[14]Cass, *Pitchfork Economics* podcast.

[15]For an interesting story of how the Trump administration attempted to disrupt the Wall Street libertarians, see Josh Rogin, *Chaos Under Heaven: Trump, Xi, and the Battle for the Twenty-First Century* (Boston: Houghton Mifflin Harcourt, 2021). To understand Biden's cabinet appointments and their connection to China, see Ben Weingarten, "Why You Should Be Skeptical of the New 'Tough on China' Joe Biden," *The Federalist*, February 17, 2021, https://thefederalist.com/2021/02/17/why-you-should-be-skeptical -of-the-new-tough-on-china-joe-biden/; and Ana Swanson, "Biden on 'Short Leash' as Administration Rethinks China Relations," *New York Times*, February 17, 2021, www .nytimes.com/2021/02/17/business/economy/biden-china.html.

[16]Phrase taken from the title of Jerome Tuccille's, *It Usually Begins with Ayn Rand* (Scotts Valley, CA: CreateSpace, 2012).

[17]Ayn Rand, *The Virtue of Selfishness* (New York: Dutton / Signet, 1992).

[18]Marilyn Moore, "Ayn Rand's Atlas Shrugged Places in the Top 20 on the Great American Read," *Atlas Society*, November 1, 2018, https://atlassociety.org/commentary/com mentary-blog/6244-ayn-rand-s-atlas-shrugged-places-in-the-top-20-on-the-great -american-read.

[19]Brian Doherty, "Rand and the Right," *Reason*, October 15, 2007, https://reason .com/2007/10/15/rand-and-the-right.

[20]Jennifer Burns, *Goddess of the Market: Ayn Rand and the American Right* (New York: Oxford University Press, 2009), 3.

[21]Burns, *Goddess of the Market*, 3.

[22]George H. Nash, *The Conservative Intellectual Movement in America Since 1945*, 30th anniversary ed. (Wilmington, DE: ISI Books, 2006), 143. For the best summary of Rand's views, see Yaron Brook and Don Watkins, *Free Market Revolution: How Ayn Rand's Ideas Can End Big Government* (New York: Palgrave Macmillan, 2012).

[23]Nash, *Conservative Intellectual Movement*, 143.

[24]Brian Doherty, "Rand and the Right," *Reason*, October 15, 2007, https://reason .com/2007/10/15/rand-and-the-right.

[25]Nash, *Conservative Intellectual Movement*, 143.

[26]For conservatives this would not do. William F. Buckley, founder and editor of the *National Review* and the leader of the conservative movement at the time, found the novel's godlessness alarming and a danger to the conservative movement, which at the time was forging an alliance between economic conservatives and religious traditionalists. Rand threated this alliance. When Rand read Chambers's review, she was furious, and from that day on she declared war on the conservative movement. Looking back, most historians of the conservative movement agree that Buckley and Chambers won, and Rand was kicked out of the movement. But that doesn't mean that Rand stopped influencing a whole generation of young people on the right.

[27]Nash, *Conservative Intellectual Movement*, 143.

[28]Burns, *Goddess of the Market*, 203. Also, for a favorable view of Rand, see Yaron Brook and Don Watkins, *Free Market Revolution: How Ayn Rand's Ideas Can End Big Government* (New York: Palgrave Macmillan, 2012).

[29]Burns, *Goddess of the Market*, 253.

[30]Burns, *Goddess of the Market*, 219.

[31]Roy A. Childs Jr., "Objectivism and the State: An Open Letter to Ayn Rand," LewRockwell .com, accessed February 27, 2020, www.lewrockwell.com/1970/01/roy-a-childs-jr/.

[32]Burns, *Goddess of the Market*, 252.

[33]Yaron Brook and Don Watkins, *Free Market Revolution: How Ayn Rand's Ideas Can End Big Government* (New York: Palgrave Macmillan, 2012), 209-21.

[34]On Rothbard's battles with Beltway libertarians, see C. Jay Engel, "Murray Rothbard Versus the Koch Libertarians," *Bastion*, February 16, 2019, www.bastionmagazine.com /articles/murray-rothbard-versus-the-koch-libertarians. To understand why libertarians are not conservatives, see Nathan W. Schlueter and Nicholai G. Wenzel, *Selfish Libertarians and Socialist Conservatives?* (Stanford, CA: Stanford University Press, 2017).

[35]To understand Rothbard's outreach to the radical Left, see Justin Raimondo, *Reclaiming the American Right: The Lost Legacy of the Conservative Movement* (Wilmington, DE: ISI Books, 2014), 248-53; and Murray N. Rothbard, *The Betrayal of the American Right* (Auburn, AL: Ludwig Von Mises Institute, 2007), chaps. 13–14.

[36]For the story of Rothbard's attempt at a paleo-libertarian alliance, see George Hawley, *Right-Wing Critics of American Conservatism* (Lawrence: University Press of Kansas, 2016), 196-201.

[37]"Our Mission, Vision, & Core Values," *Libertarian Christian Institute*, accessed February 29, 2020, https://libertarianchristians.com/mission.

[38]For a list of their resources on Romans 13, see Doug Stuart, "Romans 13 for Dummies," Libertarian Christian Institute, June 16, 2018, https://libertarianchristians.com/2018/06 /16/romans-13-for-dummies.

[39]Greg Boyd, *The Myth of a Christian Nation: How the Quest for Political Power Is Destroying the Church* (Grand Rapids, MI: Zondervan, 2007).

[40]As Boyd tells the story, when he originally preached the material that later would become the book, 20 percent of the congregation, a thousand people, left the church.

[41]Brian Doherty, *Radicals for Capitalism: A Freewheeling History of the Modern American Libertarian Movement* (New York: Public Affairs, 2007), 271-72; see also Fred Turner, *From Counterculture to Cyberculture: Stewart Brand, the Whole Earth Network, and the Rise of Digital Utopianism* (Chicago: University of Chicago Press, 2008).

[42]Doherty, *Radicals for Capitalism*, 614.

[43]Doherty, *Radicals for Capitalism*, 615.

[44]Doherty, *Radicals for Capitalism*, 616.

[45]Richard Barbrook and Andy Cameron, "The California Ideology," *Alamut*, August 1995, www.imaginaryfutures.net/2007/04/17/the-californian-ideology-2/.

[46]Barbrook and Cameron, "California Ideology," 2.

[47]Doherty, *Radicals for Capitalism*, 618.

[48]Doherty, *Radicals for Capitalism*, 618-19.

[49]Anne Case and Angus Deaton, *Deaths of Despair and the Future of Capitalism* (Princeton, NJ: Princeton University Press, 2020).

[50]Barbrook and Cameron, "California Ideology," 11-12.

[51]To understand high-tech's obsession with immortality, see Franklin Foer's *World Without Mind: The Existential Threat of Big Tech* (New York: Penguin, 2018); and Chip Walter, *Immortality, Inc.: Renegade Science, Silicon Valley Billions, and the Quest to Live Forever* (Washington, DC: National Geographic, 2020).

[52]Oren Cass, "A New Conservatism," *Foreign Affairs*, April 2020, 7.

[53]Dani Rodrik, *Has Globalization Gone Too Far?* (Washington, DC: Peterson Institute for International Economics, 1997); see also Dani Rodrik, *The Globalization Paradox: Democracy and the Future of the World Economy* (New York: W.W. Norton, 2011). For a helpful summary of Rodrik's views and the reaction they engendered, see Nikil Saval, "Globalization: The Rise and Fall of an Idea that Swept the World," *The Guardian*, July 14, 2017, www.theguardian.com/world/2017/jul/14/globalisation-the-rise-and-fall-of-an-idea-that-swept-the-world.

[54]From an interview with Asher Schechter, "Globalization Has Contributed to Tearing Our Societies Apart," *Pro Market*, March 29, 2018, https://promarket.org/2018/03/29/globalization-contributed-tearing-societies-apart/.

[55]Samuel P. Huntington, "Dead Souls: The Denationalization of the American Elite," *National Interest*, March 1, 2004, 1; https://nationalinterest.org/article/dead-souls-the-denationalization-of-the-american-elite-620.

[56]Huntington, "Dead Souls."

[57]Ross Douthat, "The Rise of Woke Capital," *New York Times*, February 28, 2018, www.nytimes.com/2018/02/28/opinion/corporate-america-activism.html.

[58]Ben Weingarten, "America Is Fast Becoming a Woke Theocracy," *Newsweek*, July 21, 2020, www.newsweek.com/1518938; also see Stephen R. Soukup, *The Dictatorship of Woke Capital: How Political Correctness Captured Big Business* (New York: Encounter Books, 2021).

[59]Weingarten, "America is Fast Becoming a Woke Theocracy."

[60]Ben Weingarten, "Woke Capitalists Sell Out US to China Behind Mask of Virtue," *Real Clear Politics*, June 4, 2020, www.realclearpolitics.com/2020/06/03/woke_capitalists_sell_out_us_to_china_behind_mask_of_virtue_513154.html.

[61]Joel Kotkin, "New-Feudalism in California," *American Affairs*, Summer 2020, Vol. IV, Number 2; https:/americanaffairsjournal.org/2020/05/neo-feudalism-in-california/.

[62]Mark Piesing, "Silicon Valley's 'Suicide Pill' for Mankind," *Unherd*, August 20, 2018, https://unherd.com/2018/08/silicon-valleys-suicide-pill-mankind; see also Nick Bilton, "Silicon Valley's Most Disturbing Obsession," *Vanity Fair*, October 5, 2016, www.vanityfair.com/news/2016/10/silicon-valley-ayn-rand-obsession; Wesley J. Smith, "The Transhumanist Bill of Wrongs," *Discovery Institute*, October 23, 2018, https://spectator.org/the-transhumanist-bill-of-wrongs/Wesley J. Smith; "New-Time Religion," *First Things*, December, 2014, www.firstthings.com/article/2014/12/new-time-religion; and Alexander Thomas, "AI and Transhumanism: Could Quest for Super-intelligence and Eternal Life Lead to a Dystopian Nightmare?" *Newsweek*, August 1, 2017, www.newsweek.com/644128.

[63]Mark E. Jeftovic, "Transhumanism: The New Religion of the Coming Technocracy," *Axis of Easy*, June 24, 2020, https://axisofeasy.com/aoe/transhumanism-the-new-religion-of-the-coming-technocracy/.

[64]Thomas, "AI and Transhumanism," 5-6.

[65]Thomas, "AI and Transhumanism."

[66]Thomas, "AI and Transhumanism."

[67]Michael Rectenwald, *Google Archipelago: The Digital Gulag and the Simulation of Freedom* (Nashville, TN: New English Review Press, 2019).

[68]See Peter Navarro's *The Coming China Wars: Where They Will Be Fought And How They Can Be Won* (Hoboken, NJ: FT Press, 2006); Michael Pillsbury, *The Hundred-Year Marathon: China's Secret Strategy To Replace America As The Global Superpower* (New York: St. Martin's Griffin, 2016); Steven Mosher, *Hegemon: China's Plan To Dominate Asia And The World* (New York: Encounter Books, 2000).

[69]Tanner Green, "It Is Time For A Libertarian Case Against China," Scholars Stage Blogspot, April 29, 2020, https://scholars-stage.blogspot.com/2020/04/it-is-time-for -libertarian-case-against.html?m=1; see also Tanner Green, "China Does Not Want Your Rules Based Order," Scholars Stage Blogspot, June 4, 2016, https://scholars-stage.org /china-does-not-want-your-rules-based-order/; "Give No Heed To The Walking Dead," Scholars Stage Blogspot, July 1, 2019, https://scholars-stage.blogspot.com/2019/07/give-no -heed-to-walking-dead.html?m=1.

[70]For the best description of the China class and those who are in it, see Josh Rogan's *Chaos Under Heaven* (Boston: Houghton Mifflin Harcourt, 2021). Also for a good overview of those in the China Class who are now in the Biden Administration, see Ben Weingarten, "Why You Should Be Skeptical Of The New 'Tough On China' Joe Biden," *The Federalist*, February 17, 2021, https://thefederalist.com/2021/02/17/why-you-should -be-skeptical-of-the-new-tough-on-china-joe-biden/.

[71]William R. Hawkins, "Plutocrats Are Only Part Of A Larger Problem," *The Journal Of Political Risk*, February 6, 2020, 3.

[72]Hans F. Sennholz, "Globalization Under Fire," Mises Institute, August 20, 2000, https://mises .org/library/globalization-under-fire.

[73]Robert Murphy, "Is There a Libertarian Case Against Free Trade?," Mises Institute, March, 13, 2006, https://mises.org/library/there-libertarian-case-against-free-trade.

[74]Murphy, "Is There a Libertarian Case?," 8.

[75]John Tamny, "Blaming Globalization for Our Society's Problems Is Just Another Version of Victim Mentality," *Foundation for Economic Freedom*, November 12, 2018, 5-6.

[76]Ryan McMaken, "The Difference Between Good Globalism and Bad Globalism," Mises Institute, March 28, 2018, https://mises.org/wire/difference-between-good-globalism-and -bad-globalism.

[77]Daniel W. Drezner, "There is No China Crisis," Reason, May 2020, 17; also see Mihai Macovei's "There Are No Winners in the US-China 'Tech War,'" Mises Institute, July 28, 2020, https://mises.org/wire/there-are-no-winners-us-china-tech-war-0.

[78]Drezner, "There is No China Crisis," 17.

[79]For the most comprehensive defense of big tech from a libertarian perspective, see Matthew Feeney's "Conservative's Big Tech Campaign Based on Myths and Misunderstandings," Medium, May 28, 2020, https://medium.com/@M_Feeney/a58160c8a785.

[80]Rachel Bovard, "We Must Break Up Big Tech: It's The Greatest Private Threat to Liberty in Our Modern Age," *American Consequences*, January 2021, https://americanconsequences.com/big-tech-rachel-bovard/.

[81]Bovard, "We Must Break Up Big Tech."

[82]Bovard, "We Must Break Up Big Tech."

[83]To understand how the Davos Men are using the pandemic to solidify their world incorporation, see Klaus Schwab and Thierry Malleret, *COVID-19: The Great Reset* (Geneva, Switzerland: World Economic Forum, 2020).

[84]Rectenwald, *Google Archipelago*.

9. Order Right 2: Poison Pill Conservatives

[1]David Neiwert, *Red Pill, Blue Pill: How to Counteract the Conspiracy Theories That Are Killing Us* (Buffalo, NY: Prometheus, 2020). While there are always people who take a narrative too far, and their theory of conspiracy doesn't hold up to scrutiny, all conspiracy theories whether on the left or the right need to be tested.

[2]Just when people might have some self-doubt, questioning whether they themselves may have succumbed to crazy conspiracy theories (yes, some theories are crazy conspiracies), the ruling elites say something out loud that they once would have whispered in private (like the Green New Deal isn't about the environment but really about massive redistribution and economic state control), see Marc Morano, *Green Fraud: Why the Green New Deal Is Even Worse Than You Think* (Washington DC: Regnery, 2021). Also consider the new election law in Georgia, passed by elected state representatives and signed by the governor. Upon ratification, Coca-Cola, Delta Air Lines, and Major League Baseball moved to punish the people of Georgia, particularly for including the voter ID provision, something that all three companies require of their employees or customers. Or consider the push for vaccine passports, threating the free movement of American citizens and the confidentiality of a patient's medical history. Or consider all the people in the Biden administration who have financial ties to China, openly defending the CCP, a transnational criminal organization that enslaves millions of its own people, see Reheem Kassam and Natalie Winters, "Revealed: China's State Propaganda Group Boasts Control Over Western Think Tanks, 'Election Integrity' Groups, and Even Joe Biden's National Security Team," *National Pulse*, April 1, 2021, https://thenationalpulse.com/exclusive/exc-china-state-propaganda-boasts-control-over-think-tanks/.

[3]For a helpful study for defining conspiracy theories, who conducts them, and for what purpose, see Lance de Haven-Smith, *Conspiracy Theory in America* (Austin: University of Texas Press, 2014).

[4]*Tucker Carlson Tonight*, March 22, 2021, https://youtu.be/6jy_oG4gcSw.

[5]Rod Dreher, "Kristi Noem's Surrender to Big Business," *American Conservative*, March 23, 2021, www.theamericanconservative.com/dreher/kristi.

[6]Rod Dreher, "The Queering of Young America," *American Conservative*, February 24, 2021, www.theamericanconservative.com/dreher/the-queering.

[7]Dreher, "Queering of Young America."

[8]Andrew Walker, quoted in Dreher, "Queering of Young America."

[9]See Ryan T. Anderson, *When Harry Became Sally: Responding to the Transgender Moment* (New York: Encounter Books, 2018); and Andrew T. Walker, *God and the Transgender Debate: What Does the Bible Actually Say About Gender Identity* (Purcell-ville, VA: Good Book Company, 2017).

[10]Margot Cleveland, "The Worst Thing About Kristi Noem's Sports Capitulation Is Her Lies," *The Federalist*, March 26, 2021, https://thefederalist.com/2021/03/26/the-worst-thing-about-kristi-noems-sports-capitulation-is-her-lies/.

[11]Emma Green, "The Christian Retreat from Public Life," the *Atlantic*, February 22, 2017, www.theatlantic.com/politics/archive/2017/02/benedict-option/517290.

[12]For a good example of a reviewer who sees Dreher as overly pessimistic, driven by fear, and joyless, see Trevin Wax, "Are Western Christians Facing a Totalitarian Threat from the Left?" *Gospel Coalition*, September 18, 2020, www.thegospelcoalition.org/reviews/live-not-by-lies-rod-dreher.

[13]Green, "Christian Retreat from Public Life."

[14]Rod Dreher, "Christian Life Under Total Surveillance," *American Conservative*, February 10, 2021, www.theamericanconservative.com/dreher/christian-life-under-total.

[15]Dreher, "Christian Life Under Total Surveillance."

[16]Dreher, "Christian Life Under Total Surveillance."

[17]Rod Dreher, "The Whale and the Net," *American Conservative*, March 8, 2021, www.theamericanconservative.com/dreher/whale.

[18]Dreher, "Whale and the Net."

[19]For an outstanding overview of critics who take on Dreher's "Christ Against Culture" view while insisting that Dreher has much in common with the "Christ Transforming Culture" perspective, see James D. Clark, "The Kuyperian Impulse of the Benedict Option," *Themelios* 43, no. 2 (2018), https://themelios.thegospelcoalition.org/article/the-kuyperian-impulse-of-the-benedict-option.

[20]Rod Dreher, "The Benedict Option: A Conversation with Rod Dreher," *Albert Mohler*, February 13, 2017, https://albertmohler.com/2017/02/13/benedict-option-conversation-rod-dreher.

[21]Dreher, "Whale and the Net."

[22]Damon Linker, a left-of-center thinker, spoke for many on the left when he said that few books on the decline of politics in our country can "match the power of the breathtakingly radical explanation contained in Patrick Deneen's *Why Liberalism Failed*. . . . It's the most electrifying book on cultural criticism published in some time, and it's hard

to imagine its radicalism being surpassed anytime soon." Damon Linker, "An Ominous Prophecy for Liberalism," *The Week*, February 22, 2018, https://theweek.com/articles /749378/ominous-prophecy-liberalism. See Dreher's review, "Deneen's Book Gets Even Hotter," *American Conservative*, February 27, 2018, www.theamericanconservative .com/dreher/patrick-deneen.

[23]Patrick J. Deneen, *Why Liberalism Failed* (New Haven, CT: Yale University Press, 2019), 3.

[24]Deneen, *Why Liberalism Failed*, 1.

[25]Deneen, *Why Liberalism Failed*, 1.

[26]Deneen, *Why Liberalism Failed*, 4.

[27]Deneen, *Why Liberalism Failed*, 4.

[28]Deneen, *Why Liberalism Failed*, 18.

[29]Patrick J. Deneen, quoted in Robert R, Reilly, "For God and Country: Can Good Christians Be Good Americans?" *Claremont Review of Books*, Summer 2017, 5.

[30]Patrick Deneen, quoted in Reilly, "For God and Country," 5.

[31]Al Mohler, "How Liberalism Failed: A Conversation with Patrick J. Deneen," *Al Mohler*, February 13, 2018, https://albertmohler.com/2018/02/13/liberalism-failed-conversation -patrick-deneen.

[32]Mohler, "How Liberalism Failed: A Conversation."

[33]David T. Koyzis, *Political Visions & Illusions* (Downers Grove, IL: IVP Academic, 2019).

[34]In an article in *First Things*, Koyzis, sounding very much like Dreher, says, "modern liberalism in its various forms—including those popularly labelled 'conservative'—has had centuries to shape and misshape our societies." David T. Koyzis, "Living Communally in God's Good Creation," *First Things*, May 2017, www.firstthings.com/web-exclusives /2017/05/living-communally-in-gods-good-creation.

[35]Deneen, *Why Liberalism Failed*, 18.

[36]Deneen, *Why Liberalism Failed*, 19-20.

[37]I am grateful to Father James Schall, one of my professors at Georgetown, who introduced me to the thought of Leo Strauss, assigning his *Natural Right and History* (Chicago: University of Chicago Press, 1999) and his *The City and Man* (Chicago: University of Chicago Press, 1978).

[38]As Deneen writes, and I think correctly, "Strauss's highly philosophic and often obscure analysis of the history of political thought proved enormously influential throughout the mid-twentieth century down to our own day. His work has inspired several generations of students who have advanced his analyses and basic premises in their academic work, but perhaps more remarkably still, has spawned countless political think-tanks, institutes, programs and centers devoted to the project of political conservativism." Patrick J. Deneen, "Week 7: Natural Rights Conservatism—The Case of Leo Strauss," *American Conservative*, March 25, 2015, www.theamericanconservative.com/articles /week-7-natural-rights-conservatism-the-case-of-leo-strauss.

[39]Deneen, "Week 7: Natural Rights Conservatism—The Case of Leo Strauss."

[40]Deneen, "Week 7: Natural Rights Conservatism—The Case of Leo Strauss."

[41]Deneen, "Week 7: Natural Rights Conservatism—The Case of Leo Strauss."

[42]Deneen, "Week 7: Natural Rights Conservatism—The Case of Leo Strauss."

[43]Deneen, "Week 7: Natural Rights Conservatism—The Case of Leo Strauss."

[44]Catherine Zuckert and Michael Zuckert, *The Truth About Leo Strauss: Political Philosophy and American Democracy* (Chicago: University of Chicago Press, 2008).

[45]Patrick Deneen, quoted in Reilly, "For God and Country," 8.

[46]For one of the best examples of the order right 1 conservative position that agrees with Deneen's declension narrative but departs from Deneen's explanation of why it happened and what the solution is, see Notre Dame professor, Vincent Phillip Munoz, "Defending American Classical Liberalism," *National Review*, June 11, 2018, https://national review.com/2018/06/american-classical-liberalism-response-to-radical-catholics/.

[47]As we will see in chapter ten, it is not only order right conservatives who push back but order right 3 thinkers who, while they agree with the poison-pill theory, differ from order right 2 by claiming they don't go far enough, are not radical enough, afraid to call for the destruction of the American system and its replacement with something new.

[48]See Robert R. Reilly, "Fools or Scoundrels? A Response to Patrick Deneen," *Public Discourse*, October 16, 2017, www.thepublicdiscourse.com/2017/10/20245.

[49]For the different Straussian camps, see Zuckert and Zuckert, "Straussian Geography," in *The Truth About Leo Strauss*, 228-60.

[50]While this is a much bigger argument than we can cover here, West Coast Straussians have had to claim that Strauss was either wrong about Locke or simply misunderstood him. But how one interprets Locke is at the heart of how one sees the founding and which side of the rupture it is on. For those scholars who hold to a "non-Locke" Locke, see Steven Forde, "Natural Law, Theology, and Morality in Locke," *American Journal of Political Science* 45, no. 2 (2001): 396-409; Peter C. Myers, "Lockeans, Progressives, and Liberationists," *Society* 50 (2013); John W. Yolton, "Locke on the Law of Nature," *Philosophical Review* 67, no. 4 (1958): 477-98; Thomas G. West, "The Ground of Locke's Law of Nature," *Social Philosophy and Policy* 29, no. 2 (2012): 1-50.

[51]For Reilly's criticism of Deneen's take on Madison, see Robert R. Reilly, "For God and Country," *Claremont Review of Books* 13, no. 3 (Summer 2013): 6-8, https://claremont reviewofbooks.com/for-god-and-country.

[52]For Reilly's discussion of John Locke, see Robert R. Reilly, "For God and Country," *Claremont Review of Books* 13, no. 3 (summer 2013): 9-14, https://claremontreviewof books.com/for-god-and-country.

[53]Patrick J. Deneen, "Corrupting the Youth? A Response to Reilly," *Public Discourse*, September 19, 2017, www.thepublicdiscourse.com/2017/09/20087/.

[54]Robert R. Reilly, "For God and Country," *Claremont Review of Books* 13, no. 3 (Summer 2013): 6-8, https://claremontreviewofbooks.com/for-god-and-country.

[55]Deneen, "Corrupting the Youth?"

[56]Rod Dreher, "Our War of Religion," The American Conservative, March 9, 2021, www .theamericanconservative.com/dreher/our-war-of-religion-live-not-by-lies-woke/.

10. Order Right 3: The Illiberal New Right

[1]Elizabeth Dias and Ruth Graham, "Millions of White Evangelicals Do Not Intend to Get Vaccinated," *New York Times*, April 5, 2021, www.nytimes.com/2021/04/05/world/millions -of-white-evangelicals-do-not-intend-to-get-vaccinated.html.

[2]To understand why conservative evangelicals don't trust the experts or their views, see Steve Deace and Todd Erzen, *Faucian Bargain: The Most Powerful and Dangerous Bureaucrat in American History* (Brentwood, TN: Post Hill Press, 2021).

[3]Many of those evangelicals who are "vaccine cautious," that is, those who have questions they want answered, have been influenced by former *New York Times* writer Alex Berenson, who since the pandemic started has appeared almost weekly on *Tucker Carlson Tonight*. See Alex Berenson, *Unreported Truths About COVID1-19 and Lockdowns: Part 4: Vaccines* (n.p.: Blue Deep, Inc., 2021).

[4]Dias and Graham, "Millions of White Evangelicals"; Jennifer Steinhauer, "Younger Military Personnel Reject Vaccine, in Warning for Commanders and the Nation," *New York Times*, February 27, 2021, www.nytimes.com/2021/02/27/us/politics/coronavirus -vaccine-refusal-military.html.

[5]See Ernie Mundell and Robin Foster, "Biden Administration Working on 'Vaccine Passport' Initiative," US News, March 29, 2021, www.usnews.com/news/health-news /articles/2021-03-29/biden-administration-working-on-vaccine-passport-initiative; Lexi Lonas, "Arizona Attorney General 'Alarmed' by Biden's Door-to-Door Vaccination Push," *The Hill*, July 7, 2021, https://thehill.com/homenews/state-watch561926-arizona -attorney-general-alarmed-by-bidens-door-to-door-vaccination-push. By the fall of 2021, the Biden administration decided the "public education campaign" had failed. Though he promised he would never mandate vaccines, President Biden changed his mind and on September 9 announced sweeping new federal vaccine requirements, Zeke Miller, "Sweeping New Vaccine Mandates for 100 Million Americans," AP News, September 10, 2021, https://apnews.com/article/joe-biden-business-health-coronavirus -pandemic-execu ve-branch-18fb12993f05be13bf760946a6fb89be.

[6]For a recent illustration of how the media criticized the Military Industrial Complex, and how even after getting caught spreading false stories they didn't apologize or correct the story, see Glenn Greenwald, "Journalists, Learning They Spread a CIA Fraud About Russia, Instantly Embrace a New One," Greenwald.substack.com/p/journalists -learning-they-spread, April 16, 2021; see also Glenn Greenwald, "The Media Lied Repeatedly About Officer Brian Sicknick's Death," at Greenwald.subtack.com/p/the -media-lied-repeatedly-about-officer, April 19, 2021.

[7]In his "What Is Trump to Us?," Angelo Codevilla contends that five years ago when Trump was elected no one would have imagined that the oligarchy would grow so strong that it now "has destroyed the American republic." American Greatness, July 6, 2021, https://amgreatness.com/2021/07/06/what-is-trump-to-us/.

[8]You may wonder why I don't address in detail the Capitol breach of January 6, 2021; after all this would seem the best place to do so, especially since a number of those involved were thought to be part of the Proud Boys and Oath Keepers and QAnon. But because at the time I wrote this chapter it was still being investigated and serious doubts existed about an organized plot by these groups, I decided not to use it. See footnote 14 in the Introduction.

[9]Laurie Clarke, "Why Scientists Fear the "Toxic' Covid-19 Debate," www.newstatesman .com/science-tech/coronavirus/2020/10/why-scientists-fear-toxic-covid-19-debate.

[10]Richard John Neuhaus, *The End of Democracy? The Judicial Usurpation of Politics: The Celebrated First Things Debate with Arguments Pro and Con and "The Anatomy of a Controversy"* (Dallas: Spence, 1997).

[11]Derek Robertson, "How an Obscure Conservative Theory Became the Trump Era's Go-to-Nerd Phrase," *Politico*, February 25, 2018, www.politico.com/magazine /story/2018/02/25/overton-window-explained-definition-meaning-217010/.

[12]Patrick J. Buchanan, "1992 Republican National Convention Speech," *Patrick J. Buchanan*, August 17, 1992, https://buchanan.org/blog/1992-republican-national-convention -speech-148.

[13]Buchanan, "1992 Republican National Convention Speech."

[14]While Buchanan dislikes Strauss, his argument here is close to Strauss's first-wave argument shared by Deneen, holding that it was compromised.

[15]Patrick J. Buchanan, *Day of Reckoning: How Hubris, Ideology, and Greed Are Tearing America Apart* (New York: St. Martin's Press, 2007), chaps. 1–2.

[16]Buchanan, *Day of Reckoning*, "The Gospel According to George Bush," chap. 3, where Buchanan celebrates Jamestown as our true founding, not Puritan Massachusetts.

[17]Patrick J. Buchanan, *State of Emergency: The Third World Invasion and Conquest of America* (New York: St. Martin's Press, 2006), 139.

[18]Charles R. Kesler, *The Federalist Papers, Introduction and Notes*, ed. Clinton Rossiter (New York: Signet Classic, 2003), 36-40.

[19]Buchanan, *State of Emergency*, 142.

[20]Buchanan, *State of Emergency*, 150.

[21]Following Buchanan's lead, Trump called for a border wall, stricter immigration control, economic protectionism, and keeping America out of unnecessary endless wars. See James Matthew Wilson, "The Triumph of Buchananism," *Front Porch Republic*, November 9, 2016, www.frontporchrepublic.com/2016/11/the-triumph-of-buchananism.

[22]Patrick Buchanan, *Suicide of a Superpower* (New York: Thomas Dunne Books, 2011), 190.

[23]Ann Coulter, *Adios, America: The Left's Plan to Turn Our Country into a Third World Hellhole* (Washington, DC: Regnery, 2015); and Michelle Malkin, *Open Borders Inc.: Who's Funding America's Destruction?* (Washington, DC: Regnery, 2019). See also George Hawley, *Alt-Right: What Everyone Needs to Know* (New York: Oxford University Press), 161-62; and William F. Buckley Jr., *In Search of Anti-Semitism* (New York: Continuum International, 1993).

[24]Tucker Carlson, *Tucker Carlson Tonight*, Fox News, April 12, 2021.

[25]For a list and description for all the groups, thinkers, and bloggers included in the alt-right, see Hawley's *Alt-Right*, particularly chaps. 1-3, 4-85.

[26]Hawley, *Alt-Right*, 4.

[27]Hawley, *Alt-Right*, 5. See Jane Coaston, "Why the Alt-Right Trolls Shouted Down Donald Trump Jr.," Vox, November 11, 2019, www.vox.com/policy-and-politics /2019/11/11/20948317. See James Kirkpatrick, *Conservatism Inc.: The Battle for the American Right* (London: Arktos Media, 2019).

[28]Angela Nagle, *Kill All Normies: Online Culture Wars from 4chan and Tumbler to Trump and the Alt-Right* (Hampshire, UK: Zero Books, 2017).

[29]Jacob Siegel, "The Alt-Right's Jewish Godfather," *Tablet*, accessed March 5, 2020, www .tabletmag.com/jewish-news-and-politics/218712/spencer-gottfried-alt-right.

[30]Rod Dreher, "Vermeule, Deneen, Pappin, Muñoz at Notre Dame," *American Conservative*, November 3, 2018, www.theamericanconservative.com/dreher/vermeule.

[31]Patrick J. Deneen, "A Catholic Showdown Worth Watching," *American Conservative*, February 6, 2014, www.theamericanconservative.com/a-catholic-showdown.

[32]Rod Dreher, "More Thoughts on Integralism," *American Conservative*, November 5, 2018, www.theamericanconservative.com/dreher/more-thoughts; While Deneen is slightly more moderate than Vermeule and the other radical Catholics, he nonetheless breaks with modernity (modernity is bad) in all its forms, and like them Deneen wants to see the end of the liberal project (polluted by all three waves of modernity) and something new take its place. So in one sense, this dialogue was unfair, it really was three Rad Trads against one (Muñoz).

[33]Edmund Waldstein, "What is Integralism Today?" *Church Life Journal*, October 31, 2018, https://churchlifejournal.nd.edu/articles/what-is-integralism-today. Dreher thought that Vermeule and Pappin won.

[34]Waldstein, "What is Integralism Today?"

[35]Kevin Gallagher, "Eclipse of Catholic Fusionism," *American Affairs*, August 2018, https://americanaffairsjournal.org/2018/08/the-eclipse-of-catholic-fusionism.

[36]Gallagher, "Eclipse of Catholic Fusionism."

[37]Adrian Vermeule, quoted in Gabriel Schoenfeld, "Don't Fall for It: The Illiberal Temptation," *American Interest*, April 26, 2019, www.the-american-interest.com/2019/04/26 /the-illiberal-temptation. To see just how far Vermeule is willing to go, see his "Beyond Originalism," the *Atlantic*, March 31, 2020, www.theatlantic.com/ideas/archive/2020/03 /common-good-constitutionalism/609037/.

[38]Vermeule, quoted in Schoenfeld, "Don't Fall for It."

[39]One critic says, "It is notable that today's anti-liberal theorists are, for the most part, rather vague about what they envision replacing the liberal-democratic order they decry. . . . One of its most aggressive critics cannot even pencil-sketch the contours of a plausible superior alternative," in Schoenfeld, "Don't Fall for It."

[40]See John McWhorter, "The Elect: The Threat to a Progressive America from Anti-Black Anti-Racists," It Bears Mentioning, March 9, 2021, https://johnmcwhorter.substack .com/p/the-elect-the-threat-to-a-progressive-755.

[41]Angelica Stabile, "Economist Glenn Loury Tackles the Issue, Impact of Race on 'Tucker Carlson,'" Fox News, June 9, 2021, www.foxnews.com/media/glenn-loury-race-tucker -carlson-fox-nation.amp.

[42]Stanley Kurtz, "Dominionist Domination," *National Review*, May 2, 2005, www.national review.com/2005/05/dominionist-domination-stanley-kurtz.

[43]Kurtz, "Dominionist Domination."

[44]Robert Gagnon and Edith Humphrey, "Stop Calling Ted Cruz a Dominionist," *Christianity Today*, April 6, 2016, www.christianitytoday.com/ct/2016/april-web-only/stop -calling-ted-cruz-dominionist.html.

[45]Kurtz, "Dominionist Domination."

[46]Michael Gerson, "A Holy War on the Tea Party," *Washington Post*, August 22, 2011, www .washingtonpost.com/opinions/a-holy-war-on-the-tea-party/2011/08/22/gIQAYRcOXJ _story.html.

[47]Kurtz, "Dominionist Domination." Also see Ross Douthat, "Theocracy, Theocracy, Theocracy," *First Things*, August 2006, www.firstthings.com/article/2006/08. See also Michael J. McVicar, "The Libertarian Theocrats," *Political Research Associates*, September 1, 2007, www.politicalresearch.org/2007/09/01/libertarian-theocrats. For McVicar's full length biography of R. J. Rushdoony, who many say is the father of reconstructionism, see *Christian Reconstruction: R.J. Rushdoony and American Religious Conservatism* (Durham: University of North Carolina Press, 2015).

[48]For a discussion of Diamond's "soft dominionism" versus "hard dominionism," see Francis Fitzgerald, *The Evangelicals: The Struggle to Shape America* (New York: Simon & Schuster, 2017), 535-36; see also Sara Diamond, *Roads to Dominion: Right-Wing Movements and Political Power in the United States* (New York: Guilford Press, 1995), 246-55.

[49]Rod Dreher, "A Defense of Jericho March Criticism," *The American Conservative*, December 13, 2020, https://theamericanconservative.com/dreher/defense-of-jericho -march-criticism/.

[50]Patrick J. Buchanan, "If We Erase Our History, Who Are We?" *Patrick J. Buchanan*, August 15, 2017, https://buchanan.org/blog/if-we-erase-our-history-who-are-we-127510.

[51]Rod Dreher, "Buchanan's Shameful Defense of White Supremacy," *American Conservative*, August 18, 2017, www.theamericanconservative.com/dreher/buchanan.

[52]Dreher, "Buchanan's Shameful Defense of White Supremacy." A few days after Buchanan's article, another conservative writer Tom Piatak jumped to Buchanan's defense. See Tom Piatak, "Rod Dreher and the Politics of Betrayal," *Chronicles*, August 21, 2017, www.chroniclesmagazine.org/rod-dreher-and-the-politics-of-betrayal.

[53]Paul Gottfried, quoted in Siegel, "Alt-Right's Jewish Godfather."

[54]Sohrab Ahmari, "Terrible American Turn Toward Illiberalism," *Commentary*, October 2017, www.commentarymagazine.com/articles/sohrab-ahmari/terrible-american-turn -toward-illiberalism.

[55]Ahmari, "Terrible American Turn Toward Illiberalism."

[56]Rod Dreher, "What I Saw at the Jericho March," *American Conservative*, December 12, 2020, www.theamericanconservative.com/dreher/what-i-saw.

[57]Dreher, "What I Saw at the Jericho March."

[58]Dreher, "What I saw at the Jericho March."

[59]For the Project Veritas three-part series release, see: Part 1: https://www.projectveritas .com/news/part-1-cnn-director-admits-network-engaged-in-propaganda-to-remove -trump/; Part II: https://www.projectveritas.com/news/part-2-cnn-director-charlie -chester-reveals-how-network-practices/; Part III: https://www.projectveritas.com/news /part-3-cnn-director-charlie-chester-says-network-is-trying-to-help-the-black/. According to Chester, CNN "played up the COVID-19 death toll for ratings, "promoted anti-Trump 'propaganda'" just to get him out of office, and "help[s] BLM," burying any and all stories that don't fit their narrative (that America is racist) or might make them look bad (like Blacks attacking Asians), and only running stories that attack Whites and divide the country.

[60]I want to thank Charlie Kirk for the Twitter guillotine metaphor.

PART THREE: FORMING THE NEW VITAL CENTER

[1]R. R. Reno, *The Return of the Strong Gods: Nationalism, Populism, and the Future of the West* (Washington, DC: Gateway Editions, 2019).

[2]Joel Kotkin, "The Pandemic Road to Serfdom," *The American Mind*, May 1, 2020, https://americanmind.org/salvo/the-pandemic-road-to-serfdom/.

11. THE NEW VITAL CENTER: THE AMERICAN SYNTHESIS AND THE FOUR SOULS

[1]Cristina Marcos, "Pro-Trump Lawmakers Form Caucus Promoting 'Anglo-Saxon po- litical traditions,'" *The Hill*, April 16, 2021, https://thehill.com/homenews/house/548731 -pro-trump-lawmakers-form-caucus-to-promote-anglo-saxon-political-traditions.

[2]"America First Caucus Policy Platform," *Punchbowlnews.com*, accessed April 30, 2021, https://punchbowl.news/wp-content/uploads/America-First-Caucus-Policy-Platform -FINAL-2.pdf.

[3]Kevin McCarthy (@GOPLeader), "America is built on the idea that we are all created equal," Twitter, April 16, 2021, 1:41 p.m., https://twitter.com/gopleader/status/13831586472 66611203.

[4]"America First Caucus Policy Platform," *Punchbowlnews.com*.

[5]Savannah Behrmann and Phillip M. Baily, "White Nationalist Language of American First Caucus Sets of New Alarms on Racism," *USA Today*, April 22, 2021, www.usatoday .com/amp/7261157002.

[6]Adam Kinzinger (@AdamKinzinger), Twitter, April 16, 2021, 3:44 p.m. Within days of it being leaked, Representative Marjorie Taylor Green, as well as other representatives thought to be behind the new caucus, distanced herself from the platform document, saying it was written by low-level staffers, was only a draft, and that she hadn't seen it until *Punch Bowl News* published it.

[7]While the AFC platform never defines "Anglo-Saxon political traditions" or exactly what they mean by it, Encyclopaedia Britannica says that "by the time of the Norman Conquest [1066], the kingdom that had developed from the realm of the Anglo-Saxon peoples had become known as England, and Anglo-Saxon as a collective term for the region's people was eventually supplanted by 'English.'" Presently, writes Britannica, "'Anglo-Saxon' continues to be used to refer to a period in the history of Britain generally defined as the years between the end of the Roman occupation and the Norman Conquest." The vast majority of the early settlers of New England were from East Anglia, a region in southeast England, who descended from the Anglo-Saxons, and these East Anglia Puritans brought with them to the new world English political traditions, many of which became the foundation for the American system of checks and balances. Perhaps the AFC platform was trying to communicate the importance of English political traditions and institutions to the founding of America, a point that no historian disputes. But the reaction might have been more favorable if they had written "English political traditions" or "Anglo-Protestant [a phrase Samuel Huntington prefers] political traditions." See "Anglo-Saxon," Britannica.com, accessed May 3, 2021, www.britannica.com/topic/Anglo-Saxon.

[8]I am aware that there is disagreement over exactly what *creed* means. For some, creed is synonymous with the freedom left 2 and freedom right 2 positions (godless constitution and libertarian freedom), what Strauss called the second and third waves of liberalism. This is what the America First Caucus meant by "abstract ideas." But there are also scholars who want to define *creed* as first-wave liberalism (something good and worth preserving) and closer to what I describe in the order left 1 position, which avoids the mistakes of the second and third waves of liberalism but in doing so doesn't throw the baby out with the bathwater. For a succinct summary of their view of the creed and why it is so important to hang on to, see Charles Kesler, "The Crisis of American National Identity," Heritage Foundation, November 8, 2005, www.heritage.org/political-process /report/the-crisis-american-national-identity-part-the-lehrman-lectures-restoring; and James W. Ceaser, "Creed Versus Culture: Alternative Foundations for American Conservatives," *Heritage Lectures*, March 10, 2006, www.heritage.org/political-process /report/creed-versus-culture-alternative-foundations-american-conservatism.

[9]Samuel P. Huntington, quoted in Peter Skerry, "What Are We to Make of Samuel Huntington?" *Society*, November-December 2005, 85, www.bc.edu/content/dam/files /schools/cas_sites/polisci/pdf/skerry/Huntington_essay.pdf. For a full account of Huntington's argument, see Samuel P. Huntington, *Who Are We? The Challenges to America's National Identity* (London: Free Press, 2004).

[10]Samuel P. Huntington, *Who Are We? The Challenges to America's National Identity* (London: Free Press, 2004), 339.

[11]Huntington, *Who Are We?*, 20.

[12]Peter Skerry, in his very insightful review (see note 8) of Huntington's *Who Are We?*, points out that critics who fault Huntington for stressing culture over creed are missing the point. As Skerry observes, for Huntington we need both culture and creed, and he actually *doesn't* prioritize one over the other. And when it seems he does, he really is just giving one priority because the needs of national identity at any given moment necessitate it. When America was locked in the cold war after WWII, which was a battle of ideas with communism, he stressed the creed, says Skerry. Now with the threats from immigration and rapid cultural change, we need to stress culture.

[13]Huntington, *Who Are We?* 344.

[14]Huntington, *Who Are We?* 41.

[15]Damon Linker, quoted in W. James Antle III, "Nationalism and its Discontents," *American Conservative*, September 18, 2019, www.theamericanconservative.com /articles/nationalism-and-its-discontents.

[16]Ultimately, even Huntington failed at holding them together because he didn't have a standard, a proper grounding, to do so. This is the problem we saw with Schlesinger and the other mid-century vital-center thinkers (chap. two) who believed we could ground our democratic republic in pragmatism shorn of any outside authority, whether revelation or natural law/natural rights. But it is a similar problem with both those on the extremes of order right and order left: both look to a form of historicism that baptizes whatever culture they most approve of, whether some moment in the past or the spirit of the times in the present. The problem for Huntington is similar: how do we know what in our tradition and history is good and what is bad? Without an outside authority (i.e., natural law, revelation, or some form of the creed), how do we know if our version of culture is just and fair? In his *American Politics: The Promise of Disharmony* (Cambridge, MA: Harvard University Press, 1983), 16, he admits this problem: "No theory exists for ordering these values in relation to one another." So Huntington wants both culture and creed, but he is not sure how to ground this balance, which leads to the continual conflict.

[17]James W. Ceaser, *Designing a Polity: America's Constitution in Theory and Practice* (Lanham, MD: Rowman & Littlefield, 2011), 7.

[18]John Adams, quoted in Ceaser, *Designing a Polity*, 7.

[19]See the discussion of this back and forth between nature and history in James Ceaser's *Nature and History in American Political Thought* (Cambridge, MA: Harvard University Press, 2006), 33-51.

[20]For his discussion on how the founders moved from history to nature, see Ceaser's *Nature and History in American Political Thought*, 22-33.

[21]Ceaser, *Nature and History in American Political Thought*, 35.

[22]Ceaser, *Nature and History in American Political Thought*, 35.

[23]Ceaser, *Nature and History in American Political Thought*, 35.

[24]Martin Luther King Jr., *Letter from Birmingham Jail* (New York: Penguin UK, 2018); Frederick Douglass, *What to the Slave Is the Fourth of July?* (Berkeley: Mint Editions, 2021); D. H. Dilbeck, *Frederick Douglass: America's Prophet* (Durham: University of North Carolina Press, 2018), 75-92.

[25]James Ceaser, "Alexis de Tocqueville and the Two Founding Thesis," in *Tocqueville's Voyages: The Evolution of His Ideas and Their Journey Beyond His Time*, ed. Christine Dunn Henderson (Indianapolis, IN: Liberty Fund, 2014), 111-41.

[26]The other being Puritan New England.

[27]Alexis de Tocqueville, *Democracy in America*, trans. and ed. Harvey C. Mansfield and Debra Winthrop (Chicago: University of Chicago Press, 2000), 31-32.

[28]While the literature on this topic is vast, for a general introduction the literature and the concept of the rivalry between Jamestown and Plymouth as the true location of the American Founding, see Ritchie Devon Watson Jr., *Normans and Saxons: Southern Race Mythology and the Intellectual History of the American Civil War* (Baton Rouge: Louisiana State University Press, 2008).

[29]As an example of how this rivalry between oligarchy and constitutional republicanism played out after Lincoln's death, see Forrest A. Nabors, *From Oligarchy to Republicanism: The Great Task of Reconstruction* (Columbia: University of Missouri Press, 2017).

[30]I want to thank Thomas West for giving me the idea of using "soul" to describe each of my four new vital center positions. See his essay, *Jaffa Versus Mansfield: Does America Have a Constitutional Soul or a "Declaration of Independence" Soul?*, https://vindicatingthe founders.com/author/jaffa_v_mansfield.pdf.

[31]For the two of the finest books on James Madison's political thought, see Colleen A. Sheehan, *The Mind of James Madison: The Legacy of Classical Republicanism* (Cambridge, UK: Cambridge University Press, 2015); and Colleen A. Sheehan, *James Madison and the Spirit of Republican Self-Government* (Cambridge, UK: Cambridge University Press, 2009).

[32]Alexander Hamilton, James Madison, John Jay, *The Federalist Papers,* Introduction and Notes by Charles R. Kesler, ed. Clinton Rossiter (New York: Signet Classic, 2003).

[33]See Ralph Ketcham, "James Madison at Princeton," *Princeton Library Chronicle* 28, no. 1 (Autumn 1966); Ralph Ketcham, "James Madison and Religion—A New Hypothesis," *Journal of the Presbyterian Historical Society* 38, no. 2 (June 1960); Ralph Ketcham, "James Madison and the Nature of Man," *Journal of the History of Ideas* 19, no. 1 (January 1958). See also Benjamin F. Wright, "The Federalists on the Nature of Political Man," *Ethics* 59, no. 2 (January 1949); and Lance Banning, *The Sacred Fire of Liberty: James Madison and the Founding of the Federal Republic* (Ithaca, NY: Cornell University Press, 1995).

[34]See Garrett Ward Sheldon, "Liberalism, Classical Republicanism, and Christianity in *The Political Philosophy of James Madison* (Baltimore, MD: Johns Hopkins University Press, 2001), xi-xvi.

[35]James W. Ceaser, *Liberal Democracy and Political Science* (Baltimore, MD: Johns Hopkins University Press, 1990), 9.

[36]Ceaser, *Liberal Democracy and Political Science*, 12.

[37]See Garrett Ward Sheldon, "Liberalism, Classical Republicanism, and Christianity in the Political Philosophy of James Madison," in *The Political Philosophy of James Madison* (Baltimore, MD: Johns Hopkins University Press, 2001), xi-xvi. See also note 23 above for more resources on Madison and the link between his faith and his political philosophy.

[38]Ceaser, *Liberal Democracy and Political Science*, 13.

[39]See Larry P. Arnn, *The Founders' Key: The Divine and Natural Connection Between the Declaration and the Constitution and What We Risk by Losing It* (Nashville, TN: Thomas Nelson, 2012).

[40]Ceaser, *Liberal Democracy and Political Science*, 14.

[41]Annette Gordon-Reed, an African American and a scholar on Jefferson and his slavery, still admires Jefferson and finds him important to study and value. See her *Most Blessed of the Patriarchs: Thomas Jefferson and the Empire of the Imagination* (New York: Liveright, 2016). Jefferson's continued importance can be seen clearly in a new book, John Meacham, ed., *In the Hands of the People: Thomas Jefferson on Equality, Faith, Freedom, Compromise, and the Art of Citizenship* (New York: Random House, 2020). On the right, see Daniel L. Dreisbach, *Thomas Jefferson and the Wall of Separation Between Church and State* (New York: New York University Press, 2002).

[42]For an overview of the debate over the role of classical republicanism in our founding and all the major historical works that grapple with this topic, see the Garrett Ward Sheldon, "Early American Historiography and the Political Philosophy of Thomas Jefferson," in *The Political Philosophy of Thomas Jefferson* (Baltimore: John Hopkins University Press, 1991).

[43]Sheldon, *Political Philosophy of Thomas Jefferson*, 141.

[44]Ceaser, *Liberal Democracy and Political Science*, 10.

[45]Ceaser, *Liberal Democracy and Political Science*, 10.

[46]Ceaser, *Liberal Democracy and Political Science*, 10.

[47]Ceaser, *Liberal Democracy and Political Science*, 11.

[48]Thomas Sowell, *A Conflict of Visions: Ideological Origins of Political Struggle* (New York: Basic Books, 2007), 21.

[49]For the definition of the constrained vision, see Sowell's "Constrained and Unconstrained Visions," in *Conflict of Visions*, 18-39.

[50]See *The Federalist Papers* 10 and 51, ed. Clinton Rossiter (New York: First Signet Classic, 2003), 71-79, 317-22. It is important to note that not all Madisonian scholars hold to the "Madisonian system" view. George Carey contends that this view is too cynical and makes Madison into a purely secular liberal, closer to freedom left 2. Also "if there is such a thing as 'the Madisonian system,' Madison never proposed it." While Carey might fault *The Federalist Papers* for not being comprehensive enough in describing the plan for a virtuous citizenry, it nonetheless "points to a positive idea of citizenship as nec-

essary for liberal democracy, though this citizenship is of a different sort than the classical republic virtue." According to Carey, in attempting to hold constitutionalism together with republicanism, Madison often comes across as ambivalent. For example, in *Federalist Paper* No. 10, elements of constitutionalism sit alongside elements of republicanism. Ultimately, for Carey, while the authors of the *The Federalist Papers* tried to reconcile the two, they realized that a virtuous citizenry would have to draw from other sources. Moreover, we know the *The Federalist Papers'* authors had a vison for virtue because they used words like *esteem and confidence* and *ability and virtue*. But even with these concerns for virtue, this group of scholars admits that *The Federalist Papers* need to be supplemented by other sources from the founding to fill out the vision. This view has over the years found a home in order right 1. See George W. Carey, "The American Founding and Limited Government," *Imaginative Conservative*, July 5, 2012.

[51]Martin Diamond, "Ethics and Politics: The American Way," in *The Moral Foundations of the American Republic*, ed. Robert H. Horwitz, 3rd ed. (Charlottesville: University of Virginia Press, 1986), 83.

[52]Diamond, "Ethics and Politics," 99.

[53]Alexander Hamilton, quoted in Diamond, "Ethics and Politics," 100.

[54]Diamond, "Ethics and Politics," 101. Thus this quadrant, freedom right 1, follows Tocqueville's view that self-interest must be allowed to flourish because it is built into human nature, and no amount of utopian thinking can change this reality. But it is not the self-interest of unencumbered self, people who retreat into their private realm of avarice and greed, people who are only out for themselves. While Tocqueville's self-interest rightly understood is not a high and noble doctrine, it gets the job done and at the same time protects individual liberty, something that republicanism couldn't guarantee. According to Alan S. Kahan, self-interest well understood "functions for Tocqueville as a secular complement to religion." For Tocqueville, the doctrine is a tool; it gets us one step closer to democratic greatness. But it can only go so far. See Alan S. Kahan, *Tocqueville, Democracy and Religion* (New York: Oxford University Press, 2015), 60.

[55]Ceaser, *Liberal Democracy and Political Science*, 166. Moreover, as we will see in the final chapter, part of the deficit weakness of the system that still remains has to do with the fact, as Tocqueville contended, that the laws (the constitution) of a country were not enough to restrain and shape a virtuous citizenry. There is a vital role that religion must play to assist "self-interest properly understood." Laws (i.e., the constitution, the creed) are not enough.

[56]Diamond, "Ethics and Politics," 108, italics added.

[57]Ceaser, *Liberal Democracy and Political Science*, 20.

[58]Alan S. Kahan, *Tocqueville, Democracy and Religion* (New York: Oxford University Press, 2015), 63.

[59]See Harry V. Jaffa, *A New Birth of Freedom: Abraham Lincoln and the Coming of the Civil War* (Oxford, UK: Rowman & Littlefield, 2000).

[60]Abraham Lincoln, "Lyceum Address," *Abraham Lincoln Online*, accessed May 3, 2021, www.abrahamlincolnonline.org/lincoln/speeches/lyceum.htm.

[61]Daniel Walker Howe, *The Political Culture of the American Whigs* (Chicago: University of Chicago Press, 1979), 290.

[62]Abraham Lincoln, "The Gettysburg Address," accessed at https://rmc.libary.cornel.edu /gettysburg/good_cause/transcrpt.htm.

[63]Abraham Lincoln, "Second Inaugural Address," accessed at https://www.nps.gov/linc /learn/historycutlure/lincoln-second-inaugural.htm.

[64]Ceaser, *Liberal Democracy and Political Science*, 20.

[65]Ceaser, *Liberal Democracy and Political Science*, 20.

[66]Rossiter, ed., *The Federalist Papers*, 9.

[67]Alexis de Tocqueville, *Democracy in America*, Translated, Edited, and with an Introduction by Harvey C. Mansfield and Delba Winthrop (Chicago: University of Chicago, 2000), 7.

[68]Nathan W. Schlueter and Nicholai G. Wenzel, *Selfish Libertarians and Socialist Conservatives?* (Stanford, CA: Stanford University Press, 2017), 29.

[69]Schlueter and Wenzel, *Selfish Libertarians and Socialist Conservatives?* 29. Here Schlueter is summarizing Robert George's argument in Robert George, *Marking Men Moral: Civil Liberties and Public Morality* (Oxford: Oxford University Press, 1995).

[70]Ceaser, *Liberal Democracy and Political Science*, 20

[71]Ceaser, *Liberal Democracy and Political Science*, 20.

[72]Abraham Lincoln, "First Debate: Ottawa, Illinois," The Lincoln-Douglas Debates of 1858, Illinois, August 21, 1858, www.nps.gov/liho/learn/historyculture/debate1.htm. As Nathan Schlueter says so well, political education is not only the task of political leaders, it is primarily the task of citizens, especially parents, teachers, pastors, and other persons in positions of authority and leadership. But as Schlueter reminds us, this soft perfectionism means that government and the constitution only play a secondary role in assisting in this task. As the Northwest Ordinance, passed by the Continental Congress in 1787, said, "Religion, morality, and knowledge, being necessary to good government and the happiness of mankind, schools and the means of education shall forever be encouraged." For all the founders, contends Schlueter, good government played a positive but secondary role in shaping a virtuous citizenry, that is, the "habits of the heart," the political culture and dispositions of its citizens that are needed to support the creed. Schlueter and Wenzel, *Selfish Libertarians and Socialist Conservatives?*, 42.

[73]Alexis de Tocqueville, quoted in Ceaser, *Liberal Democracy and Political Science*, 46.

[74]*The Federalist Papers*, quoted in Ceaser, *Liberal Democracy and Political Science*, 46.

[75]Samuel Francis Smith, "America (My Country, 'Tis of Thee)," 1831.

[76]For a helpful account on patriotism, see Walter Berns, *Making Patriots* (Chicago: University of Chicago Press, 2001).

[77]Tocqueville's phrases cited in Ceaser, *Liberal Democracy and Political Science*, 169.

12. Patriotic Citizenship: The Sweet Offer for Resident Aliens and Alienated Residents

[1]Franco Ordonez, "Almost 19,000 Migrant Children Stopped at US Border in March, Most Ever in a Month," NPR, April 8, 2021, www.npr.org/2021/04/08/985296354 /almost-19-000-migrant-children-stopped-at-u-s-border-in-march-most-ever-in -a-mon; John Kass, "Biden Called for the Border Surge. And Now He Owns It," *Chicago Tribune*, March 24, 2021, www.chicagotribune.com/columns/john-kass/ct-prem-biden -border-crisis-john-kass-20210324-s6nxh76uofgs3n53xtxcmdpjty-story.html.

[2]Todd Bensman, "Catch-and-Bus: Thousands of Freed Border-Crossing Immigrants Are Dispersing Across America," Center for Immigration Studies, March 31, 2021, https:// cis.org/Bensman/CatchandBus-Thousands-Freed-BorderCrossing-Immigrants-Are -Dispersing-Across-America.

[3]Arelis R. Hernandez, "Fewer Migrant Families Being Expelled at Border Under Title 42, but Critics Still Push for Its End," *Washington Post*, July 13, 2021, http://washington post.com/immigration/fewer-migrant-families-being-expelled-at-border-under-title -42-but-critics-still-push-for-its-end/.

[4]Two of the best are Todd Bensman (toddbensman.com) and Michael Yon (michaelyon -online.com). See also John Moore, "I'm a Photojournalist. Why Is the Administration Banning Me from the Border Facilities?" *Washington Post*, March 22, 2021, www.wash ingtonpost.com/outlook/2021/03/22/journalists-banned-border-facilities-migrants/; Gabrielle Fonrouge and Aaron Feis, "Journalists Granted 'Zero' Access to Cover Border Crisis Under Biden," *New York Post*, March 21, 2021, https://nypost.com/2021/03/21 /journalists-granted-zero-access-to-cover-border-crisis-photog/.

[5]Ted Hesson and Mark Hosenball, "US Arrested Two Yemenis on Terror Watchlist Who Tried to Cross Border from Mexico," Reuters, April 5, 2021. See also Todd Bensman, *America's Covert Border War: The Untold Story of The Nation's Battle to Prevent Jihadist Infiltration* (New York: Post Hill Press, 2021).

[6]Leah Barkoukis, "Border Patrol Official Tells 'Harrowing Stories' of Sexual Abuse Children Are Experiencing on Journey to US," *Townhall*, March 31, 2021.

[7]Andrew R. Arthur, "Rove Op-Ed Exposes Costs of Biden Border Crisis: An Open Border Is an Invitation to Criminals and a Snare for Unwary Immigrants," Center for Immigration Studies, July 9, 2021, https://cis.org/Arthur/Rove-OpEd-Exposes-Human -Costs-Biden-Border-Crisis.

[8]Emily Benedek, "Is the Religion of Mass Immigration Hurting America? *Tablet*, August 13, 2020, www.tabletmag.com/sections/news/articles/mass-immigration-america.

[9]For my analysis of the America First Caucus, especially the need to better define its grounding and its definition of "Anglo-Saxon political principles," making sure it is grounded in the new vital center, see chapter eleven.

[10]Joel Rose, "Immigration Agencies Ordered Not to Use Term 'Illegal Alien' Under New Biden Policy," NPR, April 19, 2021, www.npr.org2021/04/19/988789487/immigration -agencies-ordered-not-to-use-term-illegal-alien-under-new-biden-polic.

[11]Andrew R. Arthur, "The Words 'Alien' and 'Assimilation' Banned by the Biden Administration," Center for Immigration Studies, April 20, 2021, https://cis.org/Arthur/Words-Alien-and-Assimilation-Banned-Biden-Administration.

[12]America First Caucus Policy Platform, *Punchbowl News*, https://punchbowl.news/wp-content/uploads/America-First-Caucus-Policy-Platform-FINAL-2.pdf; Also, for how mass immigration is destroying trust among groups in America, see Edward J. Erler, "Does Diversity Really Unite Us?" *Imprimis*, July-August 2018.

[13]America First Caucus Policy Platform, page 3, *Punchbowl News*, https://punchbowl.news/wp-content/uploads/America-First-Caucus-Policy-Platform-FINAL-2.pdf.

[14]Marc A. Thiessen, "Democrats Were for a Wall Before They Were Against It," *Washington Post*, January 10, 2019, www.washintonpost.com/opinions/demorcrats-were-for-a-wall-before-they-were-against-it/.

[15]Andrew R. Arthur, "Polling Reveals Troubling Signs for Biden on Immigration," Center for Immigration Studies, February 5, 2021. https://cis.org/Arthur/Polling-Reveals-Troubling-Signs-Biden-Immigration.

[16]For thirty decades of surveys demonstrating how a supermajority of Americans want less immigration and how resentment against illegal immigration in America and in Europe is leading to the populist uprising, see Ryan James Girdusky and Harlan Hill, *They're Not Listening: How Elites Created the Nationalist Populist Revolution* (New York: Bombardier, 2020).

[17]Mychael Schnell, "100 Business Executives Discuss How to Combat New Voting Rules," *The Hill*, April 11, 2021, https://thehill.com/business-a-lobbying/business-a-lobbying/547609-100-executives-discuss-how-to-combat-voting.

[18]To see how those in the order right quadrant are working through issues over immigration and national sovereignty, see the talks at the 2019 National Conservative Conference held in Washington, DC, nationalconservative.org/natcon-dc-2019. To learn more about the book that inspired the conference, see Yoram Hazony, *The Virtue of Nationalism* (New York: Basic Books, 2018). See also Edward J. Erler, "Illegal Immigration Destroys Sovereignty: Our Ruling Classes Reject Our Right to Govern Ourselves," *The American Mind*, April 5, 2021.

[19]Christopher Caldwell, "The Hidden Cost of Immigration," *Claremont Review of Books*, Fall 2016; and George J. Borjas, *We Wanted Workers: Unraveling the Immigration Narrative* (New York: W. W. Norton, 2016).

[20]Chris Conover, "How American Citizens Finance $18 Billion in Health Care for Unauthorized Immigrants," *Forbes*, February 26, 2018.

[21]To see how illegal immigrants run a new deficit, taking more from the welfare system than the taxes they pay, see James Jay Carafano, John G. Malcolm, and Jack Spencer, eds., "An Agenda for American Immigration Reform," Heritage Foundation, February 20, 2019. See also Robert Rector and Jason Richwine, "The Fiscal Cost of Unlawful Immigrants and Amnesty to the US Taxpayer," Heritage Foundation, May 6, 2013; and Steven A. Camarota, "Welfare Use by Legal and Illegal Immigrant Households," Center

for Immigration Studies, September 9, 2015, https://cis.org/Report/Welfare-Use-Legal -and-Illegal-Immigrant-Households.

[22]Ben Popper, "Is Silicon Valley's Immigration Agenda Gutting the Tech Industry's Middle Class," *Verge*, July 3, 2013, www.theverge.com/2013/7/3/4486910/is-silicon -valleys-immigration-agenda-gutting-the-tech-industrys.

[23]Amy L. Wax, "Debating Immigration Restriction: The Case for Low and Slow," *Georgetown Law* 16, issue S (Fall 2018). See also Amy Wax's transcript from her the National Conservative Conference talk, "Here's What Amy Wax Really Said About Immigration," *The Federalist*, July 26, 2019, https://thefederalist.com/2019/07/26/heres -amy-wax-really-said-immigration/; and Edward J. Erler "Citizenship, Immigration, and the Nation-State," *The American Mind*, March 18, 2019, https://americanmind.org /features/the-case-against-birthright-citizenship/.

[24]*Face the Nation*, May 2, 2010, transcript, www.cbsnews.com/htdocs/pdf/FTN_050210.pdf.

[25]James K. Hoffmeier, *The Immigration Crisis: Immigrants, Aliens, and the Bible* (Wheaton, IL: Crossway, 2009).

[26]See Peter Beinart, "How the Democrats Lost Their Way on Immigration," the *Atlantic*, July-August, 2017, www.theatlantic.com/magazine/archive/2017/07/the-democrats -immigration-mistake/528678/.

[27]Jerry Kammer, *Losing Ground: How a Left-Right Coalition Blocked Immigration Reform and Provoked a Backlash That Elected Trump* (Washington, DC: The Center for Immigration Studies, 2020).

[28]Cited in Andrew E. Harrod, "The Immigration Problem is Worse Than you Think," American Thinker, July 30, 2020, www.americanthinker.com/articles/2020/07/the _immigration_problem_is_worse_than_you_think.html.

[29]Ann Coulter, "Bush's America: Roach Motel," AnnCoulter.com, June 6, 2007, https://ann coulter.com/2007/06/06/bushs-america-roach-motel.

[30]Coulter, "Bush's America."

[31]Ann Coulter, *Adios, America!* (Washington, DC: Regnery, 2015), 245.

[32]"Modern Immigration Wave Brings 59 Million to U.S., Driving Population Growth and Change Through 2065," Pew Research Center Report, September 28, 2015, https://pew research.org/hispanic/2015/09/28/modern-immigration-wave-brings-59-million-to-u -s-driving-population-growth-and-change-through-2065.

[33]For an oft-quoted study that shows how diversity erodes trust between ethnic groups and engenders balkanization among groups, regardless of skin color, see Robert D. Putnam, "E Pluribus Unum: Diversity and Community in the Twenty-First Century," *Scandinavian Political Studies* 30, no. 2 (2007), www.aimlessgromar.com/wp-content /uploads/2013/12/j-1467-9477-2007-00176-x.pdf.

[34]Noah Pickus, "From Them to Us," *Claremont Review of Books*, Spring 2005, https:// claremontreviewofbooks.com/from-them-to-us. See also Tamar Jacoby, ed., *Reinventing the Melting Pot: The New Immigrants and What It Means to Be American* (New York: Basic Books, 2004).

[35]Peter Skerry, "Do We Really Want Immigrants to Assimilate?" *Brookings*, March 1, 2000, https://www.brookings.edu/articles/do-we-really-want-immigrants-to-assimilate/.

[36]P. P. Claxton, quoted in John J. Miller, "Reviving Americanization: A Response to Juan Perea," in *Immigration and Citizenship in the 21st Century*, ed. Noah M. J. Pickus (Lanham, MD: Rowman & Littlefield, 1998), 80, italics added.

[37]David Miller, *Strangers in Our Midst* (Cambridge, MA: Harvard University Press, 2016), 130-50.

[38]Miller, *Strangers in our Midst*, 132. Even this least controversial option has come under fire in the years since Miller penned his book. See Peggy McGlone, "African American Museum Site Removes 'Whiteness' Chart After Criticism from Trump Jr. and Conservative Media," *Washington Post*, July 17, 2020, www.washingtonpost.com/entertainment/museums/african-american-museum-site-removes-whiteness-chart-after-criticism-from-trump-jr-and-conservative-media/2020/07/17/4ef6e6f2-c831-11ea-8ffe-372be8d82298_story.html.

[39]Alexander Hamilton, quoted in Tom G. West, *The Political Theory of the American Founding: Natural Rights, Public Policy, and the Moral Conditions of Freedom* (New York: Cambridge University Press, 2017), 178.

[40]Others who fit into this freedom right 1 are Samuel Gregg, Scott Rae, Dylan Pahman, *The Public Discourse*, and the Acton Institute.

[41]Thomas Sowell, *Discrimination and Disparities* (New York: Basic Books, 2019), and *Black Rednecks and White Liberals* (New York: Encounter, 2006).

[42]Thomas Sowell, quoted in William Vogel, "Thomas Sowell's Inconvenient Truths," *Claremont Review of Books*, summer 2018. See also Thomas Sowell, *Race and Culture: A World View* (New York: Basic Books, 1994).

[43]For proof that the largest segment of the black population is now in the working and middle class, not the lower class, see Eugene Robinson, *Disintegration: The Splintering of Black America* (New York: Doubleday, 2010).

[44]Jay Mathews, "Why Nation's Biggest Charter Network Dumped its Slogan, 'Work Hard. Be Nice,'" *Washington Post*, July 7, 2020, www.washingtonpost.com/local/education/why-nations-biggest-charter-network-dumped-its-slogan-work-hard-be-nice/2020/07/07/e7896c0a-bf9e-11ea-b4f6-cb39cd8940fb_story.html.

[45]Like Deidre N. McCloskey who rejects the idea that capitalism is built on greed and crass materialism, Sowell believes that capitalism at its best is built on a moral and ethical foundation, and when this foundation is present and continually nurtured, it will shape the very people who participate in the market economy. See Deirdre N. McCloskey, *Bourgeois Virtues: Ethics for an Age of Commerce* (Chicago: University of Chicago Press, 2016). For the role that high levels of education play in immigrant success, see Girdusky and Hill, "Legal Immigration," chapter five in *They're Not Listening*.

[46]To see how our founders understood these "middle class virtues" and the role they played in a stable constitutional republic, see chapter four, "'Happy Mediocrity': America's

Middle Class," and chapter five, "Citizen Virtue: 'Simple Manners' Among the 'Laborious and Saving,'" in Leslie G. Rubin, *America, Aristotle, and the Politics of a Middle Class* (Waco, TX: Baylor University Press, 2018), 91-118, 119-39.

[47]Thomas Sowell, *The Vision of the Anointed* (New York: Basic Books, 1996).

[48]Miller, *Strangers in Our Midst*, 133.

[49]For Galston's critique of the unencumbered self and the procedural republic, see William A. Galston, *Liberal Purposes: Goods, Virtues, and Diversity in the Liberal State* (New York: Cambridge University Press, 1991), chaps. 4-7.

[50]William A. Galston, "Public Morality and Religion in the Liberal State," *Political Science and Politics* 19, no. 4 (fall 1986): 823-24.

[51]Galston, "Public Morality and Religion in the Liberal State," 823.

[52]William A. Galston, "Liberal Virtues," *American Political Science Review* 82, no. 4 (December 1988): 1279.

[53]Galston, "Liberal Virtues," 1279.

[54]Galston, "Liberal Virtues," 1280.

[55]Galston, "Liberal Virtues," 1288.

[56]Galston, "Liberal Virtues," 1289.

[57]Galston, *Liberal Purposes*, 250.

[58]Miller, *Strangers in Our Midst*, 133.

[59]Miller, *Strangers in Our Midst*, 142. See also David Miller, *On Nationality* (Oxford, UK: Oxford University Press, 1995).

[60]Miller, *Strangers in Our Midst*, 144.

[61]Miller, *Strangers in Our Midst*, 144.

[62]Miller, *Strangers in Our Midst*, 145.

[63]Michael J. Sandel, *Democracy's Discontent: America in Search of a Public Philosophy* (Cambridge, MA: Harvard University Press, 1996), 127.

[64]Sandel, *Democracy's Discontent*, 127.

[65]Sandel, *Public Philosophy*, 10.

[66]Sandel, *Public Philosophy*, 10.

[67]Sandel, *Public Philosophy*, 10.

[68]Sandel, *Democracy's Discontent*, 14.

[69]Tocqueville, quoted in Sandel, *Democracy's Discontent*, 314.

[70]Sandel, *Democracy's Discontent*, 320-21.

[71]Thomas West, *The Political Theory of the American Founding: Natural Rights, Public Policy, and the Moral Conditions of Freedom* (Cambridge, UK: University of Cambridge Press, 2017). To see how West and other order right 1 writers address the crisis of immigration, see *The Founders on Citizenship and Immigration: Principles and Challenges in America*, edited by Edward J. Erler, Thomas West, and John Marini (New York: Rowman & Littlefield Publishers, Inc., 2007).

[72]Lorrain Smith Pangle and Thomas L. Pangle, *The Learning of Liberty* (Lawrence: University

Press of Kansas, 1993); Leslie G. Rubin, *America, Aristotle, and the Politics of a Middle Class* (Waco, TX: Baylor University Press, 2018).

[73]West, *Political Theory of the American Founding*, 169.

[74]West, *Political Theory of the American Founding*, 218.

[75]West, *Political Theory of the American Founding*, 269.

[76]See Charles Kesler, "Civility and Citizenship in Washington's America and Ours," *Imprimis*, 29, no. 12 (December 2000), https://imprimis.hillsdale.edu/civility-and-citizenship-in-washingtons-america-and-ours.

[77]While most of the historians in the documentary are on the left, most falling in order left 2, and all aware that Washington had slaves, they nonetheless don't dismiss him as a racist. The reason could be that he freed some of them during his lifetime and others at his death, and his wife, Martha, freed the rest after his death. The Washington estate also financially supported the freedman for three decades, until the support wasn't needed.

[78]See the appendix, "Farewell Address," in Matthew Spalding and Patrick J. Garrity, *A Sacred Union of Citizens: George Washington's Farewell Address and the American Character* (New York: Rowman & Littlefield, 1996), 178.

[79]Washington, quoted in Spalding and Garrity, *Sacred Union of Citizens*, 178.

[80]Washington, quoted in Spalding and Garrity, *Sacred Union of Citizens*, 183, italics added.

[81]Washington, quoted in Spalding and Garrity, *Sacred Union of Citizens*, 183, italics added.

[82]For an account of Washington's strong faith and the role it played in his own virtue and the virtue of the nation, see Michael Novak, *Washington's God: Religion, Liberty, and the Father of Our Country* (New York: Basic Books, 2007).

13. Christianity: The Second Constitution

[1]Michael Lind, *The New Class War: Saving Democracy from the Managerial Elite* (New York: Penguin, 2020).

[2]One has only to look at cities like Los Angeles to get a glimpse of where this high-tech caste society is going: thousands of homeless people camp on the sides of freeways and entire blocks of the downtown. Or look at the anger of some in the working- and middle-classes over lockdowns and constantly changing mandates that seemed to favor the elites. Or the pressure brewing over mass immigration that threatens to explode. Or the discontent of some churches who had to close due to temporary emergency powers under the pandemic restrictions, feeling their religious liberty was being threatened. Or the animus directed at Christians who hold to historic biblical views of gender and sexuality.

[3]"Supreme Court Justice Samuel Alito Speech Transcript to Federalist Society," *Rev.com*, November 12, 2020, www.rev.com/blog/transcripts/supreme-court-justice-samuel-alito-speech-transcript-to-federalist-society.

[4]Mark Tushnet, "Abandoning Defensive Crouch Liberal Constitutionalism," Balkanization, May 6, 2016, https://balkin.blogspot.com/2016/05/abandoning-defensive-crouch-liberal.html.

[5]Mark Joseph Stern, "Sam Alito Delivers Grievance-Laden, Ultrapartisan Speech to the Federalist Society," *Slate*, November 13, 2020, https://slate.com/news-and-politics/2020/11/alito-federalist-society-speech-insane.html.

[6]Matt Forde, "Samuel Alito Is Tired of Winning," *New Republic*, November 13, 2020, https://newrepublic.com/article/160199/samuel-alito-federalist-society-religion.

[7]Katherine Stewart, "The Supreme Court's Religious Persecution Complex," *New Republic*, April 9, 2021, https://newrepublic.com/article/161987/supreme-court-fulton-philadelphia-religious.

[8]This is a classic freedom left 2 argument, the godless constitution view, wanting to bracket out religion, defending the idea of the naked public square, only to have smuggled secular religions back in.

[9]John McWhorter, "The Elect: The Threat to a Progressive America from Anti-Black Anti-racists," Substack, January 27, 2021, https://johnmcwhorter.substack.com/p/the-elect-neoracists-posing-as-antiracists.

[10]Katherine Stewart, "The Supreme Court's Religious Persecution Complex," *New Republic*, April 9, 2021, https://newrepublic.com/article/161987/supreme-court-fulton-philadelphia-religious.

[11]For transcript of Justice Alito's speech to the Federalist Society, go here: https://rev.com/blog/transcripts/supreme-court-justice-samuel-alito-speech-transript-to-federalist-society.

[12]For transcript of Justice Alito's speech to the Federalist Society, go here: https://rev.com/blog/transcripts/supreme-court-justice-samuel-alito-speech-transript-to-federalist-society.

[13]James Davison Hunter, "Religious Freedom and the Challenge of Modern Pluralism," in *Articles of Faith, Articles of Peace*, ed. James Davison Hunter and Os Guinness (Washington, DC: Brookings Institution Press, 1990), 54-73.

[14]Hunter, "Religious Freedom and the Challenge of Modern Pluralism," 55-58.

[15]Hunter, *Culture Wars*, 262.

[16]Hunter, "Religious Freedom and the Challenge of Modern Pluralism," 63-73.

[17]Hunter, "Religious Freedom and the Challenge of Modern Pluralism," 72.

[18]Hunter, "Religious Freedom and the Challenge of Modern Pluralism," 72.

[19]James W. Ceaser, *Designing a Polity: America's Constitution in Theory and Practice* (Lanham, MD: Rowman & Littlefield, 2011), 16.

[20]Lindsay, *Cynical Theories*, chap. 2, "Postmodernism's Applied Turn," 45-66.

[21]Joseph Bottum, *An Anxious Age: The Post-Protestant Ethic and the Spirit of America* (New York: Image, 2014).

[22]Robert N. Bellah, *The Broken Covenant* (Chicago: University of Chicago Press, 1984), 142.

[23]Bellah, *The Broken Covenant*, 142.

[24]Charles Taylor, "Religion in a Free Society," in Hunter and Guinness, *Articles of Faith, Articles of Peace*, 105.

[25]James Davison Hunter, "Liberal Democracy and the Unraveling of the Enlightenment Project," *Hedgehog Review* 19, no. 3 (Fall 2017), https://hedgehogreview.com/issues/the-end-of-the-end-of-history/articles/liberal-democracy-and-the-unraveling-of-the-enlightenment-project.

[26]Hunter, "Liberal Democracy and the Unraveling of the Enlightenment Project."

[27]Hunter, "Liberal Democracy and the Unraveling of the Enlightenment Project."

[28]Hunter, "Liberal Democracy and the Unraveling of the Enlightenment Project."

[29]The term *court evangelicals* comes from historian John Fea's book *Believe Me: The Evangelical Road to Donald Trump* (Grand Rapids, MI: Eerdmans, 2018).

[30]For a history of the Christian Right and its connection to conservatism, see Kenneth I. Kersch, *Conservatives and the Constitution* (New York: Cambridge University Press, 2019), chap. 5.

[31]James Ceaser, *Designing a Polity: America's Constitution in Theory and Practice*, (Lanham, MD: Rowman & Littlefield Publishers, 2010), 145, italics added. For the best explanation of how the founders understood the role of religion and the first amendment, see Mark David Hall, *Did America Have a Christian Founding* (Nashville, TN: Thomas Nelson, 2019). See also Daniel L. Driesbach, *Thomas Jefferson and the Wall of Separation* (New York: New York University Press, 2002).

[32]Ceaser, *Designing a Polity: America's Constitution in Theory and Practice*, 145.

[33]See chapter 2, "The Second Tablet Project," in J. Budziszewski, *The Line Through the Heart: Natural Law as Fact, Theory, and Sign of Contradiction* (Wilmington, DE: ISI Books, 2009), 23-40.

[34]Ceaser, *Designing a Polity*, 145.

[35]James Ceaser, *Designing a Polity: America's Constitution in Theory and Practice*, (Lanham, MD: Rowman & Littlefield Publishers, 2010), 145.

[36]Ceaser, *Designing a Polity*, 145.

[37]Ceaser, *Designing a Polity*, 145.

[38]See Alan Kahan, *Tocqueville, Democracy and Religion: Checks and Balances for Democratic Souls* (New York: Oxford University Press, 2015), 68-93.

[39]For the power of prophetic Christianity in the abolitionist movement, see D. H. Dilbeck, *Frederick Douglass: America's Prophet* (Chapel Hill: University of North Carolina Press, 2018). For the widespread involvement of religious believers in the antislavery movement in Great Britain and the United States, see David Brion Davis, *The Problem of Slavery in the Age of Emancipation*, (New York: Alfred A. Knopf, 2014). For the role of prophetic religion played in the civil rights era, see David L. Chappell, *A Stone of Hope: Prophetic Religion and the Death of Jim Crow* (Chapel Hill: University of North Carolina Press, 2004).

[40]Carlos Lozada, "The Book Every New American Citizen—and Every Old One, Too—Should Read," *Washington Post*, December 17, 2015, www.washingtonpost.com/news /book-party/wp/2015/12/17/the-book-every-new-american-citizen-and-every-old -one-too-should-read.

[41]James Schleifer, "How Has Tocqueville's Democracy Been Read in America?," in *The Chicago Companion to Tocqueville's Democracy in America* (Chicago: University of Chicago Press, 2012).

[42]See William A. Galton, "Tocqueville on Liberalism and Religion," *Social Research* 54, no. 3 (1987); James T. Schleifer, "Tocqueville, Religion, and Democracy in America: Some Essential Questions," *American Political Thought* 3, no. 2 (2014); Catherine Zuckert, "Not by Preaching: Tocqueville on the Role of Religion in American Democracy," *Review of Politics* 43, no. 2 (1981); and Joshua Mitchell, *The Fragility of Freedom, Tocqueville, Covenant, and the Democratic Revolution* (Chicago: University of Chicago Press, 1995).

[43]The best account of Tocqueville's personal struggle with Christianity, see Doris S. Goldstein, *Trial of Faith: Religion and Politics in Tocqueville's Thought* (New York: Elsevier, 1975). See also Michael Zuckert, ed., *The Spirit of Religion and the Spirit of Liberty* (Chicago: University of Chicago Press, 2017).

[44]In *Democracy in America*, Tocqueville's appreciation is mainly for the Protestantism of the early Puritans that he witnessed in his travels and describes as "religion" for shorthand. In this chapter I will be using the words *religion*, *Christianity*, and *evangelicalism* to equal this pan-Protestantism, which today would also include Judaism and Catholicism (after all, Tocqueville was Catholic) as historic versions of biblical religion.

[45]Alexis de Tocqueville to Charles Forbes René de Montalembert, December 1, 1852, cited in Kahan, *Tocqueville, Democracy, and Religion*, 68.

[46]Tocqueville, *Democracy in America*, ed. Eduardo Nolla, trans. James T. Schleifer (Carmel, IN: Liberty Fund, 2012), Book 1:70.

[47]Kahan, *Tocqueville, Democracy, and Religion*, 72.

[48]Tocqueville, *Democracy in America*, ed. and trans. Harvey C. Mansfield and Debra Winthrop (Chicago: University of Chicago Press, 200), 42.

[49]Tocqueville, *Democracy in America*, ed. Mansfield, 43.

[50]Tocqueville, *Democracy in America*, ed. Mansfield, 43.

[51]Alexis de Tocqueville, *Democracy in America*, abridged with introduction by Sanford Kessler, translated and annotated by Stephen D. Grant (Indianapolis, IN: Hackett Publishing Company, Inc.), 135.

[52]William A. Galston, "Tocqueville on Liberalism and Religion," *Social Research* 54, no. 3 (Autumn 1987): 501.

[53]Alexis de Tocqueville, *Democracy in America,* ed. J. P. Mayer (Garden City, NY: Doubleday, 1969), 444.

[54]Tocqueville, *Democracy in America*, ed. Mayer, 444.

[55]Tocqueville, *Democracy in America,* ed. Mayer, 294.

[56]Tocqueville, *Democracy in America*, ed. Mansfield, 275.

[57]Tocqueville, *Democracy in America*, ed. Mansfield, 280.

[58]Kahan, *Tocqueville, Democracy and Religion*, 73.

[59]Tocqueville, *Democracy in America*, ed. Mansfield, 273.

[60]Kahan, *Tocqueville, Democracy and Religion*, 79.

[61]Tocqueville, *Democracy in America*, cited in Kahan, *Tocqueville, Democracy and Religion*, 78.

[62]Tocqueville, *Democracy in America*, ed. Mansfield, 279.

[63]Catherine Zuckert, "Not By Preaching: Tocqueville on the Role of Religion in American Democracy," *Review of Politics* 43, no. 2 (April 1981): 279.

[64]Tocqueville, *Democracy in America*, ed. Mansfield, 265.

[65]Kahan, *Tocqueville, Democracy and Religion*, 85.

[66]James W. Ceaser, *Liberal Democracy and Political Science* (Baltimore: Johns Hopkins University Press, 1990), 33.

[67]Ceaser, *Liberal Democracy and Political Science*, 33.

[68]Ceaser, *Liberal Democracy and Political Science*, 36-37.

[69]Mitchell, *Fragility of Freedom: Tocqueville on Religion, Democracy, and the American Future* (Chicago: University of Chicago Press, 1995), 206.

[70]See Harry V. Jaffa, "The American Founding as the Best Regime," *Claremont Review of Books*, July 4, 2007, https://claremontreviewofbooks.com/digital/the-american-founding -as-the-best-regime.

[71]Galston, *Tocqueville on Liberalism and Religion*, 513.

CONCLUSION: THE HEROIC ROLE FOR THE CHURCH

[1]Ilya Feoktistov, "It's Not Fear Driving COVID-19 Panic, It's Disgust," *The Federalist*, April 23, 2021, https://thefederalist.com/2021/04/23/its-not-fear-driving-covid-19-panic-its-disgust.

[2]George Orwell, quoted in Feoktistov, "It's Not Fear Driving COVID-19 Panic."

[3]George Orwell, quoted in Feoktistov, "It's Not Fear Driving COVID-19 Panic."

[4]Jennifer Rubin, "We Should Soon Stop Catering to the Vaccine Holdouts," *Washington Post*, April 22, 2021, www.washingtonpost.com/opinions/2021/04/22/soon-we-need -stop-catering-vaccine-holdouts.

[5]Josh Blackman, "Understanding Governor Cuomo's Hostility Towards Jews," Reason, October 8, 2020, https://reason.com/volokh/202/10/08/understanding-governor -cuomos-hostility-towards-jews/.

[6]Blackman, "Understanding Governor Cuomo's Hostility Towards Jews." This kind of disgust is treading on dangerous ground. For as Orwell said, when we see our opponents as "dirty" or "smelly" or a "breeding ground for disease," it opens the door "to something else," and historically this has meant persecution and pogroms. While Rubin and Cuomo are not calling for pogroms, the something else does include persecution, or, as Rubin counsels, society must "stop catering to those bent on being a danger to themselves and others" and force them to take the vaccine or else they will have their jobs, their kids' education, and the right to shop taken away, creating two classes of people.

[7]Damon Linker, "Why Do So Many Liberals Despise Christianity?," *The Week*, October 8, 2014, https//theweek.com/articles/443225/why-many-liberals-despise-christianity.

[8]Matt Walsh, "It Is Time to Face the Facts," *Daily Wire*, www.dailywire.com/news/walsh -it-is-time-to-face-the-facts-we-cannot-be-united.

[9]For examples of how these possibilities are being discussed on the right, see the pseudonym Rebecca, "The Separation: A Proposal for a Renewed America," *The American Mind*, November 30, 2020, https://americanmind.org/features/a-house-dividing/the -separation/; Michael Lind, "Showdown or Surrender: There's No Separate Peace with Our Centralized Elites," *American Mind*, December 14, 2020, https://americanmind

.org/features/a-house-dividing/showdown-or-surrender/; Michael Anton, *The Stakes: America at the point of No Return* (Washington, DC: Regnery, 2020); and David French, *Divided We Fall: America's Secession Threat and How to Restore Our Nation* (New York: St, Martin's Press, 2020).

[10]Walsh, "It Is Time to Face the Facts," *Daily Wire.*

[11]Robert Bellah, *The Broken Covenant: American Civil Religion in Time of Trial* (Chicago: University of Chicago Press, 1992), 162-63.

[12]Bellah, *The Broken Covenant*, 163.

[13]For some of the weaknesses of communitarians like Bellah, see Bruce Frohnen, *The New Communitarians and the Crisis of Modern Liberalism* (Lawrence: University of Kansas Press, 1996).

[14]Vincent Phillip Muñoz, "Defending American Classical Liberalism," *National Review*, June 11, 2018, www.nationalreview.com/2018/06/american-classical-liberalism-response -to-radical-catholics/.

[15]See Martyn Lloyd-Jones, *Revival* (Wheaton, IL: Crossway, 1987).

[16]Edmund Burke, *Reflections on the Revolution in France* (Mineola, NY: Dover Publications, 2006), 44.

[17]See Philip Gorski, *American Covenant: A History of Civil Religion from the Puritans to the Present* (Princeton, NJ: Princeton University Press, 2019), 82.

[18]Jason Willock, "A Center That Can Hold," *National Affairs*, Summer 2018, www.national affairs.com/publications/detail/a-center-that-can-hold.

[19]See Jim Belcher, *Deep Church* (Downers Grove, IL: InterVarsity Press, 2009), 181-98.

[20]For a good idea of how this is done, see Jim Belcher, *In Search of Deep Faith: A Pilgrimage in the Beauty, Goodness and Heart of Christianity* (Downers Grove, IL: InterVarsity Press, 2013).

[21]Muñoz, "Defending American Classical Liberalism," 2-3.

[22]Harry V. Jaffa, "The American Founding as the Best Regime," *Claremont Review of Books*, July 4, 2007, https://claremontreviewofbooks.com/digital/the-american -founding-as-the-best-regime.

[23]David F. Forte, "Noble Sinners," *Claremont Review of Books*, September 17, 2019, https:// claremontreviewofbooks.com/digital/noble-sinners/.

[24]See the helpful discussion in "The Civil Religion: Critics and Allies," in *American Covenant: A History of Civil Religion from the Puritans to the Present* (Princeton, NJ: Princeton University Press, 2017), 202-22 (chap. 8).

[25]See Matthew Spalding and Patrick J. Garrity, *A Sacred Union of Citizens: George Washington's Farewell Address and the American Character* (Lanham, MD: Rowman & Littlefield, 1996).

[26]George Washington, "Thanksgiving Proclamation, 3 October 1789," Founders Online, accessed May 11, 2021, https://founders.archives.gov/documents/Washington/05-04-02-0091.

Acknowledgments

[1] J. Budziszewski, *Evangelicals in the Public Square* (Grand Rapids, MI: Baker Academic, 2006), 15-37.

[2] J. Budziszewski, *The Line Through the Heart* (Wilmington, DE: ISI Books, 2011).

ABOUT THE AUTHOR

JIM BELCHER (PhD, Georgetown University) is a political philosopher, researcher, and writer. He was the founding and lead pastor of Redeemer Presbyterian Church in Newport Beach, California, and professor and president of Providence Christian College (2014–2020). He is the award-winning author of *Deep Church: A Third Way Between Emerging and Traditional* and *In Search of Deep Faith: A Pilgrimage into the Beauty, Goodness and Heart of Christianity*. For more information on the New Vital Center, go to newvitalcenter.com.

He and his wife, Michelle, live in Pasadena, California, with daughters, Lindsay and Meghan, and their two grown boys, Jordan and Jonathan, who live independently in an apartment on the edge of Old Town Pasadena, a few miles away.

ALSO BY THE AUTHOR

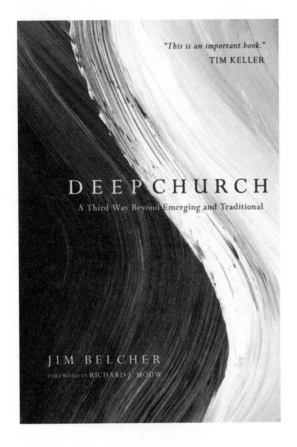

"*This is an important book.*"
TIM KELLER

DEEP CHURCH

A Third Way Beyond Emerging and Traditional

JIM BELCHER

FOREWORD BY RICHARD J. MOUW

Deep Church
978-0-8308-3716-8